The Sunday of the Negative

SUNY series in Hegelian Studies

William Desmond, editor

The Sunday of the Negative

Reading Bataille Reading Hegel

CHRISTOPHER M. GEMERCHAK

STATE UNIVERSITY OF NEW YORK PRESS

Cover art: Lorenzo Monaco, *Cut-out Crucifix*, circa 1410 (detail), Szèpmüvèszeti Muzeum, Budapest.

Published by
State University of New York Press, Albany

© 2003 State University of New York

For information, address State University of New York Press,
90 State Street, Suite 700, Albany, NY 12207

Production by Kelli Williams
Marketing by Michael Campochiaro

Library of Congress Cataloging-in-Publication Data

Gemerchak, Chrostopher M.
    The Sunday of the negative : reading Bataille, reading Hegel / Christopher M. Gemerchak.
        p. cm. — (SUNY series in Hegelian studies)
    Includes bibliographical references and index.
    ISBN 0-7914-5631-5 (alk. paper) — ISBN 0-7914-5632-3 (pbk. : alk. paper)
        1. Bataille, Georges, 1897–1962. 2. Hegel, Georg Wilhelm Friedrich,
    1770–1831—Influence. I. Title. II. Series.

    B2430.B33954 G46 2003
    194—dc21
                                                                                2002042647

10 9 8 7 6 5 4 3 2 1

Contents

Acknowledgments

Generous assistance has been offered at every stage of this journey, and I would like to acknowledge my primary debt of gratitude to Rudi Visker, my sole reader. Willing to lay aside what then was his relative indifference to Bataille, his assiduous reading and incisive commentary not only enabled the refinement of the text, but forced me to find answers to questions of which I was not even aware. I would also like to thank William Desmond, without whose encouragement it is unlikely that this work would have reached its penultimate stage.

On a more practical level, the contributions from the Katholieke Universiteit Leuven have been substantial. The final year of research was made possible by a grant from the Onderzoeksraad (Research Council) of the K.U.L., for which I am most grateful. I would also like to thank the Fonds voor Wetenschappelijk Onderzoek-Vlaanderen for providing me the opportunity to continue my research through their generous awarding of a postdoctoral fellowship.

A long-term project of this sort, while primarily a solitary endeavor, is nevertheless not to be undertaken without the support of those who are willing to offer their friendship, knowledge, and understanding. In the years that have passed from the point of conception to that of fruition, I have been fortunate enough to find individuals rich enough in character to offer their share of each. I am as well privileged to extend my warmest thanks to my families, both here in Belgium and abroad in the United States, to whom this book is dedicated. Their patient enthusiasm has been a beacon through many a dark night. How many times they heard the words, "it's almost finished," and compassionately let me think they believed it, is in itself no small feat of kindness. To each of them I extend my deepest graditude, my warmest friendship.

Abbreviations

Introduction

The text you are about to read constitutes a betrayal of sorts, one made all the more awkward because the betrayed had anticipated being handed over to an authority he did not recognize, being subjected to rules and a language he did not call his own. While necessarily missing the experience he is trying to communicate, due to the detachment and restraint that theoretical interpretation demands, neither is a commentator on Georges Bataille being just by being faithful, by reproducing his language as if it were one's own. Nevertheless, if we cannot repeat his language, we may do well to repeat his gesture—a religious one, in fact—for, like a living Zarathustra, he urgently tried to communicate a religious feeling that has been lost. And if we, the disintoxicated, are too cautious to revive those burning moments ourselves, an examination of the smouldering remains may at least allow us to realize that there is in fact something we have missed. And this, curiously enough, might just be of equal value to being caught in the moment ourselves.

It is not uncommon, for instance, to regret one's humanness in face of feral animals, those last living remnants of insubordinate nature. Such a regret, however, is founded on the misconception that those creatures actually *experience* an unalienated harmony with the world that we cannot have, that they possess their nature in opposition to domestication. In fact, their natural wildness only has significance for us, the ones who know *of* it without living it, who are separated from them by a seemingly unbridgeable gap opened by consciousness. At the same time, because of this gap, there is something in them that is enticing, something alien and unknown that we may nevertheless recognize in ourselves, something that Bataille calls "intimacy." It is for this unknowable depth that Bataille, in multifarious ways, is continually searching. And while this example is to some extent merely exemplary, it nevertheless testifies to something fundamental. If we feel melancholia when we see an animal in a cage, it is because we recognize that something in ourselves has been caged. And if they cannot be freed from their cages, it would be better to kill them—not for their sake, but for ours.

1

While such a proposal may seem appalling, we know that there was a time when the ritual annihilation of fellow-beings was a regular practice. And while we consider ourselves above such barbarity, our sadness in zoological gardens testifies to an undeniable affinity with those humans of a seemingly distant past. Their ritual slaughter of beings in which they perceived abandoned yet inalienable traces of their own nature was not only an atonement for the use to which they subjected them, but an attempt to affirm that these beings—*and thus the killers themselves*—did not belong entirely to this mundane world of work, fatigue, and concern. It was an attempt to give a sign that they themselves belonged to something unfamiliar, something "totally other," that there was a share of life, even if seemingly crushed by the weight of necessity, that could be called "sacred." The attempt to rediscover this sacred "intimacy" was the religious response to the rise of an uncompromisingly *human* nature. This attempt, in short, defines the work of Georges Bataille.

Yet, what this rather puerile primitive formula has not accounted for, and has apparently disparaged, is the very fact of the liberation that is humanity itself. Whereas the wild animal appears free, in effect it is bound by the caprice of an unforgiving natural given against which it can voice no protest. The animal world is not sacred unless and until humankind painfully extracts itself from it, destroying its links to those givens that constitute blind subordination—until, that is, natural man becomes conscious. Thus, even if in becoming conscious humankind loses its claim to the plenitude it perceives in animals, it is nevertheless the case that those animals are not as rich as the man conscious of his poverty.[1] In one and the same movement consciousness not only occults and denies, but as well defines a world that is sacred, for which it can then search as if for a lost part of its being. What humanity has the potential to gain in its loss is self-consciousness. The question is whether or not it uses this potential.

The issue around which George Bataille's thought continually circles is this dialectical tension in human life between the flight from and the search for this "sacred," "sovereign" aspect of existence: "intimacy." For if man—as perhaps Heraclitus first formulated with his perception that life is motion rather than a static possession—is the being that goes in search of itself, Bataille believes as well that man is the being that constantly goes in fear of itself.[2] That, in effect, what is considered to be a self-conscious search for oneself may in fact be a flight from oneself. This tension, more specifically, is a conflict over the very nature of self-consciousness itself. It is a tension that arises when humankind progressively defines itself, its autonomy and self-consciousness, by the measure of its conscious pursuits: its unwavering conquest of and distanciation from indeterminacy through a refinement of labor, language, and thought. Having defined the issue in this manner, by placing the question of self-consciousness at the core of our investigations, we implicitly suggest that the tension will involve the paradigmatic figure in modern philosophy of the knowing certainty of self-consciousness, namely Hegel. Bataille's challenge, concisely stated, will arise from his insistence that regardless of any claim to the fullness of self-conscious knowledge, there nevertheless persists a disturbing subterranean awareness that there is, in humanity, something irreducible, something "sacred" which defies inclusion within the parameters of self-conscious clarity. If it is thus the case that self-consciousness is founded upon a constitutional exclusion of this element, it follows then that self-consciousness is not what it claims to be.

In itself, this is not cause for alarm. One may comfortably assert that there is simply that which we know (knowledge[1]), that which we cannot and need not know (non-knowledge[1]), and all that we do not yet know (non-knowledge[2]) but will eventually come to know (knowledge[2]). Otherwise stated, there is the unconscious and unknowable state of natural abstract immediacy, animal "intimacy" (non-knowledge[1]), which is negated by the productive and intellectual action of conscious humanity (knowledge[1]), a discursive action that continuously overcomes its non-knowledge[2] until it reaches a state where it can fall together with that for which it was searching in an "absolute," self-conscious knowledge[2]. But the avidity of knowledge does not work this way, is not so readily satisfied. For one who is determined to know beyond the limits of attained knowledge, whose search for "complete" self-consciousness will not rest within such clearly defined parameters—clear insofar as the final knowledge attained here is really but the logical extension of the initial state of knowledge, profane and human, in denial of an initial natural state—this partition between self-consciousness and that with which it need not concern itself is no trifling matter. And, contrary to all ready appearances, I believe and intend to show that for Bataille, who is typically associated with obscure reflections on excessive forms of sexuality, mystical states of ecstasy, and primitive violence, the issue is to push the very limits of self-conscious awareness.

Now, given the modern position of atheism, coupled with the technical capabilities of rational humanity, it would be logical to assume that the characteristic philosophical paradigms of modern man in its search for self-consciousness would be the affirmation of an anthropological humanism and its corresponding positivist scientism—both of which effectively reduce the world and the heavens to humankind itself. One would assume, that is, that the finite individual is quite comfortable with considering itself to be the measure, the final purpose, and the highest court of appeals of all things human and inhuman. Bataille however—despite missing the cue that Hegel had already provided on this matter—believes quite the opposite. What he does believe is the following: that in confining the knowledge we have of ourselves and the world to the type of knowledge that is practical, productive, and theoretical; in restricting our knowledge to that which can be grasped by, and given meaning in relation to, our individual consciousness and its reason—insofar, that is, that we believe ourselves to be in possession of the world, and of ourselves, then we are effectively blind. In asserting ourselves as individuals, and by extending this assertion to the farthest reaches of possibility, we have lost something essential.[3]

If he then designs to extend the reaches of self-consciousness, we shall find the basis of this extension—which lurks within the very structure that he will contest—in what he named the "principle of insufficiency," an insufficiency or "incompletion" that is not defined in contrast to a model of sufficiency or completion, even if it is indissociable from the search for a completion that is necessarily denied. In more familiar terms, this principle is synonymous with desire itself, the absence of which would be worse than the absence of satisfaction.[4] The core of this principle rests on three specific notions: first, that human existence is only really human when it is putting itself in question, into play, or at risk; second, that, being desirous, *self*-consciousness always proceeds by way of an *other*, an infinite alterity and the term in relation to which insufficiency is revealed, the other that puts one's self into play; and third—which will be the crucial factor distinguishing Bataille's notion of self-consciousness from that of Hegel—that the domain in which insufficiency unfolds is incontrovertibly finite, which implies that the term that would bring the desirous being to a halt, the term to which the being could relate its life and knowledge as in anticipation of that which will complete its self-consciousness—whether this term be death or God—necessarily escapes self-consciousness.

In short, insofar as the consciousness we have of ourselves is constituted by the dismissal of that which cannot be reduced to consciousness itself, then we can make no claim to full self-consciousness. And this is the fundamental issue that Bataille addresses: we can only make a claim to have a conscious relation to ourselves, and a genuine relation to that which is beyond ourselves, if we admit that there is something—death or God—that escapes conscious knowledge, eludes our grasp, and calls our self-certainty into question. But it only escapes as the definitive point of non-knowledge, equivalent to the initial point of non-knowledge, insofar as death is considered from the perspective of an *individual self* that disintegrates. And it is this perspective that Bataille constantly, relentlessly, calls into question. If there was nothing else Bataille wished to communicate to his readers, if there is one thought that sets his thought apart from reasonable ways of thinking, one thought that is both horrifying and liberating to think, it is this: that the affirmation of the individual as an individual, while necessary, is in itself utterly insignificant. Or more accurately, it is only significant as a limit to be overcome. Consequently, all those ways by which the individual is affirmed, by which one affirms one's *self*-productive action, positive knowledge, morality, language, economic success, recognition, and even the desire to remain alive itself—all of these will be exposed as so many inevitable paths of deception, as so many forms of subordination that limit human autonomy, an autonomy that Bataille calls the "sovereignty" of being. Each, in their turn, shall be called into question.

It is difficult to overstate the significance that the insight into the insufficiency of being—from which follows the insignificance of individuality—had for Bataille, as effectively every notion he subsequently developed, every perspective that came under his criticism, is mediated by this basic premise. Yet is this rejection of individuation as first and final cause necessarily a distinguishing trait of Bataille's thought, moreover one that is absent from "reasonable ways of thinking"? Or is this not a revitalization of one of the oldest metaphysical ideas philosophy has engendered, dating back to Anaximander and periodically revived throughout the centuries and up to the present day? Is it not, that is, a restatement of the principle whereby the move toward individuation is the "primal ontological sin" insofar as it occurs at the price of violating the original ontological whole, the *to apeiron*, which is torn apart as beings differentiate themselves?[5] Is this not the ancient origin of an idea so essential for Bataille, one that establishes not only the eternal bond of *Eros* and *Thanatos*, but establishes them as conditioned by an original cleavage of an ontological whole—a schism that *Eros* strives to overcome and *Thanatos* will repair with or without a concerted effort? Now, it is not that Bataille necessarily referred to the pre-Socratics in formulating this idea, more likely taking it from Nietzsche's *Birth of Tragedy* wherein suffering is identified with individuation and joy with its destruction and submersion into undifferentiated existence. Nor did Bataille fully appreciate how much his own thought in this way followed Hegel's thought, the movement of which starts with the negation of the immediate substantial whole by determinate particularity, and continually asserts that the action of particular being will bring about its own downfall (negation) as it rejoins the universal. It must be doubted whether he recognized the Hegel for whom "the highest maturity, the highest stage which anything can attain is that in which its downfall begins";[6] for whom "self-subsistence pushed to the point of the one as a being-for-self is abstract, formal, and destroys itself. It is the supreme, most stubborn error. . . ."[7] And failing to appreciate this, nor did he truly recognize the connection with Hegel's position that genuine subjectivity acknowledges the inadequacy of trying to recognize itself as an independent individual, and rather must come to both accept and know that individuality is indeed a limit to be overcome *(aufgehoben)* so as to affirm one's social, and finally divine, nature.

Yet despite the historical precedents, and perhaps because of his insistence on breaking what he perceived to be the capitulation of modern thought to the social, economic, and post-religious conditions of modern humanity—the domination of cold economic calculation, the science of efficiency, and the loss of communal life—the conclusions to which this principle will lead him indeed seem aberrant from established ways of thinking. For instance: it will lead him to posit that the movement of life is only affirmed in a movement of ruination and decomposition; it implies that one's own death has no meaning, that the only significant death is that of another, which one should actively try to bring about; that desire desires *not* to be satisfied; that the search for self-consciousness excludes recognition and the certainty of knowledge; that ecstasis is not transcendent; that beauty is only significant as a sign of filth; that silence is the language of communication; that the highest knowledge coincides with complete unknowing. . . . If we pause over this last notion, however, we will not only find that to the dialectic of self-consciousness, a third type of knowledge and non-knowledge must be added, but we will also discover the root of another inviolable imperative.

We have already posited that the movement of self-consciousness fights its way upstream from an unqualified source to the pinnacle of complete determination of itself and its world. What Bataille will insist upon is that if the state of achieved knowledge is reached, if not by forgetting its origin, then at the price of the complete assimilation of the other to which it is in relation, an inadmissible operation has occurred insofar as the other remains the locus of something not merely unknown, but something unknowable (non-knowledge[3]). This third bastion of non-knowledge is indeed a remnant of the original, natural one, that mythical Garden of Eden. But, significantly, it is only that place insofar as we have been thrown out, and to which we can never return, even though we desire to do so. Indeed, when it does not find itself at work, Bataille believes that humanity does nothing else than try to return to this place, even if there is no possibility of knowing where it would be, or how one would get there, which indeed lends a comical aspect to mankind's attempts to coax the gods to speak. Yet with this unknowable comes another form of knowledge[3], which, I shall argue, is more precisely where Bataille situates self-consciousness. This final form is, rather paradoxically, defined as "knowing non-knowledge,"[8] conscious unknowing or the conscious experience of anticipation dissolving into nothing.[9]

From an epistemological perspective, this amounts to saying that in its truest form, knowledge is incomplete: that there is no recognizable difference between knowledge and the destruction of knowledge; or that wisdom implies a resolute hopelessness with respect to thought ever attaining its object, for the privileged object of thought is rendered elusive by the very means of trying to grasp it. What this imposes, as will be made more clear as we continue, is the relation of knowledge to a moment of experience that cannot be known and that, properly speaking, is not even experienced. From an anthropological perspective—which, as I shall endeavor to clarify, is indissociable from the epistemological—what is posited is a radically transgressive structure of desire, which is not only the lack that drives the search for an object, but is as well an excess that will destroy its object as it would transgress an opposing limit. And insofar as its privileged object is the one in which it finds itself, properly speaking what is transgressed is its own self, which is put into play, at risk, by its own desire. There where one would find oneself, one loses one's *self*.

Finally, on an ontological level, Bataille's fundamental insight is that the ground on which we stake our claim to being is no ground at all, but rather a sort of abyss over which we are suspended by our claims and means to maintain our individuality. What he endeavors to show, drawing on an obscure awareness that belonged even to humans we regard as primitive, is that we are bound to something 'in us' that we can neither know nor master, something 'in us' that exceeds us. This "something" interminably places the terms of "us"—"I" and "you"—into question, and is there the moment that "I" and "you" are not. In Bataille's lexicon, this "ground," *the Being of beings*, receives the name encountered above: "intimacy." Alternatively, it will be called the "continuity of beings," the attainment of which—should it be something attainable—is referred to as "sovereignty."

The imperative that results from these interrelated perspectives, and which serves as the active component in the search for the "intimacy" of Being, the search for the "sovereignty" of beings, is sacrifice. The theme of sacrifice was perhaps the greatest and most consistent obsession in a life replete with obsessions, forming what I believe to be the ground zero of Bataille's thought. It is the core not only of his historical reflections on religion, economics, communities, eroticism, knowledge, and literature, but more significantly, as we shall see, his analysis constantly slides from the objective forms of sacrifice to the crucial aspects of subjective life and experience.

But how are we to justify a preoccupation with such an outmoded topic as sacrifice? What does such a naïve form have to show us today, in our mature and disenchanted world where a rigorous rejection of useless pursuits and irony with respect to myth hold sway? Should philosophy be stepping outside the limits of reason and into that of violence and crime? For sacrifice is—and there is no way around this interpretation—destruction, violence, and disequilibrium brought into a relatively stable order of things. In what follows I will analyze both the success and failure of Bataille's attempt to rejuvenate modern life through the revitalization of the sovereign and sacred aspects of ritual sacrifice which set it apart from profane, economic, and "servile" existence. We shall examine why and how, through this sacrificial imperative, Bataille believes it is necessary "to regain that which our desire to survive forces us to avoid."[10] We shall see why the fear of death itself is considered to be the ultimate subordination, and the extremes to which Bataille resorts in order to reveal why this fear leads to an impoverishment of existence, Bataille's core anxiety.

Thus, if there are hesitations regarding the validity of Bataille's insistence to speak of sacrifice and its related forms, such as eroticism and mysticism, they may be answered by interpreting his evocation of sacrifice—indeed, of the multitude of heterodox notions he introduces—as a response to one of the predominant questions facing modernity and postmodernity. Namely: is there a way to confront the complacency associated with the radical, bourgeois expansion of efficient economic and intellectual-scientific life; to challenge the social disintegration linked to the economic structures of steadily advancing capitalism and its production of obedience to the economy? Is it possible to dispute a domesticated pursuit of happiness and an oft-bemoaned degradation of communal life, to infuse it with a "religious" atmosphere that transcends the designation of a particular religion, in order to rediscover some "genuine" or "authentic" experience? And if there is truly a need for something of this order, where are we to locate it? The pursuit of that which will at least express, if not satisfy, this need is, above all, the kinetic force behind Bataille's writings.

Furthermore, with respect to the internal structure of this pursuit, and therefore of his thought itself, we shall see that when sacrifice is coupled with his basic premise, that of the insufficiency of beings, the major concepts we have already encountered—intimacy, sovereignty/autonomy, self-consciousness, and their related, "inner" experiences—will take on a signification quite contrary to what they appear to be, and which may cause us to rethink the way we consider some fundamental notions. Let us take the "inner" experience of intimacy for example. There are essentially two senses which one could ascribe to the term *intimacy:* something intrinsic and personal, characterizing one's deepest and private nature; or a close association of familiarity, a longstanding friendship. When Bataille speaks of intimacy, however—which he indeed places at the very heart of our being, as that which is most intimate—he does so to emphasize its ecstatic nature. Consequently, while he refers to the experience of intimacy—among others—as an "inner" experience, the only thing inner about it is in fact the disturbing feeling that the ground is shifting beneath one's feet, that one is passing from a known world that is qualified and familiar to an unknown world that is infinite and strange. It is disturbing, that is, insofar as one desires to retain a firm grip on one's individuality and knowledge, on one's consciousness *of* oneself *as* a particular and autonomous self. What is revealed in inner experience, however, is that we are not what we assume ourselves to be. To the extent that we are at all, we are in-relation-to— or in Bataille's terminology, in "communication" with—something that escapes our grasp. And the experience of this confrontation with the unfamiliar, the unknown and inexpressible, Bataille calls the sacred. It is an experience that affirms the plenitude of being, a plenitude that he equates with the death of the isolated existence of a particular being. It is only in losing life as we know it, if only for a moment, that we approach intimacy. Accordingly, "inner experience" has nothing 'inner' about it, for there is no interior place for the subject to withdraw. Insofar as we are, we are other.

Our task will be to show the origin and efficacy of these notions, as well their labyrinthine development in a work that more resembles a midnight journey through a ravaged city than a body of philosophical thought. Bataille's thought refuses to be corralled and organized, as it is, "in a fundamental way, in perpetual rebellion against itself."[11] He writes the way children play—seemingly without rest or intention—to the growing irritation of the serious adults who must sleep because they have to work, and who work in order to sleep. Indeed, *Oeuvres Complètes* is perhaps the most inappropriate manner in which to name these *jeux incomplètes* in which contradictions, detours, and incessant reformulation reigns. It is perhaps for these reasons that Bataille has been called "intolerable to philosophers."[12] Yet despite its slippery, elusive character, there remains a certain cohesion within the apparent chaos, a cohesion of thought and experience, form and content. And if this cohesion yields ambiguous results, it is because his methodology, concomitant with its object, is fragmented, incomplete, achieving and dissolving its positions simultaneously. His object is life itself, and "my method, or, moreover, my absence of method is my life."[13] But is there anything in this life to which we can point that gives a clue to the impulse that drove him to plumb the most excessive experiences in order to compose his thought?

BEHIND THE MASK

Georges Bataille has a reputation: excrement-philosopher, modernist-mystic, postmodernist pornographer, erotic economist. Of these labels it is perhaps the first, and most immature, that is most readily recognized. It is not so seductive to consider that he spent his entire working life as an archivist and librarian at the *Bibliothèque Nationale,* that he founded the influential journal *Critique,* had two wives—his first, Sylvia Maklès, was later to become Sylvia Lacan—a son, a daughter, and tuberculosis, or that he spent the majority of his final years writing articles and books on art, literature, philosophy, religion, eroticism, and economics. Some still see him as a surrealist, a participant in secret societies and fascism, a twentieth-century Marquis de Sade. And while these perceptions are not without foundation, they do little to account for why he has increasingly come to be considered one of the major thinkers of the second half of this century, why his work is perceived as fundamental to a generation of French intellectuals: a forerunner to Foucault, Derrida, and Lacan; a companion to Blanchot; an unconscious residue in the work of Jean-Francois Lyotard; a manifest content for Baudrillard and Jean-Luc Nancy;[14] a central figure for the 1960's *Tel Quel* group which included Julia Kristeva, Phillipe Sollers, Denis Hollier, and Jean-Joseph Goux.[15]

It is not my intention, however, to trace Bataille's influence in the thought of others. What I will show is that which is essential in his own thought, with reference—at times extensive—to those thinkers who were important for him. Nevertheless, a brief account of the events and influences that contributed to his esoteric outlook, some of which will be addressed more thoroughly in later chapters, may help to bring a distorted picture of Bataille into focus. If we look past the poetic embellishments of his own account, it does seem that he simply underwent all the same difficulties that would trouble a sensitive youth of his time: a love-and-hate relationship with his parents and their religion; a struggle for acceptance in a sphere for which he was perhaps not quite ready; and above all, women and war—two phenomena, in his view never very far apart, which only lost their disturbing effect on him in his waning years. Born in 1897, son of a godless, blind, and syphilitic father, he revolted by turning to Catholicism, even considering the priesthood, briefly attending a monastery in England. This was soon to pass as he became, rather casually by his own admission, a reader of philosophy, that of Nietzsche in particular. Why he began to develop some of the profound obsessions, particularly centered around his father, that appear in his earliest writings, and which prompted a brief-tenured psychoanalysis, we shall examine at a later point. In Paris during the mid-to-late 1920s , however, the magnet of intellectual and artistic life was surrealism.

Bataille's first real step into the literary world came in the years 1929–30 with articles, primarily influenced by the surrealist movement and the current trends of Marxism, published in the journal *Documents*, of which he was the co-founder and director.[16] But the extremity and ignobility of their content met with condemnation by André Breton in his *Second Surrealist Manifesto* and the excommunication of Bataille from Breton's group. Bataille did not hesitate to fight back, accusing Breton of promulgating a metaphysical, "Icarian" flight from reality, and formed a splinter group of dissenting surrealists that included Roger Caillois, Michel Leiris, André Masson, Pierre Klossowski, and Robert Desnos, among others.[17] The allure of surrealism, while evident in his earliest writings, nevertheless faded with the arrival of the more pressing political concerns facing his generation. Intellectuals were called to respond to the tumultuous consequences of the uncertainties evolving out of World War I, which made possible such violent mass upheavals as the Bolshevik Revolution in Russia and National Socialism in Germany, the rise of which effectively sounded the death knell of nineteenth-century intellectual, political, and moral authority. Bataille's response was the formation of a group of intellectuals called *Contre-Attaque*. Joining his Marxist and Bolshevik affinities with his anthropological investigations, Bataille brought to this group the rather misguided ideal of resurrecting the primitive frenzy of festival in the form of subversive mass violence in order to overthrow the institutionalized violence of authority. Not content to stop at an insurrection in thought, but pushing it toward action, he would come to find the expressive form of his ideal in fascism.[18]

After the collapse of the *Contre-Attaque* group and prior to the start of World War II, two more projects were organized: the subterranean *Acéphale*, which, according to his close friend Blanchot, "was the only group which mattered for Georges Bataille . . ."[19] and the influential *Collège de Sociologie* whose lecture-hall format drew the likes of Alexandre Kojève, Claude Lévi-Strauss,

Jean-Paul Sartre, and Walter Benjamin. In the chapters that follow I will discuss the ideas fomenting in Bataille's mind during these years of agitation, without however specifically tying them to the groups with which they were associated. Rather, I will connect them with his work as a whole, for I believe that if we are to obtain an accurate sense of his mature thought, we must connect two periods that are marked by a profound schism—the war. If the chaos and unimaginable violence of World War I planted the seeds of his thought—horror, very real death and decomposition, and an upending of transcendental perspectives—he had to wait until World War II for it to ripen. In 1938 he states, "I MYSELF AM WAR,"[20] which is not only an allusion to his name and an affirmation of the Heraclitean principles of conflict and change, but is in anticipation of the very real events that then appeared imminent.

If I have thus far filled lines with the names of those with whom he was associated, this is not only to give an idea of the atmosphere in which he was living, but primarily—and here I am following Blanchot—to highlight the very real sense of community in which he lived, and for which he was always searching. But as community-oriented as Bataille was prior to the war, he was equally isolated during and directly after it, when literally everything around him—society, his friendships, his health both physical and mental, and the world itself—was rapidly disintegrating. Whereas previously he had infused real communities with thought gathered from rather heterogeneous anthropological, sociological, and philosophical sources, only to watch these communities fall apart, with the outbreak of the war he would take his communal perspectives into isolation in order to reflect on the ontological and subjective bases of the drive to form communities. He would never lose this concern with the community, with communication, but he would also transform it. And one of the essential precursors to this transformation was the dissolution of another community, his relationship with Laure (Collete Peignot), which ended with her untimely death, sparking—in the words of Michel Surya—a "profound crisis" in his life.

After her death, Laure—whose poetry and writings on the nature of the sacred influenced, and were posthumously published by, Bataille and Leiris—came to be for Bataille a sort of paradigm for the search for a lost object and a lost intimacy, one that received its literary precursor in his novel, *Madame Edwarda,* and its theoretical elaboration in the texts that followed, *Guilty* and *Inner Experience.* The space opened by death and loss—of a loved object, of God—is the space that Bataille's writing will thereafter come to inhabit. But it is also a space cleared by the ravages of war. He writes in the space of "catastrophe." In World War II, Bataille perceived not only the extreme consequences of a productive world without any other means than destruction for unleashing its stored energy, but also recognized the futility of continuing to commit oneself to productive *action.* Thus, at the very point where the events in the objective world became the sole point of concern for the politically minded, Bataille turned his attention to his own, "inner" experience, perceiving the burning world around him as merely a backdrop to his own personal experience.[21]

Yet there is one final, and decisive, reference point for Bataille's philosophical development, one which his thought would never cease to mediate: the interpretation of Hegel by Alexandre Kojève.[22] The lecture series given by Kojève at the *École des Hautes Études* from 1933–39 was pivotal for an entire generation of French intellectuals,[23] and his humanist-anthropological interpretation went virtually uncontested until the publication of Jean Hyppolite's *Logique et existence* in 1952, which followed from his translation of Hegel's *Phenomenology of Spirit*, the first time that text had become available to German-impaired French readers. Arguably a more accurate reading of Hegel, Hyppolite significantly proposes "to exorcise the phantom of non-knowledge as well as the phantom of the ineffable" from Hegel's text.[24] This amounts to a rejection of Kojève's "ontological dualism" of Being and Thought (*Logos*, language, man), identity and negativity, non-sense and sense, effectively clarifying for a Kojève-tutored audience that the role of human action is to be seen as a difference internal to the Absolute itself. While this reading might have caused Bataille to reconsider the way he thought about Hegel, there is no evidence to support that he ever strayed from Kojève's flock. His statement from 1946, "I would like to take this opportunity to mention that—not only on this point [recognition], but generally—my thought flows from the interpretation of Hegelianism . . . by Alexandre Kojève,"[25] therefore remained intact.

Yet there is a significant difference between Bataille and Kojève, a difference marked by the distance between a humanist atheism and an a-theological religion, which may eventually reveal that it is not necessarily Hegel, but rather Kojève whom Bataille must ultimately overturn. We shall explore this as we continue. In any event, one of my fundamental goals is to demonstrate the profound and disturbing influence of Hegelian philosophy, which—while it may seem quite distant, even thoroughly antithetical to the casual reader of Bataille—forms the very basis of Bataille's philosophical enterprise. That Kojève's reading of Hegel was an integral part of Bataille's philosophy is beyond debate. That it was *the* most decisive influence on his thought is more questionable. Nevertheless, I believe that without fully understanding Bataille's profound intimacy with, and *détournement* of, the work of Hegel, one quite simply fails to fully comprehend Bataille.

This view, which is not without precedent, has led to Bataille being labeled a "well-known subversive repetition of Hegel."[26] Just how "well-known," in the sense of correctly understood, Bataille's reading of Hegel is, however, must be questioned. For in the words of Jacques Derrida, "rarely has a relation to Hegel been so little definable"[27]—and indeed, even Derrida's reading must in turn be questioned. Perhaps this ambiguity accounts for the silence that often surrounds it, a silence that belongs primarily to his English-language interpreters and which is only slowly being lifted. Perhaps Hegel's influence has yet to be fully elaborated because it can be seen as simply one of a multitude of influences with equal claims to validity: from dogmatic Catholicism to heterodox theology; from Marxist anthropology to French sociology; from Blake to Rimbaud; not to mention Freud, Weber, and Heidegger. Or perhaps it is because our contemporary reading of the full complexity of Hegel's thought is still in its adolescence. And since one cannot 'overcome' that which one does not fully understand, there will be no talk here of Bataille as definitively 'overcoming' Hegel.

Why then center the discussion on what Derrida refers to as Bataille's "interminable explication with Hegel"?[28] While it is obvious to the "professional" reader of Bataille—as awful as that sounds—that Hegel is an opponent, that he is as well Bataille's trainer, as I shall argue, is not so apparent. And to those who are only casually familiar with Bataille, the question, "why Hegel?" may be in need of explanation, for at a glance they seem inimical to one another, perhaps even unrelated. Would it thus not be more obvious, for instance, to invoke Nietzsche, the one with whom he felt the most profound complicity? While this may be illuminating, I also feel that it would have an air of redundancy, for Nietzsche is the one accepted almost entirely by Bataille—and for Bataille, significance only arises when crossing an opposing limit. In which case one should simply read Nietzsche, a proposal that Bataille considered legitimate: "Why continue to reflect, why attempt to write, since my thought—all my thought—has been so admirably expressed [by Nietzsche, C. G.]?"[29] Why? To dig a bit deeper. If Nietzsche is the manifest content, Hegel is the underlying structure and latent core which, if not exposed, will leave our comprehension of Bataille in the dark.

The problem of excavating his relation to Hegel, however, are the layers of Kojèvian sedimentation through which we must pass. For if one follows Kojève while failing to recognize the interpretive alterations—or stating it less diplomatically, the "violence"—enacted by Kojève on Hegel's thought, then one runs the risk of simply failing to comprehend Hegel.[30] Consequently, in the prudential words of Mark Taylor, "one must exercise great caution . . . in accepting Kojève's interpretation for Hegel's own position . . . in many ways, [Kojève's *Interpretation*] [is] more interesting when viewed as an original philosophical treatise than as a commentary on Hegel."[31] Now, the latter portion of this comment certainly applies to Bataille. His work is by no means a commentary on Hegel, nor is this text to be read as a comparative study. Rather, it is an analysis of a thinker who, in the attempt to express his thought, drew upon the vast resources of a Hegelian inheritance and struggled to prodigally dissipate them. Yet if we simply assume that Bataille's allegiance to Kojève blinded him to Hegel entirely, then claim can hardly be made to a confrontation with Hegel at all. I do not believe this to be the case. Nevertheless, without some preliminary considerations of the main distortions carried out by Kojève, which certainly planted the seeds of both admiration and criticism in Bataille's thought, it may indeed be difficult to disentangle when it is Hegel that is being referred to, and when it is Kojève.

HEGEL?

It would be an understatement to claim that Kojève's lectures on the *Phenomenology of Spirit* (1933–39) and the subsequent publication of the *Introduction à la Lecture de Hegel* (1947) had a revitalizing effect on the interest in, reception of, and debate surrounding Hegel's thought in the philosophical, psychoanalytic, and literary communities, particularly in France. This effect was carried over to a broader English-speaking audience when it was published in translation (1980) accompanied by editor Allan Bloom's accolades claiming Kojève's reading to be "a model of textual interpretation . . . the most authoritative interpretation of Hegel,"[32] notwithstanding the fact that its roots branch into the soil of Marx, Nietzsche, and Heidegger. The opinion regarding Kojève's "authority" since then, however, has generally received a much more tempered response by the majority of Hegelian scholars, and while few go as far as Flay's outright condemnation (see n.30), it is not uncommon to see his interpretation referred to as "classic but highly eccentric," to the extent that "no serious reader of Hegel could fail to recognize that Kojève is as much creator as interpreter of the system he ascribes to Hegel,"[33] and indeed we must keep this in mind. Our view, however, is closer to that of Errol E. Harris who, despite his claim that Kojève's (as well as Adorno's) interpretation is "based on misunderstanding, misrepresentation, and sometimes even travesty of Hegel's thought,"[34] nevertheless claims that "Kojève's view is highly plausible, but for that reason is all the more seductively misleading. It is a brilliant but dangerous half-truth."[35] Just which half of the truth he identified, and how this half is translated into the whole, is what we now must address, albeit in its skeletal form.

    In short, there is one crucial element of Kojève's reading—one that actually derives from Feuerbach—which is indeed seductive to the modern mind, but which simply cannot be ascribed to Hegel with any claim to accuracy: namely, the assumption that theology can be reduced to anthropology, which in turn derives both from Kojève's rejection of a transcendent God, and from the view that "the only possible God is a transcendent one beyond the world,"[36] a view that Hegel, perhaps more than anything else, endeavored to rectify. Yet, ironically perhaps, it is Hegel's very insistence on undermining the notion of an abstract God situated "beyond" the world or the epistemological notion of an essential truth "beyond" appearance that enabled Kojève to derive his conclusions regarding Hegel. For if one recognizes, as indeed we must, that Hegel's notion of Spirit posits finite human existence as the external expression, development or life of the Absolute, the Concept, or God, *and* one rejects the existence of a transcendent God, then there is compelling evidence to conclude that the transcendent dissolves into the immanent (finite), and there is a compelling reason to elevate the finite (the negative) to an absolute status, as Kojève does. The 'half-truth' that Kojève asserts is thus the finite, human side of the equation, leaving God out of the picture. And while his position is perfectly legitimate, it is not Hegel. For Hegel, as his post-Kojèvian guardians compulsively repeat, neither simply effaces the difference between the infinite and finite, eternity and time, God and human being, nor does he maintain their difference in opposition. Rather, he retains their difference within their sublated identity. The human being, whose existence is in fact finite, will find the ultimate fulfillment of its finitude—and not just its annulment—when it is sublated (and maintained) in the infinite life of God, the Absolute.

We shall have more to say on this as we continue, but for now I would like to identify the three core "Kojèvisms," which, in conjunction with his rejection of a transcendent God ("the only possible God"), combine to form the root of his unconventional reading of Hegel: the "primacy" of the future, the "end of history," and most significantly, the identity of Time and the Concept, which he views as "[Hegel's] great discovery."[37] Again, out of concern for introductory brevity, we will limit ourselves to the bare bones of what is in fact a complex reading of one of the most obscure elements in Hegel, the synthesis of time and eternity. Now, in fact this reading of Hegel was not originated by Kojève, but rather by his fellow Russian *émigré*, Alexandre Koyré, whose "conclusive article" on Time in Hegel "is," as Kojève claims, "the source and basis of my interpretation of the *Phenomenology*."[38] "Curiously enough," as Kojève notes in passing, Hegel's "crucial text" on time is not to be found in the *Phenomenology* to which it is subsequently applied, but rather in the "Philosophy of Nature" from the *Jeneser Realphilosophie*. And indeed it is curious, as Philip Grier claims, that Kojève took an "obscure set of passages on time from a very early version of Hegel's *Natuurphilosophie*, which Hegel certainly rejected prior to writing the *Phenomenology*, and treat[ed] them as the basis for an interpretation not only of that work but of the whole of Hegel's philosophical position,"[39] apparently ignoring Koyré's warnings about the risk of "misunderstanding and misinterpreting" the mature Hegel by using his early works as an interpretive ground.[40] The risk, in short, is in conceiving the temporal dialectic that informs the early "Philosophy of Nature" as distinct from, and irreconcilable with, the logical dialectic of the later *Logic*, insofar as the former transcribes time as the "restlessness" *(Unruhe)* of the infinite and the latter ultimately transcends time so as to draw its moments together in the eternal present of Spirit.[41] But if a case can be made that two incompatible dialectics are indeed operative in Hegel's work, then a critical space is opened in which one may finally announce the failure of the system. It is precisely into this space that Koyré and Kojève, and subsequently Bataille, will enter.

The first issue then is Koyré and Kojève's view of the primacy of the future in Hegel's notion of time, which one may reasonably conclude was influenced by their reading of Heidegger's *Being and Time*.[42] As Koyré emphatically states, "it is this insistence on the future, the primacy accorded to the future over the past, which constitutes, in our opinion, the greatest originality of Hegel."[43] Foremost in coming to this view of the future are statements made by Hegel regarding the dialectical structure of the present instant or the 'Now'. The present, as such, is viewed as a pure moment situated between the future in the past, and therefore its content must be derived or "filled." As Koyré quotes Hegel, "The limit, or the Now, is empty; for it is absolutely simple or the concept of time; it realizes *[erfüllt]* itself in the future. The future is its reality";[44] "The present, suppressing itself in such a way *[so sich aufhebend]* that it is rather the future that engenders itself in it, is itself this future. . . ."[45] In what will become an extremely significant proposal for Kojève and Bataille, the present is "directed" toward, and derives its meaning from, the future. Yet thus defined, we are not dealing with natural time or an abstract succession of moments, but rather with the being who "searches to realize himself in the future," the being who continually transforms the present in view of the future and "who ceases to be the moment in which there is no longer any future, when nothing more is to come, when everything has already happened, where everything is already 'accomplished.'"[46] That is to say, Hegel's historical time is *human* time, finite time, and all things finite must come to an end. This "stoppage" of time will translate into the 'end of history'.

Koyré proposes that the end of history is a necessary requirement for any claim to the completion of the Hegelian system. He concludes his article with the following:

> It is possible that Hegel believed in it [the end of history]. It is even possible that he not only believed that it was the essential condition for the system—it is only at night that the owls of Minerva begin their flight—but also that this essential condition had *already* been realized, that history had effectively ended, and that it was precisely because of that that he could—had been able to—complete [his system].[47]

The completed system as the logical comprehension of the totality of the system's internal movements requires that nothing more can or will occur, that everything has already happened, an assumption without which it could never be complete. If, however, the driving force within this system is the 'infinite restlessness' of time which "is dialectical and is constructed *commencing with the future*," then time, and consequently the system, "whatever Hegel may say about it—[is] eternally unfinished *[inachevé]*."[48] This is what ultimately justifies Koyré's conclusion of "the failure of the Hegelian system."[49]

Now, Hegel, in fact, never did expressly announce the end of history. Nor was his system intended to be anything but the most adequate reconstruction possible at the time of the history or evolution of the spirit through its stages of natural consciousness, culture, art, religion, and philosophy, to the point of absolute knowing. Yet it is this assertion by Koyré that sparked the vision of Kojève and which, when joined to the notion of the complete identity of Time and the Concept, determined the path of his Hegelian interpretation. To justify Koyré's thesis, Kojève turns to a statement from the concluding chapter of the *Phenomenology: "Die Zeit ist der Begriff selbst, der da ist"* ("Time is the Concept itself, which *is there*").[50] It might, however, escape the notice of those receiving their Hegel directly through Kojève that he has added a subtle twist to Hegel's phrasing by translating this statement on time as being the concept itself "which exists empirically." And this, as we shall see, is to say that the true form of the concept as it realizes itself in time (in which the future takes primacy) is none other than self-conscious man: "Man . . . *is the* empirically existing Concept,"[51] and it is self-conscious humanity alone that will complete the developmental process of Spirit and attain absolute knowledge. The Absolute is human—nothing more, nothing less. Now, to some extent this is true, but again, it is only a half-truth.

For while the concept indeed must exist in time for it to become what it is, the concept is as well the comprehension of the temporal content of its development. Thus, it seems rather incongruous to say that time and the concept are identical, for one cannot claim to comprehend that which is still in the process of its development. If, therefore, the conceptual comprehension of the historical development of the concept can occur neither if the pair are identical, nor if they are disconnected (as with a purely eternal concept), then we must conclude that they are related, though distinct. If this conclusion fails to appear in Kojève's text, it is because this time he has carried out a critical omission. For while Hegel does say that "Time is the Concept itself that *is there* . . . ," he continues with the following: "and [Time] presents itself to consciousness as empty intuition; therefore, Spirit necessarily appears in Time, and it appears in Time just so long as it has not *comprehended* its pure Concept, that is, *[as long as it] has not annulled Time*."[52] Two things become clear: first, one cannot identify time with conceptual thought if consciousness must intuit time as something at least partially distinct from itself; second, Spirit's comprehension of itself cannot occur unless Time has been annulled, and "the inescapable conclusion would be that the comprehended concept is quite distinct from the temporal process"[53] . . . though not, of course, unrelated. Is not another 'inescapable' conclusion, however, that history (Time) must cease (be "annulled") for the system to be complete? That knowledge only relates to time as something that has already run its course, allowing for its comprehension?

To reject this last conclusion involves an act of faith in the Hegelian method. On the one hand it requires the acceptance of some rather fantastic logical inversions that endeavor to annul the distinction between the indeterminate, open-ended content of the temporal process and the logically necessary content of absolute conceptual comprehension.[54] This in turn entails the acceptance that finite human life, corporally embedded in space and time, can somehow transcend its facticity, rise above its temporal condition, and unambiguously comprehend its past and future in the present. And this, on the other hand, requires the acceptance of a Trinitarian Christian metaphysics in which the finitude of the human spirit is retained even as it is transcended in the recognition that its life is incorporated in the infinite. Finitude itself is not thereby transcended, but only its inherent ambiguity. In either case, for Hegel to be correct requires the assurance of the Absolute standpoint, which ultimately resolves the tension between finite and infinite, time and knowledge, being and thought. Resolving this tension is nothing less than the task of philosophy itself, and if it does not succeed in this task, the system will indeed collapse.

Much of the above will hopefully become more clear as we continue, but let us make a first brief attempt at sorting this out. Hegel strove to demonstrate the necessary unity of finite human endeavors and the content of religious consciousness, of man and God, difference and identity. And insofar as their unity is necessary, one-sided views that hold these forms of consciousness in opposition will never reach the absolute standpoint, will remain half-truths. One can neither posit the absolute autonomy of subjective action and knowledge, nor leave truth in some abstract metaphysical beyond, for neither constitutes true philosophical thinking: the finite being's knowledge of the infinite content of faith—God. Consequently,

> the one, that of the special sciences, could not be called a philosophy in that it, as independent seeing and thinking immersed in finite matter, and as the active principle in becoming acquainted with the finite, was not the content, but simply the formal and subjective moment. The second sphere, Religion, is deficient in that it only had the content or the objective moment in common with Philosophy. . . . Philosophy demands the unity and intermingling of these two points of view; it unites the *Sunday of life* when man in humility renounces himself, and the *working-day* when he stands up independently, is *master of himself* and considers his own interests.[55]

Here in the *Lectures on the History of Philosophy,* as well as in his *Lectures on the Philosophy of Religion,* Hegel offers two traditional conceptions whose opposition must be thought through and cancelled. One is the position of dependence or faith in which one's worldly concerns are humbly subordinated to a higher region that is spared critical reflection; the other is the position of independence or the autonomy of reason, which "restricts knowledge, science, to the *worldly side.*"[56] This dualism, as we shall see, takes shape in the philosophy of Kant, in response to which Hegel will claim that the true autonomy of reason cannot renounce knowledge of the content of religion without forfeiting its claim to autonomy.

What concerns us here, however, is what happens to "working mastery" and the "Sunday of life" once filtered through Kojève's lens. That is, what becomes of the conflict once the Sunday of life loses its religious character, when the God to whom one turns to make sense of one's workaday toil is removed from the picture? The result—which indeed constitutes the single greatest (mis)interpretive gesture of Kojève, insofar as he presents it as Hegel *à la lettre*—is that working man becomes the absolute master, and the Sunday of life comes to resemble the world presented in Raymond Queneau's book of the same title, a world of well-educated and consummately bored individuals with nothing to do at the end of history but fill their mouths, dabble in their paltry affairs, and attempt to watch time pass.[57] On the one hand, then, the following occurs: Kojève attributes to Hegel the anthropological view that humanity is defined solely by the productive manner in which it disposes of its constituent *negativity*, through which it gives meaning to the world, actualizes its own inherent possibilities, and arrives at complete (absolute) self-conscious knowledge, at which point history stops, the system closes, and man as negativity disappears into the posthistorical "Sunday of life." Bataille, in turn, adopts this presage of the modern post-Hegelian age as his starting point. Yet on the other hand, Bataille views the Kojèvian/Hegelian 'end' somewhat like the "Messianic cessation of happening" evoked by Walter Benjamin, a cessation that holds the promise of deliverance from "the homogeneous course of history."[58] And for Bataille, unlike Kojève, this deliverance will once again take a religious form—the "Sunday of the Negative."

The problematic for Bataille, then, apparently relies on the acceptance of the logical conclusions to Hegel's internally coherent system as presented by Kojève, insofar as Bataille's concern is to explore the possibilities for humanity to continue to manifest its inherent negativity, and in turn achieve self-consciousness, after humanity has completed its journey to self-conscious knowledge and history has effectively reached its end. In effect, then, Bataille addresses what humanity is to do with its negativity once the man of negativity has completed his work and finds himself with nothing to do on Sunday. His attempt thereafter seems to involve the questionable attempt to move beyond "Hegel." Yet in the endeavor to "move beyond" specifically the type of knowing self-consciousness as defined by Hegel, and to reach an alternative notion of self-consciousness, Bataille in fact adopts the structure, the movement, and the fundamental concepts of the one he is trying to escape. But is this aspect of his thought an attempt to escape Hegel, or to escape Kojève? For it is Kojève, and not Hegel, who ultimately asserts what Bataille will condemn: the mastery of work-induced human knowledge. Consequently, when we read Bataille's critique of "the sovereignty of servility" below, we should be aware of just which "Hegel" is under fire, even if we refer to him under the signifier "Hegel." Consequently, if there is any "overcoming" involved on this point, it will be of Kojève, an overcoming about which Bataille, if he indeed acknowledged it, kept silent.

Yet there is another more fundamental issue involved in Bataille's method, one that, even if it is illegitimately derived from Kojève's analysis, nevertheless arrives at a legitimate confrontation with Hegel. Namely, he will question the very absoluteness of the Absolute, which, by semantic definition or ontological status, can refer to nothing beyond itself. This will involve a question of the legitimacy of the movement of the system itself; the legitimacy of a self-mediating absolute for which nothing is irreducible; the legitimacy of the movement from otherness to dialectical difference to speculative totality; the legitimacy of eschatologically recontextualizing finitude into larger horizons of meaning until its irreducibility is usurped; or in sum, the legitimacy of the identity of thought and being. Otherwise stated, Bataille rigorously opposes the unity of working mastery and Sunday's religion, of useful pursuits as divine determination. His own conclusion will be that if there remains, after Hegel, a possibility to reveal ourselves to ourselves—which will imply the recognition of something that cannot be reduced to our reason—it will indeed take place after the working week on the day of rest, though not in worship, but rather in the "inner" experiences of risk, chance, eroticism, play, and laughter. And as he takes great pains to emphasize, these are experiences that, from the perspective of developmental knowledge, have no meaning, and are essentially useless. To insist that our actions have a meaning, he believes, is to subordinate our lives to a degrading chain of utility.

Yet there is a fundamental and inescapable tension to which these reflections point, for the human spirit, even if it desires to escape its barriers and transcend these meaningful limits, is reluctant to do so. Rather, we hold fast to our particular concerns, our goals, and our own futures with the same tenacity that we hold to life itself. Yet the impulse to do so, as Bataille will claim, constitutes a refusal to acknowledge that our particular, isolated meanings, our committed actions, are but a system of necessary illusions to hide from a more uncomfortable reality. They are in denial of the essential. And the essential is not what passes for an affirmation of individual life, but rather that which passes between individuals—in laughter, in eroticism—and annuls their isolation.

Our text consists of two parts. Part One concentrates primarily on those elements—anthropological, economic, religious, and philosophical—that form the basis of Bataille's work and the foundation of his own mature concerns. This will not be a historical survey, but rather a conceptual analysis or ideational history. Chapter 1 almost exclusively involves an extensive analysis of the Hegelian origins of Bataille's major concepts. Here we explore the tension between the "Hegel" that Bataille appropriated into his own thought, and the "immutable Hegel" against which that thought continuously struggled. Yet given the fact that this is a text on Bataille, any claim to do full justice to Hegel—when he plays a supporting role rather than occupying center stage—will be forsaken. Where Hegel is concerned, much of our reading will resemble the "left-wing" tradition of Hegelian readers with whom Bataille was most sympathetic. Chapter 2 primarily traces the development of Bataille's economic theory and the influence that a genealogy of sacrifice had upon that theory. The major points of reference here are Mauss's discussion of *potlatch*, the political questions of the mid-1930s, and Weber's analysis of the movement from a religious to an economic *Weltanschauung* which, for Bataille, had the effect of provoking a *Weltschmerz:* the rise of the bourgeois world view provoked the search to rejuvenate life with the intensity of bygone religious attitudes.

Part Two involves an attempt to give a consistent philosophical picture of the applications to which Bataille put his thought, analyzing the successes and failures of his challenge to traditional modes of thinking. The main focus of these reflections centers around Bataille's attempt to reveal the elusive experience of intimacy. Chapter 3 primarily focuses on Bataille's critique of discursive language as an attempt to secure the philosophical subject's possession of the world in its knowledge. Here the mastery of discourse is challenged with a specific notion of poetry, one that indicates the dispossession of the subject by language itself, leading the poet into a mystical form of silence where the discourse of knowledge falls mute. Finally, chapter 4 draws together the main aspects of his thought as they assemble into a unitary configuration that involves mysticism, eroticism, and sacrifice, and in particular examines the ambiguous status of representation as it pertains to these various forms of experience. And while we chart his circuitous odyssey through a variety of topics, we must never lose sight of his horizon of sovereignty and intimacy, his quest for the sacred. Ultimately, however, we must consider that what we do with our negativity on its day of rest can only take us beyond the serious, that in the end it all dissolves in laughter.

PART ONE

———

ONE

Beyond the Serious

[M]y efforts recommence and undo Hegel's *Phenomenology.*
—Georges Bataille, *Inner Experience*

The account of Hegel's reception in the last century is a history unto itself:
from being perceived as just another Romantic long since dismissed by the
advance of the human sciences, to his resurrection by the revolution-inspired
Marxists and their revival of interest in a dialectical world view; from his elevation in the middle of the century as the father of all things modern, to a
renewed attempt to bury him under the all-encompassing webs of structuralism.[1] But whether he is being praised or diminished, it is above all his system
itself that has posthumously absorbed a barrage of punches. Koyré, just one
example, remarks, "the Hegelian 'system' is dead, thoroughly dead"; "the
recent efforts to revive Hegelianism have, in our opinion, only managed to
demonstrate, once again, the sterility of the 'system.'"[2] This type of pro-
nouncement is nothing new. Writing about the reception of Hegel's thought
only thirteen years after his death, biographer Karl Rozenkranz remarked,
"one would have to be astounded by the vehemence with which it is attacked
precisely by those who declare it dead."[3] His system is often viewed as totalitarian, threatening to depersonalize the individual by turning one into a universal abstraction, to dissipate the concrete individual by absolving one from
concern with the existential dilemmas a finite individual must face to assert
one's genuine individuality, such as Kierkegaard posits. The system may also
be comforting, particularly insofar as it eases the pain of isolation, smoothes
the rough oppositions that leave one in a state of alienation, forgives one's
faults by explaining them as part of the process of development, and allows
one to feel that one is right, for one is a legitimate piece of a larger whole. Yet
the voice whispering in the ear of modern humanity will not stop insisting
that I, a trifle, am more legitimate than the whole—a tear capable of drown-
ing the ocean. And then the individual subject is but a step away from being

seized with the tormenting feeling of being imprisoned, no doors anywhere, the fluid whole becoming a suffocating swamp.

Are we to assume that Bataille is but another link in the chain of post-Hegelian philosophy—from Feuerbach to Kierkegaard, Schopenhauer to Nietzsche—that affirms the cry of a terrorized subjectivity in the face of its dissolution into the universal? To an extent, this link is inevitable: his thought contests the idealist tendency to anaesthetize the pain of finitude. His is a philosophy of the subject that trembles in anguish before the facticity of death, it is the thought of a profoundly earthbound subject that cannot escape the sting of mortality and singularity. Yet the situation of Bataille's subject is closer to that of a subject that *wants* to lose itself in the whole, to dissolve its singularity, but owing to the nature of its subjectivity, cannot. Or more accurately—at least as concerns the issues in this chapter—Bataille addresses the tension of a subject that fears the inevitable, and acts so as to avoid it, and that same subject nevertheless compelled to look that which it fears in the face—a confrontation that will lead to an altogether different employment of its powers of action.

The first task at hand, however, is to establish the field of play for this confrontation, to see why it is Hegel who has drawn the boundaries. This endeavor shall bear affinity with an insignificant incident Bataille relates to us, that of a ladybug that has alighted on a piece of paper containing the blueprint of Hegelian architecture:

> She stopped in the *Geist* column, where you go from *allgemeine Geist* [universal spirit] to *sinnliches Bewusstsein (Einzelheit)* [sensory consciousness (individuality)] by way of *Volk, Staat,* and *Weltgeschichte* [the People, State, and World History]. Moving along on her perplexed way she drops into a column marked *Leben* [Life] (her home territory) before getting to the center column's "unhappy consciousness," which is only nominally relevant to her.[4]

Wandering from concept to concept with chance as her guide, Bataille posits that this insignificant life—unaware of the compulsory movement of the structure over which it treads—is able to inflict wounds on the completed world of the system.

"Why Hegel?" Because Bataille's method of thought with its wandering ladybug-logic is the experience of life itself, and "I think of my life—or better yet, its abortive condition, the open wound that my life is—as itself constituting a refutation of Hegel's closed system."[5] Bataille and Hegel, the wound and the suture. The wound, however, is inflicted by Hegel with the sword called "negativity," the blood that flows—"desire." A conflict arises, however, in that for Hegel, the sword that opens the wound is the one that closes it, a miracle-working that Bataille greets with a burst of laughter. But must this laughter be seen to indicate that Bataille did not take Hegel seriously? Or might it betray a deep affinity? Might Bataille's laughter not be one of recognition rather than derision, one that reveals—in the Hegelian vernacular—a "pure self-recognition in absolute otherness"?[6] For the fact is he took Hegel very seriously—so much so that he could not do without him.[7] Had the line and the circle of the Hegelian system not been previously elaborated in theory and subsequently realized in modern society, Bataille's insubordination would have all the significance of a child crying that its immediate wishes were not being fulfilled. What we must see is that, taking it seriously, Bataille was forced to immerse himself in the system, to follow its reasoning to the end in order to watch it explode at the final moment by the force of its own imperative—negativity. He will conclude that if the wound can be closed then the sword did not strike deeply enough. And essentially it is these two elements that provoke Bataille into laughter: the fact that the highest of philosophical achievements may bear within it the force of its own undoing; and the pretension of the Hegelian *Aufhebung* to conceptually master every event it encounters, and thus to recover meaning even in the risible, redeeming the meaningless. Yet we must wait and see if Bataille's laughter effects a similar sort of redemption, or whether he is in fact laughing at his own failure to stop taking himself so seriously.

To reach this point we must immerse ourselves in Bataille's writings, just as Bataille realized the necessity of immersion in the Hegelian system, insofar as its organic nature precludes the extraction—the scientific isolation and examination through the microscope—of its concepts from that system. The isolation of a concept would entail the loss of its meaning altogether: "Hegel's thoughts are interdependent to the point of being impossible to grasp their meaning, if not in the necessity of the movement which constitutes their coherence."[8] And it will be principally this movement of the system, *Geist*, or the Concept, that is at issue. Likewise, the movement of Bataille's interdependence with Hegel is not made of a piece, and the sliding he introduces into Hegel's coherence is not accomplished with a single blow to its conceptual chains. While their writing is in continual movement, everything is implied in the beginning. This means one thing for Hegel—which we shall arrive at shortly—and something else for Bataille. Yet the connection of the beginning with the end means that the entirety of the Hegelian system must be put in question from the start. This putting-in-question is not, despite appearances, a rejection of Hegel. Nor, as mentioned at the start, must we add Bataille's voice to the chorus of those who sing the "overcoming" of Hegel. Rather, he seeks to reveal the profound and inescapable truth of Hegel, all the while challenging its sense.[9] That is, Bataille will propose to reveal Hegel's truth only to show how it ultimately leads to non-sense.

Alternatively, we may say that Bataille 'recommences' Hegel's *Phenomenology* to unearth the truth of its foundational concepts and their movement, only to 'undo' it in the end to rescue them from Hegel himself, from the sense to which he subordinates them. What this amounts to is in effect pitting *"Hegel against the immutable Hegel."*[10] That is, while he follows the internal movement of the Hegelian dialectic, he continuously challenges its teleology of dialectically self-mediated completion whose horizon is drawn by its eschatological orientation. Yet despite this challenge, we nevertheless find Bataille saying that "he [Hegel] did not know to what extent he was right," that is, "with what exactitude he described the movement of Negativity. . . ."[11] Bataille, taking his Hegel through Kojève without a dose of salt, will never challenge the privileged status of negativity: "[B]ut I know that man is negation, that he is a rigorous form of Negativity or is nothing." Or perhaps more appropriately, he learns from Kojève that precisely because man is Negativity, he is nothing; he is the freedom of Time opposed to Space *(Sein)*, therefore, *Nicht-Sein;* or ultimately, that man is desire, and thus incomplete. His refusal to abandon the movement of negativity, following it to the very end so as to push it beyond its place of rest, will be the crucial element in extending the scope of self-consciousness, and perhaps that of negativity as well.

Our concern in this chapter will be to delineate the fundamental Hegelian concepts which Bataille appropriates and in turn relates back to their Hegelian roots in order to create rips in the system. This appropriation and disorientation is the cornerstone of his method, for as Derrida tells us, at ground level, "[T]aken one by one and immobilized outside their syntax, all of Bataille's concepts are Hegelian."[12] In one sense then, our task is to show the extent to which Hegel, for Bataille, was right. But more importantly, we must begin to unfold the manner in which Bataille cuts his concepts loose from their moorings within the system, displaces them or puts them into play—that is, at risk.[13] This requires that we first step back to view the general outlay of the forest before we start to follow the Hegelian signs (negativity, work, desire, risk, and recognition) posted by Kojève.

1.1 THE INWARDIZING AND THE CALVARY

Hegel, who represented for Bataille the most perfect figure of Western philosophy, the "summit of positive intelligence,"[14] was curiously disturbing to one so oblivious to the demands of academic rigor. Hegel was unsettling I believe not only for the shadow he cast on the possibilities of thought after his realization of the "point where knowledge no longer needs to go beyond itself,"[15] but as well for the internal contradictions revealed between Hegel's thought and personal experience. For while the *Phenomenology* gives the "icy impression of completion,"[16] the winning of salvation in thought's satisfaction, Hegel nevertheless "touched upon the extreme . . . believed himself to be going mad," and perhaps even "worked out the system in order to escape."[17] His "madness," according to Bataille, emerged from his realization of the "impossible" yet necessary suppression of subjectivity in the universal. The brand of satisfaction that results is indeed abysmal, for it "is not in any way the forgetfulness of the impossibility from which it is born," the impossibility of actually relinquishing one's subjectivity while alive, "but is rather the image of it: an image of death and completion."[18] But in what way does this satisfaction differ from the attempts at knowledge advanced by Hegel's contemporaries?

Hegel's system is developed as a critique of the one-sidedness of both positivist Enlightenment science and the immediate intuition of the Absolute found in the Identity theories of Romantic Idealism, particularly that of Schelling. But in his own method of Science—which has been described as the search to find a proper unification of transcendental and empirical subjectivity, which is the only proper way to reach the Absolute (Substance)—he dialectically appropriated what he saw as the truth of each.[19] His particular path receives its principle in the following: "In my view, which can be justified only by the exposition of the system itself, everything turns on grasping and expressing the True, not only as Substance, but equally as Subject."[20] That is, the Absolute is to endure a process of alienation and restitutive self-realization in and through its own movement as Subject in the world.

This method, however, leads to complex tensions, perhaps even irrevocable contradiction, which I shall arrive at shortly. But of basic importance is to note that Hegel did not cut the bond between the Absolute and the experience of historical, empirically existing individuals. Not only did he not cut this bond, he posited the irreducibility of a nonidentical moment foreign to traditional Idealism, namely, the negativity that inserts Time into Being, without which Idealism—indeed, the history of metaphysics from Parmenides onward—would be right, as there would be nothing to oppose Thought and Being. Yet Hegel's historical being is problematic insofar as the living individual (Subject) is in truth the (empirically?) existing Concept which slowly and painstakingly accomplishes the reconciliation between the Absolute and its external manifestations.[21] The problem, then, as indicated above, is that insofar as the Subject is but the living manifestation of Absolute Spirit, its own internal difference, it can only be seen as a moment of the universal into which its particularity eventually vanishes.

Taking a step back, we must understand Hegel as essentially confronting the Kantian problematic found in the *Critique of Pure Reason;* that of synthetic a priori judgments faced with the irreducibility of experience, the problem of form and content expressed in the well-known formula that sums up the lessons of the Transcendental Aesthetic: "Thoughts without content are empty; intuitions without concepts are blind."[22] Kantian knowledge supposes both the Category (a priori form, advance knowledge) and intuition (content) without which thought would be vacant. The poles of form and content however are kept separate by Kant so that immediate sensation is indeterminate and unknowable until it receives the forms already existing (a priori) in the mind, in effect giving knowledge a formal and subjective character. Mind making the world conform to mind.

Kant's formal transcendental categories, translating raw sensation into spatially and temporally organized intuitions, are the possibility condition of empirical knowledge, effectively framing and editing experience. But because this epistemology digs a trench between matter and form, the intuition of phenomena does not necessarily correspond with reality, insofar as it is limited to what appears in experience. As he states, "[C]riticism has previously established our unavoidable ignorance of things in themselves, and has limited all that we can theoretically *know* to mere appearances."[23] In more formal Kantian terms: knowledge is tied to the intuition of *phenomena* (appearances), which are "middle terms" between the *noumena* (the things-in-themselves represented by phenomena) and the concepts of the understanding *(Verstand)*, which are the empty, formal constructs in need of content. The noumena, however, escape, run from experiential cognition and become the negative boundary of thought. And while the awareness of the noumena behind the phenomena does lead to Reason *(Vernunft)*, this as well is unsuccessful in reconciling the apparent and hidden worlds. This limitation, however, leaves a crucial opening, as he states, "I have therefore found it necessary to deny *knowledge* [of God, freedom and immortality], in order to make room for *faith*."[24] Or—more relevant for those twentieth-century thinkers who have abandoned their faith—the room Kant left open by limiting the scope of knowledge was in fact a space for reflection on those others of thought: the unknown, the "unthought," or, more generally, transcendence and difference.[25]

Hegel regarded this limit to knowledge, the gap between thought and the noumena (inner and outer, identity and difference) as well as the dissociation between noumena and phenomena, as intolerable. Which is not to say that he simply eliminates dualistic oppositions and their limits to reason, but rather that he posits them so as to move beyond them. His response to arguments for a limit would be that to recognize a limit is already to be beyond it. More specifically articulated, Hegel posits that the given is always already mediated, pregnant with its form, and hence is known not by imposing determinations but through a progressive dialectical process of unveiling them. This response entails nothing less than abolition of formal epistemology—the separation of the transcendental from the empirical—and the refusal of thought to be intimidated by the matter at hand, to abdicate before the task of knowing the whole of reality, including God. Essentially, Hegel does away with the barrier that is the core experience of Kant's transcendental philosophy, the experience of something that cannot be dissolved in consciousness. He thereby opens the possibility of the adequacy of knowledge to being.

It is precisely on this point that some of the most acrimonious debate surrounding Hegel flares up. *That* Hegel insists on overcoming all forms of incomplete knowledge by thought's mediation of all "apparent" difference, all abstraction, and its discovery of itself in and as the divine comprehension of the totality, is not debated. *How* he does this, and whether or not it is justifiable, is the catalyst for interpretive dispute. There are a number of ways to consider this question. One may take a quite measured approach and view Hegel as both part of, and as developing, the specific theoretical concerns of the late eighteenth century in response to what was seen as the damaging influence of the Enlightenment conception of man. As Charles Taylor lucidly analyzes it, at issue was an attempt to reject the objectifying analytic science of the Enlightenment, which not only "isolated the individual from society, and cut men off from nature," but more fundamentally lost sight of the intrinsic unity of human life itself by viewing man as a mechanistic compound of body and mind, sensibility and reason, which comports itself toward the world as an object there for its use, *à la* Descartes.[26] Two ideas were central to overcoming this distorted conception: the first is what Taylor calls "expressivism," an alternative notion of man developed primarily by Herder which saw life as an intrinsic unity that, like a work of art or Aristotelian form, reached its fulfillment through a process of unfolding or expressing itself—life as an expressive unity; the second is the conception of radically free moral subjectivity as developed by Kant in his second *Critique*. "The hope [of intellectual Germans of the 1790s] was that men would come to unite the two ideals, radical freedom and the expressive fullness [of life],"[27] to unite, that is, self-determining thought and the harmony of Greek life without, however, returning to the latter's unreflective natural unity.

Taylor boils the problem, and the solution, down to the following: "How to combine the greatest moral autonomy with a fully restored communion with the great current of life within us and without? In the end, this goal is only attainable if we conceive of nature itself as having some sort of foundation in spirit. . . . But this is to say that . . . underlying natural reality is a spiritual principle striving to realize itself. [And this] comes close to positing a cosmic subject."[28] The problem, on the one hand, is to posit nature not as a given, but as an intrinsically teleological process of development, and on the other, to posit man as that part of nature by which nature comes to conscious expression, and at the same time retain man's radical freedom. The only way to do so is to assert that "human consciousness does not just reflect the order of nature but completes or perfects it. On this view, the cosmic spirit which unfolds in nature is striving to complete itself in conscious self-knowledge, and the locus of this self-consciousness is the mind of man . . . spirit reaches self-awareness in man."[29] Man is not just a part of the cosmic whole, but is the "vehicle" for cosmic spirit to come to self-awareness. Consequently, nature's self-realization is man's self-expression. As Taylor states, "[A] conception of cosmic spirit of this kind . . . is the only one . . . which meets the requirement that man be united to the whole and yet not sacrifice his own self-consciousness and autonomous will. . . . Now it was a notion of this kind which Hegel in the end hammered out."[30] But unlike his Romantic contemporaries, Hegel strove to realize this "perhaps impossible synthesis" not through an immediate intuition of the whole, nor by recourse to the "beautiful soul" of infinite striving, but rather through the sober distinctions of rational thought and their reconciliation in reason. If we analyze certain presuppositions lying behind this aim, however, some problems emerge.

Now, it is one thing to view Hegel's thought as an ennobling, harmonious narrative of nature, humanity, and culture coming to artistically express its internal (Aristotelian) form as it climbs the ladder from raw existence to self-realization; it is another to realize that, as Aristotelian, there is teleological guidance of this raw form to its actualized perfection; and it is still another to claim that this teleology is not one of human self-development, but rather is the working out of a rational cosmic plan underlying the whole of reality, a "designed universe" whose architect—*Geist,* God, or Nature—works out the plan in the world through its "vehicles" who, in all freedom and without knowing the outcome of this plan anterior to its expression, come to realize themselves as the very self-awareness and self-perfection of *Geist.* There is a crucial presupposition at work here, one that Joseph Flay has identified as stemming from the natural, commonsense attitude with which Hegel's *Phenomenology* begins and that, if incorrect, will put Hegel's whole system into question.[31] The presupposition, in short, that there is in fact a "whole [that] also makes sense as a whole," an Absolute (Being, God) that guarantees that everything "fits together meaningfully,"[32] *and* that there is a possibility for finite being to achieve absolute comprehension of the Absolute to which it belongs, because the Absolute (Being) *fully discloses itself* in and to human thought.[33] Hegel's *Phenomenology,* which begins with this presupposition and is a reconstructive description of its process of development, is thus—as Heidegger claims—the *parousia* of the absolute, its totally manifest truth.

Before we arrive at the contested implications of this double presupposition which leads to the total comprehension of the absolute, let us restate its conditions of possibility. First of all, nature, even in its most indeterminate form, is permeated by the absolute, and humanity is the locus of development of the 'cosmic' principle of intelligibility. Thus, even in its raw, natural state humanity has access to, and is a moment of the self-conceiving intelligibility, despite the inability to recognize and fully articulate it. However, should it achieve the proper perspective, the 'absolute standpoint', it would realize that every rung on the ladder that bridges natural consciousness and absolute knowledge, every moment experienced as alienation, every object experienced as an opposed other, are actually the result of an inability to grasp the larger picture, a result of fixation on its finite perspective that separates it from the whole. Thus, failure to recognize every moment as a moment in a larger plan can only rest on an insufficient level of comprehension on the part of consciousness, because Being fully discloses itself in every moment of its worldly appearance. However, as Werner Marx suggests, "[I]f what is shown to knowledge . . . *is merely a side of Being permeated by hiddenness,* or actually 'withdrawing' itself from truth proper, we then have a thought running radically counter to the possibility that the self-conceiving concept, the self evolving toward true knowledge, should be able to rediscover itself in the complete movement of thought-determinations, *qua* systematic truth."[34] We have, in short, the view presented by Heidegger. Herein lies the locus of debate, and this debate concerns Heidegger's infamous "ontological difference" between Being and beings, the driving force of thought itself.

Heidegger's highly influential confrontation with Hegel rests precisely on this point. It would take us too far astray to fully develop his critique, so we will confine our remarks to the results. In short, both Hegel and Heidegger are ultimately concerned with the manner in which transcendent Being crosses over the ontological divide and discloses itself in and to beings in the world. Hegel is thus a profound thinker of 'the difference'. But, as the criticism goes, he thinks the difference through in order to "eliminate" it, to "absolve" absolute knowledge from dependence on anything other than itself in assuring itself of truth.[35] The Absolute, as absolute, permits nothing outside it, so "difference" is no real difference, but is merely a difference *derived* from prior unity. The Absolute *produces* difference in order to reconcile its own differences in the absolute self-production of knowledge:

> Consequently the task of the *Phenomenology* is to deconstruct the myth of the given. . . . With the collapse of the transcendent thing-in-itself into immanence . . . transcendental knowing is totally productive of the object, and has therefore absolved itself from any reference to or dependence on any given. The *Phenomenology* therefore deconstructs all forms of otherness and shows them to be immanent aspects or elements in a single overreaching thought, or absolute knowledge.[36]

It is precisely such a formulation of the issue, however, that comes under fire from the recent trend to provide a "holistic" reading of absolute knowledge which emphasizes not only the cancellation, but the preservation of difference in the absolute. Under this view, the absolute is not an 'absolute other', as this would imply an unacceptable dualism, but neither is it a transcendental subjectivity that simply produces its other. Rather, it *relates* thought and Being in manner that will not simply collapse their difference. To hold this view, however, requires a rejection of Hegel's assertion of the identity of thought and Being, preferring to see Hegel as holding them apart in an intrinsic relation.[37]

A choice is required on these matters, but in effect our present context—namely, Bataille's reading of Hegel—decides this for us: we must side with the Heideggerian reading. Having said this, we need not go to the point where we entertain the notion that this reading implies that there is simply no 'otherness' or difference, no alienation or its accompanying anxiety in the Hegelian Absolute, for otherness, alienation, and anxiety drive the *Phenomenology* forward, and constitute a number of its crucial moments. Yet neither

will we claim that Hegel does anything else than attempt to dissolve difference and opposition through the very movement of thought itself, and that
there is thus, for the philosopher, a certain predetermination of experience.
How are we to arrive at this claim, the one that will assure the philosopher
that the thing-in-itself, with which this debate began, can indeed become
available to knowledge?

To do so requires an analysis of certain elements intrinsic to his method:
the entrenching of consciousness in its object using the dialectical tool of
determinate negation; the notion of reflection particular to Hegel; and the
belief that the real is in fact rational. This analysis will eventually lead us to
Kojève. Briefly stated, determinate negation is a response to mechanistic theories of knowledge which apply their criteria from above and subsume their
object under a concept, thereby keeping its hands clean of the dirty particu-
lars. Hegel, rather, dives into the particular, giving it a lift and raising it into
its own maturity. But as this is a progressive maturing, equally implied is that
the thing is not yet what it is, that it is but an indeterminate shadow of its
future reality. Determinate negation thus goes hand in hand with reflection,
for if consciousness is directly immersed in its object then there is a likely
probability that—lacking a standpoint from which to view the action—consciousness will erroneously become lost in its own involvement. The correc-
tion of error therefore requires reflection, a doubling of consciousness: the one
(empirical consciousness) engaged directly in the world and the other (transcendental consciousness) relentlessly examining and correcting the knowledge of the former. The striving for knowledge of the former thus becomes the
"highway of despair"[38] that is self-reflective experience, as each particular conclusion is criticized, proven false, and reversed, demanding that consciousness
continue its seemingly endless work of determinate negation until it agrees
with the real. Or until—which the same thing for Hegel—thought no longer
contradicts itself.

The third presupposition is the most controversial and problematic. By
assuming the rationality of the real from the start, his method appears more
as a justification than an examination of reality, and seemingly even contradicts its experience. For the motor of the process is contradiction, a dehiscence
between subject and object. Reflection has the task of dissolving this split
through knowledge, the inwardization of the object by Spirit—Spirit being
the total movement of self-mediation, which first creates the difference
between subject and object only to negate it and consolidate all the particular
moments into a whole. As we shall see, it is the validity of dissolving the split
between subject and object *in knowledge* that Bataille, among others, continuously calls into question, thereby questioning Hegel's claim to grasp the whole
of reality.

If we follow Adorno, for example, who frequently claims that "the whole
is the false"—not only because of the falsity of the notion of a closed totality

but because he finds that Reason exerts an irrational hegemony over the non-identical—then Reason cannot grasp all of reality because that reality is not Reason. This problem does not emerge for Hegel, for if something has come to be—come to be known that is—it was necessary and finds its place in the whole wherein nothing is irrelevant or gratuitous. Indeed, more than a few evils may be justified, in fact necessitated, in this manner. But above all we must see how the previous conditions of Hegelian knowledge take their place with respect to his system's ultimate condition of meaning—circularity.

Let us take reflection, for instance. With the doubling of consciousness, we know that knowledge does not depend solely upon the relation to an object, but rather on consciousness of consciousness of the object. In effect, the object of consciousness is consciousness itself. It becomes an object to itself (self-differentiation) but with the aim of returning to itself. The obvious question is whether Hegel remains faithful to his imperative of thinking reality or whether it devolves into the divine self-enclosure of thought-thinking-itself (Aristotelian *noesis noeseōs*). This is one possible conclusion of positing the Absolute as Spirit (Science or system) as given in the formula that Substance is also Subject—or, more specifically, that Substance becomes Subject to become Substance, a movement that constitutes Truth:

> Further, the living Substance is being which is in truth Subject, or, what is the same, is in truth actual only in so far as it is the movement of positing itself, or is the mediation of its self-othering with itself. This Substance is, as Subject, pure, simple negativity, and is for this very reason the bifurcation of the simple; it is the doubling which sets up opposition, and then again the negation of this indifferent diversity and of its antithesis [the immediate simplicity]. Only this self-restoring sameness, or this reflection in otherness within itself . . . is the True. It is the process of its own becoming, the circle that presupposes its end as its goal, having its end also as its beginning; and only by being worked out to its end, is it actual.[39]

What first comes to attention is the reduction of difference implied in the self-bifurcation and subsequent self-restoration implied in the notion of Substance as Subject. But if we read carefully, this passage points as well to the possibility of the irresolvable schism within Hegelian thought which we encountered above, a tension between two different notions of History (of Time), based on two different negativities, and implying two opposing desires.

The developmental process, the Becoming of Substance, is none other than the "unrest" that is free, contingent, and finite historical living being.[40] This "restlessness" is negativity as the desire that drives the subject out of itself, giving human existence an ecstatic, transcendent, futurizing character—the openness of time. The meaning *(sens)* of this movement however is not free but has been decided in advance (its *arche*) and is guided toward its point of realization (its *telos*) by the unseen hand of Reason. The *telos* is

reached when historical negativity yields to logical negativity which internal-
izes the finite manifestation of Spirit in the world, fulfilling itself in knowing itself as having completed the process of Becoming, thereby canceling the
very negativity that drove the process onward, and canceling time along with
it. For Hegel, the essence of history—contingent, temporal change—in a
sense emerges through the annulment of its essence—in its completion or
closure. And the meaning of finite life is gained through its service to the
infinite Concept.

Yet this ambiguity within Hegelian Science has its traps. Kojève, as we
have noted, after having read Heidegger, was lured by Hegel's admission of
history and temporality into the Absolute—the finite becoming of the infinite—into offering his "anthropological" interpretation of Hegel with its
emphasis on desire, death, and finitude. And while he clearly acknowledges
the necessary circularity of the system—the teleological orientation that
inserts becoming within an anticipative horizon of closure relative to which
every moment derives its meaning—he nevertheless denies that the Hegelian
narrative transcribes anything other than *human* becoming. Against the interpretation of Hegel by, for instance, Hyppolite, who endeavored to awaken the
post-Kojèvians from their Marxist disavowal of God in Hegel, Kojève sees in
his Hegel a resolute atheist. And he asserts this specifically because of the circularity of the system, because knowledge is not related to an eternal Concept,
to something outside of Time that will serve as an exterior criterion for truth.
Rather, he sees that Hegel identifies the Concept (God) with Time (Man,
negativity), and therefore with History, so that Being (God) reveals itself to
itself through discourse in the world.[41] Alternatively, we could say that Kojève
advocated a Christian view provided that the criterion for truth is not granted
to a transcendent God, but rather to human existence in the world.

Bataille however, in one of the few instances that he directly challenges
Kojève, states, "I do not believe that Hegel was entirely the atheist that
Alexandre Kojève saw in him."[42] Now, this is hardly a daring statement considering that its referent (Hegel) is the one for whom philosophy was *Gottes-
dienst*, the one for whom the content of religion and the content of philosophy were one and the same.[43] Yet the very need for such an assertion tacitly
points to the grip that Kojève's anthropocentric interpretation had on his followers. Bataille nevertheless affirms Hegel's theism for two interrelated reasons: the first is his acute awareness that the movement of the Absolute found
in the *Phenomenology* mirrors the "life of God [Spirit],"[44] and thus that the
phenomenology of absolute knowledge is not strictly the science of finite
human being; secondly, he believes that if the movement of the *Phenomenology* is followed to its end, it reaches a state of satisfaction that could only
belong to God—namely, absolute knowledge—or a satisfaction that could
perhaps only be granted by God—namely, universal recognition—both of
which are as unknowable to humanity as God is.

The first reason is made explicit through the manifestation of Absolute Spirit (God) through the incarnation and death of Christ: the Absolute dividing or negating itself in becoming finite existence/Jesus (Subject), dying (the Calvary), and being sublated (the *Aufhebung,* or the Inwardization) into the original unity with the Absolute. First, a word on the incarnation. Hegel thoroughly opposed any notion of a narcissistic *Deus Incurvatus,* an abstract, self-enclosed (or jealous) divine which would set itself in dualistic opposition to finite life. For reasons both theological and conceptual, he rejects the Scholastic tradition of the divine as *summum esse,* stating that the life of God so conceived as self-enclosed love "sinks into mere edification, and even insipidity, if it lacks the seriousness, the suffering, the patience, and the labour of the negative."[45] Hegel prefers to view God as more of an Aristotelian actuality *(energeia),* a dynamic process of self-revelation that involves development in and through the finite. For the adequate self-revelation of God there must be differentiation and alienation: God must have a representation to overcome abstraction and become actual. Christ is this finite representation of the Absolute, its self-alienation, but this alienation cannot remain, or we would have a God with an unhappy consciousness. The Dasein of Christ must be overcome so that the meaning of Christ can be appropriated. Thus, the true meaning of Christ does not lay with his incarnation or actual existence—which is in fact a dialectically surpassable moment—but rather with his death. The absence of his actuality permits the presence of Spirit.

Now, it should be remarked that while Bataille as well affirms the transformative aspect of death, Hegel's spiritual treatment of the sensuous, tragic crucifixion of Christ may well be seen as a dividing line in their thought, similar to the one that Nietzsche posed between "Dionysus and the Crucified." That Hegel added a "speculative" to the Good Friday sacrifice implies that the negative is already a positive, that the death of Christ is the "death of death,"[46] *the death of finitude itself* insofar as through this death the finite being attains universal significance in the eternal life of Spirit.[47] The death of Christ, like every moment put to death in the system, is inseparable from his recuperation by the Spirit, for Christ's death is in fact God's "return from the state of estrangement," which is "His return to Himself. . . . Negation is consequently surmounted, and the negation [death] of the negation [Christ] is thus a moment of the Divine nature."[48] That death is an integral moment of the Spirit receives perhaps its most widely cited expression when Hegel claims, "[B]ut the life of the Spirit is not the life that shrinks from death . . . but rather the life that endures it and maintains itself in it."[49] But if life is maintained in death then nothing is truly lost. In fact the situation is quite the contrary. For while Spirit undergoes "utter dismemberment," it as well has the "magical power" that "converts [death] into being,"[50] or as stated elsewhere, converts death into *knowledge.*[51] This realization prompts Bataille to comment—leaving the obvious theological problems aside—that the tragic view of the death of Jesus partakes in comedy, insofar as it implies an arbitrary introduction of the notion that an infinitely powerful God has somehow forgotten His eternal divinity—has forgotten, that is, that finite death is but a step toward eternal life.[52]

The dialectic that drives this sublimating conversion is an essential facet of Hegelian thought that Bataille calls into question. For if the force animating the dialectic is negativity, the very force that leads Bataille to claim, "[M]an always becomes other. Man is the animal who continually differs from himself . . . ,"[53] Hegel uses the same force to claim, "[T]he power of Spirit lies rather in remaining the selfsame Spirit in its externalization [negation]."[54] The divine both wounds and heals itself simultaneously. Therefore, while Spirit's trajectory follows a path of dialectical differentiation and alienation of self in otherness, the mediation in and through the other is in the end the mediation of the self in the form of its own otherness. Spirit attains its truth through dialectical self-mediation, including a moment of otherness but ultimately subordinating that moment to the self-realizing movement of the Whole. That it remains the same, however, is only revealed at the end of the process, its internal structure consisting in a continuous process of alienation and change (History).

Bataille recognizes both of these factors as necessary: that along with differentiation into the finite (self-othering), closure or completion is a necessary constituent of meaning. He states, "[I]t was Hegel's greatness to see that knowledge depends on completeness,"[55] and further that "imagining an ingathering at the end of time (Hegel) or outside time (Plato) is surely a mental necessity. This necessity is real: it's the condition of meaning. . . ."[56] This necessity presupposes an anticipatory and closed structure, for as noted above, meaning *(sens)* implies having a sense of direction, a *telos* that gives the journey its sense—and thus its meaning. And the predetermined end of Hegel's journey is the realization of Absolute Knowledge, a "satisfaction" that "turns on the fact that a project for knowledge, which existed [from the outset], has come to fruition, is accomplished, that nothing . . . remains to be discovered."[57] Hegel knew no other aim than knowledge and it is to self-mediating knowledge that he reduced the entirety of existence, effectively crushing the distinction between being-in-itself and being-for-myself. If Being consists in being-known, and being-known is equivalent to being-mine, then all of Being is reduced to the meaning it has for knowing subjectivity. Again, an outcry from Bataille—not against the necessity of closure for meaning, but *against the necessity of meaning itself*.

The protest on this point is varied and complex, and shall guide us through the remains of our discussion. The first issue raised is Bataille's claim that it is possible to view Absolute Knowledge as simply one knowledge among others, as simply a higher, more voracious form of the common knowledge which seeks to make the unknown known.[58] Taking this principle to the extreme,

Hegel's philosophy—intending to finish the job Kant started—freely proceeds in "speculations that more or less have as a goal . . . ; the sufficient identification of an endless world with the finite world, an unknowable (noumenal) world with the known (phenomenal) world."[59] This identification, however, which essentially affirms the identity of Being and Knowledge, and which Hyppolite calls "the decisive point of Hegelianism,"[60] is what Bataille rejects.

Following Hyppolite for a moment, he points to that "through which we are able to think the unthinkable, to what makes Hegel simultaneously the greatest irrationalist and the greatest rationalist who has existed,"[61] which is the positing of the intrinsic, indeed internal, relation between sense and non-sense that delineates non-sense as merely the self-contradiction of thought, its mute double. And if non-sense (Nature, matter, immediacy) is mute, it is not for being without its proper *logos*—and thus nonexpressive—but rather that it is merely pre-expressive, and will come to speak itself in the *logos* of knowledge. The movement of thought is thus not from non-sense to sense, but rather from sense to sense: in short, there is only sense; and non-knowledge is the internal difference of knowledge.

Now, the main targets here are those philosophies that posit the limit of articulate knowledge (Kant) and those that yield to this limit and posit the direct apprehension of an inconceivable and ineffable content (Jacobi, Fichte, and Schelling). Yet Kojève, despite his adherence to Absolute Knowledge, but because of the positing of an ontological dualism between Being and Thought, must be added to this list. The essential factor here is Kojève's humanization of negativity and nothingness, his denial of negativity, and thus dialectic, to Nature.[62] Negativity, thus history, and in fact all of reality is the prerogative of the human being alone, without which Nature (non-sense) is mere Identity, an immobile rock incapable of self-differentiation. Now, Kojève does not much concern himself with non-knowledge, but one may assume that two of Bataille's critical ideas arise insofar as he adheres to Kojève's position that humanity is negativity and that it is only thanks to that negativity that Being is revealed in human discourse.

First of all, Bataille will reject the discursive 'knowability' of the sensuous, immediate unknown, the notion that the unknown is simply in the process of becoming known, that it gives itself of itself to knowledge—that it is the unknown *of* knowledge—and thus is not unknowable. Thus, with respect to a claim such as Hyppolite's—that the "phantom" of the unknowable must be "exorcised" in the name of Absolute Knowledge—Bataille will respond with the claim that it is possible to view Absolute Knowledge as merely an interpretive necessity of logic. In his view, Hegel logically coerces negativity into collaboration with the constitution of meaning through the *Aufhebung* that converts every negative into a positive, generating sense from the senseless.

The second notion—more significant for us here—is that negativity will not disappear when thought reaches its goal. That is, the notion that Being

and Thought are not identical will lead Bataille to the conclusion that there is
a residue of Being beyond Thought. And if this stain on thought is indelible,
then the subject of negativity—who thinks—and Being do not fall together in
Thought. Thought, stemming from an unsatisfied negativity, can thus no
longer be "Absolute," for "if nonsense is sense, the sense which is nonsense . . .
becomes nonsense once again (without possible end) . . . [thus] knowledge is
access to the unknown. *Nonsense is the outcome of every possible sense.*"[63] Denis
Hollier has identified the problematic—which has far-reaching implications
that we shall certainly not exhaust here—much more succinctly, claiming: "All
of Bataille's reading of Hegel takes as its main line that the subject and knowledge are mutually exclusive. This exclusion is implicit everywhere, in every
project for knowledge, but only the ambition to absolute knowledge brings it
out into the open."[64] The subject—negativity—does not come to a halt in
absolute knowledge.

Perhaps the first real attempt to take this problem seriously on Hegel's
own grounds is found in Bataille's 1937 letter to Kojève, and more importantly, the second draft of the letter which appeared in 1944.[65] This letter is
written with the assumption that Kojève's hypothesis of the end of history is
valid, which is in fact the starting point for all of Bataille's subsequent reflections. The completion of history can be interpreted in different ways. In
Kojève's terms it signifies the end of opposition: the passage into homogeneous society through the dissolution of the class conflict that drove the historical process, leaving only a resignation to the monotonous treadmill of reasonable pursuits which effectively change nothing; and the mastery of nature
by the laboring hands of humanity, so that nature is no longer alienating, pos-
ing no resistance—which is one of the notions that earned Kojève's interpretation the title of "Cartesian theology."[66] In Hegelian terms it signifies that
human consciousness has in fact become Reason (or the Concept), concluding the movement through which consciousness has sought to overcome its
difference (its object), thereby completing knowledge in the identity of
thought and being. And in general terms it signifies that humanity—negativity—no longer has anything *to do.*

This final implication is what most concerns Bataille. And what is of concern is that, given the end of resistance to human knowledge and endeavor,
the human being should be satisfied—but this is not the case. For even if
action (negativity) has vanished, and philosophy along with it, the existence of
humanity as negativity has not. The question Bataille asks is simply this: what
becomes of negativity? His answer—it remains, but is "unemployed." At the
end of history the human being is "unemployed negativity." And then further
questions arise, namely; what is to become of this "unemployed" or "useless"
negativity—if in fact it becomes something—and can it be recognized for
what it is once it no longer manifests itself in action? And if there is nothing
to do with this negativity, does our existence become a question without doors

or windows, with no way out? Does Hegel's "triumph of meaning" in the final reconciliation with all forms of otherness simply leave us at the gates of non-meaning, aimless, with only absurd pursuits to fill our time, discontented with everything because even absolute wisdom was insufficient?

Two potential solutions are offered in art and religion. We shall take these up at a later point, but for the moment we find that at least when first formulating the problem Bataille believed that neither of these solutions offers negativity the possibility to be "recognized as such," for in both it still receives an objective form, allowing it to be "introduced into a system that nullifies it, and only the affirmation is recognized."[67] As with the life of Christ, the recognition of negativity through the positive value it receives in fact precludes the recognition of the negative loss itself. Therefore, the paths available for "objectivization of negativity" that remain "at the end" are fundamentally different from those available while the gears of the Hegelian system were still in motion. The only option left at the end of History is for the man of "unemployed negativity" to become the man of "recognized negativity"—to be "recognized for what it is: negativity without content."[68] But what is "negativity without content" if not a definition of desire?

Even more precisely, it is the desire for nothing, the nothing that something or object can never satisfy, and which will become in Bataille's view the desire to lose rather than gain. Or as Bataille coins it, desire becomes "supplication without response"—the pleading with an object or God to hand itself over to the subject, a prayer that can never be answered because the object desired is no object. In fact, then, "unemployed negativity" does not become something, but rather becomes the nothing of pure desire. This too has its manifestations, found in what Bataille terms the "sovereign operation," the remaining possibility for negativity once it no longer has anything to do. With this in mind, if it manifests itself it nevertheless does not objectively present itself, does not command any action, but rather occurs as an "inner experience" which is not inner, but is rather a movement toward an infinitely withdrawing 'object'.

Negativity, desire, recognition; these notions are unmistakably Hegelian. If we are to see how Bataille subverts their meaning—or more precisely, how he shows the double sense of negativity and its vicissitudes—it is necessary to enter the dialectic in which this meaning is most evidently constituted. That is, we must enter the dialectic of Master *(Herr)* and Slave *(Knecht)*, alternatively named the dialectic of desire, or of recognition.[69] For it is truly by traveling the path of this dialectic that Bataille will open upon the clearing of sovereignty.

1.2 THE SOVEREIGNTY OF SERVILITY

Hegel's most notorious dialectic, returned to the forefront of philosophical thought in France by Kojève's teachings, had a profound impact on Bataille's thought. Indeed, traces of Kojève's interpretation of this dialectic—which he inflated into the foundational moment not only in the *Phenomenology* but as well in the movement of History—can be found throughout Bataille's works, in effect serving as a point of orientation. Indeed, Bataille posits that "the dialectic of the master and the slave . . . is the decisive moment in the history of the consciousness of self and . . . no one knows anything of *himself* if he has not understood this movement which determines and limits man's successive possibilities."[70] Thus, even if Kojève's anthropomorphic and Marxist account too heavily accents the importance of this dialectic, we are obliged to follow its path to the letter. Now, the pathways of the Master/Slave conflict are generally known to the point of being self-evident, even if its place in history is not.[71] Its evidence, however, does not necessarily imply an awakening to it. Rather its undeniable presence is like that of an unconscious residue that—when kept buried—seemingly alleviates its gravity. Perhaps this is why many readers of Bataille take Hegel so lightly. Yet it is necessary to bring this residue to the surface, to bring it to self-consciousness, for that is really the only way to lighten the load.

The Master/Slave dialectic is situated in the transition between (natural) consciousness and (human) self-consciousness, the movement toward which—for Hegel—is the path to self-certainty. In this process the subject comes to explicitly realize that which was implicitly established in the forms of consciousness (sense-certainty, perception, and understanding), as the subject comes to see itself in and behind, and thus independent of objective reality. That is, consciousness comes to see itself as the unity of the Concept which in fact creates the multiple distinctions it previously understood to be objective. The inner world of the mind and the inner being of things—previously dissociated by appearance—gradually merge together, a process which begins the dissolution of the Kantian thing-in-itself (noumena) referred to above.

If consciousness ignores itself through its immersion in the world, self-consciousness—becoming aware of (reflecting) its projection of itself in and through the appearing beings of the world—in essence returns out of the otherness of the world to grasp itself. Yet the world's otherness is, to an extent, irreducible. Consciousness is never actually separated from its object, but simply perceives it improperly, that is, in opposition to consciousness. Therefore, self-consciousness (desire)[72] brings both the awareness of self as alienated from the world and the desire to overcome this separation or dependence on externality. This dual situation is corroborated, for example, in Freud's theory that an object comes into existence at the point where being (Substance) is lost. Were Bataille to translate this theory, it would read, "[Desire] kindles desire for being at the point where being is lost."[73] In this sense, desire is both a sign of internal differentiation denoting that we have lost our 'natural' sense of wholeness, and is the source of alienation, an awareness of the external differentiation of "I" from the "non-I," the dissatisfied feeling of being-at-a-lack.[74]

Yet insofar as desire is that force that drives us from lure to lure in search of satisfaction, for Being, then it cannot simply be pure lack. Rather, as we must consider as we continue, desire may betray an overdetermination that, from the perspective of clear consciousness, may be perceived as a lack insofar as it is indeterminate, or in excess of determination. But to the extent that desire-as-lack is placed at the forefront of the investigation, a tension emerges from which escape is impossible: the inviolable feeling of human life is insufficiency. We are beings lacking Being, and are driven by a quest for sufficient, complete being, yet Being is nowhere that we could grasp it. Nevertheless, we cannot renounce the search. There is no way out.

For as we know all too well, immediate satisfaction—sexual or otherwise—is fleeting. No sooner is desire satisfied and the subject restored to itself than another lure comes around the corner and one is beside oneself once again. To truly begin the process of reconciling self and world therefore requires a specific object, one that reflects the truth of self-consciousness—a truth that is, as Hegel tells us, nothing other than Desire.[75] Desire must find its proper object for, "generally speaking, the I of Desire is an emptiness that receives a real positive content only by the negating action that satisfies Desire in destroying, transforming, and 'assimilating' the desired non-I."[76] As Desire, the subject is pure negating-negativity without content, and the object desired and subsequently negated determines the nature of the desiring subject.

Should that which is desired be a thing or a given natural object (in-itself), the subject will remain at this level. Such is the case with animal desire, which dissolves self-awareness through the immediacy of its negation of the object, plunging it back into darkness upon satisfaction. In killing, eating, or fleeing an external object, the object in which one may recognize oneself is removed—which is no problem for the animal that simply wants to stay alive. But if desire is to lead to self-consciousness, it must be directed toward a non-natural object, something capable of transcending its given reality, capable of negating itself, dying to itself. It must be directed, that is, toward another desire, toward an other which is the manifestation of the desiring consciousness itself in an external guise. Furthermore, if desire is to find itself in this other, and be recognized by the other, it cannot kill or eat it (negate it). Rather, the other must stay alive and at the same time negate itself, thereby *revealing itself* as another emptiness, another desire, a *manifestation* of the truth of the subject—negativity. In this abstract description we have found that *"second self"* [77] which is the slave.

The situation establishing the positions described above is in fact not an abstract one, but, rather, occurs in a fight to the death between the two players—a fight that Bataille obliquely, yet significantly refers to as "The game" *(Le jeu)*.[78] Conflict is the first step on the path to intersubjectivity, the sphere of recognition, for without this conflict, "the conscious subject would remain in its routine of self-certainty and subjective knowledge."[79] And this "fight"

occurs precisely because each subject involved views itself as the essential reality, independent from all otherness, a view which is then challenged by the
other who holds the same attitude toward himself. What is then essential to
realize is that the positions of this intersubjective relation are established by
the combatant's respective attitudes towards life and death, for it is above all
the disregard for life that confirms an end to otherness and dependence.[80]
More specifically: the one who becomes the slave, when confronted with the
possibility of death and propelled into anxiety at this prospect, chooses not to
take the risk of dying and opts for a life of servitude and dependence. The horror of death and subsequent flight from it is the origin of slavery in particular,
and is the precondition of conscious individualization in general.

The slave's shying away from death shows that he prefers to remain tied
to the given world, which amounts to a choice for servility over freedom,
dependence over self-sufficiency. This is negatively established through
Hegel's principle—one that is essential for Bataille—that "it is only through
staking one's life that freedom is won."[81] The slave does retain a certain freedom in the ability to negate and transform the given world, even if this is
accomplished under compulsion of fear, but in truth the freedom of negativity is hollow if it loses the strength to risk life itself. Indeed, the fundamental
condition of possibility for genuine self-consciousness is the willingness to
freely risk one's life. And the refusal to squander one's vital resources represents for Bataille nothing less than an abdication from the possibility of realizing one's ultimate truth.

It therefore seems that we should look to the other side of the equation,
to the one who accepts the possibility of death for a nonvital, essentially useless end—for pure prestige—to find the representation of freedom that
Bataille is seeking. It is the master who represents for Bataille the sovereign
attribute in Hegel's dialectic, which is "the fact of a man's having staked his
whole being" through the "reckless expenditure of vital resources."[82] And it is
this expenditure—which we will later encounter in one of Bataille's privileged
paradigms, the potlatch—that carries the connotation of sovereign freedom,
whereby one shows that one is "not attached to any specific existence . . . is not
tied up with life."[83] Or as Bataille repeatedly states; the master, the sovereign
existence, escapes the anguish of death, treating death "as if it were not."[84] We
will examine this in greater detail below.

What we must note here, however, is that Bataille could not be more clear
about the derivation of his notions of "sovereignty" and "servility" from Hegel.
He states: "In the Hegelian dialectic, the sovereign share of man has indifference to death, the risk of death confronted, for its foundation, the servile part
proceeds from the fear, or moreover the horror of death."[85] At first glance,
Bataille's "sovereignty" indeed seems identical to Hegel's mastery *(Herrschaft)*,
for both are established through risking or putting into play *(mettre en jeu)* the
entirety of one's existence. And even though Bataille again states that "the

Master's attitude implies sovereignty"[86] in the risk of death without biological reasons, it is essential for us to realize how and why these notions differ rather than simply illustrating their common origin. The first difference to note is established by two interrelated conditions of mastery: firstly, the master must stay alive despite having accepted the risk of death; and secondly, the prestige gained through his lack of concern for life is *put to use* by exerting power over the slave, by commanding the vanquished to work. The master thereby profits from his risk. Both of these conditions pertaining to Hegel's mastery thereby fall into the paradigm of Bataille's servility: the projection of the self into the future, which again implies the fear of death. Sovereignty, as we will see, must lie elsewhere.

With respect to mastery, however, the former condition—limiting the risk in accordance with Hegel's economy of life—is necessary if the possibility of reaching the truth of self-consciousness is not to be lost, for which this consciousness must be maintained. We will soon see the extensive ramifications of this imperative, but for now, we may simply posit that if one of the combatants physically dies, the dialectic that constitutes the history of meaning stops, never attaining its desired result, never profiting from the risk. Should the fight end in total loss, death would be present as nonproductive or "abstract negation" rather than the negation characteristic of consciousness, "which supersedes in such a way as to preserve and maintain what is superseded, and consequently survives its own supersession."[87] That is, biological death would not reveal the concrete, efficacious negativity that yields self-consciousness of one's own negativity, and which thereby *gives a meaning* to death.[88]

Therefore, while the master does in fact seem to rise above the concern for life, sovereignly putting that life at stake, the meaning of this risk is only confirmed if the stakes are ultimately limited. Should one drive headlong into death one undergoes the risk of losing that for which one has staked one's life—the meaning of that risk. Therefore, "in this experience [facing death in the fight], self-consciousness learns that life is as essential to it as pure self-consciousness [the realization of absolute negativity]."[89] The moment of risk is therefore only meaningful to the extent that it respects life and is in a position to profit from this risk in the future.[90] This is the comedy transcribed by reason, a comedy of compromise, which Derrida posits should elicit a "burst of laughter from Bataille. Through a ruse of life, that is, of reason, life has stayed alive. . . . Such is the truth of life. Through this recourse to the *Aufhebung*, which conserves the stakes, remains in control of the play, limiting and elaborating it by giving it form and meaning, this economy of life restricts itself to conservation . . . henceforth, everything covered by the name lordship collapses into comedy."[91] Yet again, we will have reason to question whether the reasons Bataille would laugh are those that Derrida attributes to him. Whether, that is, Bataille will resort to his own ruses in order to affirm life in complicity with death.

In any event, the profit resulting from risk is truly manifested through the second condition of mastery—one that will distinguish it from sovereignty—which is the fact that the master forces the slave to work. This condition—the origin of which lies deeper, in the relation to death—will lead to the real conflict between Bataille and Hegel. For the purity (uselessness), and consequently the "recklessness" of the master's expenditure (risk), or precisely those elements essential to Bataille's notion of "sovereignty," are compromised as soon as the risk is granted prestige—that is, once it is recognized and put to use. The sovereign excessiveness of the risk, the disregard for life for no external reason, is forfeited once it is given an end, once it enters the dialectic of recognition. Recognition indeed is one of the more ambiguous notions in Bataille's work. On the one hand he calls for the recognition of the heart of existence, yet this core must not be spatially objectified, must not assert itself or command anything—"the sovereignty [of thought] . . . hides itself. It is foreign to the desire for recognition."[92] Sovereignty—as well as lacking a sense—is in essence total powerlessness, good for nothing, *indifferent* to life. It is these two features—*powerlessness and purposelessness* (indifference to ends)—that essentially differentiate the notion of sovereignty from mastery.

Returning to Hegel, we know in principle that a desirous being is determined by the object that is desired. We also know that in the slave, the master found the object that may reflect the truth of his own self-consciousness (negativity, desire, independence), but this truth must be proven through an objective manifestation. By recoiling from death, the slave has failed to manifest his negativity, to show his independence from life, remaining tied to natural, animal existence. Slavish consciousness therefore must be induced to reveal its negativity in another way; namely, by working, by using the power within it to negate (act upon, transform) the independence of the given world to which it is bound. And it is compelled to do so through the same fear that established its subordinate position—the fear of death now embodied in the master. Yet implied therein is that the slave has found in the master—the one who manifested negativity through the willingness to risk one's life for autonomy—the object that reveals the slave's truth. The slave thus has its truth (negativity) only implicitly because it still belongs to the master. But because the "fight"—the intersubjective dialectic of death and recognition which begins the movement of self-consciousness—is a conflict of mirrors, the reflections that pass between the players undergo multiple reversals, and the positions outlined above will become no more than a ruse.

The problem hinges on the fact that the dialectic of master and slave is one of *mutual* recognition: the truth of recognition is not only recognition *by* but also *of* the other. While the master does indeed receive recognition from the slave, it is one-sided, for the master is recognized by a being that is not in turn recognized as another free existence like himself. Consequently, the recognition the master receives is of no value. One has in fact risked one's life for nothing. The risk becomes meaningless, useless. This situation is referred to by Kojève as the master's "existential impasse."[93] The sovereignty attained in the fight is degraded as soon as it has for an end the enslavement of the vanquished adversary. That is, one degrades oneself in degrading the other who mediates one's desire, by turning the other into a thing. Now for the essential reversal.

Because the recognition of the master's self-consciousness comes from a slavish object, the master's truth is slavish consciousness, is something unessential and dependent.[94] Mastery is thus constituted by servility. On the other hand, if the master is the essential-reality for the slave, being the object in which the slave's truth is revealed, then the truth of slavish consciousness is autonomous consciousness. Servility has become sovereignty. Thus, in Hegel's dialectic, it is the slave, the one who refuses the risk of life—and thus turns away from death—who will achieve sovereignty.[95] Yet the keystone of sovereignty or autonomy rests on the manifestation of negativity—the condition of possibility of self-consciousness. And the "privileged manifestation" of negativity "is death."[96] Indeed, as Kojève claims, "there is no freedom without death . . . only a mortal being can be free. One might even say that death is the last and authentic 'manifestation' of freedom."[97] Or one might say that one becomes autonomous and self-conscious "only by becoming conscious of his death," conscious, that is, of oneself as Desire and nothingness.[98] It would thus seem that Hegel's slave, renouncing death, should not be able to attain the autonomy it is granted.

Now, is it still valid, after Heidegger, to continue to pose the question of how one is to become conscious of one's own death and nothingness without dying, how one is to relate oneself, not to death as an event, but to the horizon of the sheer possibility of oneself-as-nothingness? Indeed, this is *the* question to ask, and we will encounter it again. But the question that Hegel, and subsequently Kojève, have left us to reckon with, is whether or not one can *satisfy* the desire to recognize one*self* in another Desire, in the 'revelation' of another nothingness, or in death? Does, that is, death take a form that is recognizable, and can one assume the death (desire, nothingness) of another as if it were one's own? For indeed, satisfaction of this desire would assume that one can appropriate as a possibility *for* oneself that which is in fact an impossibility for the self, which places oneself beyond any notion of self, beyond any notion of possibility altogether.[99]

It would seem then that a recognition of this sort would assume the phenomenal objectification of one's own death as an event, in which case one could propose that "the only way for desiring man to reveal himself to himself—and thus be 'satisfied', since desire of recognition is a question of self-manifestation—would be to plunge into nothingness, to die."[100] Of course, this objective treatment of death must be rejected for the obvious reason that were one to die, one would no longer be a conscious being capable of knowing that one has died. And it must be rejected for the more refined reason that were one's death to be an actual phenomenon, one would risk losing the profit—the *productivity*—of facing death, which is the development of the meaning of self-consciousness. To win its meaning, consciousness must maintain itself through death, which not only precludes it actually occurring, but as well requires that death's 'manifestation' become something recognizable, which occurs by putting this death to work.

Yet as Kojève implicitly and Bataille explicitly claim, it is problematic to assert that one's negativity is 'manifest' to oneself in death, for "death," though it may be the "privileged manifestation" of the negative, "in fact, reveals nothing."[101] And the fact that what death 'manifests' remains hidden or unknowable—a notion unacceptable for Hegel[102]—carries the further implication that the desire for complete self-consciousness cannot be satisfied, insofar as the combination of these incompatibles—death and consciousness—is the very condition of self-consciousness. Simply stated, the problem is that, on the one hand, self-consciousness is conditional upon the experience of death, and on the other hand, one cannot both die and have consciousness of dying, or so it would seem.

The solution Bataille offers for this problem is in fact but a lightly veiled testimony of his adherence to the specular structure of Hegelian self-consciousness, the mirror-play of desire in which one becomes conscious of oneself in-and-through, if not as, an other (desire) that one desires. His solution is as follows: "In order for man to reveal himself ultimately to himself, he would have to die, but he would have to do so while living—watching himself ceasing to be. In other words, death itself would have to become (self-) consciousness at the very moment that it annihilates the conscious being."[103] There is a mediating image that both draws one out of one's isolation and reflects one's desire back upon oneself, even should this desire be recognized as the desire to die. With this in mind, we are in a better position to understand why it is the slave who has the sovereign position in Hegel's schema.

The slave profits from two correlative moments: first, while it has the truth of its negativity only implicitly, it nevertheless has a 'manifestation' or objectification of death, the Negative, in the master's voluntary acceptance of the risk of life. Consequently, "he finds it only in the Other. And this is his advantage,"[104] the obvious advantage being that the slave can 'know' death, have as a representation another self-consciousness who cared not for life, all without actually having to live through death;[105] second, in the face of this murderous other, the Negative is 'manifest' to the slave in "the anguish inspired by the conscious appearance of death,"[106] that is, in the *inner* experience of trembling out of fear not "for this or that," but for the nothingness of one's own negativity itself, insofar as "Negativity taken in-itself is nothing other than Nothingness, which can 'manifest' itself as death."[107] What occurs in this double movement—ostensibly the same one that determines sacrifice—is a "subterfuge" of identification. Identifying with the one who takes the risk of life, *seeing oneself* in the other (Desire, 'absolute negating-negativity') who exists *for* slavish consciousness as its ideal representation, the slave became conscious of its own death, one's nothingness 'revealed' by the other.

In other words, death presented in the form of an other-object (the master) gave the slave *the impression* of dying, or in Kojève's words, the slavish consciousness "melted internally, it shuddered deeply and everything fixed-or-stable trembled in it . . . [an] absolute liquefaction of every stable support."[108] Quite simply, in this moment of absolute rending the slave experienced an anxiety for its very being that the master did not have, insofar as the master had no image of death—no sign of the willingness to risk one's life—in which to see itself. For the slave, then, death had become a conscious possibility, and death having become conscious, he was in a position to become fully human. Following Kojève's lead, Bataille repeats this notion in the following:

> [I]f the consciousness of death—of the marvelous magic of death—does not touch him before he dies, during his life it will seem that death is not destined to reach him, and so the death awaiting him will not give him a *human* character. *Thus, at all costs, man must live at the moment that he really dies, or he must live with the impression of really dying.*[109]

It is clear that Bataille has no intention of doubting what he will call the "impossible" Hegelian imperative to live through death. Indeed, it would take an impoverished notion of existence to think that we cannot experience and sustain numerous deaths before we physically die. But for Hegel, this is not the whole story, for it is one thing for the human being to be merely a "death . . . conscious of itself,"[110] and it is quite another for the human being to be "death that lives a human life."[111] It is on the issue of how life lives death that Hegel and Bataille will part.

More precisely, the value given to the anguish or anxiety that accompanies the moment of absolute rending *[déchirement absolu]* is the "fork in the road," the point where their paths will begin to differ. Now, Hegel has transcribed how in the fight for recognition the slave experienced a total dissolution of his stable identity. And he tells us, in his renowned statement, that the life of the Spirit "wins its truth only when, in utter dismemberment *[déchirement absolu]*, it finds itself."[112] Yet at the same time, he asserts that the life of the Spirit must "convert [the negative of this death] into being."[113] This is the pivotal disclaimer. It is this statement of Hegel's that, perhaps more than any other, Bataille must reject if he is to differ from Hegel.

The point—which we shall repeatedly encounter—is essentially this: insofar as each moment of Hegel's system is but a transformation from one state to another, unilaterally directed toward a horizon of completion that confers their meaning, then even those sovereign moments, which *should* rupture the flow, are submerged in and by the dialectical process itself.

Bataille's objection is that the moment of mortal rupture, *"déchirement absolu,"* does not break the logical chain of meaning, the teleology of wisdom. Rather, this "dismemberment is . . . full of meaning. . . . But," as Bataille hastens to add, "this meaning is unfortunate."[114] This meaning is what blinded Hegel to the truth he unveiled. And I repeat, it is *only* the meaning that Bataille will be able to contest, for in fact there is hardly a more appropriate statement of Bataille's overall intention than the one he annexed from Hegel ("spirit only attains its truth . . .").

With respect to the current context, however, we may say that it is the slave who must perform this conversion of death into being. That is, the slave must transform the negative in-itself to negativity in-and-for-itself, must objectify it, make it *real.* This is done by working for the master, transforming the given world to satisfy the master's needs for consumption, meanwhile repressing its own desire to consume, putting it off until later. Indeed, it is the master itself who unwittingly enabled not only the implicit revelation of the slave's truth through the experience of dissolution transcribed above, but also the explicit realization of this truth by forcing the slave to work.[115] Joseph Navickas provides a useful transcription of the process: "The slave is primarily and fundamentally a laborer. But that is his source of self-correcting development, of self-liberation. . . . Through his hard work he imposes his own form on the object and thus becomes aware of his own negativity." He then concludes with what we have already announced: "[The slave] cannot escape from hard labor. Nor is there any escape from fear. *But that is his salvation.* To the slave, as Hegel himself puts it, 'the fear of the lord is the beginning of wisdom.'"[116]

Thus, while the anxiety Hegel transcribed is of the same nature as for Bataille—the depersonalizing experience of facing a world that seems both overwhelming and indifferent, which throws one back upon the equally overwhelming nothingness of a self that no longer feels connected to the world—this anxiety is treated by Hegel as a regrettably necessary passageway to productive work (the possible), the form in which life lives death. In other words, the anguish felt as a loss of self, as the impossibility of continuing to confront the void that has opened before and within one—for the *object* of anxiety is nothingness, its *feeling* being the unhappy consciousness of oneself-as-nothing—this anguish is effectively avoided. And through the dialectical transformation of this nothingness/negativity into actuality through the long labor of death (action and discourse) which reasserts one's self in the world, not only is anxiety repressed, but it becomes an intermediary on the road to knowing divinity, the sovereignty of Absolute Knowledge. Economically speaking, one trembles before death and collects the wages of fear.

The response to anguish, which is in turn a response to the consciousness of death, will be a determining factor not only in Bataille's challenge to Hegelian economics, but will be essential in determining the status of sovereignty. Now, once the volatile moment has passed, and the slave has backed down from the risk of life—voluntarily choosing to work in subordination rather than die—work is no longer performed in order to avoid the immediate threat of death, but rather is infused with the conscious awareness or *idea* of death—the master internalized. The fear of death has thus become an operative principle, and by working, one will actualize for-oneself the truth that previously appeared outside in the master. It is through work—negating the given—that the slave manifests its negativity, transcends its own nature, and frees itself from the master. Hegelian sovereignty, as translated by Kojève, is achieved through slavery. Sovereignty is thereby established as the priority of productive negation over the desire for nonproductive expenditure, and over desire itself.

Now, we know that the dialectic of recognition leads to the truth of self-consciousness, and that this truth is indissociable from desire, or in fact that it is desire. But at the same time, the true autonomy gained by the slave is based upon a compromise of desire, its inhibition. Hegel is quite explicit about this.[117] He first states that work is the moment in slavish consciousness that corresponds to desire in the master's. This means that both in fact negate the thing but with a different orientation or in a different sense. The master immediately negates (consumes) the thing prepared by the slave, or as Hegel states, "desire has reserved to itself the pure negating of the object. . . . But that is the reason why this satisfaction is itself only a fleeting one, for it lacks the side of objectivity and permanence." The master consumes in the instant, gives in to his immediate desire, and nothing of the object is preserved in this consumption. We continue with Hegel: "Work, on the other hand, is desire held in check, fleetingness staved off; in other words, work forms and shapes the thing." By putting his negativity to work the slave creates a real objective world, a cultural, human, and historical world in which he will subsequently recognize the independence of his own self-consciousness. Showing his Marxist colors, Kojève states:

> Therefore, it is by work, and only work, that man realizes himself objectively as man. Only after producing an artificial object is man himself really and objectively more than and different from a natural being; and only in this real and objective product does he become truly conscious of his subjective human reality.[118]

Bataille, however, attends carefully at this point. For if he is to establish his own notion of sovereignty, he will have to challenge the glorification of work, the sovereignty of servility emphasized in Kojève's interpretation.

Yet it is Hegel himself who brings to attention the fact that the slave's work does not have merely the positive signification of realizing one's pure being-for-self (independence), but as well the negative significance of the anxiety that the master originally inspired in the slave, which made him aware of his being-toward-death. And while Hegel will posit that the fear of the master is overcome by the slave's objectification of its own negativity, taking it over from the master and "rediscovering" oneself (one's negativity) in one's products, the world one creates, Hegel has nevertheless identified the anguishing and sovereign moment of 'absolute rending'—the moment the ground gives way under one's feet, when one gains consciousness of impending death— which is so essential to Bataille. The problem, however—as mentioned above—is the framework into which Hegel places this moment. For whenever we encounter this *Erzittern*, this profound trembling in the depths of our being, it is always the precursor to pure knowledge and restored self-conscious certainty, and ultimately to the reconciliation of man and God in Absolute knowledge.[119] Now, as we shall see for Bataille, these moments of Hegelian *Erzittern*—whether they be anxiety or the abysmal feeling of the death of God—are not without their contribution to self-consciousness. But neither will these moments undergo an inversion into their opposite which reverses their meaning, as we find when "the experience of personal reconciliation with God is the inversion of the experience of the death of God,"[120] such that the loss of meaning engenders ultimate (positive) meaning. Rather, Bataille will insist in varying ways that the subjective experience of anxiety is irreducible. And in our current context, this means that work itself becomes nothing less than the fear of death—the 'absolute master'—objectified and avoided.

Or to state matters with a touch of Bataille's insouciance, in the Hegelian perspective anxiety is taken all too seriously. That is, the one who sovereignly "looks death in the face" and does so with a lucid awareness of—and *respect for*—what it implies for a finite individual, univocally experiences sadness—a reaction Bataille associates with servitude: "the seriousness of death and pain is the servility of thought."[121] In the sections that follow, we will both elaborate on these remarks, and begin to unravel the manner in which Bataille, albeit without mention, begins to move out from under the humanist shadow cast by his Hegelian mentor, Kojève.

1.3 WORK, DEATH

We have thus far established that productive action, or simply work, is conditioned by the fear and respect given to the negativity of death. Work does not signify the overcoming of this fear—or more appropriately, anxiety—but rather, from a subjective standpoint, its internalization and repression, and from an objective standpoint, its transformation into a world of things, by which it masters anxiety. At the same time, however, it is equally possible to posit that the fear of death only arises for one who is already inaugurated into the world of things, and who has become conscious of oneself as a thing among things, owing to the anteriority of work. To some extent, however, the issue of causal succession is irrelevant, for work and the fear of dying are mutually implicative, and result in the same thing: the principle of individuation and its concern for the preservation of life.

For Bataille, the question raised by this dialectical circle of anxiety and work is actually a question of human autonomy: the question is whether or not autonomy can emerge from the history of subordinations that—in his view—have been mistaken for autonomy. Now, he will not contest that the negation of the natural given to which animals are bound—the negation of which established the distinct spheres of subjects and objects—is the crucial step toward human autonomy. Yet what is troubling is that the introduction of a human world of individuals and things—and the subsequent development of work, articulate language, and scientific thought—effectively binds one to those things as to the means to some end: the development of the human freedom to transform the world has the result of subordinating *what is*, the present moment, to what will be, the future.

Yet still more fundamentally, and more radically, the subordination most expressly contested, the one that subtends all those affirmations with which Bataille will take issue—the individual, positive knowledge, productive activity et al.—is the subordination to life itself. To his thinking, the subordination to the concern for personal survival, and thus to the fear of death, is based on the misconception that individual existence, of itself, is the ultimate basis of meaning. A meaning that presumably will arrive at some point in the future. Yet if he is to contest life's drive for duration, then he must somehow contest anxiety as well, for the human being has anxiety, is in anguish—try as one will to sedate oneself to this fact—from the moment one becomes conscious of death, from the moment one realizes that one is in anticipation of some inalienable event with which every moment of life is obscurely in relation. The issue thus becomes rather murky, however, insofar as sovereignty and self-consciousness of the Hegelian variety—which are in essence the same phenomenon, sharing the same origin in the confrontation with death—must come to be opposed.

The basic data are as follows: anguish arises in confrontation with the nothing of death and signifies a concern for the duration of one's discontinuous or individual existence. Discontinuity is our fundamental reality and work is the first sign of humanity, and due to the close relation between work and anguish, in a general way anguish in fact defines us as individuals. To put it bluntly, the anguish inspired by the possible loss of one's particular existence comes from taking death seriously. While this seems obvious enough, Bataille takes a different perspective, stating:

> It is not death which is serious, it always inspires horror, but if this horror dismays us, to the point of abdicating in order not to die, we give death its seriousness, which is the consequence of having accepted work. Humanly, the fear of death not overcome, and servile labor, which degrades and levels out, are one and the same thing, immense and miserable . . .[122]

Taking death seriously, one thereby takes servility upon oneself, preferring the subordination of work over death. In anguished work, however, the slave turns itself into a thing. That is, through work the slave creates a lasting and durable world—the discontinuous objects of production—through which one in turn recognizes oneself, therefore recognizing oneself as a durable thing. The slave's negating action amounts to taking possession of the world, turning the undifferentiated, given world into a world full of human meaning and knowledge—in effect imposing an alien meaning on that which has none. But this as well is to take possession of oneself and to impose a meaning upon one's own existence: "This is the basic principle: to subordinate is not only to alter the subordinated element but to be altered oneself."[123] Through an analysis of the tool as the medium of work we may illustrate how telescoping the negativity one is toward the aim of practical knowledge involves, in Bataille's view, a self-reduction.

Work, or productive negativity, represents the most elementary separation of human and animal desire—the former negating in a way that delays the desire to consume, the latter consuming immediately. Animal negation, however, changes nothing, neither the nature of the world nor its own nature. The intimate relationship between the animal and the world or the lack of separation between "subject" and "object" (or the absence of these opposing terms) remains unaltered. The tool however not only separates the human being from the world but as well the world from its natural continuity, turning it into a world of distinct things. Indeed, "things begin to lose their natural value when they approach human endeavor."[124] That is, human endeavor turns the world into a human thing subordinate to human intentions. The tool turns humanity into a faction within the community of beings.

The tool in this process, however, is nothing but a subordinate instrument, a middle term mediating between human intentions and the reality that resists those intentions. Developed as and deriving its meaning from being a means to an end that is not its own, the tool in itself is of no value but is rather a vanishing moment in the process it serves, effaced once the end is reached. The slave is originally but a tool working for an alien purpose, its value being defined with respect to an anticipated result. The slave's subordination of the world to ends that are not its own amounts to the humanization of the world, the creation of history.[125] Therefore, history itself, the humanized world of work and knowledge—Hegelian knowledge being in fact the same negation or taking possession of the world as work—is a world of servility pure and simple.

Yet it is not only the world that is degraded through its subordination to an alien purpose. The one who acts is as well degraded. As Bataille describes the process:

> The tool changes nature and man at the same time: it subjugates nature to man, who makes and uses it, but it ties man to subjugated nature. Nature becomes man's property but it ceases to be immanent to him. It is his on the

condition that it is closed to him. If he places the world in his power, this is to the extent that he forgets that he is himself the world: *he denies the world but it is himself that he denies.*[126]

In Bataille's view, the circumscription of negativity within the confines of productive activity, whether economic—the use of resources to accumulate greater resources—or anthropological—the negation of the given to produce a world of human meaning—amounts to a self-reduction. The anthropocentric imperialism that follows from the realization of human autonomy and blindness to genuine otherness eventually leads to its own undoing:

> . . . always, everywhere,
> turned toward the world of objects, never outward.
> It fills us. We arrange it. It breaks down.
> We rearrange it, then break down ourselves.[127]

On the most elementary level, through work and the perspective that engenders it we deny our intimacy or continuity with the natural world and with other beings. Yet the autonomy from the given gained by work at the same time constitutes a self-estrangement, a denial of something in us that is transcended in becoming properly human. The tool was but the first step toward creating a world that transcends its given existence by separating it into distinct things or objects opposed to, and known clearly and distinctly by, the subject. That is, the tool is the origin of production and production is the production of the known. Yet even while separated from one's product, a separation not pertaining to the intimate world, the distance between humanity and the objects produced was progressively reduced as the human being became "more and more, and ever more powerfully, the producer of every detail in the world."[128] But it may also be true that "the closer his life comes to being his own creation, the more drastically is he cut off from that life."[129]

From the positing of the tool it was a short step to placing all natural things—previously of the same nature as the subject—onto the plane of external objects. And as self-consciousness requires the mediation of another, one became aware of oneself as a distinct thing, alienated from oneself. But of equal importance for Bataille is that—owing to the structure of work—one became aware of and anguished at the possible death of one's newly autonomous existence or one's existence as a thing. That is, once distanced from it, the indeterminate ground of intimacy from which the distinct being arose came to exert a pull on the individual being, drawing it toward what was lost in becoming an individual. But insofar as intimacy—which precedes and exceeds individuality and thus is positioned at the boundary of the distinct individual—is effectively the absence of individuality, signifying the death of individual existence, its approach is perceived in anguish. Bataille explains the dynamic as follows:

The separate individual is of the same nature as a thing, or rather the anxiousness to remain personally alive that establishes the person's individuality
is linked to the integration of existence into the world of things. To put it
differently, *work and the fear of dying are interdependent* . . . man is an individual to the extent that his apprehension ties him to the results of labor. . . .
He would have no anguish if he were not the individual (the thing), and it is
essentially the fact of being an individual that fuels his anguish. It is . . . insofar as the world of things has posited his duration as the basic condition of
his worth, that he learns anguish. He is afraid of death as soon as he enters
the system of projects that is the order of things.[130]

Bataille's assertion of the relation between work, discontinuity—individuality
or thinghood—and anguish for death is here made clear. But it is also important to note that it is essential to the meaning of a thing, or in Hegel's case,
life itself, that its value is preserved in and through its negation or consump-
tive destruction. This is the fundamental lesson of Hegelian economics, an
economy we briefly saw being played out on the cross.

In such an economy, the meaning of any negation—like the negation of
food or fuel—lies in the anticipated result. The value of the present is given in
duration, its future efficacy. What is of significance for Bataille, on the contrary, is intimacy, which *is there* at the moment the individual disappears *as an
individual*, a moment that therefore cannot arrive for that individual. It cannot arrive as anticipated because it is simply, suddenly there; it cannot arrive
because there is no longer any subject to greet it. If Bataille is to follow the
Hegelian paths of self-consciousness on the way to sovereignty, *and* open
upon the indistinct sphere of intimacy, what is required is nothing less than a
total reversal of perspective. An economic reversal such that the movement
toward sovereignty is no longer from the "impossible" (violent loss, destructive
negation) to the "possible" (servile activity, knowledge) which recuperates the
negation, but from the possible to an impossible that cannot be appropriated
as another possibility, and which thus is proposed as a sovereign end, without
qualification.[131] "Humanly," the death that is negativity is not recognized as
death, but rather as the productive labor of life; Bataille's sovereignty, on the
other hand, reeks of inhumanity.

For if we follow Kojève's Marxist account, "Hegelian" humanity is working humanity. Under Bataille's pen this becomes a life of strict *poiesis*, an
instrumental humanity of the "project" in which each action is calculated as a
means to reach a predetermined end (it is much more fruitful to see this as an
attack on instrumental rationality than any real commentary on Hegel).[132] For
one's actions to have meaning one must stay alive to see the end realized, and
so work results in anguish, the fear of death or the possibility of nonsatisfac-
tion. Yet at the same time by focusing on a future goal, work serves to keep
anxiety at bay, limiting one's concern to the possible result—in effect using
one's negativity to keep the truth of negativity in the shadows. For action

(work), insofar as it rests on the concern for the future, ignores the negativity of the present moment, its eyes being fixed on the transcendent goal. More specifically, work evades the essential moment at the very core of the working slave's experience, the *déchirement absolu* of facing death, the experience of one's radical negativity and the resulting anguish that puts one's being in question. It escapes by giving this question a necessary and sufficient answer—that man is knowledge derived through work. But an answer, the equivalent of an anticipated result, subordinates the question of human existence by closing the window once an acceptable notion has entered, effectively sealing that question off from those responses heretofore unsaid. An answer is, in a sense, in flight from the real question, eventually leaving it behind to die of thirst.

The terms we have used thus far to describe the economic orientation of working humanity—anticipation, result, duration, future—clearly betray that the question is as well one of temporal orientation. This is, as we will see in the chapter that follows, one of the underlying issues guiding Bataille's reflections on primitive ritual—particularly that of potlatch and sacrifice—where his primary concern is with the sovereign use of resources. That is, resources that were given or destroyed only within the perspective of the glorious moment itself and ideally to the exclusion of future interest. The point moreover was to *detach* the object destroyed from the real order of things and profane activity, so as to restore it to the divine order. Of course, the rituals were always limited: if one thing was sacrificed it was to save the rest; the destruction was subordinated to the concern for uniting a people and saving them from ruin in the future. Yet Bataille demotes the *interest* with which violence occurred to a secondary status, leaving the *desire* for a violent alteration of the status of the object—and the destroyer of that object—unchecked. The two worlds—sacred and profane—were not only rigorously defined in space, but as well in time. Work would always be work, but play was sacred.

With the phasing out of this mythological economy and its replacement by a mundane, rational economy, one would be tempted to announce the exorcism of divinity from economic considerations. But, as we will later investigate, the Reformation and its subsequent crystallization in the Hegelian economy will show this not to be the case. What occurs, rather, is that profane time became sacred time, and play became an insignificant diversion, serving, in fact, to augment the ability to profane oneself more effectively. For if we follow Hegel to the letter, we know that the development of history is the development of Spirit—the Absolute descending into the profane to fulfill itself as Absolute. There is no profane, finite time, nor divine, infinite time in themselves. Profane history is divine time—even if those who realize history don't know it—and the divine is fulfilled in the work of history. If we follow Bataille through Kojève, we find that the goal of Absolute Knowledge is presupposed from the start, and is achieved by the fragmented activity of fragmented individuals whose actions are added together to form a totality called history. The slave, who accomplishes this history, is "fragmented" firstly because he works upon a distinct thing or fragment—and the nature of the object that mediates the negativity of the subject determines the nature of that subject—and secondly because his activity is specialized, oriented toward a horizon of limited and specific goals.[133]

Hegel's "totality," if actualized in this manner, thereby eliminates the "total" character of the human being, a character only preserved if humanity does not separate itself into, and determine itself by, its functions.[134] As Bataille claims:

> [A]ctivity which subordinates each instant of our lives to some precise result effaces the individual's total character. . . . All action is specializing in that all activity is limited. . . . I can exist totally only by transcending in some way the stage of action. . . . When a man limits his desires . . . he knows what has to be done. . . . He inserts himself advantageously within time. Each of his moments becomes useful. It becomes possible for him to advance, with each passing instant, toward his chosen goal. His time becomes a progression toward that goal (that is what we usually call living). . . . Every action makes of man a fragmentary being. Only by refusing to act, or at least by denying the preeminence of the time reserved for action, can I maintain the quality of wholeness within myself.[135]

While not disputing Hegel's development of history itself, Bataille believes that the individual who has accomplished this history—and those who retain its principles—has done so at the price of losing the claim to moments of sovereignty. By acting, one turns one's existence into a project to be realized, one denies the time of existence itself, turns it into what Bataille calls "paradoxical time: *it is the putting off of existence to later point.*"[136] He will eventually come to call this "the absurdity of an endless deferral."[137] In contrast; the one who does not fear death need not accept the subordination of work; and the one who does not work is free to live in the present moment.

The absurdity of the slave's time is revealed most explicitly by the Hegelian system—the closed nature of his economy and the teleological unfolding of history that this implies—in which every moment of negativity is dialectically bound to the previous and subsequent moments with respect to which it is given its meaning. Every moment is therefore like a link in a chain, a chain that appropriates each link of negativity as it stretches toward the positive goal *(sens)*—decided in advance by Hegel—of Absolute Knowledge. Upon reaching that goal the chain forms a circle, the project is completed, and time stops—History becoming Being: servile History, profane existence.[138] And when all activity—as well as the society this activity serves—becomes profane, rational, and productive, the desire to *manifest* those excessive moments which disrupt the efficient functioning of that society becomes anathema.

If we may make this correlation between the Hegelian system and rational society, then denied are those moments of negativity that do not collaborate with the constitution of meaning, the paradigm of which *would be* the risk of the master—desire not yielding to the concern for preservation—*if* that risk was not used to compel the constitution of meaning, thereby turning the risk into an investment that provides its sense. In other terms, denied is the excessiveness of desire—desire that passes through and beyond any definite aim or object. For if Hegelian history is that of the working slave, and work demands that desire be repressed, then Hegelian history is the history of repressed desire—desire subordinated to meaning-constituting action. In effect, "taking work (discursive thought, project) for existence, [Hegel] reduces the world to the profane world; he negates the sacred world."[139] To be more accurate, if Hegel 'negates' the sacred world, it is in the sense that it is made commensurate with the profane world, that the two 'worlds' are actually reconcilable moments in a single process of self-mediating Spirit. Bataille, meanwhile, wants to emphasize with his notion of the sacred that there is a sacred otherness that resists integration in the dialectical rhythm of a self-mediating conceptual totality. To this end he posits the sacred as a world of excess—or that which is revealed as a result of unruly desire—that resists being reduced to the status of a thing that we can grasp in clear consciousness, and he will frequently resort to dualism in the attempt to emphasize the otherness of the sacred. He apparently had not yet become aware that eventually, as we know from Hegel, dualistic opposition ultimately collapses into a unity of differences. Eventually Bataille will have to revise his view of the sacred or divine as dualistically opposed to the world in which we live and identify another means to denote a non-attenuated sense of the sacred.

Nevertheless, at this point we must see Bataille's move as an attempt to release the excessive negativity of desire from the chains of the Hegelian system. This is one reason he evokes primitive societies. In primitive societies distinctions certainly existed among individuals, but if one acquired prestige it was due to the ability to represent the sacred time of nonproductive consumption. Hegelian truth becoming reality, society is at a loss for individuals who show disregard for the imperative to use time productively, and thus lacks manifestations of sacred time. Bataille therefore looks for the sovereign moments, fleeting though they may be, to which Hegel remained blind. The search for these moments can be read in three different ways.

First, owing to the inevitable compromises that come with the manifestation or spatial objectification of sovereignty, and the recognition received for this manifestation which establishes a hierarchy of power, a consistent reading of Bataille shows that sovereignty must not expose itself, is indifferent to recognition. Nor can it be intended with any certainty that one knows just what one is intending. There are no paths to take to reach sovereignty, for it consists in elusive, sudden movements in which the course of everyday life is interrupted and one is thrown beyond its limits. Which is why Bataille will concentrate on "inner" experiences in which not only the spatial identity (the separation of subject and object) but as well the temporal identity of the individual (connecting the present to the future) is dissolved.

Second, we may say that in these inner experiences he looks for a negativity that does not work, one that Derrida calls "so irreversible an expenditure, so radical a negativity—here we would have to say an expenditure and a negativity without reserve—that they can no longer be determined as negativity in a process or system."[140] That is, he looks for desire not to be restrained by reason, an instant of negativity so negative that it can no longer be called negativity because it does not convert itself into a positive. Should it continue to convert itself it only "proves . . . that the negation was not negative enough."[141] And finally, it may be that such an instant is only possible once history has ended, the circle closed. As Bataille clearly states:

> [A]lthough the negations and affirmations (of Kierkegaard) can be inserted into the closed circle of Hegel's system . . . because they are bogged down in history and in action, the negation I introduce takes place only once the circle is closed, beyond the domain of history and action. *In fact the instant cannot be 'most important' except to the extent that man no longer has anything to do,* when he has found Hegelian gratification in which his own dissatisfaction is no longer connected to the active negation of such and such determined form, but to the negation, which no activity can absorb, of the human situation.[142]

We have returned again to his "unemployed negativity," a negativity without content, desire without object—and hence without concern for the future, a sovereign indifference to results.

To "recognize" such a negativity therefore requires a different economy, a "non-Hegelian economy of negativity,"[143] an economy that does not relate negativity to the constitution of meaning—expenditure with a return—but one that establishes the non-relation of negativity to anything. That is, an economy related to the sovereign moments of senseless expenditure, "and finally in relation to the loss of meaning."[144] Not concerned with meaning anything, nor even with preserving oneself, the individual who unties negativity and desire from its ballast, who is not afraid to lose what could be gained from a reasonable use of one's resources, this individual does not take death seriously. Our pursuit of sovereignty shall take us "beyond the serious."[145]

1.4 BEYOND THE SERIOUS

To take the step that leads beyond the serious is to finally take leave of Kojève and enter into Bataille's thought as such. It is to move beyond the 'mortal terror' that awakens humanity from its conscious slumber and leads it to take account of the 'seriousness' of existence and articulate it in the *gravitas* of Philosophy. For despite all the apparent weight of his emphasis on death, destruction, and transgression, one may perceive the manner in which these elements have a certain levity to them, a liberating effect on the various burdens shouldered by humankind in an age of mature rationality, a blossoming of mundane life. Indeed, "the worst impotence is a seriousness succeeding at being serious."[146] His "general philosophy," as he articulates it in the most basic terms, "consists in saying that all is play, that being is play."[147] Otherwise stated, all is risk *(mettre en jeu)*, or again, all is chance.

This general definition bears affinity to the theory put forth in Johan Huizinga's book *Homo Ludens* (human being as the being who plays), which puts into question the rationalist reduction of the notion of the human being as *homo sapiens* or the naive optimism of humanity as *homo faber*.[148] In this essay Huizinga demonstrates how play takes its place anterior to—then alongside and at times above—the latter principles as a central aspect guiding civilization. Yet he also points out how play has nevertheless been degraded and ignored as civilization has become more specialized and systematically structured—that is, more serious. Without going into great detail, a few general remarks on his theory of play will be of assistance in understanding this notion and shall aid us in identifying Bataille's transcription of it.

Certain characteristics of play are irreducible: first is its freedom. While many interpretations underline the utility of play as preparation for future maturity or the "need" for relaxation, one is ultimately free to play or refuse to enter its sphere owing to a judgment with respect to the enjoyment or lack thereof that it brings. The notion of a distinct "sphere" of play is perhaps its most important aspect, for play itself implies the stepping out of or transport beyond "ordinary" or "real" life, and into another world. It therefore requires both a time and space outside of everyday existence, a "sacred" realm within which one may indeed be carried away, becoming other to one's ordinary existence, figuratively or literally donning a mask. One may be transported even if one is conscious that one is only participating in a game or illusion and that the space within which it occurs is an arbitrary though well-defined construction.

Therefore, while play is typically defined as being nonserious, at any time the game can take on a profound seriousness, most notably when it pertains to ritual in its varied manifestations, be they religious or juridical.[149] In this respect Huizinga is following Plato's "identification of play and holiness" which "exalts the concept of play to the highest regions of the spirit," and does so "particularly in so far as it transports the participants to another world."[150] Indeed this otherworldly transport is essential for Bataille, but with the understanding that it carries us to a "terrestrial beyond" *(au-delà terrestre)*, one that is accessed through danger.[151] Two final aspects of play as defined by

Huizinga are as well of great importance. The first is, as he states, that "play creates order, it is order."[152] The rules that pertain to the game are unquestionable, must not be violated if the temporary world of play is not to fall apart. He perceptively points out that those who refuse to play the game—outlaws, revolutionaries, non-believers, recluses—are tolerated far less than those who either cheat or are hypocritical. But more importantly, those who refuse to play are considered to be unwilling to take up the dare. This is the final aspect to bring to attention—that play is agonistic, is indissociable from contest and thus risk (of status, honor, wealth, etc.).[153]

Bataille holds Huizinga in great esteem for challenging the sovereignty of servility and the seriousness of labor, and he agrees with Huizinga with respect to the otherworldly and risky exuberance of play. But there are two interrelated emendations to his theory to understand if we are to correctly assess play for Bataille. Firstly, Huizinga's theory that culture is driven by play defines its own limit by its lack of acknowledgment for the role of prohibitions—and consequently for the role of work, which founded humanity and gave rise to those prohibitions. Huizinga has posited that deregulated play creates its own order, defines its own bounds, and thereby distinguishes itself from the serious. Bataille on the other hand posits that first, work has defined the boundaries of play, and second, if play contains "an element of dangerous explosive expansion" then it is necessary to limit that which it is by nature difficult to contain—the transgression of the reasonable course of the world accomplished through play.

The prohibition is therefore a necessary inhibition to play, functioning like a border guard situated in the passage connecting yet separating exuberance and fear. The violence of prohibitions and the horror they provoke in effect paralyze the movement of play through fear of death. In this sense, the prohibition is a living companion to the work that lies at its origin, and would therefore seem to have no part in Huizinga's world of play. Bataille believes just the opposite. It is only from one perspective that a prohibition suppresses possibilities; from another it shows what is possible. A prohibition would not be needed should the desire to transgress the border of work and enter the forbidden, exuberant, and dangerous realm of play not arise. This is only to be understood if it is clear that "transgression belongs to humanity given shape by the business of work,"[154] which is to say that play must be defined as a negation of that which essentially defines us as individuals. Furthermore, the limitations to play, the prohibitions that "bear witness to human exuberance," nevertheless "are not really games but the reactions resulting from a collision of useful, serious activity and the intemperate movement which animates us beyond the useful and the serious."[155] The inhibiting character of the prohibitions that effectively separate the reasonable from the forbidden, far from belonging to the world of the serious, is the negative manifestation of excessive human desire. In effect, as Bataille tells us, the lawful limits are established *in order to be transgressed.* The transgression of a prohibition is that prohibition's fulfillment.

The issue of prohibitions leads to Bataille's second critique of Huizinga; that he holds seriousness and play more as polar than as dialectical opposites. Huizinga states, "[T]he significance of 'play' . . . is by no means defined or exhausted by calling it 'not-earnest' [earnest also has the sense of work], or 'not-serious'. *Play is a thing by itself.*"[156] And while Huizinga, as we have seen, does not believe that play excludes seriousness, work does seek to exclude play. This postulate appears to be self-evident, and in fact Bataille claims that "work alone is profoundly serious . . . suppressing the elements of chance and caprice." Yet on the other hand he also posits that "work is necessary to the full affirmation of play."[157] Play is never a sphere of its own. Consequently, the type of play Bataille has in mind would not be applicable either to animals or children, neither of which have yet fallen into the trappings of death-inspired work. With a gesture toward the Nietzschean call to *become*—not merely to be—a child, Bataille would posit that play must be wrested from the dialectical economy rather than simply suppressing it.

Thus, if we are to draw closer to Bataille's notion of play, we must again turn to his confrontation with Hegel, for while he sides with Huizinga rather than Hegel, Bataille nevertheless follows Hegel in seeing the "fundamental and necessary" dialectical opposition between work and play. He thus still adheres to the Hegelian anthropology insofar as this shows the dual nature of human existence. Insofar, that is, that it is based on the contradictory principles of mastery (play, risk of death) and slavery (work, fear of death). Hegel therefore recognized the opposition between seriousness and play, and on account of its dialectical nature consequently "looked for harmony between work and play," a harmony that was to be accomplished through thought or reason that achieves completion. Yet again there is a certain agreement by Bataille: "[I]t seems to me that Hegel was right on a point: play would only know how to rediscover a place in thought . . . once, to their extreme limits, the possibilities of work have been developed."[158] But as always this agreement is limited and implies a critique. The harmony achieved through work, in effect reducing the entire movement to work, reaches fruition when work, and therefore knowledge, completes its project: "[T]o think is already to work, it is to know death and misery by giving in to them, by working *[en travaillant]*, and it is work which founds the laws of thought. Reciprocally . . . thought is in essence the negation and the active contrary of play."[159] Here again lies the primary bone of contention, for while Bataille has followed Hegel up to the point where thought has reached its limit, he nevertheless wants to avoid a dialectical reversal of the opposition between work and play into equilibrium. Play must imply something that cannot be dialectically domesticated.

Again, it is at the limit of reason's work, where the circle closes itself and thought need not go beyond itself, that Bataille situates the opening to play.

Hegel, who closes off this possibility, completing the possible in work and thought, "is not on the side of play." His thought, while not excluding play as Bataille once claimed, is nevertheless profoundly serious in the manner in which play is integrated. Bataille articulates Hegel's position as such:

> It's from the opposition of the attitude of play (or the risk of death) to the fear of death (or work under constraint) that Hegel draws the dialectical conception of human existence. But Hegel is not on the side of play. It's not Hegel who would affirm of culture, like Huizinga did, that play is its foundation or that it is a game. On the contrary, work is for Hegel the generator of all culture. It is the slave or the worker who accomplishes man's possible, who in the same time in which history completes itself, becomes completed man, who generally incarnates the totality of the possible and who becomes the equivalent of God.[160]

While this is too Kojèvian to be entirely accurate, particularly insofar as it ignores Hegel's prolific writings on religion and aesthetics, nevertheless the case may be made that, in effect, Hegel made of play—the master's risk—a moment of reason's necessity, thereby canceling the moment of play itself, submitting it to a foreign end. In other words, he made play reconcilable with the world of work and gave it a place, though limited, within the development of culture. And in a profound sense he is right, as one who adheres to this dialectic takes one's place within the majority of humanity today, for "the principle of work, anguish paralyzing the naïve movement of play, is now the sovereign principle."[161] This is based, however, upon a misrecognition of the true nature of play or a reduction of its dual sense. "Play" as an overarching term can only lead to confusion.

In fact, it is Hegel himself who allowed Bataille to define the dual nature of play. Firstly there is "minor" play as found in the Hegelian economy in which every action has future consequence. Bataille tells us that minor play is the play that survives in those who accept work, which is tolerated as long as it serves future production, serves life itself. Its meaning consists of mere relaxation within a serious life. Golf, group tourism, mollifying literature, entertaining films: these are the contemporary signs of an immense abdication, of a sad humanity that prefers boredom to chance. The cultural traps in which we are so willingly caught are a clear indication that the inmates are running the asylum. Anguish at the thought of losing that for which we have worked, of "wasting" our "free time," is the modern prohibition. It represses as much as possible the desire to manifest an "inoperable spirit,"[162] a repression designated by our inescapable anguish which indeed makes play a minor, binding humanity to seriousness.

But anguish, while binding mankind to life, work, and the prohibition, is as well the bottleneck of human possibility, the passage to the choice between two decisive attitudes: "minor" or "major" play. That is, one may either find that death and the world are serious, translating life into servility, or play in defiance of death and ruination. This choice—in fact a Hegelian impasse—is never so clearly articulated. To distinguish between the options we must look to the possible responses to anguish. We are already familiar with one response, namely, that the anguish for death is the anguish for self which constitutes our individuality, defining us as separate individuals, each one anguished for his or her own death. But Bataille opens up another possibility when he states that, "anguish is our chance."[163] Our chance, that is, for "major" play.

Like the prohibition, anguish has contradictory ramifications. Not only does it contain the significance of a limitation that ties one to life, but it is as well the sign that some truth is near yet is being kept at a distance or disguised. To recognize this truth is to recognize that—in Bataille's words—"anguish is the same as desire."[164] Anguish is a sign of the desire to transgress the boundaries of reasonable life—to "play"—a transgression that, when taken in the strong sense, amounts to death for the individual as defined by work, the loss of one's existence *as an individual,* the loss of one's existence as duration and discontinuous identity. This loss goes by the name of *"l'expérience intérieure,"* which is no retreat to the interior, but rather arises at the moment of transgression, the crossing of the limits of self-identity which puts that identity, indeed one's existence itself, into question, at risk. The only claim this experience has to being "inner" is the fact that the prohibition that one crosses does not come to one from outside but rather is manifest in anguish at the desire for transgression—for death and loss.[165] Bataille is clear about this, claiming that "man's inner experience is given in the instant in which, breaking the cocoon [the enclosure defined by anguish or prohibition, C.G.], he has consciousness of *tearing himself [se déchirer],* not an opposing resistance from outside."[166] If anguish is dissociated from the desire to transgress the self defined by that anguish, if the prohibition is seen as an external thing to be overcome, then play remains on the minor level. To simply deny the prohibition has the same result. Thus, it is only if anguish—and therefore the prohibition—*remains* when one yields to the desire to overcome it that play becomes an inner rending that gives it a "major" sense.

This is where the workings of Bataille's systematic takes on its most Hegelian nature: transgression *is* Bataille's Hegelian *Aufhebung,* maintaining the anguish of the prohibition though its overcoming: "[A] transgression is not the same as a back-to-nature movement; it suspends a taboo without suppressing it," to which he adds a footnote, "[T]here is no need to stress the Hegelian nature of this operation which corresponds with the dialectic phase described by the untranslatable German "aufheben": transcend without suppressing."[167] It is only if some limit is maintained alongside the excessive desire that pushes one over that limit that transgression can take on its sovereign or "major" sense—*despite its senselessness.* Or to put it another way, prohibitions do not arise without anguish or the fear of death, nor are they to be seen as a limitation if separated from the desire to transgress them and put one's existence at risk. Thus, one must be within the system of work and work-defined knowledge—one's existence must be bound by anguish—if anguish is to be interpreted as "our chance." Consequently, Bataille must maintain Hegel to step outside his limits, the limits of the desire he defined, for just as with Hegel the motor of Bataille's dialectic is the radical negativity of desire. But as we will see, to step outside his limits requires both a different response to anguish, and an altogether different notion of transgression—one that affirms nothing, and which thereby escapes the *Aufhebung* by which Bataille himself defined it.

Now, we have already delimited the fundamental aspects of Hegel's system that have the greatest significance for Bataille. They may be summarized as follows: anguish at the possibility of death keeps one tied to life and compels one to work; to work is to enlist one's negativity for a cause that is not one's own, to inscribe one's negativity in a "project" whose meaning is given by its future goal; the goal is decided in advance—a prerequisite for production— so while negativity is change, the anticipatory structure of the project determines the possibilities of negativity to be already-given possibilities; each moment of negativity only has meaning in relation to the preceding moments and its pre-given end, and it is in-and-as this end that one recognizes oneself—as an object of production, a known thing; furthermore, it is through his "ontology of [self] production"[168] that Hegel attributes to working humanity the development of the totality of human possibilities.

Kojève describes Hegel's working humanity as "Negativity incarnated" or, as noted above, "the death that lives a human life."[169] But the more this negativity is put to use, allowing humanity to both evade and affirm the anguish of death in work, the more is humanity distanced from recognizing the truth of negativity as pure negativity without content—or, correlatively, excessive negativity whose content exceeds the forms of thought—and the farther is negativity removed from the possibility to put one's existence at risk of death. Correlatively, if Hegelian time is the medium of realizing oneself through losing oneself or becoming other to oneself (dying to oneself), each moment of this process is dialectically recuperated and consequently is never experienced for itself. The spiritual resurrection is implied within Good Friday's execution: death is but a logically necessary moment in the immanent development of the absolute concept. Or, in a more Marxist vein, if humanity frees itself through work, and the things created are the reservoirs of the time of production, then Bataille's claim that "the product of his work becomes his master" may be understood with respect to its temporal significance.[170] Having its end outside itself in the future product, Hegel's acting, knowing subject is alienated from its present lived time. That is to say, the image of freedom embodied in the product is the image of human time as servile, profane time, of useful moments oriented toward a preordained goal. Work and its product—knowledge—are the images of humanity as fragmented, despite its claim to totality.

Because Hegel's system is the production of meaning, enlisting every moment in the campaign of meaningful work or the dialectical accumulation of knowledge, death (negativity) is always invested with profound seriousness. In a sense, Hegel is the great speculator—or better perhaps, he deals with death like the broker of life insurance, who only accepts the risk of death provided the system is capable of adjusting to and indeed profiting from the economic loss that death signifies. In effect, he minimizes any disruptive power that death might have, takes no risk at all, risk that is "first of all a refusal to take anything seriously."[171] His insistence on recuperating all negativity in service to a future gain, forcing negativity to collaborate with the constitution of meaning, effectively blinds Hegel to the very truth that Hegel himself unveiled—the priority of the risk of life over the horror of death.

On this point Bataille indeed believes that Hegel did not know to what extent he was right. But by leaving no chance that the expenditure of negativity that responds to the anguish of *déchirement absolu* could be spent to no purpose; by ensuring that in death nothing is irremediably lost, that both individual consciousness and the self-mediating Concept indeed profit from death, Hegel fulfills one imperative, only—in Bataille's view—to abnegate another. That is, he follows his own imperative to *affirm* each moment of death as meaningful, as a moment in the unfolding of Spirit. But in making each moment a necessary and meaningful moment, he limits what is "essentially unlimited," and in so limiting it effectively eliminates it: namely, chance and risk. As Bataille states, "Hegel, by elaborating a philosophy of work (I mean the *Knecht* or emancipated slave or worker who, in the *Phenomenology*, becomes God), canceled out chance—and laughter."[172] His ontology of production—the teleological movement from implicit potentiality to realized actuality in which each moment, false in itself, is cunningly revealed at the end as being a moment of the True—exorcises the disruptive moment. Or to state all that we have been saying in another way, whereas Hegel includes in his system elements of risk and exuberance that endanger one's very identity, he nevertheless aimed for a type of speculation that, as we heard above, would reconcile and unite "the working days of the week" with "the Sunday of life," that would find the unity between life's profane aspects (work, family life, fidelity, responsibility) and its sacred aspects (play, sacrificial spending, poetic exultation).[173] But the reaction this never fails to provoke—and this is not only from Bataille—is that this speculative reconciliation annuls the difference of the sacred, for the contradiction is resolved and raised into the self-presence of Spirit. Even sacred play is reduced to a conceptual or logical difference.

Nevertheless, it is from Hegel's notion of risk found in the master—*once removed from the circle of Hegel's economy*—that Bataille draws his notion of play and chance. To state the matter as directly as possible, sovereign or "major" play is the master's risk without the compromise of concern for the future, and therefore without being attenuated by meaning, or affirming, anything. From an economic perspective, "major" play is deregulated expenditure, superfluous energy spent and having "as its end the indifference to every end, being only an occasion to show a soul beyond the concerns of utility."[174] The risk of death, contrary to its apparent connection with individual glory (of the master), is not the affirmation of the individual, for glory properly understood is only the result of a lack of submission to the very tenets of individuality. It denies the anguish that leads one to take the death of one's individual existence seriously, anguish that would then imply the withdrawal from risk. Or, more precisely, the master's risk is a sovereign risk only insofar as it can somehow overcome the very anguish, the horror of death, that lies at the heart of conscious individualization: "[T]hat is why, in a fundamental sense, to live sovereignly is to escape, if not death, at least the anguish of death. . . . The sovereign man escapes death in this sense: he cannot die *humanly*."[175] Thus, even though he is "*familiar with death*," he resists individual consciousness, whose principle exists within him." The sovereign spirit refuses, that is, the servile condition of projecting its present existence into the anticipated future of its own individuality: like the master, it refuses to work. But further, it refuses the individual affirmation that governs even the appropriation of another's work, an affirmation that "is essentially the negation of play,"[176] and of chance, play's companion.

While it may appear strange to associate play with the Hegelian risk of life, this is precisely what Bataille has in mind, and he could not be more clear on this point:

> Nothing is more ordinary than this paralysis of play, which results from fear [of death]. Nevertheless, I am tempted to believe that the authentic player is, on the contrary, the one who puts his life at risk *[qui met sa vie en jeu]*, that true play is that which poses the question of life and death. . . . Far from being . . . contrary to play, the risk of death is the meaning of a movement that really wants that each of us go as far as possible in the direction contrary to interest.[177]

The logic of interest is effectively the logic of meaning. And Bataille sees the logic of meaning as effectively a logic of self. Thus, insofar as it is the meaning of the risk that is annulled in play, the sense in which the risk that is play is a "putting in question" of one's "self" may clearly be perceived.[178] Putting one's "self" into play, "to wager or question 'self,'" is a risk that finds expression in Bataille's term "chance," for "acquiring chance is what's at stake when constantly questioning yourself."[179] Or more precisely, two things are put into question: not only one's "self," but the Hegelian system in which this self receives its definition and reason. In a fundamental way, Bataille's doctrine of chance is to be understood precisely in opposition to the Hegelian economy even as it relies on an element within this system for its definition.

There are many ways in which to approach the notion of chance—and I shall not try to exhaust them here—the first of which is to say that chance assumes non-knowledge of the future. It is an opening upon unforeseen possibilities, an abrupt passage from a stable order of expectations to a world where our assurances suddenly seem deceptive: or simply, it is passage from the known to the unknowable which, not coincidentally, is Bataille's definition of laughter.[180] In this sense, chance is more an inheritance from Nietzsche than anyone else. Zarathustra, the teacher of laughter, wants non-knowledge of the future (the *Unwissenheit um die Zukunft*), exhorting others to become like the child for which "innocence and forgetting, a new beginning, a game . . . a sacred 'Yes' is needed."[181] Becoming like a child is dying to oneself, perishing through becoming-other, a bridge without end, a river never to be stepped in twice. The difference to be perceived between the two arises from Nietzsche's all-pervasive *will* to become other, to cast off the burdens of given morality and *create* new beginnings. Bataille's "chance," on the other hand, does have the connotation of being willing to lose one's preconceptions, but ultimately chance comes like a foreign invasion: "I'd have never found it by looking."[182] Is chance then simply an absence of deliberation in action? I believe it points to something much more fundamental. Still, Bataille is directed to his notion of chance by Nietzsche's aversion to goals to accomplish, and he appropriates Nietzsche's "active forgetfulness" in his notions of chance and sovereignty, so as to challenge Hegel's teleology, to challenge his anticipatory unfolding of totality with forgetfulness. That is: if Hegelian becoming is the realization of already-given potentialities through a negation of those givens, presenting us with futurizing change that is heavy with the past and bound by its future; if the Hegelian narrative is a retrospective account of an immutable historico-logical development, that *Erinnerung* or interiorizing memory which gathers and sublates all previous moments into a speculative whole; then chance signifies a break in this teleology, a forgetting of the future as well as the past, which serves to disrupt this narrative structure.

Chance only arises in the present moment, becoming a moment in which the bonds of the past and future are momentarily undone, and the individual's temporal identity along with them. Death makes no appointments. Thus, it can neither be integrated into the calculations of productive activity which subordinate the present moment to its anticipated result, nor can it be viewed from above by a conceptual process that subordinates the present to the past. Rather, death is integrated into the movement of chance, becoming a "miraculous" moment "when anticipation dissolves into nothing," undermining work and knowledge, indeed all those affirmations on which we staked our claim to self-certainty and by which we assumed our continued existence. This moment finds its expression in the phrase "impossible and yet there it is."[183]

Negativity, the organon of Hegelian knowledge and possibility, is Bataille's specter of non-knowledge and impossibility. And this, in less elliptical terms, is what Bataille attests to in his letter to Kojève, about which he states:

> I tore up (or lost) the letter to Blank, where I said that with the end of history there'll be no more use for negativity. Negativity—and I was relying on Hegel—means action that results in disruption. *Negativity that's not put to use would destroy whoever lived it . . .*[184]

Chance (play) is the guide for negativity once negativity has lost its employment. It is just this risk of destruction, dispossession, or sacrifice of the "self" that is defined and limited by anguish, yet which is a possibility only because of anguish, for anguish signals the desire to pass beyond the limits it defines. The essential in the relationship between Bataille and Hegel is this interplay between anguish and desire and its significance for chance.

As we have seen, the difference between the two comes down to a difference in orientation with respect to the notion of risk, which relies on their differing responses to anguish, and hence to ultimate chance event of death or self-loss. Bataille frequently derives his distance from Hegel specifically with respect to the possible responses to the experience of radical negativity, to the seriousness or lack thereof with which the negativity tearing apart the fabric of existence is confronted. Hegel's response is the construction of a philosophy of work or of "project." Bataille's response to Hegel is:

> The only obstacle in this way of seeing . . . is what, in man, is irreducible to project: non-discursive existence, laughter, ecstasy, which link man—*in the end*—to the negation of project which he nevertheless is—man ultimately ruins himself in a total effacement—of what he is, of all human affirmation.[185]

The obstacles to Hegel's way of seeing may be generalized under the heading of "chance," which in the broad sense opens the future beyond the closure that Hegel's project of knowledge circumscribes. But if it opens that project to a future that is unknown, it is not merely in the sense that the future always retains an element of being unknown, but rather that the horizon upon which it opens is unknowable.

That is, chance opens Hegelian self-consciousness to an unknown that it cannot affirm as another possibility, that it cannot assign a place in the system of successive possibilities. The chance moment of which Bataille speaks is such that even consciousness of it does not insert it into conscious knowledge, does not fix it as a moment that can be known—indeed, not even a throw of the dice will ever abolish chance.[186] Nor will it assuage the desire to roll the dice once again, to negate the present state of affairs without any foreknowledge of what that negation will bring. Which implies that chance is a disruption in the rational, teleological progression in the use of time and resources.

But perhaps calling it a "disruption" is not strong enough, for if we have learned nothing else from Hegel, we have learned how disruption and diremption—and if we are really faithful to Hegel, then contingency and chance as well—are the keys to the teleological process itself, a process that not only survives them, but feeds off them. Perhaps Bataille is attempting to pull off a Hegelian inversion of his own, but this time with Hegel himself as the inverted. For if, as we have heard, Bataille takes the Hegelian system and relates it to the loss of meaning; if play is the cancellation of the labor of the negative, which it requires for it to be play, then perhaps Bataille's *Aufhebung* is of the Hegelian Absolute itself. That is to say, it would follow a structure wherein the finite life of the Absolute is the negation of abstract nonsense, the progressive overcoming of limited subjective knowledge; the culmination of which, absolute knowledge, is this finite put to death (negated); the death or cancellation of absolute knowledge is then reinscribed within the horizon of nonmeaning, and the spirit recognizes itself in the absolute otherness of knowledge—namely, chance and the unknowable. In which case the process is profoundly incomplete. But perhaps there is another way to state this.

For if things are not what they are in the Hegelian movement of knowledge—insofar as each seemingly correct position will be overcome with another position that corrects it—nevertheless we can say that they *are*, if only implicitly, what they *will be*. Spirit is the self-same spirit in its negation. Its otherness is its own otherness. By introducing the notion of chance, however, Bataille challenges this notion on two counts. First, it suggests that there is no intrinsic connection between what one is and what one will be. For while chance is a negation of sorts, a becoming-other in time, it is not the Hegelian transformation of given state of being into a possibility contained within that given (dialectical negation), but an opening of present life toward an impossibility not yet given. In risk, chance or play, one does become other, but one becomes *totally other* (i.e., sacred). The other one becomes is not the other *of* oneself, but is other *than* oneself. What is revealed in chance is a perfect absence of response to expectation, a *rejection of eschatology as such:*[187] "the dice are thrown with a view to the beyond of individual being—to what doesn't yet exist,"[188] that is, toward nothing—the death of individual existence which suddenly, impossibly, is simply "there" in a roll of the dice where life is at stake.

Not guided by the hand of any available reason, chance is therefore a profound freedom, the very same freedom that Hegel showed as belonging to the one who assumed the risk of life, to the one willing to expend oneself without reckoning. The freedom of chance, however, is the master's risk stolen from the system in which it occurs. Indeed, Bataille goes so far to say—in a rather remarkable statement hidden away (in the *Post-Scriptum* to the "Dossier des 'Larmes D'Eros'")—that "my doctrine of chance is the only aspect of that which I have said which is exterior to Hegel."[189] It manifests man's *an*-economical negativity.

The second challenge chance brings to Hegelian development is perhaps more obscure. For what the moment of chance reveals is in fact not that one *becomes* other, but rather that one *is* other—now, not later. One is other, that is, to the individual one perceives from the perspective of anguish—anguish for the seriousness of death. For anguish is effectively the nullification of the moment of chance, a moment it annuls by fixing one's gaze on what one will be, to the exclusion both of death, and of what one is—a vague intimacy that is manifested in death. When, at the end of history, there is nothing more to become, no more tasks for negativity, no more productive deaths for consciousness to sustain, "complete" self-consciousness can only look for the vague intimacy it has lost insofar as it has been a self-consciousness defined by anguish. What it has lost, that is, by turning away from death. Where it will "find" what it has lost is in desire: "[C]hance is defined in relation to desire,"[190] and it is in desire where negativity will be caught once again in the movement of play.

As we will see in greater detail in the chapters that follow, the "inner" experiences of risk or chance that put our being into play cannot occur in some sort of inner vacuum, but rather are always involved in a certain type of object-relation in which desire is implied. We have already seen how human existence—negativity without content—receives its content in accordance with its choice of objects. The object for which Bataille is searching, a chance object which Bataille delineates as a sort of "Grail," cannot be known or possessed, for it retreats there where one would purport to grasp it. Bound neither by utility, knowledge, nor with any reason for being desired, the elusive and interminable object of desire opens self-conscious desire beyond those economic limits given by the concern to profit in the future, even beyond the concern to stay alive. Such an object is only to be encountered in a "privileged instant," a "miraculous moment" where the impossible—a living encounter with death—is suddenly there.[191]

It may in fact be claimed that chance as an object is the desire of desire, the desire for nothing as embodied in an ungraspable object, and which consequently cannot be satisfied. The desire for such an object turns the desiring subject into chance itself, the risk of loss found when desire wells up and provokes an exuberant moment of object-less expenditure in which sovereignty, "totality," is revealed. Or, as Bataille states, "[T]otality within myself is this exuberance: it is only an *empty yearning*, the unhappy desire to be consumed for no other reason than desire itself—which it wholly is—to burn. . . . *It has no further task to fulfill.*"[192] Sovereignty is excessive desire with nothing left to do, no one and nothing to command—*an*-economic desire.

Taking a risk or putting oneself into play rather than securing oneself through work is thus the response to desire that keeps desire—and chance—alive. Risk then becomes the fundamental imperative for, "chance—and chance alone—makes me what I am."[193] Desire without object, exuberance without end. Foregoing "meaningful action in a definite direction," it is then that:

I begin to understand totality, but as a rending movement: all existence is now beyond sense; it is man's conscious presence in the world insofar as he is nonsense, with nothing to do but be what he is, unable to transcend himself to take on sense or direction in action.[194]

To channel one's rending negativity in a certain direction or toward a transcendent object is for Bataille a flight from the consciousness of what we are—pure, rending negativity: pure desire. To the extent that desire has an aim, the grasping of which provides satisfaction, he believes that we "remain unaware of the totality of being within ourselves," or that our self-consciousness has mistaken the nature of the self of which it is conscious. Consequently, it is only when one frees negativity and desire from tasks to fulfill and knowledge to acquire, when one abandons the framework of action, that "my perfect nakedness [i.e., intimacy, C.G.] is revealed to me. . . . There is no possible outcome other than an endless incoherence in which chance is my only guide."[195] At the end of history, chance has become the guide to self-consciousness, which is then approached in play.

What follows is a sample of the general perspective that has been guiding these investigations, servile and heavy with a task to accomplish though they have been. Here we encounter something like a declaration of desire's independence, written in fact at that pivotal point where Bataille's reflections turned "inwards," and perhaps even acting as a corrective to the political commitments we will examine in the chapter that follows:

Human destiny wants capricious chance to command; what reason substitutes for the rich vegetation of chance is no longer an adventure to be lived, but is instead the empty and correct solution to the difficulties of existence. Acts undertaken with some rational end are only servile responses to a necessity. Acts undertaken in pursuit of seductive images of chance are the only ones that respond to the need to live like a flame. . . . It is, on the contrary, inhuman to abandon life to a chain of useful acts. . . . What escapes servitude—life—risks itself; in other words, it places itself on the level of chances it meets. Life risks itself; the project of destiny is realized.[196]

As we continue, we will see how Bataille sought to put in question the rational economy with practices that, from our disenchanted modern perspective, indeed seem inhuman and irrational. It will be our task not only to discover the rationale behind them, but as well to see how these "prehistorical" events somehow merge with a sense of what Bataille sees as our possibilities in the "posthistorical" world.

On the one hand, the turn to economies and actions that are bound up in a religious context may be read as a response to discontent with the irremediable idleness that prevails after the end of history, when there is no more creative action possible, and when all endeavors are thus rendered absurd. And insofar as this is at issue, the response does not significantly alter the status of "the negative" itself—it is simply placed outside the dialectical circle of the historically self-mediating absolute concept, but is still a human negative. Yet what we must account for as well is a sense of the negative that—as quoted above—would "destroy whoever lived it," which is the "effacement . . . of all human affirmation." This cannot be simply a posthistorical extension of human negativity as risk or play, a human introduction of non-being into being. Rather, we must begin to more noticeably perceive something of a tragic wisdom at stake here, a sense of catastrophe built into human self-assertion, a principle of self-destruction that is immanent to the very rationale that led to the limits of human endeavor and the "end of history," and which opens onto an impersonal and depersonalizing space beyond the limiting veils of individual affirmation.

TWO

The End of Utility

But to be constantly asking "What is the use of it" is unbecoming
to those of broad vision and unworthy of free men.
—Aristotle, *The Politics*, VIII, i.

As is often the case, the estimation of a writer tends to concentrate on a few choice aspects which consensus has deemed to be the essential, and which subsequently serve as grounds either for praise or dismissal. And while the prevailing impression may be viable, it is typically rather reductive. Admittedly, I cannot count myself among the flawless few who avoid all such argumentative expediency, for our analysis thus far may well have been complicitous in such a characterization of Hegel as the systematic thinker of the closed totality. Yet Bataille has no less been the object of such generalizations, and as fate would have it, that with which he is identified, and for which he has received his most uncritical welcome in postmodern thought, may well be the least defensible of his arguments—his notion of unreserved expenditure *(dépense)* and its corresponding economy. This notion, present from the alpha to the omega of Bataille's texts, is difficult to defend primarily in consequence of the sometimes dubious analyses by which he sought to demonstrate it. Yet despite the difficulties we shall encounter with the *economic* application of this concept, its acceptance—even should it be a false sort of acceptance resting mainly on the very seductiveness of the notion itself—nevertheless points to something that is genuinely compelling.

Bataille's notion of expenditure, properly understood, cannot be dissociated from his notion of the sacred, which is conceived both *as* unmasterable excess, and *in* excess of instrumental reason—that is, in defiance of all forms of economic (means-ends) calculation: technical-productive, religious, or otherwise. The sacred so conceived thus puts in question the self-certainty of the self-mediating subject and its rational domination of every other it encounters, the others that it encounters either as obstacles or resources. In this regard, his concern with the sacred is not altogether dissimilar in intention from Heidegger's extensive analyses of the concealment of Being. Or more accurately, his concern with the self-assertive response of humanity to the self-concealment of Being, a withdrawal that founded the productionist-calculative disclosure of entities in the world, which extends from Greek metaphysics to modern technology. Nor is Bataille's perspective distant from Weber's critique of modern, secularized salvation and the way it is played out in the capitalist form of self-justification through success.

The closest affinity, however, is with Nietzsche's tragic affirmation of life in the face of the bourgeois "last man." The condition of Nietzsche's "last man" or modern, one-dimensional humanity—infatuated with comfort, security, and moderate pleasures; staking its claim on a foundation of self-interest and individuality; acting by the logic of rationality, investment, and a belief in progress—is the condition of humanity that Bataille sought both to expose and depose.[1] For, alongside his fellow thinkers, Bataille had a profound sense that something essential was lost when instrumental rationality "disenchanted" the world and the human being justified itself as the basis for all value and truth. He was loathe of a humanity satisfied by its achievements, confident of its place in a world without mystery, a world in which God—as is all too thoughtlessly accepted—is dead, and where the finite individual is comfortable with considering itself to be the efficient and final cause of all things human and inhuman. Bataille, keeping company with Nietzsche and Heidegger, not to mention Hegel, rejected the notion of the human individual as origin. In consequence, if the original is not the human individual, and modern humanity nevertheless adheres to the assertion of self-constitution and an anthropocentric rationality of control, then at best the essential is hidden, at worst it is lost.

But rather than simply accepting this loss as being the historically determined condition of modern humanity; rather than contenting himself with transcribing the history of the forgetfulness of the essential, Bataille relentlessly tries, in a multitude of different contexts, to show how humankind has always, and everywhere, gone in search for that which it has progressively lost—a sense of the sacred, the intimacy of being. To this end, he turned to primitive cultures, alternative economies, and archaic religious practices—particularly that of sacrifice. For it is here that he found institutions that more clearly acknowledged the religious mediation between productive human endeavors that aim at finite self-determination, and excessive, divine, or mythological forces which exceed and precede every determination. Yet while he avails of seemingly irrational practices—such as the ritual release of blood and instinct—it is not the case that he will simply promote the irrational. Rather, he is seeking to discover something that is more basic than the rational, upon which the rational may be founded by way of opposition, and which humanity must conquer lest it bring disorder and destruction into its domain.

Now while less "civilized" humanity may have believed they were dealing with external, objective forces, Bataille situates the forces of disruption—inhuman though they may be—within and between the lives of human individuals themselves. But given the fact that the religious structures and cultic practices that had previously given form to these forces are no longer valid, they would be left to play themselves out among these individuals, in their social interaction, should there not be a manner by which to keep them in check. The history of this suppression of force among individuals is the history of civilization itself, and when we are talking about the social organization of a civilization that is livable for its competing units, we may then be said to be referring to the distribution of available wealth, which is the primary factor requiring regulation if a war of individual interest is not to tear apart whatever binds that may tie. Now the intent here is not to make a claim for the inviolability of a strict Hobbesian political philosophy of radical individualism with an understructure of war, for this is not our primary concern. Rather, at issue is a more general view of how certain transitions concerning the relationship to wealth and the expenditure of resources are bound to a genealogy of religious and social, political and moral developments. More precisely, at issue is the transition from a form of society in which the various bonds—economic, religious, social, and political—were integrated into a more organic whole of societal life, to a form of society in which these spheres, as well as the individuals participating in them, gradually became more autonomous.

Bataille was certainly not the first to see a potential for crisis in this transition from a precapitalist, "organic" society *(Gemeinschaft)* with its more concrete social and religious connections among persons, to a more rational civil society *(Gesellschaft)* and the rise of capitalism where personal relations are mediated by the exchange of things (commodities). More directly stated, there occurred a movement from a traditional community (based on quasi-natural and irrational conventions) to society (based on the emergence of individuality and rational systems). This transition, the "socialization of society," is indeed at the core of Marx's concerns, as well as such post-Marxist sociological thinkers as Simmel (the "tragedy of culture"), Weber (the "rationalization" and "disenchantment" of society) and Lukács ("reification"). The general problematic we find in these analyses is as follows: (a) there is a gradual breakdown in the foundations of the community; Marx attributes this to private property (and thus it may be traced back to Greek and Roman times); Weber attributes this to a process of rationalization coupled with Calvinist Protestantism which was the only religion to do away with the traditional transcendent or quasi-magical elements that held people together, (b) the result is the emergence of the individual and private interest, (c) the individual is once again integrated into society, but under the form of objective dependence on abstract and impersonal rational systems of industrial production, capitalist exchange, and bureaucracy where "integration" and "alienation" go hand in hand, (d) thus, in simultaneity with the liberation of the individual there emerged a crisis of individuality, which occurred specifically because of the new form of "integration" wherein individuals are not only dominated by, but positively contribute to a system of exchange that is their own undoing.

If we are to situate Bataille in this context, the best approximation would be to see him as taking to heart Weber's "iron cage" theory of rational, demagicized economic society, all the while pursuing Marx's vision of postcapitalist liberation, yet doing so by a return to the *spirit* of primitive "religious" practices and their extravagant use of wealth (which, one should note, is the hallmark of capitalism). Looking for a way to challenge the leveling of society to a flat plane of rational values, to find a space that may cause disruption to the efficient, nondifferentiated time of economic pursuits in which useless moments are judged to be unavoidable aberrations, Bataille will try to rediscover the hidden truths, the "unperceived laws that drove the world,"[2] in ancient practices. Indeed, it is this challenge to the prevailing capitalist economy with what will be termed a "symbolic" economy that has proven to be the most enduring element of Bataille's legacy.[3]

In positive terms, his goal—potentially misguided—is to reintroduce something sacred into a world that has lost all connection to the divine world; to find a symbolic space in which humanity may still recognize that life transcends its enclosure in the sphere of utility. His goal is to restore nothing less than the joy of spending to no purpose, the anxious intensity of wasting one's vital resources, the desire to do so effectively having been repressed, cruelly crushed, by a sort of superego economy that demands respect for the limits set by production and rational accumulation. The point, in short, is to show that *the end*—and thus the meaning—of *utility* is to be found in *uselessness*. This is the basic paradox of utility. But, as we will see, when one attempts to put the implications of this paradox into practice, a sort of performative error occurs that creates its own paradox, one that will eventually force Bataille to reassess his method and standpoint.

The waters we are about to traverse run deep and treacherous, and no claim to comprehensiveness will be made, nor is it my objective. My intent rather is to track Bataille's development as he unwaveringly followed the elusive star of a sovereign, and distinctly religious, expenditure of wealth, which he saw as the key to a revitalization of communal life. This route will take us from generosity to avaricious self-interest; from primitive plenitude to market scarcity; from ritual sacrifice to the Reformation and moral salvation; from festivals to fascism and on to the triumph of the bourgeoisie.

2.1 NO FREE GIFTS

The situation in which Bataille found himself in the 1930s, and which his writings of that period address, can roughly be defined by the two interrelated themes outlined above: the loss of the sense of community in a culture of growing fragmentation and intellectual specialization characteristic of a division of labor; and the modern hegemony of economic rationality which encouraged this fragmentation. The separation and elevation of the economic values of production and accumulation above more ethical and social concerns began with the rise of the market economy. Divested of those "irrational" and "uneconomic" desires which animated archaic exchange and gave rise to collective, communal actions that augmented social cohesion, the economy—and the individual unit within it—was able to assert its narcissistic self-enclosure, its autonomy from social concerns. To address this situation, Bataille chose to focus upon the problematic of expenditure—consumption—and the economic rationale that governs it.

If we may bracket Marxism for the moment, the pivotal source of inspiration for Bataille's endeavor to invigorate communal life is found in Marcel Mauss's considerations of the ancient practice of *potlatch* as transcribed in his essay, *The Gift*.[4] In this essay, Mauss demonstrates that economic and social life might be based on notions very different than that with which we are familiar: that the concern of economic activity may not be scarcity and the alleviation of material difficulties, but rather an excess of resources and the very real need to (apparently) waste those resources "to no end." It was Mauss who demonstrated to Bataille the existence of cultures that asserted sumptuary value over exchange value, that found it in their interest to gloriously expend vital resources rather than to save and spend to accumulate things and resources. It was Mauss whom Bataille would much later cite as a "decisive influence," particularly with respect to his own formation of a "general economy"—one that encompassed ethical, social, political, aesthetic, and religious values. And it was Mauss—although Nietzsche played a role here—that centered Bataille's concern with "total beings": that is, "beings not divided according to their faculties,"[5] which required a society that equally did not divide its institutions into independent and autonomous functions, but which treated the exchanges forming social bonds as—in the famous phrase of Emile Durkheim—"total social facts."

More generally still, Bataille sees in Mauss the opportunity to offer a critique of those ideas that subordinate human activity, and ultimately its autonomy, to ends determined by servile forms of thought. But ultimately, what Mauss revealed to Bataille was the proximity of economic and religious behaviors, provided one does not merely see the economy as a sphere unto itself, and provided that one view religion as the sphere of gratuitous consumption. Provided, that is, a very different view of the world than that which presides today.

My intention here is not to engage in an analysis of Mauss's work, nor to follow the various critiques that have been leveled against it, but rather to delineate what I believe to be of fundamental importance for Bataille—even though this may be unduly influenced by his own perspective.[6] The most read-ily ascertainable influence is the concern with the use of wealth in both quan-titative and temporal terms. Starting from a rather metaphysical "solar," "cos-mic," or global perspective which posits an overabundance of available energy, the premise with which Bataille begins is that living organisms—and this includes social bodies—receive and produce energy or resources in excess of their needs, and that this excess must be spent if not to have a deleterious effect on that body. Or more accurately, since a body cannot expand indefi-nitely, a point will be reached where its available resources exceed its needs, and thus that this excess will be lost is inevitable. The question then is whether or not humanity accommodates itself to this movement of loss, or whether it represses it. This question leads to an economic decision, and the choice faced by individuals and societies is the manner in which the surplus is to be con-sumed. That is: is it to be spent—according to an individual perspective based on the consciousness of necessity and the fear of indigence—to regenerate fur-ther growth through conquest; or is to be spent—according to a general, prodigal, perspective—in a useless and unproductive manner. More appropri-ately, the question is whether or not the *desire* for the latter can be recognized and afforded a place within the *interests* of the modern, "civilized" world. This question will, in different guises, occupy Bataille for the better part of twenty-five years.

The first systematic approach Bataille offers to the problem of con-sumption is found in his 1933 article "The Notion of Expenditure" *("La Notion de Dépense")*[7] although his concern with this issue is evident from even earlier writings. One only need look to his article from 1928, *"L'Amerique dis-parue"* ("Extinct America"),[8] to discern Bataille's fascination with and recog-nition of the basic *need* for extravagant expenditure. In this article he con-trasts the Inca civilization, whose bureaucratic organization contributed to its prolific expansion, with an Aztec civilization that, in comparison, seemed driven by death, chaos, and blood. The Incas, a culture Bataille describes as "the most administrative and orderly ever formed by men," in which "every-thing was planned ahead in an airless existence," structured and designed their society to achieve the maximum amount of systematic growth and sta-bility. While this society—like every society, including our own—had its vic-tims, they were disposed of in a manner concomitant with their outlook and architecture—like our own. Death occurred in a way that not only kept the reigning order intact, but which in fact transpired in a manner that con-tributed to the general uniformity of their "marvelous architectural wholes"—death was buried within the system.

A portrait quite different from the Peruvian Incas is offered by the Mexican Aztecs who behaved, on certain occasions, "as if gone mad," and for whom "death . . . was nothing." This society, equally cultured and wealthy, nevertheless displayed its disregard for growth and preservation of life with its extravagant sacrificial spectacles in which it slaughtered those resources it had acquired through warfare. Their pyramids—unlike the monuments in which the Incas buried the death that founded their empire—ran with blood in rituals that both offered their wealth up to the gods and consecrated those who could have been bound to slavery. Their victims represented the surplus, the "accursed share" *(part maudite)*[9] taken from the stock of useful wealth and torn away from the profane world of cold economic calculation to be consumed without profit, though their rituals indeed enhanced social order and cohesion.

Before we move on, however, I believe we should not only more sharply define the terms in question, but as well pinpoint precisely what this early article manifests. First of all, it shows us is that, from the outset, the communist Bataille introduced what has been called a "major sea-change" into Marxist economics that undermines the very foundations of praxis philosophy.[10] The cornerstone of this shift, which at least Bataille sees as consistent with Marxism, is the transformation of the use-value of labor (productive expenditure) from the realization of human life into a means for negating the cycle of production. That is, Bataille switches the emphasis from production to consumption understood as nonproductive expenditure *(dépense)*, and claims that this radical form of consumption both manifests and confirms the sovereignty of human existence. To be clear then, Bataille at least implicitly affirms—unlike "genuine" Marxists—that no mere change in the ownership of the means of production could ever alter the alienating productive rationality of modern humanity that reduces all being, including the human variety, to a mechanical process of being-produced and consumed. Therefore, while he does indeed concern himself with *who* owns the means of production, his emphasis ultimately lay in *how* production achieves its end—whether in material vitality and the golem of nonalienated production, or in communal vitality and the myth of expenditure as symbolic ritual. That is, whether production leads to productive or excessive consumption—excessive, that is, in the religious rather than capitalist sense. To analyze the principles of limited consumption *(consommation)* and excessive consumption *(consumation)*[11] I turn to Bataille's "Notion of Expenditure"[12] and its relation to Mauss.

The distinction drawn within the notion of consumption serves to indicate that "human activity is not entirely reducible to processes of production and conservation."[13] *Consommation* represents only the use or negation of resources necessary for the preservation of life in which consumption—following the principles of classical or material utility—is placed solely within the context of generating further production. This "economic" view of human activity—more specifically, the market economy view—abhors any loss that is not recuperated, for it is oriented by the fear of deficit: "[T]he market-industrial system institutes scarcity. . . . Scarcity is the axiom of our economics. . . . "[14] Scarcity, not an intrinsic motivation of production, is rather a relation between means and ends, and with the exponential increase of "vital" needs, the means are indeed perceived as inadequate, thereby encouraging further production. Simply stated, *consommation* functions as a means to the end of production that generates wealth and satisfies the vital needs of life.

This "economy of life" generated its own complement in what Bataille called "rationalism," but which is actually more akin to that bond between reason and efficiency known as "instrumental reason." With instrumental reason, thought itself becomes—in the words of Max Horkheimer—"an energy conserving operation . . . a pragmatic instrument,"[15] not only justifying but strengthening the principle of restricted consumption. As Bataille states:

> The rationalist conceptions developed by the bourgeoisie, starting in the seventeenth century, were a response to these humiliating conceptions of restrained expenditure; this rationalism meant nothing other than the strictly economic representation of the world—economic in the vulgar . . . bourgeois sense, of the word.[16]

The "rationalist" conception of activity however leads to a fundamental impasse, namely, "the paradox of absolute utility,"[17] which we briefly encountered above. The "paradox" goes something like this: productive activity is really nothing but the condition or *means* of existence, its utility being a means that serves useful ends, those of necessity; now given a sufficiently advanced state of production, the end of production, necessity, has already been secured, so that production above and beyond necessity has no other end than further production (a means); market production, in excess of needs, therefore becomes a means to a means (further production), and utility becomes absolute.[18] It is contradictory, however, to be a means to no end. Consequently, productive activity should find its true end or value "from the moment in which it *stops* working";[19] in which case, the end of *utility* is *uselessness*. In order for the value of productive activity to be consummated, Bataille believes that humanity would then have to freely, and in fact *pointlessly* spend—or better, *destroy*—that for which it has worked. What he wants to show is that if utility is absolute, then utility becomes a matter of luxury rather than necessity, or that production and acquisition are in fact "only means subordinated to expenditure."[20] The principle of absolute utility, however, reverses the roles, turning that which is in truth only a means (production) into the appearance of an end, giving the path to freedom the taste of servitude.

Leaving this rather dubiously formulated "paradox" aside, the point Bataille is making is that as long as a society remains bound to a principle requiring it to justify its losses along utilitarian grounds, as long as consumption remains restricted, that society will always betray its true needs and desires. To illustrate this point, he turns to an example frequently encountered throughout his writings and which cannot be dissociated from his personal history—the opposition of father and son. The youth is characterized by his capacity and need for "wasting and destroying without reason," precisely that activity which is prohibited by the father in whose house he is inserted, who subordinates the son by securing his basic needs. He provides for his child, therefore, with a "partially malevolent solicitude"[21]—that is, on the assumption that the son remain silent with respect to his real desires. This relationship, which Bataille finds characteristic of social conceptions in general, leads him to lament that "conscious humanity has remained a minor; humanity recognizes the right to acquire, conserve, and to consume rationally, but it excludes in principle nonproductive expenditure."[22] It is for this latter part of consumption *(consumation)*, which refuses to be a means to the end of production, that Bataille reserves the term *expenditure*.

It is Mauss—the one who told us that "it is indeed something other than utility"[23] that is at the basis of the economic impulse, that there is another imperative governing the dialectic of production and consumption—who opens the possibility of "pure" expenditure to Bataille through his writings on the archaic form of exchange known as *potlatch*. And it is in the institution of potlatch that Bataille will find a model for the general economy in which the main concern is not with scarcity and production characteristic of a "restrictive" or "closed" economy, but the wasting or expenditure of accumulated wealth not limited by particular ends. The task that Bataille takes up is to reveal, through Mauss, what this other imperative is.

Yet before we turn to potlatch itself, there is still another, more fundamental issue lurking in this dialectic of accumulation and consumption, one that will become more clear as we continue. Reflecting on this dialectic as presented in "Extinct America," Denis Hollier suggests that Bataille first describes the Inca's principles of accumulation only to invalidate them with the Aztec's drive for consumption, which leads Hollier to conclude that "sacrifice can only be produced after accumulation."[24] This viewpoint, however, is open to challenge if it is confined to an economic point of view, for there is anthropological evidence to suggest that there were societies that "sacrificed"—or more accurately, practiced unlimited consumption—without ever accumulating resources. In his text, *Stone Age Economics*,[25] Marshall Sahlins comments upon the characteristic features and prejudicial misunderstandings of the "original affluent society," or the original (Paleolithic) society of abundance. Here he describes a people whose "prodigality . . . their inclination to consume at once all stocks on hand as if they had it made" is so comprehensive that it may "carry their extravagance to the edge of disaster," for they consumed, *without reserve*, every resource available to them.[26] This society of hunters and gatherers, it is claimed, knew an abundance in their poverty that the richest producers will never know, insofar as "abundance" is defined as the equilibrium between human production and human ends. Where desires are limited, low production is sufficient. Such an abundance is necessarily denied to a society that works because of an anguished concern for scarcity in relation to infinitely expanding needs, in comparison with which the original society appeared relaxed and confident in the wealth of available resources. Consequently, they did not produce, nor did they accumulate resources, for they did not submit their activity to our economic calculations: in short, "they slept a lot."

Now, if their abundance was manifested through prodigal consumption of what were in fact scarce—though sufficient—resources, and *without concern for the future*, then it indeed seems that consumption, or the consumption that is sacrifice, need not follow upon accumulation. And to an extent, Bataille holds the same viewpoint, insofar as he views the temporal orientation of sovereign consumption as interest confined solely to the moment itself, a view that will lead him as well to posit the poverty of rich societies that indefinitely postpone the manifestation of their abundance, thereby renouncing their "abundant" existence. But I would like to raise a point here—one that will become more evident as we develop our reflections on *potlatch* and sacrifice itself—which is this: insofar as the question of sovereignty and sacrifice is posed by the purely economic dialectic of accumulation and expenditure, saving and spending, then the fundamental question is eluded, and the ability for economic analysis to get to the heart of the matter runs up against limitations.

While, in economic terms, the "original affluent society" may have practiced a more pure form of expenditure than the Aztec society, never delaying it or compromising it by ulterior considerations, this expenditure was insignificant, for they knew nothing else. Never internalizing and submitting unreservedly to the profane time of work, neither did they have a sacred time of play.[27] Rather, they merely adhered to standards of relaxation, which, while perhaps enviably immoderate, were nonetheless neutral. Not knowing profit or acquisition, they never consumed *gratuitously*, beyond the concern for vital needs. If we look to these people, who neither transformed the world, nor made provisions for life beyond the present—most likely because they had no sense of a future[28]—we may conclude that insofar as they had consciousness, it was effectively natural (an idea Sahlins rejects), living an intimacy with the world that only we, from our standpoint, can attribute to them. Yet while hunting and sleeping, *apparently* "at their leisure," in fact they were bound, like animals, by a blind servility to nature. In a way, the bourgeois world, bound in voluntary servility to production by its fear of lack, is but the flip-side of the same coin. Both societies—even the one that consumes immodestly—are profoundly irreligious; and the individuals in both—but for different reasons—have an impaired self-consciousness. And it is these issues, rather than economics itself, that are really at stake for Bataille. Allow me, if only briefly, to explain these potentially strange statements.

If we look to analyses from earlier sources with which Bataille at least had the possibility of being familiar—and here we shall follow Ernst Cassirer—we hear that there was originally a primal indivision between the subject and object such that there was no recognizable limit to the "subjective drives" of human beings, no world distinct from themselves. Their consciousness was merely of that which provoked fear or hope, satisfaction or desire—that is, purely instinctual impulses.[29] In a word, there was no sense of "self" at all, for there was nothing opposing the "self," there was no original gulf between human being and the world or the divine and the human.[30] The gulf between humanity and the world would only arise with the development of tools, which created an "inner crisis" in these early humans. This crisis occurs when intermediary steps are interpolated between immediate desire and its goal, a crisis that for the first time achieves and articulates the spheres of "subject" and "object," only gradually proceeding to the heightened sense of self-consciousness.[31]

A logical extension of this argument would lead one to conclude that if the early humans engaged in what we would call celebrations or "festivals" of some sort, which one assumes would follow upon a particularly successful hunt, the excessive consumption or in fact useless destruction involved—useless because they would have consumed beyond their needs—would be of no religious significance, for there was no objective aim, no distinct gods or purposes transcending the feast. In short, there was no sacrifice. In Cassirer's view, the essential factor in the development of sacrifice is not—as in Hubert and Mauss's logic—to create a bond between the sacred and profane, but to *first create a gulf between them*. And once this distance is imposed, "a new motif makes its appearance":

> A man's sensory wishes and desires do not flow equally in all directions; he no longer seeks to transpose them immediately and unrestrictedly into reality; rather he limits them at certain points in order to make the withheld and, one might say, *stored-up power* free for other purposes. *Through this narrowing of the scope of desire*, expressed in the negative acts of asceticism and sacrifice, the content of the desire is raised to its highest concentration *and thus to a new form of consciousness*. A power opposed to the seeming omnipotence of the I makes itself felt. But this power, by being apprehended as such and by imposing its first limit upon the I, begins for the first time to give it a determinate form. For only when the barrier is felt and known as such is the road opened by which it can *progressively be surmounted*.[32]

Now the emphasis for Cassirer is precisely this final aspect, the progressive overcoming of all those mythical elements that restrain human autonomy, effectively closing the gap—not through ritual, but through self-conscious knowledge—that it was first necessary to produce. If Cassirer plumbs the depths of the mythical thought that is at the origin of consciousness, it is in fact part of a process of removing the enemy within. That he recognizes what he overcomes is his virtue.

The point of this digression, however, is first to specify where Bataille positions potlatch and sacrifice, which only have significance, indeed, *can only take place,* once labor has established the profane world of things, and once the human being has been reduced to a thing among the things of this world. Unlike the natural consumption of the "original" humans who had no reduction for which to atone, who do represent an ideal—though unconscious—form of intimacy, the consumption that is sacrifice proper *only destroys the tie* that connects what it consumes to the world of things, the world of useful activity. This destruction, which Bataille places in the sphere of *religion*—though we may also find it in the Greek *polis*—occurs not only with the intention of allowing humanity to escape its own circumscription within the world of things by revealing its tie to a sacred realm. It as well functions to end the separation among humans beings by destroying a fellow-being—another subject—that has been reduced to a thing or distinct object, eliminating that being's usefulness, destroying the other *as a thing.* Not positing a distinct world of objects, not knowing utility, neither do the "original" humans sacrifice. In the course of our reflections, however, we will be forced to consider how sacrifice and its practitioners are nevertheless compromised by profane, economic considerations which the "society of abundance" did not know, a society that was thus, in fact, truly rich.

The second point I wish to make has a more general perspective. Insofar as Cassirer charts the development of self-consciousness, like Hegel he does so through describing the dialectical assimilation and transformation of an obscure content into a clear consciousness free of that content. The self-consciousness that results is autonomy from indefiniteness. But I repeat, and will do so again, that Bataille believes self-consciousness is limited if not aware that it is bound, despite its clear knowledge of the world, to an obscure content that eludes that knowledge. Therefore, as poor as the original humans were in self-consciousness for their immersion in the natural given and lack of an objective world clearly distinct from that 'self', so is modern humanity of clear self-consciousness—which has denied its dependence on its own nature—poor in its distanciation from an intimacy that knowledge can never grant it. Not being a return to an "inhuman" nature, our first topic of discussion, potlatch, will be but the initial step as we chart the path of a being that is irrevocably uprooted from nature by the work of consciousness as it tries to rediscover that from which it has been uprooted.

In principle potlatch signifies a system of exchanges or the circulation of wealth in the form of gifts and to the exclusion of calculated bargaining or barter. First we must note the much-contested nature of the thing given. In advanced forms of market exchange, the thing given is neutral, dissociated from the life of the provider, as is the payment for it, which serves as an abstract equivalent for the wealth stored in the object. The exchange therefore operates on a strictly profane level, having solely the sense of a calculated and formal transaction. Whereas in potlatch, according to Mauss, the thing is alive with its *mana,* its magical and religious spirit *(hau)* or force which itself obliges reciprocation. Indeed, as mentioned above, the entirety of Mauss's analysis hinges on this questionable notion of the *hau* wherein the thing itself is invested with the soul of the giver so the exchange involves a certain intimacy among the participants. As Mauss states, there is an "intermingling" in which "souls are mixed with things, things with souls. Lives are mingled, and this is how . . . each emerges from their own sphere and mixes together."[33] To keep a thing given is to hold on to another's soul and to call upon oneself the danger involved in keeping another person in a state of self-alienation.[34] Avarice in all its forms breaks the circle of the law in primitive exchange, an economic principle that in fact holds forth even with those who reject Mauss's magical/religious view of the *hau*. In more social/secular readings, the *hau*—though it is never entirely secular—is interpreted to be the increase in yield on a gift, something more akin to our notion of profit. Thus, while generosity may indeed be the initial movement, the obligation to reciprocate rests on a more directly *social* imperative—the aversion of disequilibrium which would disturb the social peace: reciprocation as aversion of war—and a more distinctly (anti-capitalistic) *moral* imperative—that "one man's gift should not be another man's capital."[35]

Now even if we cannot accept the validity of the notion of *hau* and its *mana* at face value, its significance for us is twofold: first, it implies that the object given is on the plane of the subject who gives it, that in fact it is a sign of the subject—or the clan that subject represents. Giving or destroying the object is thus a gift of self; and second, which follows from the first, is that the article exchanged was not merely a thing, was not reduced to the neutrality of the profane world, but had already transcended any function it could have. Herein lies the first glimpse of that which attenuates the excessiveness of potlatch—what is given is useless from the start. In principle, the goods that are exchanged are not done so for their use or exchange-value, for these goods had already been set aside just for the purpose of the potlatch, which for obvious reasons then cannot be conducted out of concern for acquiring wealth. Yet it is utterly senseless to give, and in fact we would never do so, should there be no trace of gain involved.[36] But since—as we just noted—the issue cannot be mere acquisition, then the reward for the gift must be linked to the dissipation of wealth. How does this work?

The crucial feature of potlatch is unveiled when one considers that there is no such thing as a private potlatch. One of the virtues of potlatch, indeed one of its central elements, is the fact that the subject who gives surpasses itself, both crossing the narrow field of individual interest and entering into a personal relation with the one to whom the subject gives. This is why this form of exchange differs from the "vulgar" practice of the bourgeoisie, who do not exactly consume only for themselves—there is an image to worry about—but who do so in accordance with an impersonal market, "behind closed doors," as it were. But the very fact of its public nature brings about the downfall of its ideal nature as a pure loss or destruction, for while it cannot—like the form of exchange we know—be reduced to the desire to gain, neither is it reducible to the desire to lose.[37] For by showing a willingness to lose or dissipate one's wealth, one gains the prestige of being perceived as above the concerns of life. Indeed, for Bataille, the fundamental element of potlatch, the very reason for which it is carried out—namely, recognition—is the very thing that compromises it.[38] Because of recognition, the gift, in Bataille's words, becomes "absurd."[39]

But for what reason does Bataille make claims for its apparent absurdity? After all, Mauss himself recognized the contradiction in the very notion of "gift," but did not see that as grounds for absurdity. As Mauss states:

> All in all, just as these gifts are not freely given, they are also not really disinterested. . . . Even pure destruction of wealth does not signify that complete detachment that one might believe to be found in it. Even those acts of greatness are not without egoism. The purely sumptuary form of consumption . . . in which considerable amounts of goods that have taken a long time to amass are suddenly given away or even destroyed, particularly in the case of the potlatch, give such institutions the appearance of representing pure lavish expenditure and childish prodigality. . . . But the reason for these gifts and frenetic acts of wealth consumption is in no way disinterested . . . through such gifts a hierarchy is established.[40]

He knows that prestige, superiority, and the acquisition of rank and power are indissociable from potlatch; he knows as well that the obligation for the receiver of the gift to return it with interest, negating not only the first giver's "loss" but even more painfully, his prestige as well, are laws built into the exchange; yet he still is able to see in it a more generous and humane form of contract, one that brings people's lives together into a stronger sense of community than the type of exchange practiced today. For while the potlatch may contain ambiguous motivations, it is still far from the triumph of profit and individual interest that has overtaken the use of wealth. Bataille, while appreciating this aspect, did not truly take it to heart until much later.

Nevertheless, what Mauss brought to his attention was a problematic with which he would forever be preoccupied. For the essential lesson Bataille drew from Mauss, one that will in fact take him beyond his mentor's framework of economic restitution, was the fundamental importance of the desire to lose, to risk oneself unconditionally in an expenditure that was without concern for anything beyond the moment of loss itself—which is why the sphere of sexuality came to be such a focal point for Bataille. He would come to apply this principle of loss not only to our resources, but to our "selves": the risk that the potlatch will not be returned will become the risk that desire remain unsatisfied, that desire end in the death of the self. This risk or chance, a putting-one's-self in question, is the "inner experience," the "need" on which not only potlatch, but in fact the "sovereignty" of existence, rests. And it is the lack of restricting conditions, the lack of *meaning* for the loss, that differentiates Bataille's sovereign *dépense* from Mauss's *don*. Because Bataille sees *the* imperative of potlatch, indeed the condition of sovereignty, in the risk of loss without return, he believes that the *use* to which potlatch is put and which retroactively determines its meaning brings human existence into contradiction and absurdity.[41] That is, he sees in it the comic situation that "one wants to be unlimited and limited at the same time."[42] One apparently loses, but this loss is illusory. One unveils the value of life in negating the servile use of one's possessions, one asserts one's sovereignty in the *useless* disposal of one's life, only to negate this sovereignty by putting it to use. It is the problem of an unrestricted human nature bound by a restricted economy.

Now, the economy Mauss describes is obviously not restricted in the strict sense of the word, but nevertheless, despite itself yet because of its restitutive imperative, it contains the element of symbolic recuperation that provides exuberant loss with meaning. Yet it is Mauss himself, realizing the effect of the obligation to reciprocate, who leads Bataille to his foundational principle when he states, "the ideal would be to give a potlatch that is not returned."[43] Functionally, this would assure the prestige of the one who gives, for his "rival" would not negate this gift with his own. Yet more important for Bataille is that the value of the act would be consecrated solely in the instant itself, an instant of total surrender that abandons considerations of a higher purpose or future interest. In which case he will be able to assert his principle that "desire demands the greatest possible loss."[44] It would allow him to take desire out of the economy.

As it is a matter of desire, however, the issue has the potential to become clouded, for empirically speaking, once desire is involved one has already started down the road to acquisition of an external object, whereas the issue is in fact the sovereignty of self-consciousness independent of external determinations, of tasks to accomplish. The real task will be to find a moment of *pure* expenditure, *pure* loss. Bataille describes the dilemma as follows: insofar as we are beings who search for that which will raise our lives beyond mere subsistence, our autonomy—our sovereignty—is compromised, for it is guided toward something in the future. "In reality," as he claims, our resources for life itself "should be situated in relation to the moment in which it will resolve into a pure expenditure." This reality, however, is not so easily accessible:

> But this is precisely the difficult transition. In fact, it goes against consciousness in the sense that the latter tries to grasp some object of acquisition, *something,* not the *nothing* of pure expenditure. It is a question of arriving at the moment when consciousness will cease to be a consciousness of *something;* in other words, of becoming conscious of the decisive meaning of an instant in which increase (the acquisition of *something*) will resolve into expenditure; and this will be precisely *self-consciousness,* that is, a consciousness that henceforth has *nothing as its object.*[45]

A number of issues deserving our attention hereby present themselves. First of all, it is striking that on the final page of study devoted to the objective, historical forms of political economy and their religious counterparts, Bataille concludes that objective forms and external determinations of the issue only lead one away from what is at stake, that "an antiquated teleology" of religion and economics is but the starting point of the larger question of self-consciousness itself.[46]

Secondly, there is an unequivocal—though not specifically articulated—assertion that the problem of expenditure is a problem of desire: desire not for some object but for the nothing that is desire itself; desire that thereby is equated to *Hegelian* self-consciousness.[47] The difficulty announced is thus the search, perhaps "absurd," for unrestricted expenditure or an "open" notion of desirous self-consciousness that has as its basis and structure a desirous self-consciousness that is typically considered restricted or "closed." This is the conflict to which his study of Mauss will lead, and the problem is unchanged: how to offer a gift that is not returned; how to desire outside of a symbolic system of recuperation? In effect, the use of expenditure for rank, or of desire for empirical acquisition, is a result of the "stubborn determination to treat as a disposable and usable *thing* that whose essence is sacred, that which is completely removed from the utilitarian sphere."[48] It is a matter of a human attitude that is perhaps unavoidable, a "compromise in our nature" itself: "It is not enough for our left hand not to know what the right hand gives: Clumsily, it tries to take it back."[49] It tries to grasp the ungraspable, to use the useless. It is only on a strictly economic level, however, that this dynamic is so clear-cut.

And as we will see, Bataille himself is not exempt from this sort of recuperation. In his case however, when the left hand gives, the right hand that takes it back does not belong to the same person. When—as in the potlatch—one places oneself at risk, even if that risk is recuperated and thereby seemingly annulled, one nevertheless *becomes other* in the process. This dynamic shall inform a large part of the chapters that follow. But before we move on, it will be of interest to indicate the political and moral conflicts into which Bataille entered as he himself tried to employ the violent and sovereign impulses found in potlatch within a homogeneous society characterized by a functionalist rationality. Such an attempt is one way to describe fascism.

2.2 UNHOLY ALLIANCES

Bataille's first theoretical approach to fascism, found in his 1933 article "The Psychological Structure of Fascism,"[50] reveals an element of attraction that this repulsive phenomenon had for Bataille. He was seduced in effect by the connection he perceived between the *Führer* and traditional forms of sovereignty, those individuals and institutions that, with respect to everyday existence, represented something heterogeneous, totally "other"—something sacred. Yet he as well saw fascism as delineating the sacred with respect to the other "other," those others made "heterogeneous" by the fascistic principle of exclusion.[51] For in these excluded, prohibited others—and what is prohibited is also sacred— were perceived those non-assimilable elements which were considered dangerous to the social order, elements that he saw as capable of provoking an affective reaction. It is this definition that allows Bataille to place the *lumpenproletariat* and noble leaders alongside menstrual blood and dead bodies, which are traditionally subject to taboo. With respect to the *Führer*, however, the aspect of forbidden attraction was his sacred function of both serving as a stable point of unification for the diverse affective forces of the masses and as a provocation to their release.

Consequently, when the *Führer* and his followers with their mass rituals and contempt for democratic principles practiced their *Blitzkrieg* politics, Bataille only saw the possibility of a rebirth of ancient values, apparently missing the uncompromisingly rational nature of the fascist program itself. The potential for this rebirth he found in the image of the fascist leader as a "pure" sovereign whose power—like that of ancient priests, military nobility, and monarchs—rested on mass acceptance of their divine, symbolic status, which placed them above men and required no rational legitimation.[52] Essentially it was the potential for a politics relying on a sacred element dissociated from the cycle of production that was enticing to Bataille. But two problems immediately presented themselves: how to reconcile fascist politics—which reduplicates the tendency of royal power to concentrate both military and religious power to oppress and negate human beings—with the socialist revolution; and correlatively, how to conceive the possibility of keeping political sovereignty pure from a connection with profane, exploitative, and repressive power. Strictly speaking, if history is the measure the latter possibility proves virtually unrealizable. All forms of historical sovereignty, even if based on purportedly "pure" or disinterested sovereign activities or individuals, form their links to profane power. This is made evident, for instance, by the power and recognition associated with potlatch, in which a seemingly radical example of careless destruction cannot be dissociated from the rank and acquisition that is its end. Historically speaking, then, utility always seems to prevail even in the most radical forms of its negation.

With respect to the former problem we see Bataille the communist concerned with retaining the elements of subversion that are quashed by fascism, which, by his definition, merges the heterogeneous with the homogeneous. Seen idealistically or aesthetically, such a fusion could lead to the liberation of the oppressed, "lower" heterogeneous, but functionally (that is, in reality) it leads to the exploitative assimilation and neutralization of the lower productive elements to the aggrandizement of their leaders and those who benefit from a centralized power structure. Fascism therefore ultimately reproduced the capitalist gesture but under the mythical guise of racial unification, as "the imperative presence of the leader amounts to a negation of the fundamentally revolutionary effervescence that he taps. . . ."[53] That is, fascism ultimately cancels the very subversion upon which it was founded by channeling it into profane power.

Bataille nevertheless tentatively pursues—within the fascist framework, though with a decidedly Marxist influence—the possibility that the violent, nonabstract negativity of the volatile masses may realize the Final Revolution. At which point the proletariat, the "lower" class, will take control not only of the means of production but as well the means of expenditure traditionally offered for consecration to the imperative, "higher" class. This possibility is made evident by his proposed unity of the impoverished forms of heterogeneity and the imperative forms characterized by kings, royals, fascist or totalitarian leaders. Yet because of this very fragility in the distinction between the imperative and impoverished forms of heterogeneity, this theory carries the implication that revolt may easily slide into another form of fascism, one in which the subversive forces achieve a reversal and occupy the vacated position of the privileged rulers: "[T]he necessity inherent to subversive forms requires that what is low become high, that what is high become low."[54] Now this by definition is not necessarily a fascist upheaval, and is in fact the noble intention behind the uprisings of many a disenfranchised peoples. Yet there is a distinct possibility that if the "lower" heterogeneous form of the proletariat, stimulated by "renewed affective forces," should serve as a "point of concentration for every dissociated social element that has been banished to heterogeneity,"[55] then we indeed have a situation that reflects his description of the attraction of imperative fascist leaders.

He does take care, however, to add that the "imperative attraction" that these new forces acquire would be such that it "no longer immobilizes those who are subject to it," and with this in mind he will later—in the *Accursed Share* (1953)—offer the Soviet model as a possible, although flawed, solution. The problem of the conscious elevation of the revolutionary classes, however, remains the same: on the one hand, the revolutionary group has the obligation to replace the overthrown order with its own order and power structures—so sovereign violence once again cedes to profane power; and on the other hand, once accomplished, labor power must use the tools at its disposal to remain in power. That is, it must institute a world of labor which once again excludes the value of unproductive expenditure so essential for Bataille. Yet it is in this very exclusion that he saw the possibility of its reversal.

He interpreted Soviet Marxism as founding an exclusively functional and economic society with the goal of unlimited development of the forces of production. Yet he believed—in a gesture reminiscent of Heidegger's views on instrumental rationality and technological production—that when productivity reached its pinnacle with the total liberation from material need, it would also imply the independence of humanity's religious, affective, and sacred elements from profane economic activity. But rather than concluding that these religious impulses would fall by the wayside, he suggested that the radical expansion of functional society and its separation from the sovereign sphere would prompt a release of unrestrained expenditure. And this, as he rather vainly hoped, would somehow rescue humanity from the dynamics at work in the disenchanted world of rational production and consumption. He suggested it, however, without ever explaining *why* unrestrained expenditure would then occur, save for the assumption that since so much surplus would result, *dépense* would be inevitable.[56] The difficulty in following this theory is that in his political writings Bataille too often tries to articulate his view of expenditure by means of actual material practices and ideologies and to the exclusion of the real moving forces behind those practices. Whereas the problem in fact lies in the very composure of humanity toward the world and to others, which Bataille fails to analyze in his political writings. And when we combine this lack of analysis with his rather problematic conflation of ontological and political analyses—his tendency to articulate his politics with more "existential" views—we have an idea why he involved himself in some rather suspect engagements.

Nevertheless, he did not remain unaware of the possible fascistic reversal that could result from the violent agitation he promoted,[57] and in a sense, the founding of the secret group *Acéphale* (1936) along with a public review of the same name, can be seen as a response to the fascistic tendencies of his own *Contre-Attaque* group (1935–36). "Acéphale" or acephalous means to be without a head, or equivalently, without a leader. On the one hand, this name was chosen as a rejection of fascism, a paradigmatic example of a monocephalic structure in which the head or leader of state represents the entirety of subjects under its command and expels those not fitting into the centralized schema. The move toward an acephalous structure—chopping off the head—always involves some form of liberation of forces kept in check by the power of the symbolic order. The festival, where all social roles and restrictions were turned upside down, traditionally followed the death of the king. On the other hand, insofar as the head symbolizes reason and calculation, "Acéphale" was chosen in order to show that humanity and its reason is not the measure of all things: "Human life is exhausted from serving as the head of, or the reason for, the universe. To the extent that it becomes this head and this reason, to the extent that it becomes necessary to the universe, it accepts servitude."[58] He concludes here that to escape from one's head is as if to escape from prison. What the deprivation of the head truly addresses, however, is not simply the primacy of what the head symbolizes—reason, power, calculation, leader—nor is it a mere call to a free release of passion. Rather, the issue is the principle of exclusion itself, specifically insofar as it is used to define an individual in opposition to, and to the exclusion of, another individual. I am anticipating the later concerns of Bataille here, but significantly, what Acéphale is in anticipation of is the opening of the space of intimacy between mutually exclusive subjects, an exteriorization of interiority.

For while *Acéphale* was a protest against the stultifying web of social relations, this group did not directly engage in political action. They had entered what Bataille had earlier called the "postrevolutionary phase" in which destructive negativity *is no longer in service* of social and political revolution—the "revolutionary phase"—but is rather operating on the margins of society, in brothels and artistic activity.[59] What is posited here is *separation* between economics and politics on the one hand, and "religious" activity—insofar as religion involves orgiastic destruction, sacrifice—on the other. It is this separation that I will call the *an*-economy of sacrifice. Such a separation of economics and sacrifice, however, is in fact a chimera in the history of sacrifice, and the search to effect such a separation runs up against difficulties when considered within a genealogy of sacrifice itself.

The primary difficulty—briefly mentioned at the opening of this chapter, and which we shall extensively analyze in what follows—is the overcoming of an individual perspective. Using the model of "scissiparity"—the reproductive process of unicellular organisms in which one cell effectively disappears in becoming two—Bataille's view is that in sacrifice, as in any intimate affair, individuals must tear open their "selves" and annul their self-enclosure in order to form the community. He thus contests the notion that groups are formed simply from a collection of individuals who maintain their individuality while contributing it to something that transcends them, as in human reproduction where two self-identical individuals produce an offspring that contains parts of, yet is distinct from, its parents. Given Bataille's view then, it would seem obvious that in sacrifice the individual perspective yields to a general perspective, but this is not necessarily the case. Let us look to his principle and its tensions. He states:

> I propose to assume as a law that human beings are never united with each other except through tears or wounds, an idea that has a certain logical force in its favor. When elements arrange themselves to create the whole, this is easily produced when each of them loses, through a tear in its integrity, a portion of its particular being for the benefit of the communal being. Initiations, sacrifices, and festivals represent just such moments of loss and communication between individuals.[60]

The differing connotations within this statement point to a methodological impasse: on the one hand, people congregate for festivals and sacrifices in order to satisfy their need for expenditure; on the other hand, these expenditures merely serve to propitiate the needs of the community and ensure its duration—a future-oriented perspective that is proper to an individual.

Should the latter be the case it is thus simply a matter of substituting one individuality for another, replacing the individual-self with the community-self that transcends it, but in which the individual lives as an individual. Expenditure is then nothing but a means to the ends of the community, in direct contradiction to Bataille's goal of expenditure having no end outside itself. But if this principle is met, then to what extent does individual experience border on utter meaninglessness? And then again, is this tension merely overlooked when the extremes of experience are banished from contemporary society like Antigone at the hands of Creon's edict of juridical-social conformity? This impasse—lose to no end or lose for the ends of community, practice expenditure or accumulation—is, as he states, nothing less than the "ultimate question of being," the perhaps irresolvable tension of existence and one to which Bataille will only be able to respond by redefining the notion of community itself.

More accurately, however, this "ultimate question" refers to a still more fundamental tension, one that occurs between individual isolation, separation, or "discontinuity," and the loss of individuality in "communication," "fusion," "intimacy," or "continuity." Bataille spells it out as follows:

> Thus each man must consider both confining himself in isolation and escaping from that prison. He sees, on one side, that which is foundation, that without which nothing would exist, a particular existence. . . . He sees, on the other, a world whose splendor is that of communicating elements that fuse with each other like . . . the waves of the sea. . . . Between these irreconcilable poles a man is necessarily torn, since he cannot decide for either direction. He can renounce neither his isolated existence nor the exuberance of a world which cares nothing for that existence and is prepared to annihilate him. A daily dispute between tiny enclosure and free space goes on: first of all between others and one's self, between generosity and greed.[61]

Indeed, the duality of the direction in which human life is torn cannot be escaped. It is a fundamental impasse that belongs to finite human existence itself, and which Bataille will illustrate with varying modes of sacrifice. It is an impasse between the "spirit of sacrifice" and the relatively stable order of things which sacrifice endeavors to secure.

This "spirit" can be identified as central to Bataille's thought from as early as 1930, and is found in a reflection not on economics or religion, but on Van Gogh. In his article, "Sacrificial Mutilation and the Severed Ear of Vincent Van Gogh,"[62] Bataille draws a close association between the painter's tormented personality and his sunflower/sun paintings produced prior to the automutilation that has become the most famous gift in recent history. Referring to his "solar" model of expenditure, Bataille goes so far as to say that "it is possible to see the painter himself as an overwhelming incarnation of the candelabrum of sunflowers, attaching to his hat a crown of lighted candles and going out under this halo at night in Arles."[63] Interpreting this beautiful scene, Bataille equates the painter with the sun, a connection that signifies the "striving for dislocation" that animated his paintings of flaming flower-suns. As we read on, "dislocation," the expression of an "inner rending" that throws individual integrity into disequilibrium, becomes the last living remnant of the "spirit of sacrifice."[64]

The emphasis is then placed on sacrifice simply as the rupture of individual stability, a *self*-mutilation, through the projection of a part of oneself outside of oneself, an ecstatic loss of being that receives the paradoxical title of "inner" experience. What sacrifice does liberate are those same violent, immoderate internal forces of destructive consumption that "original" affluent humanity unleashed, but which they unleashed *without mediation*, and thus without those spatial or temporal limitations that are indissociable from sacrifice proper. This is the key, as well as the difficulty, to the matter at hand. If Bataille evokes sacrifice, it is precisely—contrary to Hubert and Mauss—to emphasize the aspect of automutilation, the "radical *alteration*"[65] of one's own being. And in relation to this alteration, the ends for which the sacrifice was performed acquire a secondary status. We thus see from one of his earliest articles how he was preoccupied by a search that would continue until his final days.

But insofar as we may claim that Bataille recognized very early on his ultimate imperative of self-alteration through expenditure divested of its aims, and guided by this notion is able to offer a critique of Mauss, at the same time his political affinities of the same period testify to the fact that he had not yet fully incorporated the lesson to be learned from Mauss, nor indeed from Kojève. At least until 1937, he apparently did not appreciate the implications that the application of his ideas to a real political situation could have. He had not yet recognized just how important the "end of history" would be, nor had he realized how extensive the paradox of recognition that emerged in the potlatch really could be. This is not to say that he did not realize that the sovereignty of human existence loses its sovereign status once it has recognition, and inevitably power, as its goal. That is, insofar as it is subordinated to any goal, as Bataille continually repeats, expenditure is an abdication of sovereignty full stop.

Yet the structure of symbolic recognition is perhaps more ensnaring than Bataille at first realized. For should an action that is *not motivated* by recognition nevertheless be granted recognition, it is a challenge to retain the autonomy of the original impulse from the prestige—and the inevitable gains that come with it—that is conferred upon the one who carries out the action. This, I believe, is the ultimate challenge of retaining the purity of any impulse one acts upon—whether it pertains to artistic or philosophical activity, love, and even—as Freud exposed—acts of kindness. Yet this autonomy from recuperation—symbolic or otherwise—this demand that one knows not what one does, or if one knows, one somehow maintains an absolute indifference to the result of an action, remains the *sine qua non* of the morality of sovereignty, and of sacrifice, that Bataille is advocating. To see the difficulties in asserting such a morality in the current times, let us turn to the genealogical development of the history of sacrifice as a prelude to the search for an escape from its compromises.

2.3 TAKING SACRIFICE INTO ACCOUNT

The question of ritual sacrifice is seemingly outmoded to our way of thinking. That its consideration has been primarily confined to the fields of ethnology and religious anthropology, relegated to the narrow realms of specialized research, is perhaps due to a tacit acknowledgment not only of its fundamental ambiguity, but as well of its incommensurability with Occidental reasoning and practices. So remote is it from our common sensibility, so unacceptable is it to our moral landscape, it is a topic that remains, despite our liberality of thought, a sort of forbidden domain. And perhaps because of its apparent remoteness, it is also a widely misunderstood phenomenon, having been watered down to a more recognizable form, becoming a notion that manifests a Judeo-Christian morality in the form of altruism or self-surrender: one "sacrifices" one's life for one's child, one "sacrifices" one's freedom for a principle; or, in an even more common vein, one "sacrifices" a well-paying but stressful job for more free time, etc. And while these examples may share a similar root as the question at hand, such common conceptions nevertheless miss the mark.

But what conception of sacrifice would justify Bataille's claim that the ritual annihilation of one being by another is "the enigma which is the key to all human existence"?[66] How may we take him seriously when he claims that, despite having "fallen into disuse," the practice of sacrifice has been, "due to its universality, a human action more significant than any other"?[67] "Due to its universality": veiled in this phrase is the key to unlocking the enigma of its significance, insofar as it rejects the notion that this significance can be unveiled by examining the particular aims for which sacrifice has been undertaken. It is the essence of sacrifice that is at issue, not its secondary efficacy. The difficulty in unveiling its essence, however, lies in the fact that its endoskeleton has been hidden by the clear consciousness of its visible effects. For while the awareness of the aims of sacrifice initially lagged behind the moment of the material event itself, they gradually came to have priority of importance and took root in consciousness with a fixity that can only pertain to abstractions.

To the extent that we want to uncover its essence, what must be called into question is the evolutionist interpretation—whether it be sociological, ethnological, or philosophical—that traces the growth of moral sacrifice directly down to its roots in ritual sacrifice, or that in effect makes primitive ritual sacrifice the equivalent of modern moral sacrifice, its heir.[68] It is this homogenization, enabled through a progressive atrophying of the possibility to unleash transgressive violence, which Bataille will call into question with the intention of unbinding the moral and ritual interpretations of sacrifice, or better still, of opposing them. More specifically, what he opposes is the application to ritual sacrifice of an interested, hypothetical *economy* of morals in which a present action is justified by the future end that both transcends and subordinates the present action, favoring instead a categorical notion of sacrifice independent from self-interested concerns.[69] Bataille's interpretation of sacrifice therefore requires not only a reexamination of ritual sacrifice itself but as well of the moral value associated with it, for if a value is given to sacrifice, then it seems that it cannot be pure of causal motivations. Yet since we have already seen, with respect to potlatch, that there would be no gift if there was no lure of gain, then the assertion that there must be no motivation for the act is not entirely accurate. Rather, the question is which value wins out: the religious or the economic; the community or civil society.

If—following Max Weber—the latter is victorious, then, as we will see, the religious essence of sacrifice is integrated into the productive world, which sacrifice will in turn have to challenge if its is to be restored to its religious essence. And the "essence" of religion, Bataille tells us, is "the search for lost intimacy,"[70] the central moment of which is always a sacrifice. Or again, "religion in general," he asserts, "answered the desire that man always had to find himself, to regain an intimacy that was strangely always lost. But the mistake of all religion is to always give man a contradictory answer: *an external form of intimacy*. So the successive solutions only exacerbate the problem. . . ."[71] The dynamic is as follows. Bataille posits that the human being is, obscurely, an intimacy that it has rejected in becoming conscious, bound to a world of things that consciousness itself constitutes. And indeed, "consciousness could not have become clear . . . if it had not turned away from its awkward contents,"[72] from its intimacy. Yet it is precisely these "awkward contents" that consciousness seeks to regain so as to have complete self-consciousness. The problem, however, is that consciousness is resolutely facing the other direction, toward an external world of clearly posited things and goals which intimacy, should it resurface, would only serve to disrupt. And herein lies the problem of sacrifice.

Sacrifice—or equivalently, the festival—opens the floodgates of expenditure where the distinctions of individual consciousness melt into an indeterminate field of intimacy. Now, this is only possible if consciousness has ceased to be clear and oriented toward the determinate world—the house it has built and in which it feels at home. What this implies, however, is that what sacrifice unleashes cannot be integrated into consciousness. As the story goes: if intimacy—through sacrifice—is there, clear consciousness is not; if clear consciousness is unyielding, then one cannot take account of intimacy. What this leads to, however, and what it will be our primary task to explain, is a "fatal misunderstanding of sacrifice."[73] That is, insofar as it is with a clear consciousness of its transcendent value and purposes—moral or economic—that sacrifice is undertaken, it necessarily turns its back on intimacy, yet at the same time it purports to regain intimacy through the practice of sacrifice, thereby landing itself in contradiction. This contradiction, which shall guide us through this discussion, is perhaps unavoidable once sacrifice is approached from the perspective of clear, modern consciousness.

To restate the problem in a way that should offer some clarification, I will first attempt to elucidate the meaning of a term Bataille uses in a variety of contexts, yet which he never precisely defines: transcendence. When Bataille uses this term, which we will encounter again, it is generally in a narrow sense upon which he passes a pejorative judgment. He tends to reduce transcendence to its "horizontal" orientation, the projection of the self—or in the case of ritual, the group-as-entity unified in interest—toward finite objects and goals, which, once appropriated or attained, allows the self to retire into its identity after a brief and relieving escape from itself into externality. One escapes from oneself into the world, but the world encountered is of the nature of a detour which eventually leads one back to one's self-determined path. In this sense of the word, the subject transcends itself toward an other that is only moderately other, toward an other that is effectively a term of self-mediation, which allows consciousness the change involved with progressive movement, yet which leaves it essentially unaltered. In short, horizontal transcendence is mediation of self through a clear and distinct object.

The problematic Bataille introduces into sacrifice, however, rests on a problem introduced into the notion of transcendence, which is the extension of "horizontal" transcendence onto the "vertical" plane of transcendence. Vertical transcendence, the projection of a finite subject toward the infinite, a search for the ground of existence or a transcendence of finite concerns and an opening to the ultimate, will thereby sink into profanity. His criticism of organized religion and its morality, or sacrifice and its efficacy, is essentially that they instrumentalize the divine by making it too accessible, too accommodating, in effect viewing the divine as a terminus into which infinite desire can submerge confident in the promise of wholeness regained. The God of vertical transcendence thusly understood is, in short, not transcendent enough; or it is assumed to *give itself* to finite spirit as just another object—albeit higher—of self-mediation. The otherness of the divine is illumined in the light of the finite spirit, "but from the very fact that it is illuminated one encounters it as if it came from us."[74] In other words, it is not completely other. Or in another line of reference, we may posit the "weak" notion of (vertical) transcendence—into which Bataille will implicate all transcendence—as the successful overcoming of the impasse of Hegel's "Unhappy Consciousness,"[75] an overcoming of the unhappy situation in which a divided consciousness fails to recognize itself in the Absolute, a recognition that would unify its finitude with divinity.

Without venturing too far into Hegel's analysis—which always risks subjecting the dialectic to a too-homogeneous interpretation—a few critical points may provide a useful reference for Bataille's religious orientation of sacrifice. The main coincidence to note is the mutual drive of sacrifice and unhappy consciousness to bridge the divide between the finite (perceived as inessential) and an infinite which is located in the transcendent 'beyond'. In both cases, the worldly side of the equation trembles before what it perceives to be the excessive magnitude of its sacred other. And while both bring themselves into contact with the sacred through a representation, the sacrificial cult believes that it mediates the dangerous excess of its Other through tangible manifestations and elaborate rituals, thereby crossing the divide. In a sense, however, the belief of the cult in the efficacy of the rituals, like the Christian representation of God in a finite form, may expose that the sacred is not so completely other after all. The cult, however, necessarily believes that their offerings are commensurate with the expectations of the beyond, whereas the more spiritually subtle Christian, despite the element of faith, trembles before the capriciousness of a final judgment one cannot influence. Absent from sacrifice is thus the despair that pertains to unhappy consciousness, which suffers the feeling that its finite existence is nothing in relation to the infinite with which it cannot find the proper mediation, insofar as it holds to a dualistic notion of the difference between itself and the plenitude it desires.

Of course, unhappy consciousness is but a moment in the course of Spirit, though it is a moment—it must be said—of extreme dissatisfaction. Its dissatisfaction, however, is founded on a misrecognition which will eventually be corrected. The correct view will reveal that the dividedness experienced as alienation from the Absolute is in fact a self-division of the self-same Spirit, an experience of itself in an alien form.[76] Thus, while the experience of unhappy consciousness combines the extremes of finite emptiness and infinite desire for a transcendent other, neither this experience, nor the (vertical) transcendence of the other, are necessarily affirmed in themselves. Rather, they are affirmed as stages on the way to Reason which will recognize that the divine—the "God of reason" as Bataille calls the Christian God—is not radically other to the self, recognizing instead that the "other" is but a momentary other in the dialectic of *self*-mediation.[77] Unhappy consciousness, which fails to dissolve itself in the Absolute, will nevertheless prepare the victory in which the beyond is dialectically appropriated into self-consciousness, dissolving the tension of unsatisfied desire. It may be claimed, then, that the feeling of finite nothingness, which opens consciousness to vertical transcendence, is ultimately annulled with the dissolution of the vertically transcendent Being into the finite being's horizontal drive for knowledge.

Now, while Bataille consistently positions his desiring subject in the unhappy situation of consciousness, and critically addresses the attempts of the desirous subject to escape its predicament and claim a sense of wholeness—either through the flight into horizontal (worldly) or vertical (metaphysical) transcendence—he will nevertheless repeat the gesture of escape, as well as that of the search for a more profound sense of being, but with a significant difference. The difference lies in his affirmation of the unresolved tension between desirous finitude and infinite satisfaction, his refusal of a reconciliatory economy between the self and the other which nonetheless does not imply a lack of contact with that other. Indeed, the contact involved is of a more extreme nature, one in which the other confronted is excessive to the point of denying consciousness the possibility to master it, and which renders the desiring subject—if not destroying it altogether—profoundly altered. And while there is no satisfactory outcome available, this need not be an occasion for uncompromising despair, for the threatening yet transformative relation to the sacred can be, as we shall see, an occasion for joy.

The point of this discussion is as follows: while Bataille repeats the gesture of finite desire transcending itself in the attempt to regain an originary, indeterminate sense of wholeness (intimacy) from which it has been alienated; and while he will duplicate the sacrificial structure whereby the sacred other manifests itself in some determinate form; it is nevertheless the case that this other—though it may well be the subject's own otherness—will not come to be known in the light of the subject's comprehension of itself. Unlike the horizontal transcendence toward object-things, or the vertical transcendence toward a God who annuls the radicality of His own transcendence by giving Himself to be known in a finite form; unlike, that is, those forms of transcendence whose weak alterity is a road back to the self, Bataille's "transcendent" other will put the subject infinitely into question, offering no response to its supplication. In effect, he points to what Hegel may well have revealed only directly thereafter to conceal—the notion of a beyond that resists the reduction of dialectical appropriation. In Bataille's scenario, the (horizontal) "object" of desire, like the properly transcendent—or "transascendent"—God, withdraws from its manifest presence, is in excess of any determinate manifestation or representation, and disrupts the circular paths of self-mediation. Equally affirmed, however, is the excessive nature of the desiring subject itself, its "transcendence" of "thingly" determination, which Bataille will not refer to as transcendence, but rather as intimacy—the threatening yet life-affirming annihilation of the individual-as-separate individual.

Returning to the problematic of sacrifice itself, we should be in a better position to see the problem that, traditionally, human beings sacrifice with consciousness of its transcendent[78] aims and utility, subordinating the sacred to its own profane interest, all the while seeking a sacred, intimate nature. Now, from a conscious perspective, intimacy is something like a "poetic fallacy of animality,"[79] an image of unbroken immanence with the world which is fallacious once broken by consciousness. Nevertheless, "the animal opens before me a depth that attracts me and is familiar to me. In a sense, I know this depth: it is my own. It is also that which is farthest remove from me, that which deserves the name depth, which means precisely *that which is unfathomable to me.*"[80] The misunderstanding of sacrifice, however, is the belief that human beings can fathom these depths, which are not definable in space and time, through a practice of sacrifice that is governed by those particular aims for which it consciously searches. The tension that emerges for Bataille is between the essence of sacrifice and its integration into the world of productivity, or alternatively, between its "purity" and its symbolic efficacy.

This is the general outlay of the issue. To address this "misunderstanding," we will first turn to the structure of primitive sacrifice as presented by Hubert and Mauss, and then to Bataille's treatment of the successive religious solutions as documented by Max Weber.[81] The historical development of sacrifice that runs between the primitive and more modern conceptions will lead Bataille to define the "fundamental problem" as follows: "*How can man find himself—or regain himself* [his intimacy, C.G.]—*seeing that the action to which the search commits him in one way or another is precisely what estranges him from himself?*"[82] How, that is, can one find one's intimacy—which is never a thing—through action in the profane world of things?

The answer lies in that which may be identified as the fundamental unity of all sacrifice—literally, the act of making sacred *(sacer-facere)*—which is the principle of destruction, or equivalently, negation. As Hubert and Mauss tell us, by destroying a victim that, of necessity, is taken from the profane realm, one undermines the victim's circumscription within the profane world of production and utility, restoring that victim to the divine realm: "There is no sacrifice into which some idea of redemption does not enter."[83] Leaving the literal sense of destruction aside for a moment, however, we shall be in a better position to identify the meaning of sacrificial destruction, for it is not specifically of importance that a living victim physically die in order for it to become sacred. Rather, what it is necessary to destroy, to *negate*, are the links that bind the victim to the profane order of useful things and productive activity. That is, it must be destroyed *insofar as it has become a distinct and profane thing.*

What this first implies—as noted previously—is that a previous negation has already taken place: the negation of an original state of primal indivision between the subject and object where the objects destroyed—that is, killed and eaten—are not objects or things in the proper sense, for in fact, they are not distinct from the being that destroys them. The destruction involved here—*immediate,* animal destruction—*has no meaning* beyond the need it addresses. But when this original state of animal immanence or intimacy is negated—a negation that sacrifice then serves to negate—there arises an objective world of distinct things transcending the subject, with a meaning beyond their immediate consumption. Now, this transition from animal to human destruction, bringing with it the world of objects, came about with the use of the tool, a mediator between the subject and its goal. The tool betrays the fact that consciousness had reached the stage where it could view things and activities as relating to other things and purposes quite distinct from that which is immediately perceived. With this as a basis, Bataille is able to claim that "the objective . . . positing of the world of things has duration as its foundation: no *thing* in fact has a separated existence, has a meaning, unless a subsequent time is posited, in view of which it is constituted as an object. If it is destroyed as food or fuel is, the eater or the manufactured object preserves its value in duration; it has a lasting purpose. . . ."[84] A number of implications hereby arise.

First of all, it implies that the sphere of sacrifice is an advanced, dialectical form of destruction: it negates a negation already carried out; it is a negation of the transcendence that negated a state of immanence; a restoration of the thing's immanence which had been lost. Secondly: insofar as it arises at the relatively advanced stage of thinghood where the thing sacrificed is determined by its usefulness; insofar as the thing sacrificed is by definition useful, of vital interest for the human life in relation to which this thing has its meaning; and insofar as sacrifice is specifically oriented toward negating the thing's usefulness, and thus toward disrupting the subordinating chain of efficacious activity that serves human needs; then the sacrifice *apparently* occurs without concern for oneself. Sacrifice always involves the renunciation of a sensory desire, and is thus equivalent to a self-renunciation.[85]

Two final notions must be added to complete the scheme of sacrifice. We have already posited that first, an intimate world has become a world of things, and second, that sacrifice serves to redress what is considered a wrong by destroying the thing as a thing—that is, destroying its useful value given in the future. Now, while it is true that sacrifice is the destruction of a thing—or a human that has become a thing—it is as well an automutilation, not only because one gives up what one could use for life, but because of the purported identity between the sacrifier and the victim-god.[86] Indeed, the one who sacrifices does so with the intent to address one's own reduction to a thing, but the very manner in which one has become a thing, the very nature of individuality itself, contests the notion of self-destruction: "The separate individual is of the same nature as the thing, or rather, the anxiousness to remain personally alive that establishes the person's individuality is linked to the integration of existence into the world of things."[87] Insofar as one is an individual, one takes account of one's continued existence, renouncing death and destruction; if one does then "destroy" the thing-self, it must be with sights set on the future.

This notion is reinforced by what is in fact an anterior, constitutional possibility of sacrifice as proposed by Ernst Cassirer.[88] His claim is that when humankind was lacking a fixed mythical image—a god with a name or specific function—toward which it could direct its activities, when consciousness did not face a world "split into determinate, enduring, and unitary forms," there was no consciousness beyond the immediate sensory stage. In effect, lacking was individual consciousness. In order for consciousness to "arrive at a clear division between the different spheres of activity and between their divergent objective and subjective conditions," in order to clearly posit a world of the subject and object and the conscious activity that belongs to it, it was necessary to "refer each of these spheres to a fixed center, to one particular mythical figure . . . [through which man] also perceives himself in the concrete diversity of his functions." According to Cassirer, humanity was in need of gods to become distinctly human, for only with determinate forms guiding its activity could humanity move beyond an unconscious state in which its activity is guided by unformed feeling. Consequently, sacrifice only became a possibility once there was something to which one could sacrifice—the deity, which was to become the community over which that deity presided.

The point is this: there have always been periodic conflagrations that occur when human beings unite, but these "festivals" were not specifically *human* until they were *limited* by consciousness of the aim of the conflagration. Until, that is, the orgy "is limited by a countervailing prudence."[89] A provisional dualism is thereby established between a divine, intimate world of untrammeled violence and contagion manifest in the sacrifice, and the beginnings of a profane order of limited violence and transcendent purposes toward which this violence is directed. Needs are served on both sides. What must be emphasized, however, is the universal occurrence of an irreversible economic compromise of the purity of self-renunciation and expenditure. All claims to pure disinterest must be placed in question, a point that certainly did not escape Hubert and Mauss. Again, once there is an efficacious benefit that pertains to the sacrifice, the self-renunciation involved in sacrifice may never be considered pure: "[D]isinterestedness is mixed with self-interest."[90] They are unambiguous on this point:

> In any sacrifice there is an act of abnegation since the sacrifier deprives himself and gives. . . . But this abnegation and submission are not without their selfish aspect. The sacrifier gives up something of himself but he does not give himself. Prudently, he sets himself aside. This is because if he gives, it is partly in order to receive.[91]

Like the potlatch, sacrifice involves a contract, it is an interested exchange in which every player gets his due: "Expiation is the condition of enjoyment,"[92] self-renunciation merges with prosperity. This is the basic economy of sacrifice, an economy that—if it holds to its claims of truly being a disinterested "gift" economy—is indeed a "comedy."

For while the goal is not exclusively economic, nevertheless one limits the loss, mediates it not only by interposing a victim but by relating it to a future good, to revitalization, rebirth, or redemption.[93] If one destroys one-self—or what is useful to life—it is to preserve oneself on a higher level: if one destroys the first fruits of the crop, it may be to drive out a dangerous spirit (desacralization) so that the crop may be consumed, or to appease the god of the field to ensure the next year's harvest; if one relinquishes one's personal distinctions, as in military or ascetic milieus—not to mention the contemporary trend-culture of lifestyle consumption—it is to become part of a larger community. In short, if there is some future gain, automutilation is justified: *it has a meaning,* its value consummated in its utility. Bataille's conclusion is that sacrifice comes to be enmeshed, integrated into the world of production, "the world of things." Its internal violence, the condition of intimacy, becomes externally directed and attenuated by considerations of future prosperity. And thus,

> its intimacy is dissolved in the real and individualized positing of the ensemble that is at stake in the rituals. For the sake of a *real* community . . . a thing—of a common operation in view of a future time—the festival is limited: it is itself integrated as a link in the concatenation of useful works. . . . In the end the festival itself is viewed as a [productive] operation and its effectiveness is not questioned. The possibility of producing, of fecundating the fields and the herds is given to rites whose least servile operative forms are aimed, through a concession, at *cutting the losses* . . .[94]

In short, an activity whose purpose was to cancel the effect of profane activity on the sacrifier and victim, ends by affirming their continued efficacy within the profane order, even as it raises the sacrifier and victim above their immersion in that order by bringing them into contact with a sphere of divine violence. This is the weakness of sacrifice: its nature is compromised as its virtue for the community is affirmed.

We must keep in mind, however, that the reduction of the sacred nature of sacrifice, at this early stage, is never total. Even if the ritual is highly structured according to the pretext under which it is carried out, it is never entirely explained by its effectiveness, nor can it ever be in full, conscious control of the elements it brings into play. Indeed, the ritual itself, its rigorous rules and structures, betrays the fact that there are elements involved that are mysterious and dangerous. The ritual then is a mythical form of language that attempts to mediate something beyond the player's control. It first places at a distance, and then reorganizes and integrates the sacred that it evokes, for that sacred—if left in the darkness of incomprehension—is capable of unleashing a plague amongst the living, devouring it from within. Efficacy never erases the deeper meaning of the ritual sacrifice, which is not simply the continued life of the elements involved, but rather the fundamental coincidence of life and death, the affirmation that life extends beyond a world that is clearly defined, stable, and secure.

Two specific changes, however, started humankind down the one-way street that led to the desacralization and rationalization of its religious activities: there was a shift in the moral consciousness of human activity in the world-below; which flowed from a change in the representation of the divine world. If we turn to Nietzsche's view of the moral development of mankind as presented in *The Genealogy of Morals*,[95] we find that prior to the positing of even a primitive notion of salvation in the form of recuperation or renewal of spent resources, the violence and cruelty of festival was characterized by its "naïveté," its "innocence," and manifested a "disinterested malice."[96] The cruelty and violence of those involved was not only considered "normal" and pleasurable, but—when compared to "modern men," those "tame domestic animals"—was an affirmation of human strength that, in his eyes, is so painfully lacking in a world misguided by weary notions of "good" and "evil." But whether it was a matter of spectators, spectator-gods who "see even in the dark," or the tragic community—all precursors to the Christian God of salvation—some response, some purpose, had to be conceived for the gratuity of the violence and suffering found in primitive festivals. For "what really arouses indignation against suffering is not suffering as such but *the senselessness of suffering* ... [and] it was with the aid of such inventions that life then knew how to work the trick which it has always known how to work, that of justifying itself, of justifying its 'evil.'"[97] But justified evil is not evil. It is good. This is the "trick" that is at issue, the trick that leads from ritual destruction to morality.

When coupled with the transformation of the divine world itself, however, it will not be the case that violence is merely justified, rather, it is effectively eliminated. The divine world itself was previously ambiguous, combining a pure or beneficent aspect and an impure, malefic, and dangerous aspect. It is this second, contagious notion of the sacred that was of greater importance to the primitive consciousness, a situation soon to change.[98] And with this change comes a decline of the interior violence of the festival. To illustrate this change, Bataille looks to the nature of the sovereign individual who is sacrificed in the festival. In the properly religious order, it was the king, the symbolic representative of the people itself, who was destined to be the victim. His destruction symbolized the unleashing of sacred violence within the community itself, its own destruction as a condition for its rebirth. Eventually this practice was condemned, the king being replaced by the "carnival king," a slave temporarily assuming a sovereign status. And while the sacrifice of the slave was an internal violence insofar as the slave could be made to serve the community, in effect this substitution, this refusal to gloriously expend their own king, to make their community *acephalous*, was a rejection of internal violence.

A crucial reversal thus occurred: the sovereign representative of the people was spared from violence, and the integrity of the community—assured by the intact head of its leader—was no longer ruptured. From this point onward violence was directed outwardly, from one community to another, in the form of military conquest with the aim of accumulating resources—resources that would no longer be spent in a manner reflecting the malefic and dangerous sacred, but calculated to provide the maximum yield. In the transformation of the divine world itself, leading to an essential reconfiguration of the relationship between the divine and the profane, Bataille sees a decisive *economic* reversal. Nonproductive, sovereign expenditure was gradually removed from the world, leaving worldly sovereignty in the hands of mundane, productive, rational, and ultimately servile activity. This is, as Bataille sees it, an essential historical step toward the hypertrophy and reification of the profane sphere, and toward the desacralization of life. But crucial to recognize are the final steps by which rational productivity came to have a *moral* value, to serve as a reconciliatory mediation with the divine, as a means to salvation, eventually becoming sacred in itself.

Bataille identifies two specific religious ideas that contribute to this development: the sacrifice of the god, and subsequently the more radically dualistic notion of divine transcendence. Thus far we have identified two fundamental developments within ritual sacrifice: a spirit of renunciation or inhibition of immediate, sensuous desire as it became directed toward specific interests (the god, the community, redemption); and the notion that there is economic restitution granted from this renunciation. Yet one may as well posit that a new form of consciousness arose from this spirit of renunciation, a moral consciousness associated with the economic notion of indebtedness to a creditor-god in which Nietzsche sees the origins of guilt or "bad conscience." This guilt would not have been so pronounced had the renunciation transpired solely through the contractual and mutually beneficial sacrifice *to* the god. However, the situation was exacerbated with the parallel notion of the sacrifice *of* the god in which "the idea of sacrifice attains its highest expression."[99]

As the sacrifice of the god is willingly undergone by the victim, this "sacrifice" is more precisely a suicide, the sacrifice of the god by itself without calculation or expectation of return, the "one case from which all selfish calculation is absent . . . for the god who sacrifices himself gives himself irrevocably."[100] If humanity is to reconcile itself with this pure gift, it must make an equivalent sacrifice, but we have already seen how primitive sacrifices fail to achieve this measure. And with the god's suicide, the situation becomes even more problematic, the debt seems even more difficult to annul, for the auto-mutilative violence humanity had previously undergone in order to restore the bonds with the divinity has been assumed by the divinity itself. A double effect results: the direct link between the divinity and the world is broken, and the violence without which intimacy cannot be achieved—for intimacy requires violence to the individual as individual—is displaced into a world beyond. The search for favor in the eyes of the divine nevertheless continued, being refined by Christianity.

The motif of the sacrifice of the god, its cancellation of mankind's debt is not—despite Nietzsche's claim that it is the "stroke of genius on the part of Christianity"[101]—a solely Christian concept. Rather, "this motif of the god's sacrificial death is among the truly elementary mythical-religious ideas of mankind."[102] What Christianity does bring to this notion however, "is not so much the content of the motif as the new, purely spiritual meaning that is gained from it,"[103] the self-sacrifice of the Christian God being "the ideal limit of abnegation."[104] The spiritualization of sacrifice—and of religious experience in general—implies two significant developments: firstly, the overcoming *(Aufhebung)* of the sensuous world as merely physical existence, or the raising of physical existence as a means to spiritual existence through the early forms of ascetic practices; and secondly, the transformation of sacrifice from a physical mediation directed toward particular, immediate desires and relative goods, into an actual correlation between the human and the divine through the direction of sacrificial activities toward an absolute good in an attempt to equate one's activities with the will of God.

Bataille summarizes the basic conditions of spiritualization as follows:

> The shift to spiritual forms requires one main condition, since a pretext would be necessary before rejecting sensuality. . . . Whatever the case, we escape a giddying sensuality only by representing for ourselves some good situated in a future time, a future that sensuality would destroy. . . . So we can reach a summit beyond the fever of the senses only provided we set up a subsequent goal. Or, if you like . . . we reach a nonsensual, nonimmediate summit only by referring to a necessarily higher end. . . . Beyond sensuality, beyond the reply to desire, we are in fact in the realm of the good—which is the primacy of the future against the present, the area of being's preservation, contrasted with its glorious loss. . . . When we feel our strength ebbing and we decline, we condemn excesses of expenditure in the name of some higher good. . . . Now, to the extent that a spiritual summit . . . becomes revealed in an unfolding action, it's associated with efforts that desire to gain some good.[105]

We have here a clear, though perhaps too simple, perspective on the initial connection Bataille perceives between what he terms (in *On Nietzsche*) a "spiritual" summit and a morality of "decline." The "decline" involves resisting the temptation to immediate and unrestrained expenditure, the decrease of sensuous "intensity" by binding it to ideal motivations. Its "morality," in a phrase borrowed from Nietzsche, "simply is weariness."

Henceforth, insofar as the natural instincts to expenditure have not disappeared, having merely been inhibited, the result is that they are internalized, turned against oneself in the self-abnegation to be found in the voluntary torments of monastic asceticism. The early forms of asceticism were essentially useless in the world itself, and this uselessness was equated with sanctity or holiness, the transcendence of the world-below to mediate with and glorify God in a sort of disinterested counter-gift. But, as Kant points out,[106] there is a "deception" involved here, for while one could believe that the suppression of all (self-)interest in the ritual of ascetic sacrifice gives to this act a pure or categorical moral intention, in fact this is just an appearance. Not only is its purity abdicated in the attempt to please the divinity, but it is further sullied by the fact that the real aim of self-sacrificial asceticism is salvation. In this sense it is a work like any other:

> In theory, *salvation* in Christianity liberates the end of religious life from the domain of productive activity. But if the salvation of the faithful is the reward for their merits, if one can achieve it through one's works . . . these *works* by which a Christian attempts to achieve his salvation can in their turn be taken as profanations.[107]

Or in more Kantian terminology, "apparently disinterested religious sacrifices are a deception . . . which tries to make an action submitted to a *hypothetical* imperative pass for an action which would be directed by the *categorical* imperative."[108] That is, it mixes interestedness with purposelessness. This mixture, as we have claimed above, is not confined to the realm of sacrifice, but is a portrait of life in general.

But of greater interest to Bataille than this otherworldly asceticism, which retained the magical—that is, sacrificial or ritual—belief that one could redeem oneself in God's eyes, that one could exert an influence over His apportionment of grace, is the this-worldly asceticism that is the byproduct of Luther's Reformation. Whereas the medieval Church manifested an extravagant use of wealth unknown to the world of utility that followed, nevertheless by transforming its excess from a sign of God's glory reduplicated in the world, into a means for this world to reach God, it "succeeded less in making earth heavenly than in making heaven banal."[109] Prompted not only by what he perceived to be the scandalous, wasteful practices of the Roman Church, but more precisely by this notion that through the use of such practices one could gain heaven, Luther sought a more stringent transcendence of God, a more radical separation of God and human activity, such that all activity herebelow was to be seen as futile.

All Bataille seemed to see in this, however, was a deprivation of the glorious possibilities of wealth: "Luther's doctrine is the utter negation of a system of intense consumption of resources."[110] Rejecting the system of indulgences and asserting the notion of predestination, Luther effectively sought to put an end to divine-profane mediation. For while "the world exists to serve the glorification of God and for that purpose alone,"[111] there is no connection with worldly activity to salvation: one is either of the elect or not. On the other hand, the deep meaning of Luther's protest, which Weber—and subsequently, to his detriment, Bataille—failed to take into account, is a direct result of his insistence on the *incommensurability* between God and humanity, from which Kierkegaard drew so much inspiration. Luther in fact helped to shape the existential modern consciousness not merely in the way that Weber ascribes to him—as starting the trend toward the industrious self-production of salvation—but rather by the initial moment of extreme anxiety regarding salvation, and the emphasis on one's earthly finitude and radical aloneness before God, which received its first formulation in the pathetic cry: "Why hath Thou forsaken me?" And if God is radically transcendent, then there is nothing one can do to be certain of salvation: one may turn not to action and the Deed, but to introspection and the Word, and take a leap of faith—which is only a leap if it is taken without foreknowledge.

This did not, however, stop Luther's followers from taking to heart his impulse to bring about one's own salvation, for if one cannot rely on a divine causal agent, one must rely on oneself. Thus, the futility of works did not erase one's *moral* responsibility to succeed in worldly activity, for even if one cannot please God through earthly activity, one is obliged to regard oneself as chosen, and to perform "good works" in one's worldly "calling" as a sign of having faith in being of the elect; faith, necessary for salvation, that God is working through one and guiding one's actions.[112] The believer must refashion the world in accordance with the divine purpose and design, a design of "rational . . . wonderfully purposeful organization . . . to serve the utility of the human race." Consequently, "this makes labour in the service of impersonal social usefulness appear to promote the glory of God and hence to be willed by Him."[113] In effect, this idea represents Calvin's extension of Luther's rejection of useless expenditure taken to its extreme, for it was Calvin who took Luther's emphasis on radical divine transcendence and introspection and turned it into an emphasis on one's righteous *character* as a sign of divine election. The hard-working, thrifty, and ascetic ones who were devoted to improving the human lot in accordance with God's will effectively practiced their worship on an everyday basis, not earning but rather testifying to their salvation literally "on the job." It is this which prompts the claim that Calvin promulgated a "morality of commerce."[114] If the glorification of God is still the issue, it is henceforth only to be sought in the profane world of productive action. Or as Bataille concludes:

> Limiting man's possibility to useful works, what [Calvin] offered man as a means of glorifying God was the negation of his own glory. The true sanctity of Calvinist works resided in the abandonment of sanctity—in the renunciation of any life that might have in this world a halo of splendor. The sanctification of God was thus linked to the desacralization of human life. . . . The decisions to rescue divine glory from the compromises in which the Church had placed it could not have had a more radical consequence than the relegation of mankind to gloryless activity.[115]

In short, one profanes oneself to glorify God. Yet soon enough, with the demand for divine purity as a catalyst, the glorification of God will fall by the wayside and economics will assert its true independence from moral concerns. The Calvinist "work ethic" is internalized and secularized, no longer needing its religious supports.

With the dualistic separation of the beyond and the here-below, the schism between divine intimacy and the world of things will effectively be complete. And in respect to this final state of affairs, there is one specific idea from Weber that makes its way into the very center of Bataille's analysis, albeit in a veiled form: namely, the transition from isolated and irrational acts of redemption, the periodic discharge of sin which Weber sees as specific to Catholicism,[116] to the systematic, continuous rational activity that governs the worldly life of the Protestant with an ironclad mechanical consistency. With this shift in the very *temporality* of religious pursuits will come an equivalent shift in the orientation of economic pursuits. These changes rest on the move from the provisionally transcendent divine to which humanity is ritually restored by a violence that *momentarily* ruptures the order of things, to the unwavering transcendence of the god of reason, intelligibility, and the calculated exclusion of the violent sensuous world. Or, as Bataille claims, the dualistic shift by which the divine becomes rational and moral

> undoubtedly has the same intention as archaic sacrifice, which is . . . to lift and preserve the order of things. But if it lifts that order, it is by raising it to the negation of its real effects: the transcendence of reason and morality gives sovereignty . . . to the sanction of the order of things. Like the operation of sacrifice, it does not condemn, in themselves, the limited unleashing of *de facto* violence . . . but defines them as evil as soon as they place [the order of things] in danger. . . . Hence there is given . . . an empire of the real order that is *a sovereignty of servitude*. A world is defined in which free violence has only a negative place.[117]

That is, a capitalist world from which nonproductive activity is forbidden as economics is king. Here, the dangerous sacred no longer penetrates the profane world, for the law has been founded on an unambivalent sacred that has been "spiritualized, and made univocal, individuated, and concentrated as the personal God in a beyond."[118] Thus, the play between the law (prohibition) and transgression—previously at the origin of religious consciousness—has ceased: the law has become reason and morality has become autonomous, standing in a purely negative relation to excessive experiences.

The conclusion to be drawn from the moral renunciation of excessive expenditure, the freedom of production from its archaic purposes, however, is not only human autonomy from the divine sphere and vice-versa, but rather human subjugation to the world of things. Now, insofar as Bataille tries to contest this subjugation solely with the evocation of a different economic practice, he will land in difficulties. For the question must be asked: "[H]ow do we reconcile the affirmation that capitalism represents an unprecedented break with all archaic (pre-capitalist) forms of expenditure *and* the postulate of the necessary universality of spending as pure loss?"[119] How, that is, are we to challenge an uncompromisingly profane economics with a sacrificial economics when, as our analysis has shown, every attempt to "make sacred" through sacrifice has ultimately ended in a "profanation," some sort of interested exchange or a morality of "decline" in which the moral value resides in some *future* good. When, that is, we have seen how the spiritual evolution of sacrifice has led to an economic morality that weaves together the rejection of sensuality (the present moment), the restricted expenditure of work, self-preservation, and the integrity of individual being—the person, the community, the State. Or again, when we have seen that there has always existed a certain imperative to give oneself, but quite simply this imperative has never been categorical enough, for this gift has a subterranean, a posteriori content, the duration and value of the person or system to whom the benefits accrue.

The problem, in short, is that "throughout history—and in the process of making history—there developed *reasons* to proceed to the summit and risk ourselves. The difficulty beyond this is to proceed to the summit without motivation and without pretext."[120] That is, to the *an*-economy of sacrifice. Now it would seem, from our previous analysis, that for reasons both social and moral, as well as in principle, the history of sacrifice in its objective forms is at an end. Indeed, sacrifice seems impossible to undertake without canceling its principle of "making-sacred," without annulling its aim of redressing the reduction of the sacred to profanity, and without foregoing the desire to raise humanity out of its enclosure in the world of things. It would seem in fact that the economizing of sacrifice has sacrificed sacrifice. In a Hegelian movement, it has cancelled the core moment of sacrifice, death itself, by denying it the significance of annihilation, effacing the trace of death by raising it to the sense of preservation, either of the communal or individual good. Or in Bataille's view, insofar as sacrifice has been consistently undertaken for the greater good, carried out for universal, ethical, or moral ends, it has ended in "failure," the "elementary" "instinct" to introduce threatening elements into life has been functionalized, canceling its essence.[121]

In the face of this degradation, is it still possible, as Bataille contends, to have an *experience* of sacrifice, and if so, of what would this experience consist, and how might it occur given the fact that the communal ferment of sacrifice and festival has been displaced and dispersed onto the individual level? The question, in fact, remains the sovereignty or sovereign intimacy of being, a sovereignty that assumes "the power to rise, indifferent to death, above the laws which ensure the maintenance of life,"[122] above calculation and concern for the future—and thus above economic considerations for the continuation of being. If we are to find the origins of this *an*-economy, it seems that we must look for the roots of sacrifice in a source other than the history of sacrifice, its "antiquated teleology."

Now, if the historical notions of the Reformation have ceased to have any direct hold on our activity, it is nonetheless difficult to deny that, on an individual level, its principles have survived in modern consciousness and are more profoundly sedimented in thought than in practical principles. Might it as well be the case that archaic principles, abandoned in practice, still persist in modern thought despite all its rigor, its increasing clarity and self-conscious knowledge? Might it be that a self-consciousness at the extreme limit of clarity has not abandoned its basic desire to find its sovereign intimacy, to find another way to discover the essence of sacrifice: the heightening of self-consciousness through the exposure of humanity to its own negativity, its own intimacy, and its own death? This is, indeed, Bataille's supposition. But while Mauss may have cleared a path in the search to contest the givens with which we are familiar, the givens that he presents to us are so unfamiliar that they appear metaphorical and anecdotal. Thus, if we are to address the ubiquitous problematic of sacrifice we must recognize that the heart of this problematic—and thus the very foundation of Bataille's reflections—is the Hegelian problematic of negativity, "that Hegelian doctrine of death,"[123] but that this problem is perhaps not best, and certainly not fully, addressed by recourse to the expenditure of material resources. Rather, if we are to follow Bataille's shadow-dance with Hegel, it will serve us well to take the anthropological grounds we have established and place them on more familiar terrain. Our first task will be to follow the language of this game, which involves the interplay of discourse, poetry, and silence. Yet silence will not have the last word. Rather, it will lead us to our final chapter where an unrepresentable and unutterable truth may indeed call for a language and a representation in order to bring us face to face with that which would otherwise escape us.

PART TWO

———

THREE

Logomachy

Through Discourse to Poetic Silence

All this business of a labor to accomplish, before I can end, of
words to say, a truth to recover, in order to say it . . . before I can
be done with speaking. . . . All lies. I have nothing to do, that is
to say nothing in particular. I have to speak, whatever that
means . . . none will ever know what I am. . . . I won't say it, I can't
say it, I have no language but theirs, no, perhaps I'll say it, even
with their language . . . so as not to have lived in vain, and so as
to go silent . . .
　　　　　　　　　　　—Samuel Beckett, *The Unnameable*

I have cautioned you about language. I must therefore caution you
against my own words. . . . I have been trying to talk a language
that equals zero, a language equivalent to nothing at all, a language
that returns to silence.
　　　　　　　　　　　　　　　　—Bataille, *Eroticism*

In the previous chapters we went to great lengths in an attempt to identify the
elusive phenomenon Bataille calls sovereignty, which is certainly tied to the
human being's extreme possibility, but in such a way that it is not a possibility one can call one's own. The sovereign self-consciousness does not take
death into account, its impossibility is not a possibility. To some extent, then,
we have only been able to speak of sovereignty negatively, in opposition to
Hegelian philosophy as Bataille construes it: the unity of seriousness, action,
and discourse, the nucleus of concepts defined by humanity's constant proximity to, and mastery of, death—the negative. The action of the negative, a
civilizing freedom, has been identified as the imperative to give meaning to
every moment, sense to the senseless, form to the formless, as it strives toward
the universal affirmation of death as revealed in the discourse of Wisdom

where death achieves its fulfillment. And while the movement of this philosophy may be irrefutable, Bataille constantly reminds us that it involves an elision of what cannot be placed in its system of symmetrical oppositions. And "the only obstacle to this way of seeing . . . is what, in man, is irreducible to project: non-discursive existence, laughter, ecstasy. . . ."[1] In a word, what is irreducible is sovereignty. This of course does not make Hegel "wrong," but rather indicates that he effectively removed the obstacles to the project of knowledge, to the unity of humanity, slave, and God, given in a discourse become absolute, noncontradictory, and dead.

At the same time we should remember that Hegel did not exclude sovereign moments from his account of history, in particular those of mastery and its risk, the "absolute rending" of the slave and the "depths of the night" of Unhappy Consciousness grieving for the death of God.[2] The problem, rather, is that these moments are inscribed within and revealed by a totalizing discourse, contributing to "man's intelligence, his discursive thought," which "is developed in terms of servile labour," and consequently, "insofar as discourse informs it, that which is *sovereign* is given in terms of *servitude*."[3] That is, it ceases to be sovereign. Quite simply, as a manifestation of meaning—which Bataille equates with servility—discourse is a loss of sovereignty, which means nothing and affirms nothing, least of all itself. For sovereignty, as we may recall, renounces being recognized. Occurring solely in the instant, it does not place itself in an objective spatial location, does not maintain itself in duration, is not—unlike informed discourse—a position of mastery.[4]

Yet while this ban on adding words to the negative instant effectively signals an attempt to cancel the symbolic efficacy of language, its ability to reintegrate an inexpressible experience which would be overwhelming should one lack the means to place it, Bataille then—in a potentially paradoxical move—sets about the "impossible" task of writing sovereignty. That is, he attempts to write that which is not of the order of possibility, to write that which undermines the linguistic mastery of the negative—a negative and a mastery that enabled one to write in the first place. The "impossibility" of this task thus rests on the notion that, like the "Nothing" of negative theology, sovereignty resists positive signification, is no state that can be identified and immobilized, is a disappearing goal, is nothing to appropriate for oneself. In other words, just as the "instant" is not a moment of full self-presence, there is no notion of "sovereignty," no conceptual nucleus, no definable or sustainable position. In short, it is not a discursive reality. It is not graspable. Were it to be discursive or graspable, it would become another figure of dialectical appropriation, would be a foundation both grounding activity and that at which one could aim: *it would mean something.*

Bataille was certainly not unaware of this predicament, acknowledging that "I cannot speak of an absence of sense [*sens*] without giving it a meaning [*sens*] that it does not have."[5] Or in a similar vein, "one cannot speak of the sovereign moment without altering it . . . insofar as it is truly sovereign . . . to speak of it, to *seek* these movements is contradictory. At the moment we seek something, whatever it is, we do not live in a sovereign fashion, we subordinate the present moment to a future moment that will follow."[6] Consequently, it would seem that one cannot speak of sovereignty without eclipsing it, for indeed, "sovereignty isn't speaking—or it's deposed."[7] How then may one expect to inscribe in language that which exceeds the concepts of that language? How is one to use the instrument of meaning to forego meaning anything? It would seem that the attempt to designate "sovereignty" or the "sovereign operation," "meditation" or "inner experience," only reveals the futility of trying to designate it in words. The sliding of sovereignty out from under any word that tries to grasp it only expresses "the bothersomeness of using any words at all."[8] The problem, in short, is that discourse implies an originary experience, thing, or event, but always misses it, for once described it is no longer the thing itself. A double divestment thus occurs: the event is divested of its sovereign status, and words are divested of their pretension to attain the originary. To the extent that Bataille wants to actively disrupt the discursive neutralization of experience, he must therefore disrupt discourse itself, silence its meaning. Poetry is to be the ghost in the machine.

"Only sacred, poetic speech," Bataille claims, "limited to the plan of impotent beauty, would safeguard the ability to manifest full sovereignty." But is the silencing of discourse itself a manifestation of sovereignty? And if sovereignty is manifest does it not once again risk becoming meaningful, risk making sense? If the speaking subject survives the sacrifice of its words, is the risk that is poetry not a fictional risk? And correlatively, would poetry, objectifying its risk in the poem, not preserve that which does not want to be preserved: the sacred, sacrificial instant; the writing subject itself? "I write. I don't want to die."[9] This final possibility leaves Bataille open to criticisms such as that of Sartre, who claimed that Bataille unwittingly committed the same error he criticized, the hypostatization of the ungraspable.[10] And indeed this may appear to be the case insofar as poetry—in the narrow sense—is a use of words, and "the glue of words makes an entity, a durable being . . . of what *is* not . . .": the instant, the sovereign subject, Being.[11] But to write in such a way so as to affirm nothing, to intentionally withhold words from an abysmal reality, depriving negativity of its mediating function, is to leave one's writing, and oneself, prey to the promiscuous and deadly force of negativity—or desire—itself. This is the risk of sovereign writing.

The questions above remain to be answered, as does the thought that poetry—to which Bataille assigns the task of leading the discourse of knowledge into non-knowledge, of leading discontinuous beings to ecstatic experience, putting the subject of language at risk—is merely the next act of the comedy that is unfolding, the one in which the ineffable comes to be spoken. But if poetry seems to be burdened with responsibilities beyond its means, this assumption may have to do with our conception of it, which is why it will be of pressing importance to thoroughly elucidate its means and ways—as well as its possible failure. The possibility, that is, that it will only preserve what does not want to be preserved. The risk that writing, the play of presence and absence, will turn definitive absence into just another possibility to be mastered in the work of art. The risk that poetry will succeed in presenting the unpresentable, fulfilling its obligation and bringing the wandering spirit, the exile of language, to a stable place; or that in failing, will leave the poet at the mercy of the impossible, silent, lost in the foreign lands which are nonetheless the poet's proper home:

> . . . we are not really at home in our interpreted world
> . . . there is no place we can remain
> . . . Strange to see meanings that clung together once, floating away in every
>   direction.[12]

3.1 A CONTRADICTORY PROJECT

When referring to a sovereign experience, event, or "object," are we referring to something that is prediscursive and is on its way to finding a language to express it, or do we mean something that is inexpressible and for which the silence of words is the final word? Must there be an adequate expression for either wonder or horror—two reactions that while different in tone, are kindred in philosophical spirit—or does the attempt to give them an articulate tongue reveal but a human response to the anxiety of facing a meta-human reality? Let us be aware from the start that when Bataille refers to silence it is the silence that interrupts the discursive order of words—and thus of self-conscious knowledge—and which serves to indicate that there is an indistinct and elusive aspect of human experience before which discursive existence falls mute, as in shock or awe. Silence therefore points to that which language is powerless to identify and grasp, that which remains at the limit of the seemingly limitless scope of words. But if the silence that follows a risk of language is to have any significance for self-consciousness, then a recognition of the extent to which language is our being requires elaboration. There must at minimum be an acceptance of the fact that human existence is in language, that it is language, irrevocably, until death do us part.

Bataille is aware that the contours of human existence are defined by the use of language: we mediate Being, establish our autonomy, relate to others, and distinguish things through language. There is in fact but a brief period of prearticulate life when we are truly facing outward, into an open world. Our first words begin to erect the boundaries that define our existence. For we use words to define a world of objects that are the mere reflections of their own freedom, which we progressively confine with our concepts, concepts that offer us clarity at the price of rendering opaque the open world. Poetry, as a risk of language, is a risk of being.[13] The *usage* assigned to words however is only one aspect of the gift of language, one in which its luster has been tarnished like the hands of young laborers grown callous after too much travail. The *work* of words is discourse, words not uttered like some bird in directionless flight, but words that are a trap lying in wait for the sovereign share of existence, a trap whose jaws are set from the moment one says "I."

The tension Bataille confronts is the inability to live outside of language and the necessity to somehow escape its work, all the while recognizing that we cannot—like some agonizing yet cunning fox—bite off the leg that is ensnared, separating language from our existence.[14] Rather, the question is the ability to find some language that would no longer serve a theoretical, discursive function, a function we may define as a process of clearly distinguishing and separating (naming) isolated moments—sense impressions and concepts—and then relating them to one another in a progressive synthesis so as to gather them into a union that presents a coherent picture of the totality. The "discursive," as Cassirer claims,

> treats the immediate only as a point of departure, from which it can run the whole gamut of impressions in various directions, until these impressions are fitted together into one unified conception, one closed system. In this system there are no more isolated points; all its members are reciprocally related, refer to one another, illumine and explain each other. Thus every separate event is ensnared, as it were, by invisible threads of thought, that bind it to the whole.[15]

Removed from their sensual immediacy, isolated elements may be organized into a noncontradictory binding-system of significative concepts capable of being intelligibly transmitted. The function of discourse, in short, is the constitution and transmission of knowledge, knowledge that is coextensive with its condition of possibility—discourse.

But in fact, the question posited above—that of finding a language that would not be discursive—is not an accurate representation of the issue, as I will explain below. What I will first draw attention to, however, is the seemingly paradoxical nature of Bataille's enterprise itself. For Bataille, who wanted to silence discourse, "the miserable possibility of words,"[16] was above all a writer. He reaches us through words alone. But what he tries to bring us to, and communicate to us, is experience, which is silent. This tension between the experience he is trying to communicate and the mode in which this experience receives its expression is a problem frequently addressed in his writing. And the problem, more specifically, is this: there are levels of experience that are heterogeneous to *logos* itself, but there is only one language in which to evoke them. In short, the problem—as we will hear again in different contexts—is that his method, "writing," is "always only a game played with an ungraspable reality."[17] Writing is to relate in discourse that which precedes discourse. There is always the chance, however, that writing will succeed in taking the ungraspable reality out of the game.

Indeed, it would seem risible to attempt to evoke the "heights" of an (sovereign) existence that is neither subordinate to any necessary concerns, nor erects knowledge as the ultimate goal, in a language of well-defined possibilities, in discursive knowledge. Recognizing this impasse, Bataille states:

> I would provoke laughter in the reader who notices that I discuss, write and make erasures without knowing how to emerge from such a manifest contradiction: how, if I write, can I attain these heights, when what I write commits me to write no longer? If I talk of the heights, or would attain them, I would immediately cease to talk; otherwise I would betray the heights I talk about.[18]

Bataille would indeed seem to betray himself in the very attempt to express in his discourse the sovereignty that exceeds discourse, and he was acutely aware of this dilemma, stating that "the only way of expressing myself would be for me to be silent, hence the flaw. . . ."[19] If sovereignty is truly to retain its purity from concern, its total indifference to results and recognition, then it should apparently preclude linguistic articulation, for as soon as one starts speaking, the intimacy of Being is broken. One opens one's mouth and negates self-coincidence. This is the power of language. It gives determination to the undifferentiated continuum of Being, tearing apart that which does not welcome separation, whether this be the external world or one's own internal affectivity. Such is the content, however, of Bataille's writing.

Rather than seeking to flee from contradiction—or equivalently, refusing to submit to a logic of noncontradiction—Bataille, however, embraced a certain "cohesion of contradictory ideas."[20] This cohesion is dissimilar to that of harmonic equilibrium toward which one proceeds measure by measure until—like an architectural construction—the opposing forces cancel one another out achieving a stable yet petrified whole, "the mummy-like afterlife of the thing written down."[21] If Bataille builds an edifice it is for the pleasure of destroying it, his words and projects like castles of sand, their meaning both cancelled and affirmed by the waves of time. Or more exactly, the meaning of Bataille's construction *as* a completed project, *as* a goal reached which retroactively confers meaning on the activity of building, is that which is annulled. What it affirms, on the contrary, is continual incompletion, unending disagreement with itself. For the word that puts an end to words, and to which they are all directed—namely, God—is lacking.

Or more appropriately, as we will see in greater detail in the chapter that follows, Bataille places the keystone of language—God, the guarantor of the coherence of meaning—at the very center of his architecture, only to negate it as a support, so that the meaning of the individual bricks, words, collapses, and the conceptual edifice along with it. In Bataille's writing we find the continual reemergence of his peculiar and radically *empty* formulation of the Hegelian *Aufhebung* in which the play of contradictory elements—destroying and building, canceling and affirming—affirm and achieve nothing. Is it a contradiction that he writes to say nothing, to fall silent? Not in his eyes, at least: "[T]hese judgments should lead to silence and yet I am writing. This is in no way paradoxical,"[22] because "the inadequacy of all speech . . . at least, must be said."[23] Which leads to the conclusion that simply saying he "embraced" his contradiction is not strong enough, but rather that it constitutes the project of his writing itself. The project of writing sovereignty.

His project, in short, is contained in a writing that would ultimately efface itself, *and its author along with it,* by refusing to maintain itself in the coherence of meaning, and in the stronger sense, by denying that the individual who is writing *affirms himself.* For in writing, the absence who writes, like the absence of the thing in the word, nevertheless becomes a presence in his affirmation: "[I]nk changes absence to intention,"[24] or as Lacan cheekily suggests in one of his seminars, say the word *elephant* and here comes a herd trampling through your living room. But truth, if we are to follow the suggestion from Walter Benjamin, is "the death of intention,"[25] the implicit awareness of which leads Bataille to claim, "I should have kept quiet but I'm speaking. . . . There are such contradictions in my attitude! . . . To write is to articulate an intention," to affirm oneself and one's presence. Yet when Bataille writes, it is so that "my death and I slip away together into the wind from outside where I open myself *to my absence.*" What his writing makes present is his absence itself. Bataille is continually attempting to express in his own way the double bind of language itself, for "writing and speech can entail *either* mastery or dispossession—the dispossession of the self,"[26] its dispossession by the objectivity of language, which subverts our meanings and escapes our control, and implies that all attempts at discursive mastery are, by definition, subverted before they even begin.

That his writing may be called a "project," however, should itself give us reason to pause, for have we not already identified the realm of project as that of servility, well-defined future aims, *discursive* experience aimed at knowledge? The lessons Bataille integrated from Kojève are resolutely unambiguous on this point—(Hegelian) humanity is discourse and discourse is project, is work pure and simple.[27] Hence the difficulty in articulating non-servile or sovereign experience, for servility and discourse are thicker than thieves, conspirators in the dialectical constitution of meaning. Consequently, "that which is not servile is unspeakable *(inavouable):* a reason for laughing . . . that which is not useful must be hidden (under a mask),"[28] and the effort to say in the language of servility that which is not servile seems to become an inaccessible possibility. The problem, however, does not adhere simply to the articulation of experience, but to experience itself, which remains—if not "contested" in some way—on the discursive level, caught in the webs of meaning.[29] For the moment, however, let us remain with the issue at hand, Bataille's "project."

I proposed above that Bataille, in order to circumnavigate the servile aspect of language or the "discursive thought of man," seeks another language, one not so readily put to use. One will now notice that this proposition has been slightly, but very significantly, altered. We now see that the task is to say in discursive language that which is not servile: sovereignty or inner experience. His project in short is this: "to emerge *through* project [discourse] from the realm of project."[30] Or to restate it in another manner, "I enter into its game [that of consciousness] in order to fight it with its own weapons."[31] The game is Hegelian discourse, the discourse that is both constituted by, and equivalent to, the omnipresent *Aufhebung* that makes every experience (negativity) collaborate with the constitution of meaning (positivity), the project or process in which every moment of experience serves the *telos* of knowledge.

Bataille, reversing the roles, seeks to make discursive thought "the servant of experience."[32] What is more, he follows the paths of knowledge in order to lead discourse to non-knowledge, to silence. It is therefore not necessary to reject reason and its language—or joining these two, *Logos*—in order to invoke a more volatile realm of experience. As he explains: "[I]t is nevertheless by a contempt not of reason itself, but of the narrowness of its commands, that we find the strength to return to the world of death and enchantment of which we deprive the exclusive commerce of reason. . . ."[33] In effect, he proposes to follow reason and its language to its own threshold where reason itself will take the leap that will reverse its direction and lead it into the unknown, the unknowable, where all knowledge dissipates save the recognition that one is passing from the known to the unknown. At this point it will be "as if the language of philosophy must, I say neither always nor from the first, but finally become mad. Not from a madness open to the arbitrary, but mad in that it is fundamentally lacking in seriousness . . . where thought only searches for the vertiginous fall of thought." Assuming the passage has occurred, then "the final word of philosophy is the domain of those who, *wisely*, lose their heads."[34] Hegelian madness, reason expending itself and its discourse and beginning the slide into the realm beyond discourse. But this is a comedy. It is a comedy in the form of a parody of Hegel.

The parody of Hegel, more specifically of Absolute Knowledge—or "extreme knowledge" as Bataille sometimes uses in order to indicate that discursive knowledge has reached its frontier—is a central feature of Bataille's method. It is in fact this method that was so influential for Derrida and his "strategy" of deconstruction, the entrance of the deconstructionist into a text so as to dislocate it with its own internal difference. For indeed, it is through "miming" Absolute Knowledge that Bataille perceives that "circular, absolute knowledge is definitive non-knowledge."[35] I will reserve a more detailed explanation of this view for later, but for now two propositions—both of which are provocative in their puerility—given within the context of his Hegelian shadow-dance should suffice to reveal how Bataille may envision the inversion of knowledge.

The first critique—one not foreign to more rigorous Hegelian critics—is that if one strictly adheres to the dialectical movement constituting knowledge and is not to abandon its integrity then one must admit, contrary to Hegel, the final contradiction and recognize that even absolute knowledge, should it be attainable, will in turn negate itself.[36] Or, in Bataille's logic, "[E]ven supposing that I were to attain it [absolute knowledge], I know that I would know nothing more than I know now."[37] Consciousness of absolute knowledge implies consciousness not only of that which it encompasses but as well a zone of obscurity outside its confines. Therefore, dialectically speaking, if there is "all that I know," this cannot but imply "all that I do not know," and interminable desire comes to replace satisfied knowledge. The intellectual powers of Hegel certainly would have presented this contradiction to him, and Bataille believes that Hegel did in fact discover that "the satisfaction of knowledge turns into its opposite"[38] whether he in fact included this moment in his system or not. Bataille does, however, suggest that Hegel's implicit recognition of the reversal of knowledge played as central a role in his temporary "madness" as did his recognition that the realization of his system implied the necessary suppression of subjectivity, more precisely his own.

But in order to discover this for himself it is first of all necessary that Bataille fictively repeat Hegel's experience of "becoming absolute knowledge"—negating one's individuality by "becoming everything (becoming God)."[39] That is, while recognizing that he himself could not achieve the knowledge Hegel claimed, he could nevertheless imagine it,[40] and did so to the following end: "[I]f in this way, as if by contagion and mime, I accomplish in myself Hegel's circular movement, I define—beyond the limits attained— no longer an unknown, but an unknowable. Unknowable not on account of the insufficiency of reason, but by its nature. . . ."[41] Bataille does thus not intend to question the efficacy of reason within its own domain, but rather the attempt to extend it into a domain of alterity or nonconceptual difference that resists the mastery of reason. The "unknowable" is in this way an other of thought that is not in contradiction to thought—for contradiction can always be resolved into a unity of differences—but is rather a realm of being that can only be experienced rather than known, a realm whose being is not attributable to its being-known.

Secondly, in this mime is accomplished Bataille's further critique which is posed in the form of a question: even if one may suppose oneself to be in possession of absolute knowledge, one may still ask, "Why must there be *what I know?*"[42] This question cannot be answered from within the confines of a universal science, for while such a science may adequately explain why the real is rational and the rational is real, it cannot explain why the real *is*, why *Being* is. But more significantly, language itself, specifically the language of speaking individuals in the form of the discourse that is both constitutive and expressive of Absolute Knowledge, is quite simply inadequate to Being—as Bataille conceives it. There is, if we wanted to term it thus, a heterogeneity of language (knowledge) and Being, language and experience (the subject)—the real is not necessarily discursive.

As Denis Hollier defines the problematic, Bataille enacts a "war between copula and substance,"[43] or more specifically, between the "logico-grammatical" and the "lexical" function of the copula which, I suggest, parallels the conflict between the subject and its knowledge. The copula, the nonsubstantive verb "to be," in its lexical function becomes *the* crucial element in the discursive constitution of meaning by linking unrelated words to one another, finally in relation to the final word. This verb, *to be*, meaning nothing in itself, nevertheless receives its lexical *sens*—its meaning and direction—by the system of signification that orients it toward the ultimate horizon of meaning—substance, Being, the transcendental signified. Thus, "the nonsubstantive becomes substantive ... that which had no meaning becomes the sign of meaning."[44] The verb to be confirms an identical meaning on that which it relates to Being—in particular, the *knowing* subject who speaks. In its grammatical function however—the function coextensive with the subject as such—the copula retains merely its function of copula-tion, the communication between terms without consideration of the meaning that results—and thus an erotic rather than reproductive copulation. Without a goal, a signified, a point of stoppage, there is no stopping the unruly play of language, no guiding thread in the metonymic labyrinth of words. Copulation never finds the object that ends desire, and the discursive knowledge of Being remains eternally unsatisfied, incomplete, as does the subject who supposes oneself to know.

Being, in short, is elusive, is *"nowhere,"*[45] emerging from, rather than exerting a magnetic pull upon, the erotic copulation of words, the metonymic interplay of beings. Being is the loss of Being as substance: "man *is* what he lacks," and the copula ("is") shows its function again, this time revealing man as insufficiency, insufficient unto itself, finding itself, its "being," as "being in relation to," in communication. The human being's existence in language is in defiance of self-presence. And while this is true of discursive language as well, its "lexical" function nevertheless aims to produce the closure of meaning in the substantial presence of Being, while Bataille's labyrinthine function of writing produces absence and opens language through the rupture of meaning. If, therefore, Hegel—our paradigm of meaning—relates discourse to a horizon of knowledge, Bataille will relate discourse, and the subject who cannot but fail to master it, to one of non-knowledge. The method by which he does so goes by the name of poetry.

The path taken in this chapter will reflect the play of operations in question. We start where every subject starts, the verbal articulation of self and other known as language—or, for our purposes here, discourse. It is not my intention to overestimate the value of discourse by giving it some privileged, fetishized place in thought, nor to enter the domain of those who refer to varying discourses like independent existences fighting for supremacy on the ideological battleground. I intend, rather, to get down to basics and show the fundamental effects that discursive articulation has on our relation to the world. To this end I shall first outline the elementary features of Hegelian discourse—resorting mainly to Kojève's discussion of the issue—and in connection with this task will offer a brief analysis of Hegel's notion of the sign itself. The point is to identify those aspects of discourse which Bataille finds contemptible even if unavoidable, ultimately to open the question of knowledge and non-knowledge.

The section following that on discourse places poetry where it belongs, at the outer edges of discourse and on the way to the death of words, the silencing of their meaning. Here I will offer a detailed analysis of Bataille's notion of poetry, its method of practice, its difficulties and limitations. This will prepare the way for our final chapter where poetic silence takes on a mystical slant: the mystical in turn an erotic significance; and the erotic a fictional, sacrificial structure.

3.2 HEGELIAN DISCOURSE: A "DOG" EAT DOG WORLD.

It is not an original position to make a claim for the paranoid nature of Hegelian Desire and its articulation in the discourse of self-consciousness, a discourse that draws everything it encounters into its self-referential system of meaning. Indeed, if we were to search for an aphorism to encapsulate Hegel's unparalleled tenacity for knowledge, we may well look to a phrase from another notable and clever paranoiac, Daniel Schreber, who uttered the pathological battle-cry, "*Aller Unsinn hebt sich auf!* (All nonsense cancels itself out! [is annulled, rises, is transposed]."[46] There is no abstract immediate given, no senseless sensual being, that can resist the magical power of the concept, that can fight for its meaningless life and reject the articulate death that transposes it into the universal significance of the "discursive real."

In a fundamental way, Hegelian discourse mirrors the self-referential structure one finds in his dialectical structure of perception in which the objects of the material world are transformed into dusty mirrors that gradually become more polished as the subject awakens to self-consciousness. That is, the subject that first perceives the objective given as standing opposed to it eventually—through a process of reflection upon consciousness itself—comes to see itself in and behind the reality it had perceived as alien, and thus comes to know the world as its own. And indeed, discourse in all its forms is essentially a story of the knowing eye. Its essence is the annulling of ambiguity resting on a dual origin of separation: the separation or discontinuity of the I and the non-I known as self-consciousness (or Desire);[47] and the congruent separation of indeterminate, identical, or natural Being into distinct moments capable of being conceptually restructured and known—that is, perceived and revealed by discourse. Without the first visual separation there is indeed neither subject nor object but rather the night of prehistorical or mute animal darkness. This visual separation goes hand in hand with verbal determination or nominalization as one not only distinguishes a thing but identifies and stabilizes it—knows it—by attaching a word to the thing. Indeed, "one opens [one's eyes] and thinks in words."[48] That is, one moves from an ambiguous vision to an articulate vision.

Bataille, in a characteristic use and abuse of his Hegelian inheritance, yet in an uncharacteristically sober self-evaluation, claims that "if it is necessary to give myself a place in the history of thought, I believe it would be for having discerned the effects, in our human life, of the 'vanishing of the discursive real', and for having discerned a vanishing light from the description of these effects."[49] Bataille stakes his claim at the point where Hegelian discourse has nothing more to accomplish, where negativity has been made redundant, having established a real, consummate world and a knowing humanity. But if a light is to be cast on the intimate order, the "fundamentally *unreal*,"[50] which has heretofore been submitted to the principles of the real, discursive order, then it is not enough to simply claim that intimacy is immediately accessible because discourse has "vanished." Rather, it must be made to vanish, which implies "self-consciousness taking up the lamp that science has made to illuminate objects and directing it toward intimacy." Not, however, in a manner so as to suspend intimacy, but so as to bring it into discourse, establishing an "immediate coincidence of clear consciousness and . . . the intimate order," manifested, for instance, in the "prolonged stammerings" of discourse. The point is thus to establish "a recognition of its obscure nature, of the night that it opens to discursive knowledge."[51] Yet the intimate night that is supposedly opened to discursive knowledge is at least in part the same night of natural immediacy to which consciousness was originally in relation, but in a relation of productive negation diverting its immediacy toward duration in consciousness.

If we are to bring to light the effects that result from a reversal of viewing the intimate order from the perspective of the discursive operation, then it is to the very earliest stages of Hegel's science—the immediate relation to the world in which the dialectic of vision and discourse begins to unfold—that we must turn. As it is a dialectic, this implies that it must be approached from both sides. The first aspect requiring attention is that knowledge is impossible without the looking-glass, the moment of reflection or alienation when the I sees (itself as) another, the moment Lacan designates the "ontological structure of the human world."[52] Or, at least, the Hegelian world, in which Being—

and indeed any being—must manifest, present, or appear to itself by dividing (negating) itself in order to know itself—to see itself. This is just another way of stating what we should remember from above, namely that Substance becomes Subject or that the Absolute is the True only as result, that it therefore is constituted by a movement of self-differentiation and return, and that the end is only the beginning fully articulated.[53] But if adequate articulation is constituent of truth, the visual realm of self-division and return is insufficient in itself. Rather, the final coincidence of Substance and Subject (Absolute Knowledge) occurs in the Subject's adequate description of the total dialectic of Being and the Real in a fully coherent and complete discourse. This is why Kojève frequently repeats that truth is not simply reality (Being, the Real), but rather it is *revealed* reality. That is, it is reality *plus* the revelation of reality in human discourse.[54] This is why the Real is a "discursive real."

From these rather general remarks we may now begin to distinguish some specific aspects of the nature of Hegelian discourse. The first point to note is that what may appear as an ambiguity with respect to discourse is in fact what may be identified as—in keeping with Hegelian systematics—its dialectical *and* circular economy. That is, discourse must be understood as both negativity and movement opposing the Subject to the Real (Nature, given Being) as well as the completion or closure of this movement in a complete coincidence of the end with the beginning. At the point of coincidence discourse ceases to be dialectical, is no longer in error, is satisfied. I will begin briefly with the latter character of discourse, which was emphasized by Kojève and had a strong influence on Bataille. A summation of the situation by Kojève shall point the way:

> The perfect and definitive adequation of Being (= Substance) and of Discourse (= Subject) can therefore only occur at the end of time, when the creative movement of Man is completed. And this completion is revealed by the fact that Man no longer advances and contents himself to travel again *[de refaire]* (in his philosophical thought) the path already followed (by his active existence).[55]

Hegel's discourse in the end is just this retranscription of the entirety of historical developments, is a mere description of what he already knows in the form of the book which is the new and eternal presence of the spirit—eternal because it no longer creates, acts, or changes.

Implied therein, however, is something else we also know from Kojève, namely, that the end of history is the death of humanity—not of its animal existence, but of the properly human sense of existence as negativity or action. "True knowledge," or absolute, final knowledge in which the subject no longer opposes an object, "is selfless—that is, inhuman."[56] *Where there is true knowledge there is no longer a subject,* a desiring, temporal being, but rather an existence become past and preserved in the word, in the book. It is this which leads Bataille to his vision of the old Hegel who, effectively dead—that is, satisfied with the knowledge he has accumulated—represents the opposition of knowledge and the subject:

> Hegel's desire thus resolves itself in a knowledge which is absolute, which is a suppression of the subject . . . who knows. *One no longer exists* in these conditions, history, above all, is presupposed [to be] completed just as the life of the individual subject must be. Never, if one thinks about it, has one conceived of anything more dead . . . toward the end of his life, Hegel no longer posed the problem: he repeated his courses and played cards.[57]

Kojève adds his own authority to this image in a statement that should arouse the memory of our earlier analysis: "Hegel no longer discusses [*dialégesthai*, from which *dialektikè* is derived]. . . . And if, having nothing more *to do* . . . it is because he profits from all the actions effected throughout history. His thought simply reflects the Real."[58]

Properly speaking then, and Kojève says this directly, Hegelian discourse in itself is not dialectical, "it is neither a dialogue nor a discussion,"[59] for in the end it admits no contradiction. If it were to acknowledge a thought, an event or moment beyond its circle—and Hegelian discourse by definition encircles *all* the possibilities of thought—if the final synthesis could admit negation, it would once again be in error. It would forfeit its claim to completion—or equivalently, to *eternal* truth. The theological undertones here are by no means accidental, but rather establish the essential framework for a later discussion. The fact that Hegelian discourse abandons dialectic, however, should in no way lead one to think that it is dissociated from dialectic or from humanity's constituent negativity. On one level the fully adequate description that occurs at the end of history merely *presupposes* the real dialectic of fighting and work, of desire and recognition, as its infrastructure. Yet on another level, discourse incarnated in the speaking being is immanent to the historical process, and is essential to the point of being equivalent to the very negativity that drives the historical dialectic onward. Kojève is quite clear about this.

We already know that the human being is negativity incarnate, acting upon given-being and separating it from its natural support to develop it as conceptual or spiritual being. Now we hear that the human being—negativity—is discourse, and that the thought that arises from its action is essentially discursive: "The miracle of the existence of discourse, which philosophy must reckon with, is therefore nothing other than the miracle of the existence of Man in the world."[60] It is the precise nature of this "miracle" that it is now for us to comprehend, and to do so we will be driven back to the beginning in order to describe its becoming.[61] The beginning I have in mind is the initial section of Hegel's *Phenomenology* entitled "Sense-Certainty" in which we are presented with a basic yet extremely significant argument: the inability of language to express the immediate, and consequently the relegation of the immediate to untruth.[62] Contained in this brief moment of the Spirit's passage are notions so essential to the unfolding of the discursive process, and to Hegel's ontology itself, that they cannot go without mention.

The first is the following: in the attempt to know the immediate—sensuous being or a moment in time—which seems to be "the *richest* kind of knowledge," the knowledge of what *is* and what is essential, as soon as this "sense-knowledge" is put to the test by language, it contradicts itself. Try Hegel's test: write "Now it is noon"—a simple, immediate truth—go get a cup of coffee and then read what you wrote. It is no longer true, for noon no longer is. The "Now it is noon" does preserve itself, but as something that is past, vanished, that is not-noon, and the new "Now" is what it is through mediation with what it is not—noon. This process of mediation is the path by which the particular moment becomes a universal, and language only ever utters the universal:

> It is as a universal too that we *utter* what the sensuous [content] is. . . . Of course, we do not *envisage* the universal This or Being in general, but we *utter* the universal; in other words, we do not strictly say what in this sense-certainty we *mean* to say. But language . . . is the more truthful; in it, we ourselves directly refute what we *mean* to say, and since the universal is the true [content] of sense-certainty and language expresses this true [content] alone, it is just not possible for us ever to say, or express in words, a sensuous being that we *mean*.[63]

In other words, "pure being," the unmediated essential object of sense-certainty—that which we *mean* when we say "Now" or "This"—can never be said in its immediacy. That is, in saying the essential, we make it vanish, and preserve it only in our words, through mediation with what it is not. This process involves a fundamental reversal, which is as follows: no longer is the truth of Being to be found in the fact that Being *is*, rather, it is found in being-mine, through its preservation in my words, in the fact that I know it.[64]

Of course, a simple shift of essentiality from the object to the subject is too one-sided to be acceptable for Hegel, and he will subsequently undermine this position to show that it is the whole structure or movement of the subject-object relation that is at issue. Truth does not reside in one individual's opinion, in what one means or intends. Nevertheless, there are two lessons to be drawn from the dialectic of sense-certainty. The first, as indicated above, is that the sensuous particular or the moment itself cannot be reached by language, for "in the actual attempt to say it, it would . . . crumble away."[65] Properly speaking, then, the moment itself is unutterable, and "what is called the unutterable is nothing else than the untrue."[66] We will return to this below. The second factor worthy of attention is that if truth is the discursive revelation of that which is, then in fact the unutterable moments belonging to sense certainty must indeed come to be spoken. This requires a bit of miracle working. The general heading for this process is *Erinnerung*, the internalizing memory which we previously encountered. Its fundamental activity, here as elsewhere, is for the content of sensuous externality—the objective real—received by immediate intuition to be negated as immediate and internalized in the form of a concept freed from the intuition. It may then be reworked by consciousness and manifested again for the first time but now in a form accessible to thought, for the content has already been spiritualized. That which has both the capability of negating the immediate world, conceptualizing it, and manifesting it once again, is language.

We find an increasing momentum on the discursive level of the same devaluation of present sensuous reality that occurs in the field of vision, as Hegel claims that "language is the disappearance of the sensuous world in its immediate presence, the suppression of this world. . . ."[67] This appropriative gesture would be inadequate if it remained on the level of consciousness or the earliest and most abstract level of reason. That is, if it remained bound to and dependent upon the external objects it passively observes despite its empty certainty that—having appropriated difference as its own—it is all of reality. The specific power of language, however, is not only the suppression of the spatial object but the ability to raise it into the concept (the word), into the fluid, creative freedom of human intelligence or into time.[68] It is, then, in the higher unity of the thing and self that is the concept (the word), that the subject can represent itself both to itself and to others rather than simply re-presenting the given intuition, the particular intuition that is put to death and resurrected as universal in the name. For transcription of this double process I shall turn to Kojève's presentation of the issue.

The dual process of tearing elements of the world from their natural support only to reunite them once again but as revealed or true reality, a process known as discourse, has negativity as its power.[69] Kojève's adroitness in dealing with the *Phenomenology* is made explicit by the location from which he specifies discourse as negativity, as the power of death—namely, from the text of "capital importance" found in the Preface (§32) which makes no mention of discourse, but rather cites the Understanding *(Verstandes)* as "the tremendous power of the negative."[70] Kojève cites this text in its entirety. I shall offer that portion relevant to us here:

> The activity of separation *(Scheidens)* is the power and work of the Understanding, the most astonishing and mightiest of powers, or rather the absolute power. The circle that remains self-enclosed and, like substance, holds its moments together, is an immediate relationship, one therefore which has nothing astonishing about it. But that an accident as such, detached from what circumscribes it, what is bound and is actual only in its context with others, should attain an existence of its own and a separate freedom—this is the tremendous power of the negative; it is the energy of thought . . .[71]

It is here, in a text emphasizing the power of intelligence, the power of abstraction, that the core of discursive activity emerges.

To express this core as succinctly as possible, the word or concept—metaphorically speaking—kills the sensuous, living thing, and in fact becomes that thing without being tied to either its spatial material support or its existence in the present. "In a general manner," as Kojève claims, "when one creates the *concept* of a real entity, one detaches it from its *hic et nunc*. . . . Thus the concept 'this dog' differs in no way from the real, concrete dog to which it 'refers' except that this dog is here and now, whereas its concept is everywhere and nowhere, always and never."[72] This is why Kojève claims that all conceptual understanding is equivalent to a murder.[73] The word is the death of the thing. Kojève illustrates this with the dog that is continually being put to death in his *Introduction*.

The real, living dog is inseparable from its material existence and all that sustains that existence, it exists in its environment without fissure, a self-enclosed circle, a senseless and simple being. To separate it from these links and keep the dog alive, to retain its essence without its existence would therefore be an "astonishing" feat, yet this is what discourse purportedly does. This is not to say however that the "dog" now exists as some celestial idea, a Platonic dog, outside of space and time. It does exist as a "meaning" *(sens)* or "idea," but is embodied in the word spoken by the speaking being, the new, non-natural support of the dog in the world. Consequently, the natural world becomes subordinate to the desires, concerns, and necessities of the one with the ability to speak of this world, the one who effectively "destroys Nature by reducing it to his own ends."[74] Bataille illustrates this dynamic with an example of a fly and a biologist.

The fly, like Kojève's dog, or Hegel's "Beauty" (from §32), is powerless to be other than it is. It is inseparable from its environment, with which it is in continuity. Left to its own devices, death does not strike the natural elements. "Without doubt, the individual fly dies," but given that this fly is no different in kind from the ones living last year, or the ones to come, "*nothing* has disappeared. The flies remain, equal to one another like waves in the sea," intimate to one another. The fly only dies when the biologist enters the picture, for the biologist separates the fly from its immersion in the elements, but he separates it "for *himself*, not for the flies," and he does so by naming it. The point Bataille is making is that death is solely human death. The monstrous power of the understanding, of language, alone founds the separation of elements, and it is only by considering something as individualized that death may be seen to strike it.

The word separating the individual fly from the immensity of nature is a word spoken by a being who not only "kills" the fly through one's act of conceptual separation, but who in acting and speaking *separates oneself* from one's own natural support. One isolates oneself from Nature, and thus from one's present situation, to live with respect to a future, to become other than one is, to die. In Bataille's words, "in this play [of language] the human animal discovers death: he specifically finds human death, the only one that frightens . . . but it only frightens . . . the man absorbed in the consciousness of his future disappearance, as a separated and irreplaceable being. . . ." It is thereby only in virtue of existing in language that we have consciousness of death. But the flip side of this is that one only exists as an irreplaceable and specific individual—the prospective death of which frightens, provokes anxiety—insofar as one keeps a firm grip on the language that establishes one as this individual. One articulates one's self so as not to die, at least on the discursive, profane level. On another level, however, language is the sacred communication of intimacy or the absence of self—and this is the level that Bataille's writing seeks to attain, a fictional writing that reveals the loss of individuality itself, the loss of its linguistic mastery in its relation to an unutterable God.

Still, writing need not admit that there is a reality that escapes it, for with the power of the Understanding in one's possession, one may separate, recombine, and rearrange the world as one sees fit. This power, while belonging to the workings of fiction, "is in no way fictive or 'ideal'. For it is in separating and recombining things in and by his discursive thought that man forms his technical projects which, once realized by work, actually transform the given aspect of the natural World and creates a cultural World in its place."[75] The language of self-conscious knowledge may well put the ultimate death off until a "later" that never arrives. For to speak of the world and of one's self is to transport both into an artificial space of that which is-not, to project one's existence into the future, to master death. As Kojève reminds us, action (negativity) reverses the natural course of the world, introducing the future into the present, "and it's as [a] *discursive project* that the future is *actually present* as the future . . . which subsists in man under the form of discourse. The real created by Action is therefore a real revealed by thought, or speech."[76] Correlatively, the real dog is not only the dog, it is also the "dog": the "dog" I will buy for my brother's children, the "quadruped" that kept me awake last night with its barking, and so on. The dog no longer is what the dog is, rather, it *means* something, it has become determinate. The essence of the real dog can offer no resistance to the word endowed with a meaning, to the abstract concept that exists not in the dog—as evidenced by the fact that one may speak of some future "dog" not yet in existence, or of a "dog" that never dies—but in the thought of the speaking being. An analysis of the Hegelian sign or name will make this apparent.

For the sake of brevity I will only consider two interrelated aspects of the sign, its general character as an *Aufhebung*, and its arbitrary nature. The first characteristic is that which I sought to underscore with the quotation from Schreber: in the word, all non-sense (undifferentiated, immediate being) is banished and raised into the concept, the presence of spirit. The sign is the manifestation of self-presence, the spirit that "plants the symbol of its sovereignty on every height and in every depth,"[77] even if the I that speaks is present as vanishing, or whose existence in language is living through dying. Hegel:

> In speech, self-consciousness, *qua independent separate individuality,* comes as such into existence, so that it exists *for others.* . . . The 'I' that utters itself is *heard* or *perceived.* . . . That it is *perceived* or *heard* means that its *real existence dies away* . . . and its real existence is just this: that as a self-conscious Now, as a real existence, it is *not* a real existence, and through this vanishing it *is* a real existence. This vanishing is thus itself at once its abiding; it is its own knowing of itself, and its knowing itself as a self that has passed over into another self that has been perceived and is universal.[78]

We see here that "real" existence for Hegel is not sensuous, immediate, or finite existence, but existing for others in a concept-form. In language, one's bodily reality is overcome, a concept does not decay. In this statement, however, we find both a crucial difference and similarity with Bataille's notion of linguistic existence. The communicational structure of this existence determines that one is indeed nothing as a separate individuality, that one does not exist except with others, as other. The "vanishing" involved for Bataille is indeed the vanishing of separate existence, but rather than this turning into duration for-another as another self—another, higher form of the same individuality—Bataille believes that, in a particular form of language, one exists as absent. The vanishing of the discursive real thus does not imply the conceptual presence of that which vanishes into discourse, but rather asserts the absence of an "independent separate individuality" by returning, after discourse, to a prediscursive reality.

The Hegelian subject, on the other hand, manifests itself, its negativity, in the sign by effectively reducing reality, and itself, to a concept. As Hegel states, "the intuition—in its natural phase a something given and given in space—acquires, when employed as a sign, the peculiar characteristic of existing only as *aufgehobene* (sublimated and suppressed). Such is the negativity of intelligence."[79] It cancels the immediate given, sensual, brute reality. This power of spirit or its freedom from the given is more forcefully demonstrated by the arbitrariness *(Willkür)* of the sign from which Saussure and then Lacan drew such great significance. I do not wish to enter the extensive complexities and ramifications of this topic about which so much has been written, for it is a topic conspicuously absent from Bataille's work, so I will only offer the most basic of remarks. The arbitrariness of the sign expresses the lack of natural relation between the signifier and signified, the famous bar that keeps them apart and which testifies to the inadequacy of the signifier to reach the signified as it is in-itself. Taking one of Lacan's innumerable comments upon this dynamic, "when one talks about the signified, one thinks of the thing, whereas in fact signification is what is involved."[80] The word (signifier) therefore does not necessarily refer to the thing but rather to another signification, another signifier. It is in fact the word itself and the relations among words that brings the thing into being, that give it a human meaning. The word replaces the thing. This is one of the many lessons Lacan drew from Hegel, as he states, "Hegel puts it with extreme rigour—the concept makes the thing be there, all the while, it isn't."[81]

A passage from Hegel makes this substitution explicit:

> Language . . . gives [the thing] a name and expresses this as the being of the object. What *is* this? We answer, It *is* a lion, a donkey, etc.—it *is*. Thus it is not . . . something on its own, [existing] independently. Rather, it is a *name* . . . and this [as named] is its true *being*. . . . By means of the name, however, the object has been born out of the I [and has emerged] as *being*. This is the primal creativity exercised by Spirit. Adam gave a name to all things. This is the sovereign right [of Spirit], its primal taking-possession of all nature—or the creation of nature out of Spirit [itself]. *Logos*, reason, the essence of the thing and of speech . . . this is the *being* of the object. Spirit relates itself to itself: it says to the donkey, You are an inner [subjective] entity, and that Inner is I; your being is a sound which I have arbitrarily invented.[82]

Objects are inconsistent, fleeting, uncertain, and unknowable entities if not accompanied and designated by words, the most effective tools of appropriation in the spirit's arsenal. Through nomination one gives a greater consistency to the knowledge gained on the visual realm, giving the object a temporal duration without which neither an agreement between individuals upon the object would be possible, nor would the object have any meaning *(sens)* as its experience would be confined to a fleeting succession of instants.

But beyond the obvious efficacy of words, Hegel makes the claim for an absolute subsumption of the thing into the name where it vanishes without a trace. The name then literally banishes the nonsensical aspect of experience (the signified), and in Derrida's opinion, "the irreducible privilege of the name is the keystone of the Hegelian philosophy of language."[83] Bataille will not challenge the notion of nominalist linguistics itself by returning to some outdated naturalism. But were he to address it, and to the extent that he does—with respect to scientific articulation—he would argue against the mastery involved, the inward spiral of meaning. In his view, language, rather than a tool of possession, is a crucial aspect of communication—dispossession of one's self-as-isolated-individual. One is relieved of one's self not only by the opacity of words passing between speakers, the inability for a self-identical subject to make transparent an ideational message to another self-identical subject. Rather, it is the excessiveness of language itself, its density, its multiplication and instability of meanings as it "floats" around an unknown signified, that may dispossess the self-certain subject. That is, the "floating" of the signifier above the signified may allow the creation of meaning from out of the concatenation of signifiers, but it may as well push language to the point of meaninglessness in its relation to the infinite withdrawal of the ultimate signified.

Having already specified the core of Bataille's criticism with respect to both scientific and Hegelian thought, the fundamental polemics that he himself will raise against discourse should be readily apparent, and the features I have attributed to discourse already bear the insignia of those polemics. The argument that circumscribes his particular criticisms is that discursive language, quite literally the *work* of knowing, is existence as project—the project of knowledge which relegates the immediate to insignificance. To know is to relate to the known, and that which is properly known is a thing produced by conscious, futurizing action. What we have seen here however is that, insofar as it is the word that produces the thing by negating (killing) it and replacing it with a word, knowledge is not an adequation of word (concept) and reality, word and experience, but the swallowing of reality. Knowledge then becomes the logical relation of words to words, signifier to signifier. But insofar as words cannot grasp the immediate—or if they do, it is only by turning it into an object—knowledge is effectively placed at a remove from evanescent experience, from a truth to which Hegel's method blinded him.

Or perhaps more accurately, the language *of knowledge* trivializes the truth of sensuous reality, which only emerges in the effect—desire and/or repulsion, if not indifference—this reality has upon us at the moment it is experienced. It trivializes experience insofar as it turns it into an object of knowledge. The lie of Hegelian discourse, however, is to speak truth and call it knowledge. For he unveils the truth of language—negativity, death, and desire—only to cancel it by bringing it to a halt in the satisfaction of the word satiated by the thing. The truth discourse announces therefore is a truth that, even while it may emerge through words, nevertheless evades—and is forbidden to—the grasp of words. It is a truth that "loves to hide" from knowledge, or more paradoxically, a truth that emerges in discourse but which is unveiled only when its words fail us.

The word relegates the present intuition, internal or external, to the past, a past contained in the presence of spirit, then externalized in the word, which bestows meaning upon the intuition by projecting it into the future of the subject. Knowing (naming) therefore not only eschews the immediate, not only entails the cutting up of the confused, undifferentiated continuum of the material world into discontinuous things (words) but as well the organization and mastery of this world through the construction of a logical chain of signification in which every word, thing, and moment has its specified place. The determination of this place clearly belongs not to chance, but to the work of reason.[84] Leading the dialectic of discourse to a complete adequation of word and thing, subject and object, thought and being, reason confers a divine authority on the language of the philosopher. Or quite simply, the discourse of the speaking subject which orders the world into a closed system of sentences admitting no contradiction, which in effect encloses the totality of being, turns the speaking being into God.

The general line of argumentation should be apparent. Discourse entails a suppression of confused and senseless nature, a suppression that lifts it out of immediacy and into human meaning by naming and separating it into distinct objects. Death, to the fly that does not speak, and hence does not know itself as distinct, has no meaning. But equally and perhaps more importantly, discourse entails the autonomy from one's own animal nature, an autonomy that is necessary to establish the limits of propriety which define one as an individual. To articulate oneself is an attempt to separate oneself from the abyss of an intimate and confused involvement with both internal and external nature, an attempt to protect oneself from the loss of individuality, from death. Or perhaps more precisely, it is to ensure that one's death has a meaning, that one remain beyond one's disappearance, that death may be recuperated.

Bataille posits that the intellectual autonomy that comes with the discursive challenge to natural existence, the attempt to free oneself from death and from the chance occurrences of life, may be seen as an attempt to repeat God's autonomy from the world. In a sense, both language and the God of reason are seen as "middle terms" which respond to the vulnerable self's desire to be *taken out of play*.[85] But this sort of autonomy, the type "to which the human mind aspires, isn't its own autonomy but that of a purely speculative existence." That is, it is an unreal autonomy founded upon that which the Hegelian sign made clear, "the attribution of being to words,"[86] the replacement of the real with the discursive real, an unreality. This linguistic gesture, however, is seen as a "Christian" gesture: "[T]he truth of language is Christian," namely, a "doubling the real world with another world,"[87] a doubling intended to evade the hazards of existence by narcissistically thinking up a God who is just like the self—and who is never at risk.

Bataille summarizes the positions I have outlined in the following passages:

> Clearly, in the two cases (God and Reason) this type of breakthrough into unreality is a result of the substitution of language for the immediacies of life. Man has doubled real things—and himself—with words that evoke them and signify them and outlive the disappearance of the things signified . . . these words themselves make up an ordered realm, *adding*, to precisely translated reality, pure evocations of . . . unreal beings. *This realm replaces being insofar as immediate being is sensible consciousness.* For the formless consciousness of things and oneself there is substituted reflective thought, in which consciousness has replaced things with words. But at the same time that consciousness was enriched, words . . . took the place of the sensible world.[88]

Here we have Bataille's transcription of Kojève's "dog" eat dog, and there is no doubt that the target of this quotation is Hegel, specifically the Hegelian dialectic of *logos* and nature. In short, Bataille claims that for Hegel, reality is *logos* or reason, and that reason is no unreal abstraction but that "a human being of flesh and blood is reason incarnate."[89] This leads him to conclude that Hegel "was the first to resolve a demand for autonomy," which develops through the negation of nature. The point he wants to make is the following: "[W]hether it's God who's in question or pure reason or Hegelian reason, there is always *logos* substituted for man seeking autonomy,"[90] *logos* replaces sovereignty.

The essential to be retained from these reflections is that the activity of discourse, which liberates the speaking being from the material world and establishes the autonomy of that being, not only subordinates the world to the one who possesses it in one's discourse but quickly translates into what Bataille frequently refers to in *Inner Experience* as the "desire to be everything," to refuse one's limits, to become God. That this is the omega of Hegelian knowledge should be evident, as it is consistent with the specular structure of his dialectic of Desire, which in turn has prompted various authors to stress the "paranoid" nature of Hegelian knowledge.[91] That is, whether it is the move from basic intuition to the world of human meaning, or from the discursive character of Hegelian sight to its encapsulation in the language of absolute knowledge, there is a self-referential structure to Hegelian knowledge. Seeing and speaking the world is seeing and speaking oneself. That which one sees and says is therefore—notwithstanding the fertile "slips" and silences of speech—that which one already has in mind.

This type of self-observation that grounds the intellectual operations of philosophy not only reflects, as Freud claims, "the characteristic tendency of paranoiacs to construct speculative systems,"[92] but as well the schizophrenic tendency to abandon the world in favor of words that represent oneself (a "hyper-cathexis of their own ego").[93] Or in a more Hegelian vein: the temporary sojourn of consciousness into material difference will always yield to self-conscious desire and its return out of difference into unity, a unity accomplished through the "middle term" of language which resolves the alienation of the subject and reestablishes the presence of Spirit. What this notion of the self-conscious spirit banishes, however, is the response of language to what Bataille would call the poetic experience, the "inner" experience around which words circle, words like fingers that cannot grasp. This response cannot be the willful mastery of the poetic "genius" who can point the quill at any reality and make it fly, but rather like a poetic archer pointing her arrow into the night, reaching its goal the instant it is lost. The poetic experience brings the element of chance into language: the poet at the mercy of the play of words . . . words at the mercy of an elusive reality. If the final word of Hegelian discourse gives a sufficient and necessary answer to the question of Being, then the poetic response which prolongs the question is eliminated—taking chance along with it: "The absence of poetry is the eclipse of chance."[94] No word abolishes chance. Self-consciousness, which cannot be satisfied by clinging to the known, may do well by a share of poetry.

3.3 THE HATRED OF POETRY

"Poetry," in the sense in which Bataille uses the term, is not to be understood as some-thing upon which to reflect, as having some proper and narrow place within culture and language like that of the *"belles lettres."* To the extent that this is poetry, it is already poetry's negation,[95] the "hatred of poetry." *The Hatred of Poetry* (*La haine de la Poésie*, 1947) was the original title of what came to be called in the second edition (1962) *L'Impossible.*[96] The provocative original title carries this double sense: that traditional literary poetry is an object of hatred because it respects aesthetic conventions, and because it attempts to eternalize and affirm both that which is expressed and the poet expressing it; but it as well signifies that poetry in Bataille's sense is that which actively reveals the hatred for traditional poetry, is poetry hating poetry with the violence of tragedy. It is the second sense that articulates the true sphere of his "poetry."[97]

He clearly expresses this view of poetry in an article on Jacques Prévert's *Paroles*, where he states that "Jacques Prévert's poetry is poetry precisely as a living denial—and derision—of whatever congeals the mind in the name of poetry itself," and further claims that Prévert's poetry "is poetry because, in itself, it harshly effects the ruin of poetry."[98] What it ruins in poetry is that which resists change and outwits death, in particular the laws of rhythm which are technical prerequisites given to poets to master, and the themes given to poets from the stock of "noble" or "majestic" feelings prevalent in a given society, which it wants to maintain even if these elements no longer predominate.[99] The dislocation of forms, the purveyors of a monumental sovereignty or of themes guaranteeing the unity and reassuring certainty of traditional foundations, is not, however, to be found solely in written forms of poetry. And it is in fact in his book on Manet where these ideas come most explicitly to the fore.[100] A brief glance at some themes in this text should give us a clear indication of the general sense of poetry at which Bataille is aiming.

The main line of argumentation in *Manet* is as follows: art prior to the modern period was determined by an exterior signification, generally of mythological or theological content and its correlative conventions, which effectively filled the forms on the canvas—sovereign, royal, or divine forms—with a traditional and determinate symbolic value. In effect, premodern painting narrated a story told from beyond present-day life, from beyond this world, with art serving as the conservator of the past. The turn to the modern period—which Bataille locates not with the favored father of modern art, Cezanne, but rather with Manet—was signified by the birth of painting that refused any signification foreign to the painting itself, which effectively suppressed the signification of its subject. Or as Bataille repeatedly states, the subject of the painting became a matter of indifference, a mere pretext for painting. In which case the naked sensation of the play of color and form came to replace the eloquent verbiage of a "majestic"—the noble sense of "sovereign"—discourse. The raw materiality of what was depicted, as well as the physical texture of the paint itself—and here Cezanne should be cited as the original instance—emerged in place of transcendent ideas which were effectively silenced. This, in Bataille's view, is the essence of modern painting, and Manet achieved a "supreme indifference."[101]

Now, while Manet is identified as the turning point to the modern period, Bataille fortunately does not fail to include Goya in the revolution. The distance between Goya and what Bataille saw as the essence of modern painting was due to two factors—his narrative approach (with exceptions such as the "black" paintings), and his emotive stance. And while Manet's *The Execution of Maximillian* (1868) is identified as a reproduction of Goya's *The Third of May* (1814), ("minus what this painting signifies" [Malraux]), the narration of a political event is expressed with outrage by the Spaniard, while the death painted by Manet is executed with the same indifference with which one would paint a fish.[102] Manet does tell a story, but it is told with total indifference to the event. However, the raw passion and refusal of eloquence found in Goya's work effectively achieves the same silence as that of Manet, though it is an excessive silence that depicts death with the outrage of a scream. Therefore, while Goya may maintain the means and conventions of edifying painting, he nevertheless "undermined the foundations from within."[103] Or if the temple, the house containing an edifying theological resident, had the mission to protect and reassure, Goya is "the temple fire in the night." But the question we are asking here is in what sense is Manet's indifference poetic?

The suppression of traditional sovereign themes given from outside has its counterpart in the necessity to "rediscover," independent from conventional sovereignty, a "secret royalty" that "belongs . . . to the passion of the one who attains in himself a region of sovereign silence."[104] The sacred or sovereign element is expressed by bestowing sight upon the affect (horror, desire, etc.) that an immediate relation to the object evokes, and by rendering the hidden power of the object to evoke this affect tangible. The point is to find through the forms of the present world—or of the world present in the imagination of the artist—an obscure sacred, obscure and silent because it is not joined to a discourse that situates its meaning. Modern painting is poetry for poetry is the silencing of this meaning.

Bataille demonstrates his viewpoint with an analysis of Manet's painting, *Olympia* (1863), which is a reproduction of Titian's *Venus of Urbino* (1538).[105]

The Italian's work, however, had no element of the scandal with which Manet's reproduction was received. Bataille attributes the scandal of *Olympia* not specifically to her provocative, knowing eyes which show her recognition and return of the viewer's lustful gaze, but rather to the general fact that it overwhelms expectation, presenting something outside conventional frames of reference as it unleashes the subject from its mythological moorings. One *expects* to see a goddess. What one sees is nothing but a naked girl. One sees *what is*. Here one may be reminded of the powerful painting by Hans Holbein the Younger, *The Body of the Dead Christ in the Tomb* (1522), which is composed entirely of a scarcely covered corpse—and we only know it is Christ from the title—laid out on a slab, pinned down from above by the heavy mass of the tomb. No Christian symbols adorn the painting, there is neither the passion nor the glory of the crucifixion, not the slightest hint of transcendence or impending resurrection—an anti-Hegelian Christ. What is depicted rather is an excruciatingly human death, the non-narrative death that awaits us all, neither as punishment nor in extreme anguish, but as testimony to our very condition as human beings subjected to death. With this painting we may grieve for our finitude, which lacks the anticipation of a radiant beyond, yet may still come to a sense of our intimacy with our death and humanness. With the breakdown of transcendence we find a transformative breakthrough to an intimacy with existence.[106]

Through a destruction of reference to a transcendent world of signification, one leaps from one world to another, from the past and its transcendent future, to the present here-below, and it is here that the sacred must manifest itself—without subtitles. Like Holbein's Christ, the girl depicted by Manet is not a symbol, she is present as what she is, naked and provocative—more naked, if you will, than the unclothed Venus who is kept at a neutral distance by the veils of tradition. "*Olympia*, like modern poetry, is in the end a negation of this world" [the world of convention, the mythological/theological world that provides assurance through its stability of meaning].[107] Furthermore, "poetry is in the end the negation of all imaginable convention . . . it only draws its *magic* from itself," a magic found "in the immediate, absurd given."[108] The divine figures liberated of their foundations do not, for all that, cease to be divine. Their divinity, however, no longer refers to a discourse beyond what one sees, but is brought into the *hic et nunc*, is something within humanity that can be evoked by a naked woman as well as a sunflower, a seascape, or a poem. Whether it pertains to painting, music, or a written poem, "poetry gives expression to what exceeds the possibilities of common language. It uses words [or colors, etc.] to express what overturns the order of words. It is the *cry* of what, within us, cannot be reduced; what, within us, is *stronger than us*."[109] Poetry evokes this overwhelming and undefinable otherness.

These remarks may provide an opening to the general nature of "poetry" envisioned by Bataille, but we cannot substitute preliminaries for understanding, so we must enter into the specific workings of poetry and the methods by which the "overturning" of the order of words is to occur. The suppression of the subject—or equally, of theme or meaning—is a critical step, one by which poetry becomes a "play without rules."[110] This privative notion, however, must be joined by the operation through which this suppression occurs—sacrifice. To understand poetry requires an understanding of the logic of sacrifice, which functions by drawing a victim from the profane, useful realm in order to mediate with the sacred, intimate realm by being put to death, negated, or expended. In principle, it is only what is useful that is destined for sacrifice. In sacrifice, an internal violence is unleashed upon elements of the real, calculated world, elements whose immediate, sensible value has been reduced to their use value, a tendency which "deprived the world of poetry."[111] "Primitive" societies used sacrifice to redress this reduction of sensible, immediate, or sacred value to productive value—even if it served to propitiate a god to secure the god's beneficence for further production.

The victim in poetry is the word. For "poetry," as Bataille claims, is the "sacrifice in which words are victim."[112] And, like a sacrifice with respect to the useful things it involves, "poetry is the path followed at all times by man's desire to redress the abuse which he makes of language."[113] It goes without saying that the abuse of language in question goes by the name of discourse, which effectively uses language as a tool, the paradigm of servility. One common way of illustrating the servility of language is by association with the "language" of bees. This indeed is a language in the sense of having a fixed correlation of signs to a variety of elements signified. The sign itself is fixed in its function as *a means* of transmitting practical information (knowledge), and this function only makes sense within a limited referential horizon of productive activity. The sole significance of the sign is a means subordinate to the communication of a message, the sign itself being a hollow shell to be discarded once its function is fulfilled. This illustration is loosely congruent with Heidegger's analysis of equipment or the "ready-to-hand" *(Zuhandenheit),* into which language (the sign) falls.[114]

Heidegger's analysis is particularly relevant to Bataille as it highlights the fact that the awareness of what is closest is passed over in favor of that toward which our interest is directed. The proximity of equipment and language as the way of disclosing the world becomes distanced through its absorption in its referential matrix, the common example being its context of assignments or its functionality.[115] Correlatively, the ready-to-hand disclosure of the world relies on a more primordial relation to the world which is presupposed and effectively hidden by the totality of involvements or assignments constituting our concernful dealings with the world. Indeed, the foundational "worldhood of the world" can be unveiled from within the system of relations with the world, but the primary manner in which this unveiling occurs—on the level of equipment—is when these relations *break down.* It is essentially when the equipment facilitating our functional relationship to the world becomes unusable, its efficacious activity disrupted, that the tool itself "becomes conspicuous"[116] and the phenomenal content of the world, along with the Being of the being in this world, is for the first time—although not fully—unveiled.

Like Heidegger, Bataille does not dispute that the neglect of our own existence, through our absorption in the functional horizon with which we originally discover the world, is an essential structure of our existence. His style and method being different, Bataille nevertheless searches for those points at which the functional, "servile" relationship to the world is disrupted. And when it is a matter of language used as a tool, he actively attempts to sever these meaningful relationships with poetry, with his writing: "I write in order to annihilate the play of subordinate operations [in myself]";[117] "words—we use them, we make of them the instruments of useful acts. We would in no way have anything of the human about us if language had to be entirely servile within us."[118] This returns us to the active opposition to the use of language oriented toward practical ends, language that—insofar as it defines the category of subject-object, of the subject considered on the plane of objectivity, of clearly and distinctly known objects—effectively establishes the world of things, the known, and whose usage transforms the speaking being into a thing.[119] In other words, through opposition to the linguistic function of relating the unknown to the known, we are brought back to poetry, to sacrifice.

From our brief look at the Manet text we were able to delineate some of the general tendencies of poetry. Implied within this analysis was as well the sacrificial movement constitutive of poetry itself, taking an element from one realm and delivering it to another. The two paintings mentioned (*The Execution of Maximilian* and *Olympia*) explicitly borrowed from previous paintings that rested on the pillars of the tradition. Manet did not challenge these paintings by escaping them, rather, he effectively transformed painting from within, using its established means and ways. This is in fact the work of poetry:

> If poetry introduces the strange, it does so by means of the familiar. The poetic is the familiar dissolving into the strange, and ourselves along with it. It never dispossesses us entirely, for the words, the images (once dissolved) are charged with emotions already experienced, attached to objects which link them to the known.[120]

Already from this definition we may begin to apprehend the limitations of poetry. If it introduces an element of the unknown, the manner in which it does so—by means of that which still retains its links to us, by means of what we already know—involves a sort of compromise. Poetic images—whether they involve displacement, combination, or distortion—are drawn from the words of discourse. If they disrupt the fortress of discourse, they nevertheless arrive in a Trojan horse, in a recognizable form that only causes disruption from within the city walls.

Recognizing this situation, Derrida for example emphasizes that the writing at which Bataille aims is not another discourse that may be placed alongside or outside meaningful, significative, Hegelian discourse, for "there is only one discourse, it is significative, and here one cannot get around Hegel."[121] Rather, Bataille must search for those elements within every discourse that make it slide toward the loss of its meaning, that transgress its meaning—and in this sense he must be seen as a forefather of "deconstruction." But as we have already established, when it is a matter of transgression, one may only temporarily exceed the law, one cannot suppress it. Poetry therefore cannot overthrow discourse, meaning, knowledge, reason, or utility, and establish itself as the new autocrat of truth. Poetry in fact cannot claim to be any more true than discourse, just as one cannot act as if meaning and knowledge did not exist. There can be no dualistic abyss between poetry and discourse, and consequently there can be no idealistic reduction of sense to non-sense. One cannot simply leave one realm to take up residence in the other, for if the fictive freedom of a comprehensively destructive and nonsensical language became a reality, madness would reign, and if language was constrained solely to make sense, servility would be sovereign. The fictive play of poetry is therefore limited to a movement from one realm to the other, it is "the use of a function detached (freed) from the servility *from which it springs [qui en est le principe]*,"[122] which cannot avoid falling back into the normal pattern of life once it subsides.

Bataille illustrates both the play and impotence of poetry with a rather simple example, using the ordinary words *horse* and *butter*. The farm girl or stable boy, when they say "butter" or "horse," know butter and horse, and "the knowledge which they have of them even exhausts the idea of knowing, for they can make butter or lead a horse at will. The making . . . the using, perfect and even found knowledge (the essential links of knowledge are relations of practical efficacy . . .)."[123] Should these words enter a poem however, they are "detached from interested concerns,"[124] are liberated from the practical ends and referential context with which the boy and girl understand them. That is, the poem can introduce a significance outside that of utility or clear and distinct knowledge, simply by introducing the image of a "butterhorse." In doing so, Bataille says that one is placed before "the unknowable." But what has occurred?

> No doubt I have barely enunciated the words [butterhorse] when the familiar images of horses and butter present themselves, but they are solicited only in order to die. In which sense poetry is sacrifice, but of the most accessible sort. For if the use or abuse of words, to which the operations of words oblige us, takes place on the ideal, unreal level of language, the same is true of the sacrifice of words which is poetry.[125]

In this case, the poetic image has indeed displaced the words from their discursive habitat, and condensed them into a fictive evocation of a new reality, but it would be frivolous to assert that it has touched the reality it concerns (butter or horse). At least this would seem to be the case—but I would like to cast a shred of doubt.

Toward the end of *Theory of Religion,* Bataille bemoans the fact that—like the fictive freedom of poetry that can only alter the world of words—religions have submitted to the order of things without trying to modify it. And in fact, it is neither a possibility or a necessity for them to do so. Nonetheless, there does appear to be a way for a type of destruction to occur by reversing the movement of clear consciousness and, as sacrifice does, returning the real world to intimacy. As religions tend to do this on the level of unreality, Bataille will descend to the lowest level of the human reduction to thinghood to show how this might occur. In one's room, one may look at the objects that surround one and determine their meaning, as well as the web of relations they involve. One sits at the table, a table for which one had to work in order to buy, to compensate for the labor of others, a table that allows one to work in order to pay butchers, farmers, clothiers, to ensure one's survival and continuation of one's work, etc.:

> Now I place a large glass of alcohol on my table.
> I have been useful. I have bought a table, a glass, etc.
> But this table is not a means of labor: it helps me to drink alcohol.
> In setting my drinking glass on the table, to that extent *I have destroyed the table . . .*
> At least this table in this room, heavy with the chains of labor, for a time had no other purpose than my breaking loose.[126]

In both the ordinary and strong sense of the term, the table is now there to consume, to waste (time and labor). The previous moments of activity, the clear consciousness of the table—and oneself—as belonging to the world of work, are lost in the careless flow of alcohol. Of course this is a futile moment, one will sober up and take one's place in the real order, but the seed of intimacy has been sown in the destructive moment. I will return to this shortly, but first let us again consider the poetic image of the butterhorse.

The image created out of two known terms may bring some havoc into the discursive order, insofar as it tears the words out of their context and ruptures the sense in which they are known, but this does not make poetry equivalent to a "holocaust of words."[127] Not only does the image remain linked to the known from which it arises, it even, like a sacrifice, restores that which it undoes, and "from this it follows that poetry is almost entirely poetry in decline. . . ."[128] That is, while the butterhorse may be the ruin of "butter" and "horse," it nevertheless erects itself on the ashes of the old as a new, poetic, reality. Similarly, Manet did not destroy painting. He opened a new age on the ruins of the old, maintaining his predecessor's influence as he transformed it. But the new itself became a foundation, the standard bearer of impressionism, which in turn would yield to postimpressionism, expressionism, abstract expressionism et al. Indeed, "it is difficult to no longer possess anything but ruin, but this is not to no longer possess anything—it is to retain with one hand what the other hand gives."[129] As we see from this quite Hegelian statement, poetry does not seem to be without reserve. It is, as Bataille claims, a "minor" form of writing, a minor that is "inserted" in the world like children in the house—subordinated, neutralized, to be seen not heard.[130]

A fitting example of this tendency is one of the most famous poems written when poetry was no longer possible,[131] Paul Celan's *Todesfuge (Deathfugue)*. This poem is a lyric witness to the horrifying experience of death-camp reality, centering around the staggering fact that orchestras of Jewish musicians in the camps were ordered to play tangos and nostalgic songs while others were digging graves:

> . . . He shouts jab this earth deeper you lot there you others sing up and play
> he grabs for the rod in his belt he swings it his eyes are so blue . . .
> He shouts play death more sweetly this Death is a master from Deutschland
> he shouts scrape your strings darker you'll rise then as smoke to the sky . . .[132]

Containing other disquieting metaphors such as black milk the prisoners drink and drink, graves dug in the air, hair of ash, this poem is a bitter condemnation of an unspeakable atrocity. Nevertheless, the musical rhythm and fugue-like repetition of this *danse macabre* almost seem to disguise its fury, to sublimate the raw matter of Auschwitz, although this does not seem to be its intention.

Some years after its initial reception, when it was established enough to be taught in German schools, the poem indeed came to be read as one of reconciliation.[133] For example, the closing lines evoke both Goethe's heroine from *Faust* and the Jewish beloved from the Song of Songs: "Your golden hair Margareta/Your ashen hair Shulamith." The hair of the latter stained by ash from incinerated bodies is a negation of the Aryan prototype that does not insinuate dialectical recompense, although it could be distorted into doing so. The truth is, the poem came to be appropriated. The transposition of horror into art came to be seen as a purification of the event, an objectification that achieved annulation by enabling its reader to grasp, master, and overcome the pain with the full force of dialectics. Here we see at work the universalizing function of language, economic equilibrium reestablished through an adequate response to a particular event—economic neutralization. If poems are, in a compelling phrase Celan borrowed from Rilke, "enclosures around the limitlessly wordless," perhaps the enclosure effectively imprisons the ineffable, unwittingly immobilizes it with words.

But perhaps, in a more generous light, the poem is a witness to the ability of language to enable one to live with that which, should it not receive some representation, would leave one sunk in an inward spiral of uncomprehending despair. And we need not conclude that Celan found such an adequate representation of the unrepresentable horror that confronted him that all its brute absurdity was annulled—he did, after all, drown himself in the Seine. It may rather be that his representation, rather than fixing the event in question, points beyond itself to the unrepresentable at the same time as it orders it and makes it bearable. This transformation need not be, however, such a successful *Aufhebung* that the meaningless is rendered entirely intelligible. And while I find a proximity of the poem to a ritual or myth—which in effect give a rhythm and language to anxiety or a senseless experience that would otherwise be devastating—it need not be seen as so effective that it completely absorbs the heterogeneous, rationalizes the incongruous, or translates the other into the language of the same.[134] That is, it need not be presumed to merely bury the unrepresentable under a soothing phraseology and hand it over to a system in which everything is meaningful. Rather, it may be closer to the Nietzschean sense of the tragic (of which lyric poetry is one example) in which Apollinian illusion and Dionysian horror work together in an aesthetic affirmation of existence. For here the Apollinian illusion enables a confrontation with the horror of existence by giving it a beautiful form, yet this illusion truly serves to illuminate the Dionysian abyss from which it arose. We shall have more to say on this later.

I have raised the example of Celan's poem because it quite explicitly reveals the dangers Bataille associates with language, and it as well indicates the direction we are heading. But for the moment let us focus on the manner in which Bataille looks for poetry to lead language into the "limitlessly wordless," into the dark wellsprings of poetic silence. To the extent that writing does not sufficiently challenge the entirety of Hegelian discourse, put it at risk, it remains a minor form of writing and risks itself being inserted into a meaningful discourse. To the extent that writing is to become a "major" form of writing, it must bear the stamp of the point of no return, which severs all ties with the reappropriative constitution of meaning. As we saw with both Manet's painting and Celan's poetry, the work produced in the break from the prevalent mode of expression nevertheless maintains itself as a recognizable form of writing, even if these works arose from a sovereign protest against complicity with a neutralizing significative discourse.

The painter, however, was more effective in silencing meaning through indifference to his subject matter, an indifference unavailable to the Jewish poet in the face of an event that called for a response. Painting may in fact retain this advantage over language, for it does not speak *about* violence or passion, light and color, but allows them free rein to speak themselves in a language the viewer may quite simply not be prepared to understand. Even if, as Bataille points out, Manet desired to paint only what he saw, it is not necessary for the painting to take on a recognizable form or re-present a given reality, as the painter has at his disposal a polymorphous methodology that can express pure sensibility without a universalizing judgment, is free to play with the inarticulate and unknown. To the extent that poetry is to follow suit, it requires its own methodology, a strategy that "annihilates the play of subordinate operations," that is "liberated from the servility from which it springs," a strategy that Bataille enunciates as follows: ". . . these words! which exhaust me without respite: I will nevertheless go to the limit of the miserable possibility of words. I want to find words which reintroduce—at a point—the sovereign silence that interrupts articulated language."[135] Again, he wants to find words and concepts, drawn from the realm of significative discourse, that make this discourse slide toward the loss of its meaning. But first let us look at this strategy for a moment to try to more accurately define what is at stake.

The first thing to notice is the precondition of a nonpracticable journey to the end of efficacious language, of language that works. In fact this is a formal gesture, as it rests on an assumption that a systematic reflection on the entirety of discourse, an exhaustion of philosophical and scientific pathways, is to be carried out by Bataille. In actuality, this achievement is attributed to Hegel, and Bataille has merely assimilated his thought in order to reflect on a discourse that has reached its limit. Nonetheless, it indicates that discourse is to be followed to the point where it puts itself at risk of falling into nonsense and exhausting itself. This view is expressed in *"Hegel, l'homme et l'histoire,"*[136] where the end of history is rightfully equated with the view of a totality so complete that no constitutive element can be separated from it, a totality adequately circumscribed in the discourse that articulates it. Bataille claims, "I can imagine—and represent—a completion of discourse so perfect that afterwards, other developments would no longer have any meaning,"[137] and furthermore, that this void at the end of discourse is "the final problem of Hegelianism." Or more correctly, this is not a problem for Hegelianism as such, but for those who want to escape it. It is a problem for poetry.

Poetry is assigned the task of relating meaningful (Hegelian) discourse to the point that opens the void, becoming a language that leads nowhere, asserts nothing, thereby constituting a language not drawn into the dialectical play of a self-mediating absolute. Quite simply, it is to be "a language belonging to a brief moment."[138] First some general remarks. The desire for an immediate writing that escapes the project of writing—a project constituted by the progressive accumulation of successive phrases, the present phrase related to future phrases which seal its meaning—is revealed both through Bataille's use of and fondness for the fragment (here his affinity with Nietzsche resurfaces), as well as for the "automatic writing" of the surrealists. If "the present is always unavailable to thinking," because "thought and language have no interest in the present—and at every moment substitute a vision of the future,"[139] then automatic writing—which he sees as the foundation of surrealism—has as its "principle . . . to have done with goals."[140] Escaping the servitude of subordinating language to some ulterior goal, or quite simply of language that works, "what has proved to be simultaneously attained and realized [by automatic writing] is nothing other than the *instant*."[141] Furthermore, attaining the instant, "it extricates the human mind from any end other than poetry."[142] Poetry is an attempt to write the instant.

Of course, the obstacle is one we have already brought to attention, namely: how to affirm the (sacred) value of the instant without fixing it in a recognizable form, without making it a thing, a problem Bataille quite simply articulates in stating that "ink changes absence to intention."[143] Discursive language never has the present instant as its object, one cannot speak the present instant any more than one can speak death. Or rather, simply by speaking, one speaks death, in the sense noted above where the word ("dog") was the death of the thing (dog). But poetry, wanting to write the instant, in effect wants to write death in another way. It wants to write the instant which is akin to death in that it does away with the knowing subject at the same time it faces a vanishing object. Therefore, if poetry involves death, it is the death of words which rely on a discontinuous subject, fix the object of reference, and ensure the survival of the thing named and negated. If poetry brings death it is to the extent that poetry murders words: sovereign, sacred, or poetic writing is "analogous to a suicide [of language]." Or rather, poetry is to cease being language that designates things, in order to become that which bestows sight *(donner à voir)* on what—in the object, in language, and finally in human life itself—is not reducible to utility. Poetry is to awaken one to the sacred domain of sensibility, the mythical immersion in overwhelming reality—"or if you prefer, of *interest confined to the instant itself*."[144] But to what extent does it succeed?

Let us choose a simple example, the word *wind*. Scientific language can designate wind as a thing, can isolate it, explain its causes and specific effects, predict its occurrence, ultimately with the intention of either using it or protecting against it. But it can never express the feeling of standing on a pier in a gale, nor can it account for the intangible emotion arising from an ordinary breeze on the face, any more than one can explain how Pachelbel's "Chacone in F minor" can transport one from one's armchair and into another world. Quite simply, it cannot grasp the experience of wind, for wind is only ever experienced by its effects, which may arbitrarily change from moment to moment. Such is the case as well with the word *silence*, which, "among all words . . . is the most perverse, or the most poetic."[145] It is "silence," a word that in fact only indicates an absence (of sound)—although it can yield to subjective evocations such as an "overwhelming," "tangible," or "deathly" silence— which Bataille chooses as a "sliding word."[146] Is this sliding a loss of one's footing or a sliding toward something? One must conclude it is both. One loses one's grasp on the world of things, of the known, of subject and object, when the attention given to words which solidifies this world is silenced. When, for instance, one "cannot find the words" to express an event, to grasp, articulate, and ultimately distance oneself from what has befallen one. The correlate is thus that one is transported from the world of things to an "inner" state—which is not exactly "inner" because we know that inner experience is an ecstasis without object or subject, hence without words.

But if poetry indeed murders words that establish the domain of subject-object, it consequently should be the death of the discontinuous being, of the self as a distinct subject (consciousness). But it is not. It occurs, unlike sacrifice, in the realm of unreality. This seems obvious enough. Sacrifice proper is a topical, contextual event, limited to a particular domain, and is absent from the world in which we live. If it does occur in our world, it does so on the plane of fiction or literature. Nonetheless, literature or poetry can be a sacrifice, even if it is available without limit, without a topical reference, in that it is "directed towards the same aim as sacrifice: it seeks as far as possible to render palpable, and as intensely as possible, the content of the present moment."[147] But the problem we have repeatedly encountered again shows its face, for in the end, "poetry ultimately accepts poetry" and "when to accept poetry changes it into its opposite (it becomes the mediator of an acceptance)! I hold back the leap in which I would exceed the universe, I justify the given world, I content myself with it."[148] One should not fail to notice herein the standard criticism of Hegel as justifying every moment as a reasonable moment.

In other words—and here I am anticipating a discussion yet to come—the more one approaches poetry, the more one misses it:

> What once *bestowed sight* is exactly what later prevents it. It was soon apparent that poetry is also the enemy born of poetry: in being born it turns away from poetry to mingle the cry with the desire for permanence. . . . In fact, such is the poverty of poetry that in using words to express what happens it tends to stifle the cry of an actual emotion under the disguise of a museum face. Poetry, proclaiming the suspended instant, by the fact that the affecting order of words will survive it, tends to express only a durable meaning: it fixes it in a funereal solemnity.[149]

Here we touch upon an essential point—which has been indicated in reference to poetry in general, to Celan's poem, and which we shall see in relation to Levinas's *il y a*—which is as follows: by situating in words that which, in the moment, gives rise to a cry of an existence at the borders of dissolution or death, one tends to outwit this experience by the survival of the individual secured through the mediation of words. The survival, that is, of the individual as individual, through the survival of poetry as poetry. As Bataille claims in his article on Baudelaire, "[P]oetry which survives is always the opposite of poetry for, having the perishable as its subject, it transforms it into something eternal."[150] That is to say, having "impossible" existence lived to the point of death as its subject, it turns this existence into an existant.

This is the criticism of Baudelaire offered by Sartre from his essay in which Bataille recognizes a certain profundity, but not enough to entirely accept it. Baudelaire is said (by Sartre) to have wanted to *attain* what Bataille calls the "ultimate definition of poetry"—and, I add, the ultimate aim of sexuality—which is the "impossible" fusion of the being and existence, of subject and object. Poetry, however, "limits it and transposes it into the realm of the impossible and the unsatisfiable."[151] Sartre's view, as Bataille quotes him, was that Baudelaire's "dearest wish was to *be* like the stone, the statue, in the repose of immutability." Bataille replies that this may be so, but

> the images which [Baudelaire] left participated in a life which was open, infinite in Baudelaire's sense of the word (in the sense of that which is not subordinated to anything other than its primary impulse and which is indifferent to every external consideration), that is to say, unsatisfied. It is therefore misleading to maintain that Baudelaire wanted the impossible statue or that he could not exist, unless we immediately add that he wanted the impossible far more than he wanted the statue . . . [although] Sartre is justified in claiming that Baudelaire *wanted* something which seems *ruinous* to us.[152]

It is in fact the point, which I have and will continue to emphasize, that desire remains unsatisfied insofar as it wants a ruinous possibility—the impossible—and that, insofar as writing seeks an identity between what is reflected and the consciousness that reflects them, it inhabits the realm of failure. As we will see in the chapter that follows, it is ultimately survival that is at stake in erotic experience and the writing that evokes it.

The poverty of poetry therefore means that while it may suppress objects insofar as they are knowable and useful, the poetic itself is finally transformed into an object. This movement denies its essence, for "nothing is more essentially fleeting than the *sacred* or the poetic,"[153] whereas poetic moments, upon their disappearance, leave a residue or trace that can be repeated. Should one say or write "silence," one is not thrown into silence, one pauses before the word. This indeed seems to be an inextricable impasse. The ability of poetry to live up to Bataille's demands indeed seems *impossible*. Words, drawn from the sphere of discourse, always risk meaning something, risk making sense, being brought back into discourse. If words have succeeded in killing discourse through poetry, they have nevertheless neglected to bury it.

The question that remains, given the endless contradictions involved in the play of discourse, poetry, and silence, is whether words can in some way lead us to some unsayable or unnamable which words would negate should they say it. At least this seems to be the issue if we agree that it is untenable for silence to be the only measure of that which cannot be a determinate object of thought, or if we agree that there can be a search through language for nonlinguistic experience. This seems to be no less of an impasse, but it nonetheless defines the space in which Bataille's writing inserts itself, one from which he cannot extricate himself once he is committed not to exclude the unknowable from his reflection. Ultimately, Bataille's writing searches for God in the space left by the absence of God. The game that henceforth is announced is the attempt at a movement from the "hatred of poetry" to "the impossible," impossible because it attempts to express what, if expressed, is altered or missed: "My idea is that the particular human experience called the God experience is altered by naming it."[154] If his writing evokes God, it calls upon God's overwhelming presence, which, because it overwhelms, leaves one absent; he writes for deliverance from self and a God that can be known, "whose presence is manifest in sentences,"[155] or in the project of discourse.

If I have led one to believe that Bataille makes a coherent attempt to either solve or avoid this contradiction, perhaps I have posed the dynamic badly. A satisfying solution to the problem would end the play of writing itself, which—to the extent it is not just work—always chases an ungraspable reality. The only criterion that would be acceptable to Bataille is whether or not his thought and writing is in harmony with the "object" it seeks, if form and content are as one, or if it alters what it seeks by making it known. I believe the same criterion is poignantly expressed by Celan, who in reflecting on the progression of his own work says, "[i]n my first book I was still trans-figuring things," which does not coincide with his later view on the paths of poetry: "[P]oems . . . are making toward something . . . they are the efforts of someone who . . . [is] most uncannily *[unheimlich]* in the open, goes with his very being to language, stricken by and seeking reality."[156] These final words, perhaps more evocative in the original German—*wirklichkeitswund und Wirk-lichkeit suchend*—show that one is to pursue in language the very reality that has wounded both oneself and language, to pursue an overwhelming reality in a language that "had to pass through its own answerlessness, through fright-ful muting,"[157] to somehow reach what ordinary language or transfiguring poetry leave in darkness.

I believe it is in this respect that Bataille places emphasis on "the point" he seeks, the point that would interrupt or "mute" articulated language by denying its capacity for completion or even temporary rest. This capacity is in fact undermined by what it seeks, for unable to actually reach this point, the point becomes a point of loss, of loss without reserve. The meanings of dis-cursive language, in relation to this excessive point of loss, are extinguished, burnt like copper ingots in the ceremonial fire. Strictly speaking, the meaning of endeavors—whether they be tasks of writing, action, thought, morality—is given in relation to moments of completion, where movement gathers itself and subsides. This, I believe, is what underlies his critique of poetry—it sus-tains meaning even if it transforms the meaning of the elements utilized. If it wounds words poetry nevertheless closes the wound which drove one to write.

The foundation of Bataille's "hatred" of poetry is thus not the relation of poetry to a determinate, known object which it transforms into a poetic real-ity. Rather, what really enables poetry to come to rest is the reduction of an ungraspable, nondiscursive reality to the level of knowing humanity. Or more simply stated, it is poetry's attempt to be a prayer, the insolent endeavor of taking an unattainable God into one's mouth like bread, for people only pray for what is on the level of human possibility, calling on God whenever we see fit. The "sovereign" writing at which Bataille aims thus may be seen to put the entirety of the Hegelian writing we have examined at risk, for if Hegelian writing gathers all its sentences in logically continuous relation until it reaches the final sentence where God becomes articulate and revealed in absolute knowledge, Bataille will take the entirety of Hegelian discourse and, at its limit, relate it to what exceeds this limit—the evanescent, mystical God which admits of no distinction, the blinding darkness in which nothing is revealed. He relates absolute knowledge to a God—or its erotic equivalent—that does not collaborate with the constitution of meaning. Self-consciousness becomes divine in the experience of this limit.

Simply stated, sovereign writing relates to the sovereign moment, the point of non-reserve, the beyond of absolute knowledge.[158] This is "the point" that makes articulate language "slide" towards non-meaning, a "point" that is an unmasterable other that exceeds dialectical articulation and which deprives language of its mastery. The writing of sovereignty, however, is no more a state of sovereignty than the general economy is risk itself—for as we know, writing still maintains itself, while sovereignty or risk, unlike mastery, maintain nothing, renounce being recognized. Rather, one may say that sovereign writing follows the same operation of the general economy:

> The science of relating the object of thought to sovereign moments, in fact, is only a *general economy* which envisages the meaning of these objects in relation to each other and finally in relation to the loss of meaning. . . . The *general economy*, in the first place, makes apparent that excesses of energy are produced, and that by definition, these excesses cannot be utilized. The excessive energy can only be lost without the slightest aim, consequently without any meaning. It is this useless, senseless loss that *is* sovereignty.[159]

Bataille's writing takes its (discursive) resources in order to expend them without recuperation or aim, hence without meaning. One may not say that his writing is non-meaning itself, or that it actually describes the ineffable, or that it *says* "silence" or "non-knowledge." It is a "relation to" the unknown—the inarticulate and unmasterable other—to the loss of meaning or useless expenditure. But this relation is one that—precisely like sacrifice, precisely like the relation of the table to the glass of alcohol which helps one break loose rather than work—destroys the usefulness of the elements involved.

In searching for some unknown yet tangible presence that does not disclose itself, this relation lets language go dark, effacing itself in its utterance. One may object: Bataille has not effaced his own language, he wrote and did so profusely, and we can identify the methods at work in his writing, identify his themes and concerns. But perhaps this is to miss the point, for as he admits, "I could not avoid expressing my thought in a philosophical mode. But . . . ," he takes care to add, "I do not address myself to philosophers."[160] Philosophers struggle to make sense, to find meaning in whatever presents itself. To the extent that Bataille wants to undermine this attitude, he adds to his own writing what he—perhaps unrealistically—demands of poetry if it is to avoid discursive assimilation, namely, "the commentary on its absence of meaning."[161] It is perhaps for this reason that Bataille, displaying his affinity with Socratic irony, constantly reminds us that he knows nothing, asserts nothing: *"I don't lead anywhere."*[162] But he is not unaware that his "leading nowhere" will in fact lead to something, namely, misunderstandings:

> The disorder of my thought, what it has of irreducibility to clear sight, hides *nothing. I know nothing.* It is true that the harrowing cry *[le cri déchiré]* that announces it is also silence, if I wish. But finally I protest, anticipating the will to reduce this screaming silence or this inaudible cry, which steals every conceivable possibility from me, to some state of intellection: it is this will and this will alone that masks my writing.[163]

That is to say, it is those of us who read Bataille solely from the standpoint of philosophical or significative discourse that commit the error that Bataille—like Eckhart, as we shall see—wanted to avoid: the adding of determination (words) to that which is truly revealed in silent experience, in the absence of distinction, without subject or object. This error is committed insofar as one approaches his works from the outside.

Responding to Sartre's criticism that in *Inner Experience* Bataille transposes the mystical God into a foundation under the guise of "the Night," Bataille replies, "[W]hat I tried to describe in *Inner Experience* is a movement that, as it loses any possibility of coming to a halt, falls easily under the attack of a criticism that thinks it can effect a halt from the outside, since this criticism itself isn't *caught* in that movement. . . ."[164] This point warrants repeating:

> One must *live* experience. It is not easily accessible and, viewed from the outside by intelligence, it would even be necessary to see in it a sum of distinct operations. . . . It is only from within, lived to the point of terror, that it appears to unify that which discursive thought must separate. . . .
>
> It is the separation of terror from the realms of knowledge, of feeling, of moral life, which obliges one to *construct* values uniting *on the outside* the elements of these realms in the forms of authoritative entities, when it was necessary not to look far; on the contrary, to re-enter oneself in order to find there what was missing. . . . 'Oneself' is not the subject isolating itself from the world, but a place of communication, of fusion of the subject and the object [a fusion leaving outside only the discourse by which one tried to separate these objects].[165]

Herein lies the real efficacy of Bataille's writing, the creation of a space into which subject and object, writer and reader, are drawn so as to fuse or "slide" together, to "communicate." He attempts to create this erotic space by transgressing the subject of knowledge, or more precisely, by transgressing the borderlines that keep experience on one side and knowledge on the other, a breakdown of borders which will lead to the eroticization of knowledge, or self-consciousness through eroticism.

The transgression involved in his writing is therefore a transgression of the discursive law that keeps the subject and object, word and reality named, apart. Or more precisely, since I noted above that the word subsumes the thing, the transgression is of the discursive distance between the word-as-thing-known and the thing-as-affective-experience. This is why one cannot know the unknown, or God, by saying "the unknown" or "God." One can only "know" them through their effects. "All that I can know of the unknown is that I pass from the known to the unknown."[166] In this margin of passage discourse is abandoned. But if poetry as well has abandoned or led discourse to ruin, why is it impoverished? Bataille's response: it does not accede to "the inner ruin which is access to the unknown,"[167] for inner ruin (sovereignty) maintains nothing of the ruins, casts them into the void.

The writing which delineates a space of communication between subject and object, which searches for the innermost wound, one that is approached in the ambiguous light of terror (anguish) and desire, is erotic writing. It is a writing that intends to catch one in its movement, in which anyone whose "attention is given entirely to the world of objects by way of words,"[168] is—as in ecstatic, mystical vision—absorbed to the outside, lacking the words and "missing a God" to catch one's fall. Indeed, "eroticism is the substitution of the instant or of the unknown for what we have believed ourselves to know,"[169] the substitution of experience for words. But given its manifestation in words, is this substitution any less of a ruse than poetry, which could only evoke the unknown? "Poetry is not a knowledge of oneself, and even less the experience of a remote possible . . . but rather the simple evocation in words of inaccessible possibilities."[170] Or finally, "[P]oetry was simply a detour: through it I escaped the world of discourse. . . ."[171] But to understand why it was only a detour—on the way to eroticism—one must realize the following: "Poetry reveals a power of the unknown. But the unknown is only an insignificant void if it is not the object of a desire."[172] A desire for what? To communicate, to lose oneself in the unknown—a desire not for "God," but for GOD.

Ironically perhaps, it is a poem that indicates the move from "the hatred of poetry" to the "impossible," from the maintenance of ruins to the risk of being ruined. This poem is significantly entitled *The Book (Le Livre):*

I drink from your slit
and I spread your naked legs
I open them like a book
where I read what kills me.[173]

The closed book, the Hegelian mausoleum, is opened, its pages spread apart
to reveal the crack in the system. But more important to realize is the play
between knowledge and eroticism. The book, the locus of knowledge, is eroticized. Knowledge is eroticized and erotic knowledge can be deadly. The
déchirure is indeed absolute—if, that is, one can move beyond the sacrificial
economy of poetry. For the profound meaning of poetry, as we have heard, is
that it is a "sacrifice in which words are victims," a sacrifice that brings profane discourse and its knowledge of objects into contact with the unknown
and dangerous "sacred." The poetic image that results however, even if it ruptures the bond between life and profane knowledge through its sojourn into
the unknown, still yields its results for self-consciousness, both protecting it
from sinking into the abyss of unmediated emotion, and yielding an obscure
possession and control of that which threatens one with utter ruin. Yet if this
is the efficacy of poetry, if poetry can do this for us, there should be no reason
to condemn it as Bataille apparently does.

Yet his condemnation, viewed correctly, is only partial: the limited nature
of his condemnation is betrayed, on a basic level, by the fact that Bataille himself avidly wrote poetry. What his condemnation really addresses, however, is
the notion that poetry and its exercise, while destroying the unambiguous, discursive quality of words, nevertheless leaves the individual—reader or
writer—intact: "[C]ertain that the sacrifice of objects [or words, C.G.] is powerless to truly liberate us, we often experience the necessity for going further,
right to the sacrifice of the subject."[174] He wants the sacrifice of object and
words to slip toward inner ruin, "the author put to death by his own work."[175]
There is, however, another way to express this death, one that has a very positive sense in Bataille's vernacular and which is announced in a term that plays
upon the efficacy of language—"Communication."

In a word, Communication is the grail that Bataille's writing pursues
through the labyrinth of words.[176] He states this in no uncertain terms: "literature is communication"; "poetry is communication or nothing."[177] Communication is for Bataille one of the essential ways to assert the structure of Being
in that it denies the integrity of discontinuous existence, denies individuality
itself by leaving the being in play "naked" or "wounded" rather than closed in
upon itself. Writing as Communication therefore fundamentally differs from
communication understood as a well-defined message sent from one intact
being to another, communication that preserves the individual agents in a
state of isolation. "Communication, in my sense of the word, is never stronger

than when communication, in the weak sense, the sense of profane language . . . fails and becomes the equivalent of darkness,"[178] for, as he states elsewhere, "contrary to what is admitted, language is not communication but its negation. . . ."[179] The "profane" notion of language signifies a discourse of control, of "minor" sovereignty which is, more precisely, that sovereignty we previously equated with servility. Communication, on the other hand, is that which puts the subject and object, as well as the discourse binding them, at risk. But in putting at risk their isolated, individual nature, it reveals an intimacy between beings—it reveals, as I suggested above, the Being of beings.

Nevertheless, writing is a form of production, is one of the ways to produce an objective realm in which the subject manifests and stabilizes itself. What Bataille aims at, however, is a strange, poetic production oriented toward loss and incompletion—toward expenditure.[180] Bataille, failing to complete many of his texts, produced incompletion. His production of incompletion bears witness to the "principle of insufficiency" we encountered earlier. The insufficiency of isolated existence in turn bears witness to the following: "I am sure about one thing: humanity is not composed of isolated beings but of communication between them. Never are we revealed, even to ourselves, other than in a network of communication with others. . . ."[181] At the *instant it occurs*, there is "no difference" between this Communication and sovereignty, and sovereignty, as we know, involves the power to transcend the laws that prescribe the maintenance of life, involves a risk of self in a chance moment when limits become blurred. To the extent that sovereign writing is Communication, the writer places oneself on the level of those sovereign moments in which he or she, as well as the reader-object, is lost, one's individual existence in language put at risk by the very excess to which it is in relation—a sacrifice.

Writing, like sacrifice, is the way to found a community among beings, to end their isolation in this profane world of personal concerns by revealing the human province as bound to something we cannot master. Something that, insofar as one holds to *discursive* self-consciousness, is discarded to the junkheap of nothingness. Sharing the basic impulse of the great modern poets, and in a gesture that—surprising as it may be given the standard image of Bataille—he calls "friendship," Bataille wants to expand self-consciousness to include its dark companions: perhaps then one may "arrive at the *self-consciousness* I speak of, because reason, being consciousness, is fully conscious only if it has for an object that which is not reducible to it."[182] He writes lest we forget what we must forget in order to live.

Given these basic elements that define Communication, coupled with the notion that Bataille intends his writing itself to be Communication, we shall be in a better position to comprehend the essence of his mystical-erotic texts. Indeed, writing as Communication defines writing as erotic. It is ultimately his erotic texts, or better, the sacrificial imperative of literature itself, that reveals Bataille's motives. For sacrifice, like writing, plays on the limits between law and transgression, individual life and self-loss: "I do not dispute knowledge [and consciousness], without which I would not be writing, but this hand that writes *is dying*, and through this death in store it evades the limits accepted in writing (accepted by the writing hand but refused by the hand that dies)."[183] The limits accepted by the writing hand are the limits of individual life and the discursive language which founds and envelops it. If one is to Communicate, to reveal the intimacy among beings and their intimacy with that which exceeds them, one must leave oneself naked, open to laceration, to the risk of death.

Writing, in this way, is the kindred spirit of eroticism, and of sacrifice. All of these practices aim at Communication through putting into play the very subject who enters the game. The game of Communication, however, is the game with death, with "a suppression so perfect that at the pinnacle utter silence is its truth. Words can't describe it. . . ."[184] Yet the question of Bataille's language, if it can say anything, is not saying the unsayable. It is rather the evocation of silence through the relation of words to a moment of mystical, erotic, or sacrificial Communication. How this relation may occur is now the question.

FOUR

Mysticism, Eroticism, and the Sacrificial Ruse

It may well be a desire to die, but it is at the same time a desire to live at the limits of the possible and the impossible with ever-increasing intensity. It is the desire to live while ceasing to live, or to die without ceasing to live.

—Bataille, *Eroticism*

Human life resides in an impasse. It maintains itself in the midst of profoundly conflicting desires and contradictory impulses. In innumerable ways we try to escape our finitude, to deny our limits—we dream, gamble, read, desire other lovers—yet we are reluctant to release our hold on our individuality, our own particular future. We want to be everything and be ourselves, to break our barriers yet escape the terminus of death: we simultaneously want to transcend and maintain our limits. That the profoundly religious desire to send oneself reeling toward the beyond of individual existence, to some unknowable continuity where life as we know it is at risk, may adhere in the depths of every human being, does not necessarily entail that each human has the unambiguous desire to die. We simply want to become *other*, for life to burn beyond its daily concerns, and live to tell about it.

The "it" in question, the "it" of the opening quotation, I have intentionally left without definition. For "it" is an ambiguous desire which has never been lacking as long as humankind has had consciousness of its individuality, and consciousness of something beyond this consciousness. And while the "it" cited above is apparently in reference to eroticism, the referent is not so stable, for "it" may be identified as the desire that unites sacrifice with eroticism, and eroticism with mysticism. And while there are certainly differences between these manifestations of the desire to die without dying, to "regain that which our desire to survive forces us to avoid,"[1] their inner unity to some extent renders these differences negligible.

For instance, the mystic, Saint Theresa of Avila, could "die for not dying"; "eroticism," Bataille claims, "is assenting to life even at the point of death";[2] and sacrifice, as we have heard, brings a violent, sacred world into profane life, "reveals to the living the invasion of death."[3] Their unity is a convulsion of life, a *violation* of the individual participant's being as self-possessed, discontinuous being, a dissolution of stable individuality in the face of something overwhelming. And it is in such a convulsion—an "absolute dismemberment" as we heard from Hegel, the "absolute liquefaction of everything stable" as Kojève has described it—that we "receive being in an intolerable transcendence of being, no less intolerable than death. But since, in death, being is simultaneously given and taken away, we must seek it in *the feeling of death*, in those unbearable moments where we seem to be dying . . . *where horror and joy coincide*."[4] This feeling, in Bataille's view, is the experience of the sacred, of God—God as the final negation of every *possible* object.

Now, the seductiveness of Bataille's writings resides in just this sort of amalgamation of heterodox realms which are generally considered radical or "other" from the perspective of sober thought. Who with a taste for the unusual can resist the allure of a thinker that unites self-consciousness with sacrifice and eroticism with atheistic mysticism? Yet if we are to avoid falling into a naïve and idle attitude that bathes in Bataille's dark sunlight we must affirm these various realms for what they are, and not for their face value; we must expose their differences as well as their unity; we must address them not to immobilize them, but to show where they are leading us. We must try to identify what, if anything, it is at stake. And we must identify Bataille's method of ceaselessly trying to raise those stakes, to put more and more on the line, into play, at risk.

The major terms in play—mysticism, eroticism, sacrifice—as I have suggested, have a unified orientation, which is best defined as follows: they are "limit experiences" which Bataille calls upon in an attempt to affirm unemployed negativity.[5] We have arrived back at the point from which we started, the problem posed by Hegel. Now when Hegel, with his "unheard-of audacity,"[6] asserted that he had reached the admittedly devastating position of perfect self-consciousness, "*wanting* nothing, *desiring* nothing . . . *satisfied* by what he is,"[7] he perhaps made the mistake of the subject who supposed himself to know. But because of the perfect internal consistency of his system itself, he as well dug a trench around those who, arriving after the limit was reached, had to face what to do with desire and negativity. And this, as Blanchot argues, is still the problem:

> At present, the problem brought forth by the limit-experience is the following: how can the absolute (in the form of totality) still be gone beyond? Having arrived at the summit by his actions, how can man—universal, eternal,

always accomplishing himself, always . . . repeating himself in a Discourse that does no more than endlessly repeat itself—not hold to this sufficiency, and go on to put himself, as such, in question? Properly speaking, he cannot.[8]

He cannot, that is, without reassessing the notions of desire or negativity itself, such that they no longer aim at the reconstitution of self-presence arriving after the experience of the "manifestation" of death. Without, that is, a thoroughly catastrophic vision of a death that nothing would follow, yet without being the dissolution of physically dying, without reaching the final equilibrium.

Now, such a notion is dubious at best, and nothing short of untenable if taken strictly in these terms, yet it is to this demand that Bataille's notion of sacrifice and its more directly lived companions, mysticism and eroticism, respond. If, that is, we take the "radical" approach to Bataille, which—I would suggest—is not specifically the road Bataille takes. For if he wants to affirm the principle that "desire demands the greatest possible loss,"[9] which would be the annihilation of the desiring subject, in order to affirm it the subject must be *conscious* of that loss. It must maintain itself at the border, even if it is no longer concerned for maintaining itself, even if the consciousness of itself-as-individual has lost its appeal. His approach, which is most readily ascertainable with respect to sacrifice, is actually . . . much more *Christian,* though with a decidedly pagan twist, an atheistic core, and a rejection of its morality. How then is this Christian? The answer lies in the need for *representation,* a *spectacle,* a *fiction:* the "knowledge of death," and thus self-consciousness, "cannot do without a subterfuge—the spectacle."[10] Christ's spectacular death on the cross—the moment that fulfills for Christianity what Bataille believes is the essence of every religion, "the search for lost intimacy"[11]—was not only the most significant myth for Hegel, it was profoundly influential for Bataille, though with a decisive difference.

The difference, in short, relies upon the drama of transgression enacted on the cross receiving an improbable atheistic, rather than a theistic, interpretation. Such an interpretation will in turn alter the type of dialectic involved, which is not to say, however, that Bataille's atheistic version will eliminate the notion of divinity, nor, strangely enough, even that of God. Rather, he will attempt to reconfigure, according to a negative, a-theological schema, the experience of a finite being confronting the "manifestation" of divinity, which in turn will bear upon the way one experiences one's own finitude. Now, without entering into a full-scale theological debate, we must nevertheless delineate the positions of atheism and theism, which may be clarified in light of the different responses to one's finitude, to the irreducible fact that one will eventually "be other" to one's existence in the world.[12] That is to say, due to human finitude, one is given to oneself in relation to one's being outside the world, in relation to death, the passage to the beyond of being. This "being other" to one's worldly existence is, in short, the passage to God—the "other" than worldly being.

Now a theist carries two beliefs along with one's finitude: the first is the belief in the immortality of the soul, the second is the belief that the "other" is Something (Being, *noumena*) rather than Nothing. The passage through death to God is thus not simply becoming-other to finite worldly life, it is a passage to oneself-as-*something*-other in God. The process of becoming-other in death is thus a homogeneous transition from life to death, wherein one finds oneself *as oneself* in God, in and with the other, and the mortal terror of death is effectively suppressed.[13] In effect, the dialectic of Christ's death on the cross symbolizes to the theist the reduction of the transcendence, the being-other of God, insofar as Christ's passage to the "other than being" is commensurable or reconcilable with God's transcendent otherness. Through the incarnation and crucifixion is revealed an ontological commensurability between the finite and infinite, human and divine. Christ's death thus both mediates and attenuates the horror of becoming-other, that is, dying, for it represents a bridge thrown over the ontological abyss between finitude and eternity, which effectively cancels and lifts the mortality it manifests. The finite spirit is essentially vaporized and absorbed into the infinite, in one sense losing life, yet in another risking nothing with respect to the principle of life, for the individual spirit maintains its individual life infinitely in the universal, in God.

The atheist, on the other hand, who asserts that all one's relations are finite relations to beings within the world—yet for whom the "beyond" of finite existence is as well posited in the inevitability that life will eventually "be other" than life—definitively rejects the idea that Something is to be found beyond death. Rather, the transition of death is viewed as the change into nothing, one's becoming-other to worldly existence which is not becoming one's *own* other, but rather becoming totally other. Death is thus a terrifying experience for the atheist, for one is either unable or unwilling to posit the continuation of one's own life beyond death. The death manifest on the cross is thus viewed solely as the violation of a worldly being incarnate, affirming that there is nothing subtending the being put to death on the cross, that there is simply the being and his unknowable beyond. This is not to say, however, that the manifestation of death affirms absolutely nothing, for the finite being put to death not only affirms his finitude, but as well reveals the finite, in the experience of its limits, as sacred.

If Bataille then evokes the paradigm of Christian sacrifice, it is primarily for the indissociability of this sacrifice with the notion of the divine, the sacred "other." Yet because the God he conceives is truly, infinitely "other," in effect *any* victim will suffice as an opening to the divine, for any victim can bring us face to face with the totally other, and no victim has privileged access to reconciliation with God. As Bataille conceives it then, the search for God, like the erotic search for satisfaction, is both promiscuous and dependent upon chance. Every object of desire is potentially an opening to the beyond of being(s)—to God—yet none provide the satisfaction of falling together with Being. For this to be otherwise would require the affirmation of a God whose transcendence is already assumed to be commensurate with, and attainable by, a finite being passing beyond its finite limits. It would require, in other words, the positing of God as an extension of self, a God in relation to which the subject may enter a dialectic of self-mediation, just as it does with any other profane, clear-and-distinct object.

Thus, while Bataille follows the traditional dialectic of sacrifice wherein a finite being is negated in order to be restored to divinity, at the same time the synthetic moment of reconciliation is emptied of its content, and consequently brings no reassurance to the spectator. Or more accurately stated, God as the being-other confronted through the consciousness of death is *in excess* of any notion of transcendence commensurate with a *self*-that-dies, is in excess of any notion of a transcendent Some-thing conceived in the light of finite understanding. Furthermore, by focusing on the all-too-human element of laceration in sacrifice—the wounds inflicted on the body rather than the transition of this body into spirit—Bataille affirms that beings communicate with their beyond through wounds alone, that they communicate with one another through the ruptures inflicted upon individual integrity. This is the path to (divine) intimacy, the annulment of the type of transcendence conceived as the separation between merely opposed—and thus reconcilable—individual/things, and the expansion of transcendence into a mutual absence where God is experienced.

The reinstatement of the Christian theme of representation is thus used as a means not only to challenge the "weak" notion of transcendence that posits God as a separate thing commensurate with the knowledge of finite things, and which is thereby reassuring to the finite self; but also to challenge the manner in which Hegel posits the successful overcoming of Unhappy Consciousness or the separation of divine essence from human consciousness, namely, by rejecting the God of abstraction placed in the "beyond," and positing a God whose real conscious existence (and not just its imagined "shape") is the actual self-consciousness of the human being, and whose real essence is finally revealed as actually present in the conceptual (i.e., nonrepresentational) thought of that being.[14] To reiterate, in order to overcome abstraction, Hegel's Spirit creates its own representations—the most essential being the religious representations which depict the content of the absolute, though in an inadequate form—and the path to absolute knowing is the long process of overcoming all representation to reach the pure presence of Spirit in thought. When Bataille evokes the penultimate Christian representation however, it will be to show how the sacrificial-erotic structure of desire opens, through representation, upon a more excessive notion of God, one incommensurable with thought.[15] Consequently, the sacrificial-erotic "object" toward which desire aims will reveal itself for what it is—an indeterminate totality disguised by its determinate form—and the unrestricted nature of desire as pure ecstasis as well reveals itself as it purely is—for there is nothing that arrives to stop it.

What Bataille does, in fact, is to associate carnal lovemaking with divine love, less the notion of divine perfection or feminine purity, which would restrain His/her violation—God becomes a whore, and the whore a path to divinity:

> My desire today is focused on a point. This object without objective truth is the most awesome I can imagine—and I compare it . . . to the transparency of the beloved. No embrace can attain this transparency (it's specifically what flees at the instant of possession). It's lacerated by a desire that I've seen beyond any desirable presence. . . . This is the object I recognized, that I awaited so long . . . the beloved is someone expected. . . . Still, the woman I hold my arms eludes me . . . only absence, *through feelings of lack,* continues to attain this object.[16]

A distinct conflict is thus implied here with the Hegelian-Christian notion of a sensuous representation *(Vorstellung)* and its beyond, one that will deserve greater attention as we continue. As our analysis will show, following the movement whereby an artistic or religious representation must shed its veils of opacity and hand its content over to the speculative concept, Hegel posits that the beyond of representation is actually a release from its form which enables the content to be preserved in the *presence* of the knowing spirit—a union of content and mind which Hegel will name as "mystical." It is, let us reiterate, not the case that Hegel rejects representation altogether, for in a way it is the very life of Spirit. Rather, he sees in it a potential source of opacity, an objective misrepresentation of the absolute. Such is the case, for example, with the Catholic sacrament of the Eucharist, where it is believed that Christ is actually present in the material reality itself, a notion Hegel (rightfully) finds to be "fetishistic."[17] That is, he finds that such an approach fixes the infinite in an outward form that cannot be fully appropriated, and posits that the sensuous should rather be a sign pointing beyond itself to its spiritual transparency. This type of transparency is not what Bataille has in mind. And while it may be difficult to specify just what "transparency" signifies for Bataille, it is not the *noetic* transparency or presence of the beyond-of-representation to the knowing mind which we find in Hegel. Rather, Bataille will attempt to undermine the implicit spiritual guarantees of representation by substituting an erotic encounter for God. For both Hegel and Bataille, then, though with different emphases, a sensuous representation is not merely a limit, but is rather an opening to the divine.

In Bataille's view, the object of desire, God or its human derivative, exceeds its representation, which is but a lure perched above a nothingness that puts the object and the desiring subject—its knowledge, its language, its identity—at risk. Extending like some symbolic iceberg into dark depths, which one assumes must be present, yet which one can never encounter without going under, sinking, the depths of God finally remain—not unknown—but unknowable. Yet as indicated above, the path Bataille takes to this impossible encounter with the unknowable is specifically the path of self-conscious knowledge as defined by Hegel, and as practiced by religions. Bataille's path retains its link with representation on the way to an abysmal truth, the search for an intimacy that is always lost, the impossible "rediscovery" of which would be the summit of self-consciousness. The problem, however, is that the consciousness of intimacy—self-consciousness—is no longer intimacy. And a successful fusion of subject and object, a complete "mystical" union of being, would dissolve the self-consciousness that was the condition for the search. Self-consciousness resides in an impasse.

The problem, which leads to a series of contradictions of which Bataille was fully aware, is the fact that the "original" intimacy for which humankind has always searched, *never was*, that discursive consciousness is indeed the *condition of* intimacy: "[W]ould the summit be approachable if discourse did not point the way?"[18] That is, intimacy would never have been considered as intimacy except from the perspective of a singular, discontinuous being conscious of itself as discontinuous and having a vague feeling of having lost something. Like the paradox of longing for childhood innocence, which is irretrievable once one knows one is no longer innocent, yet where this knowledge is the condition of the longing, as soon as one consciously tries to find what was lost—intimacy, sovereignty—all one achieves is its burial, its irrevocable loss. Nevertheless,

> man is always in pursuit of an authentic sovereignty. That sovereignty, apparently, was in certain sense originally his, but without any doubt that could not have been in a *conscious* manner, and so in a sense it was not his, it escaped him. We shall see that in a number of ways he continued to pursue what forever eluded him . . .[19]

Self-consciousness is incomplete should it not take account of intimacy. However, the intimacy for which consciousness searches is compatible neither with the functioning, the temporal orientation, nor the language of clear consciousness: "[I]ntimacy cannot be expressed discursively."[20] Again, clear consciousness even occasions the loss of what it seeks to recover, for it is founded on *respect:* for the prohibition, for individual propriety, for the God of transcendence, for *life*. Intimacy can only be approached through transgression, despite ourselves.

Yet why, we must ask, would the "knowledge" of intimacy gained through transgression, through death and erotic desire, be any different than the philosophical desire for, and path to, absolute knowledge, complete self-consciousness? For as we have already heard from *The Philosophy of Religion*, the *Phenomenology*, and even the *Logic*, the final waystation on the path to knowledge always serves up death, downfall, and the deepest sorrow. Furthermore, "Hegel's desire," as Bataille suggests, "resolves itself in a knowledge which is absolute, which is a suppression of the subject . . . who knows,"[21] a suppression that sounds remarkably like the intimate, erotic moment of "fusion" which Bataille frequently evokes. And indeed, what emerges as one of the dominant motifs in his erotic novels, a phrase we hear again and again, is the desire TO KNOW: "How lovely it is, how dirty it is to know. Yet I wanted it, I wanted at all costs TO KNOW! . . . The lowest whores certainly don't behave any more obscenely than we do, but they aren't lucky enough TO KNOW IT."[22] In *Story of the Eye*, Bataille establishes a metaphorical and linguistic equivalence between the ocular and the genital, elaborating an erotic discourse that transgresses the function of the eye—knowledge. The eye transgressed and sexualized, knowledge is eroticized—one *knows* through transgression.

This is indeed a sticky web that he has woven, and is the most elusive aspect of his work. The way he approaches non-knowledge is always threatening to turn into another form of knowledge. His solution, however, is not to terminate the subject in either knowledge or non-knowledge, but rather to assert that "knowledge is access to the unknown,"[23] to an unknown that, should it become known, again would open upon the unknown. The process is interminable, the naked truth loves to hide:

> Non-knowledge is a process of stripping bare. This proposition is a summit, but has to be understood in this way: stripped bare, therefore I *see* what knowledge kept hidden till this point. But if I see, I *know*. Indeed, I know, but what I have known is again stripped bare by non-knowledge. If nonsense is sense, the sense that is nonsense is lost and becomes nonsense again (without any end to the process).[24]

Sartre's conclusion: "Mr. Bataille has escaped." That is, "if he reifies non-knowing, it is with a certain wariness: in the manner of a movement, not a thing. And despite all, he pulls the trick off: the nonknowing that previously had not been *anything* is always becoming the beyond of knowing."[25] The beyond of knowing is beyond Being as we know it, beyond our language of knowledge, beyond our self-conscious knowledge.

Yet the issue is still one of self-consciousness, and self-consciousness always requires an object commensurate with itself, in which it can find itself. For at the basis of human life is the principle of insufficiency: "[T]he mind awakening to inner life is . . . in search of an object . . . cannot do without an object: its existence cannot close in on itself."[26] The need for an object is the need answering the necessity to take leave of oneself, to "Communicate" with the beyond of individual being. This object, to be precise, is God. What we must always keep in mind when reading Bataille however, is that even at the height of self-consciousness, there is still incompletion, dissatisfaction. "Incomplete" is the first and final term, Bataille's *alpha* and *omega:* "[T]o be disappointed is life's bottom line, it's core truth,"[27] and the attractions of completion—God or a woman loved, knowledge or death—come from its inaccessibility. We neither fall together with continuity, attain a unity of being, through dissolution, nor in perfect consciousness. We exist on the border between continuity and consciousness. If life is to retain its intensity, we can neither renounce the desire for the former, nor abandon the latter.

Mysticism, sacrifice, eroticism—these are the ways Bataille identifies to unsettle life as we know it with the consciousness of intimacy. If they rely on representation, Bataille will attempt to pass them *through* the mirror; if they rely on language, Bataille attempts to reduce the meaning of coherent discourse to incoherent stammering and fertile silences. In effect he will use the paths of self-conscious knowledge in an attempt to achieve *conscious non-knowledge*, relating desire and consciousness, language and knowledge, to that which withdraws from all relation. His writing almost uniformly addresses the problem that the image of happiness, of satisfaction, chased by desire through the labyrinth of words, can by necessity never be grasped by words. His writing takes the form of a mystical, erotic, "inner" experience—the pursuit of an unrealizable object of desire, a vain search for a satisfaction one could both realize and survive intact.

Our first task is to examine the efficacy of, and limits to, Bataille's evocation of mysticism. At stake in mysticism is the status of God, and consequently that which God guarantees: the coherence of language and knowledge; the position of the knowing subject and object known. To orient our discussion we will focus primarily on the mysticism of Meister Eckhart, the appropriation of Eckhart's thought by Hegel, and its relevance for a very different appropriation by Bataille. It will then be our task to show how Bataille's fiction, particularly *Madame Edwarda*, roughly charts a mystical path to an obscure lucidity—"[U]tmost lucidity . . . happens when lucidity fails: the night has to fall before knowledge is possible."[28] In Bataille's view, if self-conscious knowledge is to attain the extreme limits and encompass "the totality of that which is," it must include the night from which it proceeds, which implies a necessity for knowledge—the movement from the unknown to the known—to "inverse itself at the summit and go back to the unknown." Absolute knowledge, the summit of intelligibility and clarity, eventually returns to the night.

4.1 I Pray to God . . .

Bataille roughly equates inner experience with mystical experience but hesitates to fully commit himself to mysticism.[29] His hesitation is due not to the experience itself, but rather to his very questionable view that mystics enter and ultimately draw from their experience a reassurance given in advance. "A 'mystic' sees what he wants . . ." as Bataille claims, "and in the same way, he discovers—what he knew."[30] The mystic has a presentiment of what experience will disclose because this experience occurs within a known, theological horizon, and "he who already knows cannot go beyond a known horizon."[31] This view as well is not only questionable, but—even according to his own principles—is effectively wrong. We thus must guard against taking Bataille's understanding and critique of mysticism in too strict a sense, and rather see it as informed by his own principles. To identify his perspective, we need to draw a line between mystic experience on the one hand, and on the other, that which it reveals.

For I believe that it is in fact on the issue of revelation, and in particular Hegel's interpretation of mystical experience—most notably that of Eckhart—that the lines of distinction between Bataille's view of mysticism, and the Hegelian interpretation which Bataille associates with theistic mysticism, can be drawn. The fulcrum on which the issue rests is the nature of the divine itself, its mode of manifestation, how this manifestation is interpreted, and the effect that the experience of the divine has on our language. To state the matter succinctly: Hegel's view is that the divine (the absolute) is positively revealed and conceptually known, which both enables our discourse to articulate the truth and requires that our discourse be an adequate manifestation of the divine. Bataille, contesting the movement of revelation from sensuousness to conceptualization, thereby calls our knowing discourse into question.

His critique then, grounded on the view that the ecstatic abandon of mystical visions retains an aim, is that "classic" mysticism is ultimately a work in progress in order to arrive at a state of possession of and by God (mystical union), even if this most valuable of objects possessed is called "Nothing."[32] Contrasted with this is Bataille's own idea of mystical or "inner" experience, which he wants "to lead where it would, not to lead it to some point given in advance."[33] He wants experience to be fully in the hands of chance, for "non-knowledge to be its principle," without a goal, without the evasion known as salvation, in effect to be its own authority—but one that expiates itself, that founds nothing, gives no assurance, puts everything in question.[34] He thus seeks to remove the hidden yet undeniable presence of some essence in the Nothing—which is not to say, and we must be careful here, that the experience is of nothing at all—but that it is nothing which is revealed.

To this extent even the negative theologians at times are not immune from occasional criticism. For while he praises the experience of mystics— "their life is *aflame* and they *consume* it," their experience enacts the "complete destruction of the world of common reality"[35]—and while mystics know that to speak of God is a negation of his negative essence—"without form or mode"—that leads toward God's positive assimilation in the finite world, Bataille nevertheless believes that their experience is oriented toward an end. Eckhart says that "God is nameless. . . . If I say God is a being, it is not true: he is a transcendental essence, a *superessential* nothing."[36] He could therefore be seen as reserving, beyond all positive predication and distinction, the touchstone of meaning. His radical negativity may ultimately be a moment of positive theology. To prevent the possibility that the negative of negative theology would be positive enough to give some assurance to experience, to try to assert the essential which he does in fact attribute to mystic experience, Bataille proposes a mysticism "beyond classical mysticism," an "a-theology,"[37] founded on an "experience . . . [that] is not merely negative within certain limits: it is totally negative."[38] The *effect* (or *affect*) of extreme, "totally" negative experience, the effect of unknowing, is none other than God. And should our language (signifiers) be related to such a horizon, it would inevitably slide toward the loss of meaning *(sens)*, having no aim, no signified, at which to stop.

In *"Hegel, la mort et le sacrifice"* (see n.37) Bataille quotes Kojève: "[T]he mystic flees the idea of death and speaks of Nothingness itself as something which *is*" (author's emphasis). Bataille believes, however, that Kojève has made a mistake in "not envisaging, beyond classical mysticism, a 'conscious mysticism,'" or an a-theistic mysticism. He states:

> The atheistic mystic, *conscious of himself,* conscious of having to die and disappear, would live, as Hegel says—*evidently about himself*—'in absolute rending' *[déchirement absolu]*; but for Hegel, it was only a question of a phase: as opposed to Hegel the atheistic mystic would never emerge from it, 'contemplating the Negative quite directly', but never able to transpose it into Being, refusing to do so and maintaining himself in ambiguity. (author's emphasis)

We may see then how Bataille's "mystical" experience challenges two related traditions. It contests traditional theology—and its mystic counterparts—by removing the transcendent "beyond." And it contests Hegelianism, which locates the "beyond" within the sphere of discourse, the "magical power" that adds determination and differentiation to Being/Nothing, and thereby "converts it into Being," into knowledge.[39]

The two traditions in question, each in its own way, rely on a particular Christian notion of revelation, one in which sensuous externality withdraws into spiritual appropriation where its eternity is confirmed. Speaking of Hegel, Bataille states, "[O]ne believed in the answers of reason without seeing that they only hold water by according themselves a divine-like authority, by mimicking revelation. . . . What one couldn't know: that only revelation permits man to be everything, something which reason is not."[40] In his own view, "at the extreme limit of knowledge, what is forever missing is what revelation alone provided: an arbitrary answer. . . . Without this answer, man is dispossessed of the means for being everything, he is a bewildered madman, a question without a way out."[41] Discourse, which leads to absolute knowledge—"the extreme limit"—relies on a term of closure to assure the coherence of meaning. Lacking the word that gathers all the others together, "even if the coherence of discourse was absolute," the meaning of that discourse would come undone.[42] The inviolable coherence of discourse is perhaps most striking in Hegel's *Logic*, where the categories are in fact predicates of the divine, and whose internal relation constitutes a categorical genesis of the divine from which no deviation is possible. Should the matrix wherein Being leads to Essence and Essence to the Concept, or the movement from Essence to Appearance to Actuality be altered in any way, Hegel's *logica divina* would break down, and the intelligibility of the divine along with it. Our question, however, is whether the final term which seals this movement is available to discourse?

This is where we must situate our discussion, namely at the level of the very condition of possibility for Hegel's claim to the absoluteness of discourse, to the completion of knowledge, and Bataille's challenge to these claims. The fundamental issue around which his challenge occurs is the following: does the claim of knowledge to absoluteness, one that necessitates a final term of closure (God), ultimately rest upon an inappropriate discursive assimilation of nondiscursive and unknowable experience; or is the final term of such a nature that God can be fully comprehended, known and articulated in the thought and discourse of a finite being? Simply stated, is the experience of God one of knowledge or non-knowledge? One should have no doubt from the outset— Bataille's position is the latter. I will elaborate this position first through a brief summary of his critique of Descartes, and then through a more rigorous analysis of Hegelian discourse as an ontotheological narrative, focusing on the interpretation of the term *mystical*. We shall then be able to address what Bataille calls the "new theology (which has only the unknown as object)," in which "knowledge is access to the unknown. Nonsense is the outcome of every possible sense."[43]

Bataille provides no thorough analysis of Descartes, and when he brings Descartes into his sights it is essentially to emphasize one point: the questionable evidence of the intuition that founds discursive knowledge. Bataille interprets this as questionable insofar as Descartes is presented as transcribing a circle in which a finite project of scientific investigation is required to demonstrate the certainty of an infinite knowledge which that project presupposes in the first place. Thus, there is both an immediate intuition of God's existence, and at the same time this intuition is an extrapolation from a demonstration of its finite epistemological effects. What Bataille is aiming to show is that the indefinite experience of finitude may draw solace from the intuition of an "intellectual nature considered without limitation," but it is illegitimate to extend this unlimited intellect into the finite practice of science which, once set in motion, is no longer in need of the original intuition, but rather anchors all being in itself and effectively becomes unlimited in its autonomy.

The movement Bataille identifies in Descartes is that the *cogito* (finite, discursive knowledge) serves as a model for infinite knowledge. He points out, however, that the transcendental ego and its project of determining being—while desiring to be so—is not the experience of infinite knowledge, which can only belong to the infinite. He expresses this problematic by emphasizing that even if Descartes posits an unlimited extension of the intellect to the knowledge *of* God, this cannot be equivalent to the knowledge God has of himself. Bataille's text emphasizes this point quite clearly. At issue again is the possibility of infinite knowledge, and as Bataille states, "in God, *true knowledge can only have as object God himself.* Now this object, whatever the accessibility which Descartes imagined it to have, remains unintelligible to us."[44] He thus implicitly points to an ontological difference between God's knowledge of Himself and our understanding, concluding that "divine nature . . . escapes man's understanding."[45] In a sense, then, Bataille is repeating the criticism of Descartes as found in Pascal, who derided the reduction of the enigma of God to the God of philosophical rationality; who rejected the philosophical replacement of passion with the certainty of the intellect. In short, Bataille joins the critique of the hubris of the intellect and its claim to comprehend what is other to reason. Descartes's flaw, as Bataille sees it, is therefore the introduction of

a confusion by means of which thought slips soundlessly from the discursive level to the non-discursive. God no doubt can know himself but not according to the discursive mode of thought which is ours. The 'intellectual nature without limitation' finds here its final limitation. I can . . . represent to myself . . . the limitless extension of my power of understanding, but cannot pass from there to the knowledge which God must have of himself. . . . Even 'without limitation', understanding cannot go beyond at least the (discursive) mode without which it would not be what it is.[46]

As indicated above, Bataille wants to show that an inadmissible assimilation of the nondiscursive (God) into the discursive has occurred. And if it is inadmissible, then God is ultimately unintelligible for discursive thought, is non-knowledge. Is this, however, something Descartes would deny? May it not be the case that Bataille is in fact criticizing Descartes for implying what Bataille himself wants to affirm? Indeed, even Aquinas, who looks to the effects in the world-below in order to proceed to the existence of its proper cause (God) which necessarily preexists the effect, claims that "man reaches the peak of his knowledge of God when he realizes that he does not know Him, understanding that the divine reality surpasses all human conceptions of it."[47] Bataille nevertheless sticks to his guns, believing that if our miserable imperfection, our unhappy consciousness, necessitates the postulation of God—or the more universal substitution of empirico-epistemological project for God—this is none other than to "succumb by a rather vain flight to submit the unknowable to the necessity of being known."[48] It is an evasion of God.

As he sees it, an unquenchable thirst for knowledge—which belongs not only to Descartes and Hegel, but as well to Bataille—drives us not only to pass from finite knowledge to infinite knowledge, but from there "as if through an extension of limits, to a different, non-discursive mode of knowledge."[49] Herein lies the fundamental impasse, in that the latter condition is not knowledge in the proper sense, but rather the night of non-knowledge. For in Bataille's view, total knowledge—whether Hegelian/dialectical (the cohesion of every possible thought) or scientific (proceeding from general premises to precise ends)—involves an equivalence with its opposite.[50] Nevertheless, it must be made clear that this "night" is not to be dissociated from the pathways of knowledge, for it is "the passion of knowledge," the erotic insatiability of knowledge, that "alone has the force to lead knowledge to the moment where it dissolves."[51] Perhaps Descartes, with his passion for knowledge, indeed acknowledged a greater knowledge than that of which he could be entirely certain from the discursive perspective, precisely because of the manifest external relation of the divine and the finite, for which he came under fire by Hegel. Perhaps Bataille is in fact *closer* to Descartes and Aquinas than his own project would allow him to recognize, and would do better to look to them in support of his fight against Hegel.

For the criticism Hegel leveled against Descartes and the tradition of Enlightenment rationalism is that they did not enable the infinite to come across the ontological divide with *enough* rigor, so that a gulf persisted between the finite thought developed in project and infinite thought which could only remain immediate and abstract—or unknown.[52] It was therefore a short step from the criticism of Enlightenment thought to Hegel's primary target, Romantic Intuitionism, which Hegel identifies as the theology of the "Unknown God"[53] or negative theology. The central axiom of Intuitionism is that no discursive knowledge of God is possible.[54] I will now try to explain, as briefly as possible, why Hegel thinks this position is not only untenable but a perversion of the truth.

The central point at issue is the undermining of ontological difference and correlatively the ability of discourse (knowledge) to in fact know the infinite, to cognitively know and articulate God. And the issue we must subsequently address is one that is the explicit concern of Heidegger, who cites the "danger" of the Hegelian method in which "everything ontical is dissolved into the ontological (Hegel) . . . ,"[55] which may occur insofar as Hegel lacks a proper investigation into the ground of ontology itself, factically existing *Dasein*. A proper investigation, however, may just reveal the real "danger" that haunts the finite being, which is more precisely the simultaneous impossibility and threat of the dissolution of the finite into the ontological. But for now let us remain with Hegel.

Hegel was a self-professed Christian philosopher, and in his eyes the true nature of the Christian religion—the "revealed" religion which rests upon

God as *Deus Revelatus,* the self-revealing God—is the ability to discursively know and articulate God.[56] And this, in turn is possible because "revealed religion is manifested religion, because in it God has become wholly manifest. Here all is proportionate to the notion; *there is no longer anything secret in God.*"[57] This is not, however, to insinuate that his contemporaries—Jacobi, Schelling, Schleiermacher—were distanced from Christianity. Rather, they adhered to the Kantian restrictions on the limits of knowledge, assigning discursive knowledge to a finite horizon and leaving the infinite to mere conviction based on feeling or intuition, effectively performing—in Hegel's view— a sacrifice of the intellect's ability to disclose the truth of reality.[58] In other words, while they posit *that* God is, they fail to fully designate *what* God is, which is a result of failing to adequately surpass their adherence to a philosophy of *Verstand.*

Hegel is explicit in his criticisms of Intuitionist or Identity-philosophy, as is easily evidenced in both his *Phenomenology* and his *Logic.* In the Preface to PS (§18–25, 10–14), after a rather scathing summary of intuitionist thought, he offers his own view of the necessary development of philosophy, the movement from Substance to Subject. He leaves no question here, however, that the whole that is the True is none other than God, or more precisely, that God is Spirit. That is, God as Spirit is the whole given and constituted by differentiation in and through finite spirit (Subject), which in the course of its development raises itself to the divine (Substance) which is its beginning and end, *alpha* and *omega.* This differentiation—which involves a confrontation with the initially alien other of finite spirit—does seem to imply that God as infinite would have to cross over to the finite which is not one and the same with the infinite.

The real emphasis however is that the divine, like any subject, is not immune from the necessity of development, rupture, or even death, and that the narrative development of finite subjectivity transcribed in the *Phenomenology* is none other than the manifestation/revelation and development of God. Therefore, even when Hegel avails of the possibility that "God is dead"[59] with the death of "the Mediator" (i.e., Christ), this is not to assert God's absence but to reveal that death is a moment of divine becoming which will be appropriated in the fully disclosed and developed presence of Knowing. In short, the narrative development of man-in-the-world is the narrative of God. The ontological framework functions to secure the efficacy of the historical narrative, ensuring the meaning and precluding the opacity of any and every moment of experience, thereby eliminating the possibility that an experience may remain unintelligible. If Reason in the *Phenomenology* is cunning, working out its own aims and drawing every developmental "error" into the orbit of eventual knowledge, then God of the *Logic* is "the capacity of absolute cunning."[60] His cunning assures that human activity accomplishes God's realization of Himself in the world, which in a sense undermines at the same time it affirms the demythologizing process of the Enlightenment by asserting that finite action is nothing more than God's manifestation.

It is therefore an empty assertion to simply say the word *God*, just as it is only in anticipation of the truth to speak of notions such as "Being" or "the One," for they are terms evoking the Absolute in an immediate and abstract manner, as something simple and at rest. Hegel makes the inadequacy of such an articulation explicit when he states:

> When the notion of God is apprehended as that of the abstract and most real being, God is, as it were, relegated to another world beyond: and to speak of knowledge of Him would be meaningless. Where there is no definite quality, knowledge is impossible. *Mere light is mere darkness.*[61]

Or in another well-known formulation—which rejects the notion of God or the Absolute as indefinite and immeasurable—to speak of mere Being is the equivalent of speaking of Nothing. The task of his *Logic* is then to show how the closed, finite totality of logical categories and their unbroken interrelation form an integrated whole equivalent to the absolute that they articulate—or that God is in fact the logical structure of the world. In other words, as Heidegger along with many others have claimed, Hegel's *Logic* is an onto-logic, a *logica divina* with divinity as a final coincidence and closure of conceptual categories, exorcising any nonlogical element such as the unknown God.

The point to which I have been leading this discussion is now at hand. Upon examination one must conclude that Hegel effectively banishes any remnant of negative theology, or anything that falls under the rubric of mysticism. But in a rather curious move, Hegel reads the mystics—notably Meister Eckhart and Jacob Boehme—as articulating a positive theology, as expressing the truth of Christianity—the religion of revelation—which assumes the ability of discourse to name the divine, or more accurately, of the divine to speak itself in self-conscious discourse. This tendency is revealed in Hegel's definition of the mystical *(das Mystische):* "for the mystical is not concealment of a secret, or ignorance, but consists in the self knowing itself to be one with the divine being or that this therefore is revealed."[62] Central to this formulation is Hegel's reliance on the Christian doctrine of the Trinity, a representation that emphasizes differentiation within the divine sphere and enables not only manifestation or emanation but the self-reflexivity of divine self-consciousness in and through the finite.[63] Indeed, Hegel refers to the Trinity as "the mystery of God,"[64] or more appropriately, the mystery of the self-revealing God which, in its revelation, will cease to be a "mystery" at all.

Of interest in Hegel's articulation of the self-revealing God, however, are the sources from which he gains support, of particular concern to us being Meister Eckhart, the father of the language of German mysticism who was "almost unique in escaping any kind of censure by Hegel."[65] Now it certainly cannot be called a mistake on Hegel's part to read in Eckhart the possibility to "know" God—and when we speak of "mystical" knowledge, whether of the Eckhartian or Hegelian variety, we refer to the ability of the "finite" being to attain a union with God, thereby implying an ontological commensurability between the finite and infinite. Indeed, the thrust of the mystic's speculation is in fact to lay hold of the (ontological) ground, to become one with the One, a union that occurs in the "intellect." Rather, Hegel's error may have been in attributing to Eckhart a mode of knowledge that Eckhart did not in fact affirm, for it may be the case that Hegel appropriates that which is conducive to his method and marginalizes what is not, which in Eckhart's case can be extremely misleading. It is misleading for a number of reasons, among which include: the nature of the God with which the soul is unified, the nature of this unification, and the activity as well as the nature of the intellect in which this union occurs, all of which involve a matrix of interrelated distinctions forming a core of his mystical experience which Hegel would seem to ignore.

Yet let us first propose a few possible explanations for Hegel's high estimation of Eckhart, the first being a view identified as central to Hegel, namely, the "divinization" of the human being or the undermining of ontological difference. Eckhart says, "[F]or as true as God has become man, [it is] as true [that] man has become God,"[66] a conception supported by his frequent evocation of Augustine's notion of the identity of the one who loves with the one that is loved. Eckhart's identity or union of finite humanity and God, in which literally "there is no distinction," rejects any notion of similitude or resemblance.[67] Nevertheless, in articulating this "union," he will refer to it as "image," a term typically understood to fall within the realm of representation or similitude. Therefore, Eckhart's "union" and "image" must belong to a different order.

A second possible explanation for Hegel's sympathy to Eckhart is another manner in which Eckhart speaks of the operation that establishes the identity of God and human being, namely the Word. The Word, at other times referred to as the "divine birth" in the soul, is not so much an event of birth as a testimony to the eternal divinity of the finite. It is through the Word that God is present in the life and intellect of finite being. Indeed, one of the scriptural passages frequently cited by Eckhart is John 1.1: "In the beginning was the Word . . . and the Word was God." When Eckhart comments on the significance of this initial word however, he turns to the Book of Exodus (3.14), where God reveals himself to Moses by claiming, "I am who am."[68] A revelation of this sort, Eckhart believes, is in fact a concealment of God's name, or is a revelation but of an indefinite existence without quality. Indeed, if one feels a presence in a darkened room and asks, "who is there?" is not the response of "I am who am" that of one with something to hide?

From a mythological perspective, for instance, it is indeed fortuitous for gods to hide, insofar as the Word in mythico-religious thought is not only endowed with power but is the name of the deity, and knowledge of the name gives the one who knows it power over the god. One may call to mind the Egyptian legend of the sorceress Isis and the sun-god Ra. In this story, Ra says, "I am he with many names and many shapes. . . . My father and my mother have told me my name, and it has remained hidden in my body since my birth, lest some sorcerer should acquire magic power over me thereby."[69] Isis, however, cajoles his name from him by creating a poisonous serpent to strike him, and then tells him that his name must be known so the gods can relieve him of the poison. Possessing his name, she then gains power over him and the other gods. Eckhart's God is indeed wise to conceal his name lest humanity diminish Him by putting Him to use for their own purposes.

If we look to Eckhart's analysis of the structure of God's response to Moses, he notes that should it have stopped at "I am," this would indicate a subject that is predicated by a denomination of being, but as such remains incomplete as a simple negation of the unity of the "I." By adding the second "am," the initial negation is denied, and it is as a negation of negation that God is properly conceived as the One or pure unity, and so the response constitutes an affirmation. That Eckhart asserts unity through a negation of negation certainly would have appealed to Hegel. But rather than invoking Exodus, I would speculate that Hegel—after John 1.1—would have turned to John 1.14: "And the Word has become a human being of flesh and blood and has come to live among us." I justify this speculation for two reasons: the first is that it would be indicative of his reading of Eckhart, which emphasizes the relational, Trinitarian God derived through the notion of the "divine birth" in order to dispel the notion of an unknowable God; and secondly, it is in keeping with the affirmative double negative of the Word, whereby God's Word is negated (bifurcates) in becoming human articulation, an affirmation that in developing to completion becomes one with the original Word of God.

However, as a reading of Eckhart's sermons undeniably reveals, occluded from the sort of positive revelational account presented here are certain foundational distinctions which all but overturn the type of knowledge Hegel sees as imperative—discursive knowledge. The first of which, one that, as it were, casts the first stone, is the distinction Eckhart posits between "God" and GOD (the "Godhead," the "Deity").[70] That is, on the one hand there is the Trinitarian God and creator, the God that relates to creatures as their cause and toward which creatures aspire in their works and knowledge. And on the other hand there is GOD as the "simple ground" prior to and refusing particular creatures—a refusal extending even to the three Persons of the Trinity[71]— described as the "thing which is no thing," which "is what it is," an ineffable reality that Eckhart evokes by images such as "the silent desert" or "bottomless abyss," the "unspotted mirror." Failing a recognition of this difference—a failure that resulted in the condemnation of many of his statements—the mystic can scarcely be understood. I shall briefly explain, beyond the strangeness of the terms utilized, the ramifications of the divine dehiscence.

The one issue focusing the rest is that the emphasis placed on the Deity as a nonrelational unity and abysmal foundation precludes distinction within GOD, representation and predication of GOD. The iconoclastic gesture of mystical thought is in fact to purify religion of representation and God of human determination, under which certainly falls denomination. Indeed, "God is inexpressible."[72] Otherwise, GOD is a "place" in the sense of ground where all things and creatures reside, the place that gives them life and order. This place is not named, or as Eckhart says, "[T]his place is God. . . . The place remains unnamed and no one can say an appropriate word." No image or name can be an adequate expression in the place of GOD. The text continues:

> Every word that we can say about him is more of a negation, concerning what God is not, rather than an affirmation of what He is. This is what a great master [Heraclitus] understood; it seemed to him that everything he could say about God by means of language could not truly express Him without always having something false about it. This is why he kept silent, without ever wanting to pronounce a single word. . . . *For this reason, it is much better to keep silent on the subject of God than to speak of him.*[73]

It is for similar reasons that Bataille believes God to be best encountered in silence, and why he suggests "the complete humour of the situation. Hegel. God. It's the transgression of all language. God is this transgression."[74] The comedy is then that Hegel's discourse articulates the transgression of all discourse, and by bringing it into his discourse can only transgress his own discourse. Similarly, it would therefore seem paradoxical that Eckhart should ever speak of GOD in relation to the Word, as well as claiming that this Word is spoken to finite being—but then again, Eckhart was never one to shy away from paradox or contradiction. We must therefore clarify the nature of the Word and the intellect that receives the knowledge of GOD.

When Eckhart speaks of the intellect or "head of the soul," it is not what we would imagine to be a capacity of the mind for knowledge, but rather refers to the eternal existence of human being which is in fact anterior to its created, worldly, spatio-temporal existence. The intellect is humanity's highest power, is the place of the true union between or "birth" of GOD in the soul. And if this union is identity, and if GOD—to still be GOD—can be touched neither by time or creaturely existence, by anything exterior, then the intellect as well operates above time, and renounces all commerce with the exterior world.[75] Obviously this has profound implications for human thought, will, and desire, which exist in time and to each of which belongs the power to turn toward the exterior and the particular—and thus away from GOD. For to think of GOD through various determinations, "to think goodness or wisdom or power, is to hide his existence, to obscure him by this thought. A single thought added hides existence."[76] But how then may there be "knowledge" of GOD when knowledge implies separation, and what must one do to gain access to this knowledge? In short, one must "detach" oneself from oneself, create "a void in oneself,"[77] a place left clear for GOD to spread Himself out into oneself, and for one to Communicate with GOD. We shall shortly see the strong affinity between the mystical experience of GOD requiring a detachment from self, and Bataille's notion of divine experience as it occurs in eroticism. This is perhaps the single most striking coincidence between Bataille and Eckhart: *GOD is experienced when the self is no longer there*, literally in ecstatic self-abandonment.

The question I have left unanswered is how—if one must separate oneself from everything exterior, remove all distinction and thought, become undivided, atemporal, etc.—does the intellect receive the Word of GOD, know and grasp GOD? The Word certainly is not the word as we know it. Rather, it is the "eternal" Word, the "image" of GOD, GOD's "birth" in the soul. This "birth" is at one point (Sermon 32) described by analogy with a wax seal (the soul) and a stamp (GOD), in which the stamp imprints itself in the wax so completely that nothing remains of the wax outside of the imprint. The personality is literally subsumed, submerged by a divinity whose overwhelming and indeterminate presence renders the soul absent. A more pertinent example, however, is when Eckhart describes the Word or "image" as pure light, with "birth" being a "little spark" in the soul, the way in which the soul "knows" GOD. Eckhart says that while the soul is formed after GOD, "God is formed after himself, he draws his image from himself and from nothing else. His image, by which he absolutely knows himself, is nothing but light."[78] On the next page of the same sermon, he says, "[W]hen the soul devotes itself to the knowledge of the authentic truth, to the simple power by which one knows God, the soul is called a light. And God also is a light, and when the divine light pours itself into the soul, the soul is united to God *like a light in a light.* . . ." It is hard to see how this would not be the immediate, intuitive certainty of the absolute for which Hegel criticized the romantic intuitionists, how it would not be the pure light that is nothing but darkness, for "when the soul remains in the light of God and in the silence of pure repose, *it is the night.*"[79] The Word speaks directly to the interiority of the soul, to the intellect, is born in the soul prior to its creaturely, historical, speaking existence.

An even more provocative image follows: "[T]he intellect grasps God in his vestiary, in his nudity, as he is One, without distinction."[80] The intellect, by which one "knows" and is one with GOD, clearly is not the discursive knowledge which develops over time, which separates the absolute into specific determinations, which is the work of finite intelligence, for "there where knowledge and desire come to an end, is darkness, and there God shines."[81] When we encounter GOD in Bataille's writing, it will be in the erotic night, in the blinding, dazzling light of nudity, in the silent experience of non-knowledge.

We have obviously traveled a great distance from Hegel's definition of "the mystical" as being-revealed, from our words, concepts, and actions being the self-conscious articulation of God. The mystical path foregoes conceptual distinction, precludes the separation of the One into graspable categories, as determination can only blind one to the truth. Eckhart's GOD is the great iconoclast: GOD hates any image of "God," hates any knowledge of "God," for GOD does not reveal Himself as such. Should humanity continue to try to name, place, or know GOD, the union can never take place, GOD cannot be born in man's soul. This is why, in a remarkable and almost shocking admission, the mystic says, "I pray to God that he liberate me from 'God.'"[82] It is only shocking, however, if misunderstood. For as should now be clear, that which is prayed for is a liberation from the barriers—the qualities, determinations, attributes, and moreover, the words—that the finite understanding applies to GOD in an attempt to grasp Him, yet which only prevent true access to GOD.

Nevertheless, there are profound similarities between Eckhart and Hegel which we should not fail to underscore, for they will have further bearing on our analysis of Bataille's relation to Hegel. As much as it is the case with Eckhart, so is it with Hegel that the categories and predicates of the divine, in themselves, are inadequate. As mentioned above, to adhere to divine predication as if one is providing determination for an external reality is to remain stuck within the limits of *Verstand* (understanding), and to be blocked to the infinite self-consciousness or *Vernunft* (reason) where thought and the absolute are properly unified. More accurately, given the commensurability of the finite and infinite, in *Vernunft* is where the finite being attains self-conscious knowledge of partaking in the absolute self-consciousness of spirit. The main difference here is Eckhart's relativization of the dynamic historical or Trinitarian development of the finite to infinite self-consciousness, placing it rather in an immediate, atemporal intuition; and from the other side is Hegel's relativization of the radical transcendence and negative aspects that are essential to Eckhart's schism between the Godhead and the Trinity.

Of increasing importance for us, however, will be the imperative found in both to transcend the limits of representation, which is viewed as an insufficient form of the absolute content with which it is concerned. The difference, if I read Eckhart correctly, is that the mystic does not posit a dialectic of finite form and infinite content, such that one may lead to the other. Rather, an immediate leap must be made from the image to the imageless, finite to infinite such that the finite is only affirmed in its infinitude and not in its finiteness. The finite does not run up against a limit, but is simply dissolved in a mystical vision. Whereas for Hegel, the mystical vision is the elevation through and beyond representation and into the pure realm of the concept (spirit).[83] Hegel does not delete the finite representation, but rather sees the infinite therein imprisoned by the sensuous from which it must be released. The finite sensuous form must be cancelled and raised to its non-sensuous, spiritual truth. The representation—think here of the body of Christ—is not just a limit, but is the gateway to the absolute in its negation (death). There is a movement not only through the image to infinity, but through suffering to divinity. To anticipate our later discussion, we will find Bataille actually drawing closer to Hegel on this point, even as his rejection of a conceptual appropriation of the beyond-of-representation aligns him with Eckhart.

And it is this which leads us back to our original question, whether the first and final term of discourse is available to discourse. Eckhart's standpoint should be clear: the first and final Word or name is that which is above all names, for His name is "The Unnameable," is that which cannot be pronounced, which is revealed as it was to Moses—revealed as concealed. Thus, the experience and "knowledge" of GOD may only occur in a realm beyond the positive conceptual knowledge of speculative theology. Bataille adds his voice to the critique of the final term of knowledge: "[W]e cannot add to language without impunity the word which transcends words, the word God. As soon as we do so this self-transcending word vertiginously destroys its own limits."[84] Yet this is precisely Bataille's purpose in his aphoristic, poetic, and fictional writing: it aims at saying the first and final word, to bring GOD into discourse in a way that destroys the discursive limits of meaning that God defines. He incessantly tries to add GOD to language so as to transgress "God."

The reading of Eckhart that I have proposed and which Bataille loosely follows calls into question not only Hegel's reading of Eckhart but the efficacy of discourse itself. Discourse is put into play, at risk *(met en jeu)*—as I stated from the outset—when God is reconceived. And the entirety of Bataille's writing will rest on this fundamental question: is discourse related to a horizon of knowledge or non-knowledge in the form of experience? If it is the latter, if one therefore arrives at the extreme limit of discourse, but at the end cannot claim "the Absolute," or "God," or "Logic," then one is left probing the night, supplicating, and receiving no response, realizes one's utter abandonment. It is important, and shall become more so as we continue, to note here the double sense of the phrase, being abandoned.

Abandonment can be understood in two senses which, taken together, emphasize the radical nature of Bataille's mystical gesture. The first—not to be dissociated from laughter, drunkenness, orgasm—is the commonplace experience of effusion or abandon, taking leave of oneself for a moment which is the basis for the ecstasy that various mystics related in describing their visions. Ecstasy in this sense is the experience of *ek-stasis*, a movement that carries one beyond limits—particularly the limits of self, and consequently those of knowledge or *Logos*. And while he may conceive this experience as "religious" in nature, for Bataille "there is no question of a foundation of a religion. No, there is no foundation, since there is no possible presupposition; there is only a possibility of experience."[85] The lack of foundation leads to the second sense of being abandoned, which for Bataille means that in the ecstatic night one is entirely without assurance. That some presence is there is certainly a possibility, yet no reassuring voice comes out of the darkness, this "presence" yields nothing of itself. God may well be there, but from the perspective that seeks some reassurance, some recognizable sign onto which our anxiety can grasp, is as good as absent. The gaze that implores the night to yield even a shadow of a tangible presence is absorbed into the darkness, into too loud a solitude.

Understood in the strong sense, this realization is intolerable—especially if He is there yet refuses to present Himself—and the human response is to continue the attempt to see in a way that picks out objects in the night so as to orient oneself as a subject, to speak in a way that names what we fear so as to control it. Indeed, does not language at its very origins arise from a need to deal with abandonment or its threat? Is this not what Freud teaches us in telling the story of the little boy with his wooden reel and piece of string, *"Fort/Da,"* disappearance from sight yet there in representation? Does the boy not come to words in order to mediate what Freud calls "some overpowering experience" of being abandoned, using words "so as to make oneself master,"[86] rendering absence present, providing assurance in the anguishing night? It is apparent that our mystic realized this as well, or more specifically he realized that the human tendency to hold to language in order to name and thereby tame the abysmal experience in the end hides a truth that is immediately there, and he resorts to pleading to be relieved of that which constructs oases in the desert so as to live in the truth.

It is for similar reasons that Bataille invokes violent, ecstatic or "mystical" experiences, such as when he comments on Levinas's *"il y a,"* the traumatic experience of an anonymous, exterior invasion, an experience of pure existence which depersonalizes the subject and eliminates precise objects in a night of obscure presence, the night in which there is no longer this or that, no subject or object, but rather an absence that invades as a presence.[87] The movement involved in the *il y a,* the movement in which the existant is dissolved into existence, repeats the movement of chance from the known to the unknown, the sacrificial movement from anguish to ecstasy, or the a-theological "movement which carries us to the more obscure apprehension of the *unknown:* of a presence which is no longer in any way distinct from an absence."[88]

In an experience such as this, knowledge goes the way of discourse, which in turn goes the way of the knowing subject itself, which is dissolved, depersonalized. Such is Bataille's "inner experience," an experience that—as bears repeating—has nothing "inner" about it, for it designates the ecstatic loss or depersonalization of self. Drawing an analogy between "inner" experience as a mystical experience of GOD, and Levinas's *il y a,* Bataille states, "[I]t [the *il y a*] is immediately there. *There is no discourse.* Nothing responds to us, the voice of silence is heard and frightens like 'the silence of infinite space' of which Pascal spoke."[89] It is perhaps an understatement to posit that knowledge is dissolved along with our capacity to name and immobilize the experience, for there is—at that moment—not only an absence of discourse, but there is no subject of discourse, there is no "us" to which the *il y a* could respond.

Yet in spite of, in fact because of, this harrowing experience, the adherence of a temporarily overwhelmed subject to its discourse is not relaxed, for the experience cannot be tolerated, cannot be both maintained and survived—so it must be mediated. The experience in question is not the idyllic submersion into a Nirvana-like state of non-desire, although Bataille at times drifts toward its allures. Rather, it is anguishing to the core. For on the one hand, it involves the anguish of the discontinuous being sliding toward an unknown, an anguish that drives one to evade the unknown by linking it to the known through discourse, so as to regain control, to find a hook that stops one's sliding. And on the other hand, there is the anguish of a being that desires to disappear, to merge with the night and escape one's individuality and finitude—but is unable to do so. Quite literally, the individual is hung in suspense between the threat of disappearance and the inability to disappear. It is this tension that articulates the ecstatic core of the "inner," sacred experience, a tension that will be articulated in his erotic texts, and in sacrifice.

That Bataille is critical of the tendency to treat the nondiscursive in discursive terms, to alter the sacred, the intimate, by discourse, is thus not to say that it is avoidable, or indeed even undesirable. Rather, as he sees it, the real problem is the one we identified with respect to poetry, namely, the inability to Communicate the experience of intimacy because of the inability or unwillingness to find a language that could express it without altering it, without turning it into another object of knowledge.[90] The problem, in short, is how to communicate in words an ineffable experience for which no discursive equivalent is possible, which conscious discourse omits from its chain of meaning. The problem, in short, is this: the expression of thought should reflect experience, but the words of discursive thought turn experience into an object of knowledge, thereby evading the experience through its mastery. Such, as Bataille's view goes, is the work of discourse in us. Yet it is imperative to recognize that there are experiences that discursive language and thought cannot grasp, which it can reflect upon from outside, but cannot integrate into thought. The paradigmatic example is death, for one may speak of death like an object of knowledge, but one can never speak of its experience without being in error. Quite simply, there is no one who has experienced death and lived to speak of it, so strictly speaking death can only be an experience of non-knowledge.

This problematic goes as well for violent, inner states such as eroticism, which "is as if it did not exist as far as our existence is present for us in the form of speech and language."[91] And this is as well why the experience of God, even were one to take the leap that equates it with God's experience of Himself, is the night of non-knowledge. "Non-knowledge," as Bataille claims in a statement reminiscent of the Eckhartian intellect seeing GOD naked, "lays bare,"[92] and so one would seem to see and know what was hidden behind the veil of "God." But then Bataille concurs with Eckhart in that what is laid bare cannot be grasped knowledge, cannot be named, is not a point of rest, and non-knowledge again strips one of knowledge. "Should I speak of God?" Bataille asks. Not if God is the *telos*, the satisfaction of discursive knowledge, for God is "unthinkable, a word, a way to forget the eternal absence of repose, to forget the absence of satisfaction implied in the search for what *we are*. The impropriety of thought which gives itself a stopping point in the word God [conditions its own undoing]. Ecstasy is the undoing of thought."[93] GOD is this ecstasy encountered by the mystics, is the truth content of eroticism.

The *dissatisfaction* involved must then be properly understood, for it does not relinquish its share of pleasure. What dissatisfaction implies is that the ecstatic movement does not stop: it achieves neither the peculiar satisfaction of death itself—the absence of desire—nor the satisfaction of grasping the terminal point—the satisfaction of knowledge. But does Bataille's thought, as immediately related to a God posited beyond a thought proclaimed absolute, betray Bataille as an abstract intuitionist equally susceptible to Hegel's famous criticism that they relegate the Absolute to "the night in which . . . all cows are black,"[94] the night of Being which is indistinguishable from Nothing, in defiance of all determination and knowledge? Does it make Bataille a "new mystic"?[95] In a single statement which—to my knowledge—has been overlooked by Bataille's readers, Bataille both rejects the first criticism, and specifies the extent of his culpability with respect to the second: "Entering into non-knowledge, I know that I efface the figures on the blackboard. But the obscurity that thus falls is not . . . the 'night in which all cows are black'. *It is the enjoyment of the night.*"[96] With a nod more than anything else toward Nietzsche's notion of the Dionysian mood in which the painful collapse of the *principium individuationis* is mixed with rapturous delight or a "mystical feeling of oneness"[97] with "the primordial unity" *(das Ur-eine)*, Bataille's mysticism culminates in the painful, mystico-erotic pleasure of the loss of self, "where horror and joy coincide," in silent anguish.

It would indeed seem an impossible, or at least "paradoxical" task to express in words that which is situated beyond words, that which eludes thought and language, yet this is precisely what Bataille's literature endeavors to do. And if, in the analysis of literature that follows, I give a certain priority to vision, it is to emphasize two specific points: the first is the emphasis Bataille will place on vision when it comes to inner experience, which he rarely dissociates from a spectacular or theatrical—or as Bataille claims, sacrificial—representation; the second is how this experience bears such a close affinity to a blind or "affective"[98] identification which precedes any opposition of self and other, subject and object, that it may almost be seen as its derivative.

Thus, in what follows, Bataille will be seen—both in his erotic writing, and in sacrifice—to evoke something similar to that which Nietzsche affirms and Hegel condemns, namely, the mystical night of pleasurable abandon where one feels an unmediated union with the indistinguishable totality. Yet all the while, we shall see Bataille approaching the divine (or "mystical night") in a structurally similar way not only to Nietzsche, but as well to Hegelian self-consciousness. The mirror in which one sees the divine in the world is, however, profoundly altered, cracked, and the image one receives as well reflects oneself as one is when facing GOD—utterly shattered. In a way, then, the ecstatic culmination of the mystical and erotic are made of a piece, for in Bataille's view, mysticism—while not reducible to the erotic—is but another expression of an erotic search, minus the sensuous reality of its erotic object—GOD. But to arrive at mystico-erotic joy, we must take a detour through the theatre of sacrifice.

4.2 EROTICISM AND SACRIFICE: THE BODY AND THE FICTION

Awakening to intimacy requires seeing what we must not see if we are to respect the limits of our integrity which anxiety—the desirous fear of the unknown, of death, of our own animal nature—prescribes. To become conscious of the intimacy *that* we are—to become self-conscious, to KNOW—therefore requires facing up to *what* we are, even if it frightens.[99] Indeed, were it not threatening to our selves, intimacy would not be sacred, would be merely animal. Likewise with sexuality or the object of desire. Sexuality without anguish is not erotic, it is mere animal sexuality, "unleashing the beast within us." Eroticism, rather, is our own animal nature—negated because of the horror humanity feels at being dependent on its natural, bodily mortality[100]—transfigured by its negation, and reemerging as desirable. Eroticism involves a fundamental coincidence of filthy nature and desire, death and life. And the most common experience Bataille privileges with the capacity to awaken us, to allow us to recognize what we are, is eroticism.

Anguished and filthy as it may be, eroticism, like religion, is a search for lost intimacy, a search for GOD. But as I pointed out above, eroticism—and thus intimacy or divinity—is as if it did not exist for language, "the articulated language on which [clear] consciousness was founded."[101] Consciousness therefore could only know intimacy—an experience—by reducing it to an object of knowledge, which it is not. This I have sought to make evident in the preceding section. What I will now try to delineate is not only how Bataille conceives the erotic search for intimacy as resting on sacrifice, but how he attempts to portray this in his writing—a writing that, like the life of the Spirit, "wins its truth only when, in utter dismemberment *(déchirement absolu)*, it finds itself."[102] We must pause over this phrase however, for it is crucial to an understanding of sacrifice, and we will encounter it again shortly. Yet it may be more ambiguous than it seems.

Does it mean, on the one hand, that the subject finds *itself* in *its own* absolute rending, the subject itself torn to pieces, sinking directly into nothingness? Or does it mean that the subject must *find* itself, outside itself, in a reflection of its own nothingness, a reflection of itself torn to pieces? If the former is the case, the proposal becomes untenable: if "the condition in which I *could see* would be to die," then "I will not have, at any moment, the possibility *to see*"[103]—if death is Nothing, how does it illuminate life? And if the latter is the case, there is the possibility that the nothingness reflected will be merely treated "as if it were nothing," for the "content" of the reflection is Nothing—death, "absolute rending." Indeed, the desire for death or self-destruction tends to elude us if it is not "tinged with eroticism."[104] Consequently, it must be represented in captivating image. Still, if Nothing is a captivating form, how is it Nothing? To answer these questions requires first that we specify Bataille's use of these terms with as much rigor as possible.

Death: it is not an event. From the subjective pole, death is a break from isolation, is ecstatic movement toward nothing that can be anticipated, an opening of individual consciousness to something beyond itself that it cannot reduce to itself, or to what it has excluded in order to live. From the objective pole, death is nothing, not pure nothingness. It is a provocation and an infinite withdrawal. Nothing: it is a presence that is no-thing, an absence that can overwhelm, a complete lack of response to expectation, in itself silent and invisible. Nothingness:[105] it is the limit of individual existence that one's limits—in time and space—define; a transcendence of individual limits beyond which individual existence no longer exists (as individual). It is in the sphere of nothingness (transcendence) where an object appears.

The subject can be lost in transcendence toward an object, or reduce the object to immanence, both options having two derivatives. The object as active or "superior"—a person, a god, a state—necessarily undoes one's individual existence, can reduce individual existence to an inferior nothingness and make it serve its own purposes. The individual is lost in transcendence. With an object as passive or "inferior," one can do to it what the superior reality does to the subject—reduce it to one's own limits, make it immanent. The question, however, is of an object that is a subject equal to oneself, a "second self,"[106] a "no-thing," in which the terms *transcendence* and *immanence* lose their oppositional stability, in which transcendence becomes immanence and immanence transcendent. This is, as we saw earlier, the efficacy of sacrifice. A being is torn from immanence, transcending its natural continuity with the world and with its fellow beings, to become a separate object, a thing among things; struck down, the object is restored to its immanence, becomes no-thing.

Now with respect to the subject/sacrifier in relation to this thing become no-thing—as we saw with the mystical situation—one is still lost in transcendence toward the object. But the object, transcending its empirical limits, has become unlimited in space and time: it cannot be reduced to the limits of the subject, nor the subject to its limits, for the subject and object, along with their limits, have momentarily disappeared. "The isolated being *loses himself* in something other than himself. What this 'other thing' represents is of no importance. It is still a reality that transcends the common limitations. So unlimited is it that it is not even a thing: it is *nothing*."[107] This object—sacrificial, erotic, mystical—is of no importance in itself, just as the subject is in itself of no importance to the object. Of importance is the Communication, actually a type of love, passing between this subject and this object. What Communication unveils is that neither the subject nor the object in question are in-themselves at all. The object for the subject is rather "the extension of an existence first revealed within myself."[108] It is an extension of—I would suggest—an "initial inner experience,"[109] of an ecstatic intimacy from which an object only becomes an object, from which a subject only becomes an separate thing, by transcending. The question at issue, one that can only be asked once the position of mutual transcendence has been established, is how this immanence, this intimacy, is restored within a relation of transcendence. We have said that this occurs through sacrifice, yet the question is one of Communication, which in turn is one of desire for that "other self": a self more Other than any particular other; a Desire that is more a non-relation of immanence than it is the condition of relational transcendence. Yet it is important for us to clear up any final equivocations with respect to Bataille's attempt to have Communication emerge from the Hegelian, sacrificial imperative that lies at its foundation. This will be essential in delimiting not only the distance Bataille finally takes on his proximity to Hegel, but as well in judging whether this distance is wide enough for Bataille to feel comfortable.

So let us once again consider sacrifice within the perspective of the Hegelian prerogative to manifest and recognize "the Negative," but let us try to take this discussion out of the strangling hands of economics. To do so requires a notion of sacrifice that has no justification, no transcendent concerns, thereby allowing its structure alone be revealed. Not pertaining to *any* good, sacrifice must therefore be evil in Bataille's sense of the term: a crime or transgression of the human law of non-violation, of respect for life and for others which protects and secures individual being. Sacrifice must be disrespectful of limits if it is to be an opening to the beyond of being-as-isolated existence—to Communication—without serving the survival of some entity, independent of concern for life in the future. It must be a categorical transgression, without reserve. If we are to continue to speak of sacrifice at all, it seems then that we must look for another dynamic than that which guided traditional, ritual sacrifice.

For we have made clear that the ritualization of naïve sacrifice only served to discipline and domesticate the sacred it evoked with respect to its end, that in fact ritual sacrifice never escaped moral, economic, or social justification, and that any justification is interpreted by Bataille as obliterating the truth of sacrifice: the heightening of self-consciousness through the exposure of humanity to its own negativity, to its own intimacy, and thus to its own death. This is what is at play in sacrifice. But can one both enter the game and play by its sovereign rules? Can one reach the "impossible" without dialectically turning it into another "possible"? Or more to the point: can a subject maintain a self-conscious relation to its truth, to the truth of its Desire, when this truth requires that one go to the point where one risks losing oneself as a subject? This is in fact the Hegelian question that Bataille addresses.

For sacrifice, as we heard earlier, "is always a question of manifesting the Negative," the "privileged manifestation" of which "is death," where nothing is revealed. The question of sacrifice turns on the Hegelian problematic of negativity, "that Hegelian doctrine of death." Bataille sums up the situation as follows:

> Concerning sacrifice, I can essentially say that, on the level of Hegel's philosophy, man has, in a sense, revealed and founded human truth by sacrificing. . . . Actually, Hegel's problem is given in the action of sacrifice. In sacrifice, death, on the one hand, essentially strikes the corporeal being; and on the other hand, it is precisely in sacrifice that 'death lives a human life'. It should even be said that sacrifice is the precise response to Hegel's requirement, the original formulation of which I repeat: 'Spirit attains its truth only by finding itself in absolute dismemberment. It does not attain that (prodigious) power by being the Positive that turns away from the Negative . . . no, Spirit is that power only in the degree to which it contemplates the negative face to face (and) dwells with it . . . .'[110]

Hegel has revealed how life lives and dies in one and the same motion, a motion essential to self-consciousness and which, when extended, transcribes the arc of Spirit. And in the sense that Bataille's interpretation of sacrifice involves a revelation of one to oneself—self-consciousness—his aim is not strictly opposed to that of Hegel. The problem, however, is one with which we should already be familiar, namely, the possibility that Hegel may, in effect, turn away from his own requirement, that he avoids—or at least delays—death (the Negative) by integrating it into the teleology of Spirit (the Positive). Or to restate this in a manner more pertinent to us here, the fundamental question is whether Bataille can adopt the Hegelian structure of self-consciousness by which one sees oneself reflected in and by another, yet avoid circumscribing this reflection within a dialectic of self-mediation. Is it possible, that is, to address the dialectic of representation not as being overcome by a higher, conceptual self-mediation that has left the sensuous behind like a *caput mortuum* whose spirit has been extracted, but rather to view the self-mediating representation as a manner to pass beyond self-mediation and into the nonconceptual and unmasterable beyond of all representation? To begin to unfold this crucial issue we must now address how Bataille interprets sacrifice as a means to both fulfill Hegel's requirement—"finding oneself in absolute dismemberment"—and escape Hegel; we must decide whether or not his attempt succeeds where Hegel's might fail; and ultimately, we must decide whether it is indeed the same self-consciousness, the same "oneself," that is at issue.

First things first: is Bataille able to conceive of sacrifice in a way that avoids its reduction to an interested exchange? Can he find a way for sacrifice to be sovereign—autonomous, disinterested, or pure—which, in fact, precludes it from having a meaning, insofar as "the logic of meaning is itself nothing but a logic of interest"?[111] If this requirement is to be fulfilled, it is imperative—though not sufficient—that it not be conceptualized by discursive thought: "Sacrifice . . . is a *sovereign, autonomous* manner of being only to the extent that it is uninformed by *meaningful* discourse. To the extent that discourse informs it, what is *sovereign* is given in terms of *servitude.*"[112] The reasons for undermining discourse in Bataille's schema we have already established, and are in no need of restating. I will simply say that the problem for Bataille is that sacrifice would become just another element in the realm of the "possible" as defined by discourse and productive action, and thus its manifestation of death or negativity would be indefinitely delayed. That is, it would be displaced along the chain of relations among objects or submerged in the knowledge that is coextensive with productive activity and which weaves a "fabric" *(tissu)* that veils both the radically empty negativity of Desire, and the truth of "what is" *(ce qui est).*[113]

If this is what must be avoided, the assumption is thus that sacrifice would be a "pure revelation of man to himself,"[114] free of meaning, motive, and utility—in a word, sovereign—were discourse not to interpret it as a means to some end, making it one possibility that it relates to further possibilities. While this proposition may retain a certain validity, it is nonetheless equivocal. And with respect to this equivocation, I will restrict my comments to this: it would seem that Bataille conceives sacrifice not only as an unmotivated event that suffers discursive reduction, but as well as a "remedy" for the reduction already carried out by discursive intelligence on "the impossible" intimacy originally belonging to every human being. That is, he sees sacrifice not only as a pure, disinterested revelation, but as that which responds—after the fact—to the necessity to break the discursive integration of an incommensurable particular into a transcendent universal. As he states, "[O]ne remedies the empty character of the transcendent world by sacrifice. By the destruction of an object of vital importance . . . one breaks, at a point, the limit of the *possible. . . .*"[115] Indeed, in place of a transcendent, discursive bond, sacrifice establishes "a link of immanence" or intimacy, it is the point where "*the impossible* is . . . laid bare *(dévoilé)*."[116] But must we say that sacrifice is necessarily put *to use*, as Bataille fears, if what it reveals is not a possibility that can be appropriated in the developmental self-mediation of a subject, clan, or people? Is it compromised if what it unveils only sends the search for intimacy beyond what can be seen or known?

In sum, the equivocation we have introduced is whether or not sacrifice may be used, once discursive consciousness already has it in its grasp, to restore the sovereignty assumed to have belonged to sacrifice prior to the discursive awareness of its meaning. Is it a failure if it is used *as a means* to reduce the reduction, to negate the negation of intimacy which discursive consciousness is to have carried out on the "pure revelation" of intimacy that Bataille believes sacrifice was originally purported to achieve? This equivocation, however, is in fact built on a misunderstanding, for as we have already pointed out, the "original" intimacy for which sacrifice searches *never was*, that discursive consciousness is indeed the *condition of* intimacy insofar as it would never have been considered as intimacy except from the perspective of a singular, discontinuous being that had lost it.

Sacrifice would in fact be a failure, a deception or ruse, if Bataille were to claim that it can be used for the purpose of returning lost intimacy to the possession of self-consciousness. What he does claim, however, establishes a position that may prick up the ears of the devotees of Lacan, for what he says is this: "sovereignty," or intimacy, "is the object which eludes us all, which nobody can seize: we cannot possess it like an object, *but we are doomed to seek it.*"[117] To seek it, that is, in-and-as something that it is not: in-and-as an object to be possessed, a promise of satisfaction. For in a crucial—though in fact quite obvious—statement, Bataille acknowledges that "it is not that simple to bring about an abyss,"[118] by which he means that one cannot confront "the beyond of being"—that is, Being—immediately and directly, without detour, any more than Desire can aim at the Desire of the other without an other desired. What can be said of the erotic object applies as well to sacrifice. The very deception, the promise of satisfaction offered by the object, is the lure needed to enter the game.

If one is to lose, there is always a lure of gain which renders the loss acceptable—there is value in exchange;[119] if one is to approach intimacy, there is always a detour through the thing that is mistaken for intimacy—the value is imagined as inherent in the object (fetishism). Consequently, following the logic whereby the prohibition is the ineradicable gateway to transgression, the interest with which sacrifice is undertaken is a mediation necessary for the violent expenditure that, unwittingly, unveils the impossible, even if this interest involves, as far as Bataille is concerned, a fundamental misrecognition of the Desire in question. A misrecognition, that is, of the fact that Desire wants to go as far as possible in the direction of loss. Yet in another sense, this misrecognition attests to something that Hegel knew very well, namely, that the path to truth lies in error and deception. The movement of self-conscious

Spirit progresses through a history of successive identifications, a "gallery of images"[120] or of others which are manifestations of consciousness itself in an external guise, the negative of itself.

What needs to be emphasized regarding this movement, and which is most evident in its origin—the intersubjective dialectic of death and recognition—is the problematic dynamic of identification and the experience of anxiety at its core, two elements that are clearly recognizable as the very foundation of Bataille's mature notion of sacrifice. That is, sacrifice not considered simply as extravagant, wasteful expenditure, but as adhering to the structural development of self-consciousness itself. Having said this, I want to leave no doubt that, despite the "profound difference"[121] Bataille claims between his notion of sacrifice and that of Hegel, the reading of Bataille's sacrifice given here proposes the assimilation of critical moments of Hegelian self-consciousness: Desire looking to recognize itself as manifested in an-other Desire; the confrontation with "absolute dismemberment" (death) and the anxiety it provokes as the path to consciousness of self; and the projection of what is revealed in anxiety onto the plane of representation, the in-forming of an abysmal negativity. This is not to suggest, of course, that Bataille will draw the same conclusions.

He does, however, attribute to Hegel a profound awareness of what is at play in sacrifice, claiming, "[O]ne cannot say that Hegel was unaware of the 'moment' of sacrifice; this 'moment' is included, implicated in the whole of the *Phenomenology*—where it is the negativity of death, insofar as it is assumed, that makes a man of the human animal."[122] And, we should add, it makes a "God-man" of the finite spirit. In Bataille's eyes, Hegel rightly identified the central role sacrifice has in human life insofar as sacrifice can be equated to the "manifestation" of negativity, the condition of possibility of self-consciousness. The real question is how this manifestation occurs, for nothing is manifest if one plunges headlong into death and winds up dead, in which case one would lose whatever it was for which one was risking one's life.

We already know Bataille's answer to this question, one that bears the indelible imprint of his Hegelian heritage: the "manifestation" occurs in the mirror-play of Desire in which self-consciousness sees itself in-and-as the other, the "second self." His solution: one would have to die watching oneself dying. But this is a comedy, a fiction, an "inevitable deception" arrived at through the affirmation of the alienating structure of self-manifestation. The fiction is nonetheless necessary: "man searching for the secret of being in death and finding nothing, for he lacks the power to simultaneously know and cease to be: [therefore] he must satisfy himself *(se contenter)* with a spectacle."[123] In short, he affirms the need for a *representation* of that which, if lived, would kill the one who lived it, of that which, if experienced, would put an abrupt end to experience—a representation, that is, of non-experience. Yet to what extent is this "satisfying," and how do we delineate the Desire that it satisfies?

Desire, taken in the Hegelian formulation, which has yet to be overturned, is emptiness, nothingness, perpetually in need of something other than itself. Yet what Desire desires is to free itself from all dependence on otherness, which will require that it recognize itself in-and-as another Desire, for that Desire to cease to be alienating. But if Desire truly is, in Kojève's formulation, a "revealed nothingness, an unreal [revelation of an] emptiness, the presence of the absence of a reality [a thing],"[124] then Desire desires to recognize itself not as any identical *self*, but as nothingness. If we could pare the opaque sensuousness of the object-representation away, then we could recognize Desire as a relation of a desiring subject to itself as nothing—a non-relation, pure ecstasis—rather than a relation to this or that desired object. A strange relation indeed, for if we follow the definition formulated above, then Desire as a relation to nothing is essentially the Desire for death. In which case the absolute satisfaction of Desire would be the absolute dissatisfaction of self-consciousness—it would be death itself. Hegel's solution—or more precisely, Kojève's: the satisfaction of Desire is in *knowing of* one's death and nothingness, not in dying. "If man is essentially finite, he can become completely self-conscious only by becoming conscious of his death. Thus, only in knowing himself to be irremediably *mortal* can the Wise Man attain the fullness of satisfaction."[125] Self-consciousness is not satisfied in death, but in the subject *knowing* that it is the object of its own desire, namely, death.

Bataille concurs and disagrees in one and the same gesture. For self-consciousness still needs an object, a sign, a representation in which to recognize itself. But what it recognizes is in defiance of every possible image: every image of, every possible knowledge of *self*. An impossible manifestation. It may have a mirror, but it is a mirror that reflects nothing that can be grasped by knowing consciousness, a mirror reflecting oneself in the depths of the darkest night, reflecting oneself as absent. As we hear again: "nothingness, *which isn't*," which is the beyond of the limits of individual existence, which is Desire as pure ecstasis, nevertheless "can't dispense with a sign . . . without which nothingness (since it isn't being) couldn't attract us."[126] But the sign, the object—in order to provoke Desire, the desire to Communicate with the beyond of individual being, death, or nothingness—necessarily lies. It presents itself as graspable or knowable, but its reality—(excessive) nothingness—escapes our grasp. Death is ungraspable. It can be lived, but then it is never known. It can be known, but on the condition that it is never lived. The time has come to affirm the truth of the lie.

Communication requires both the body and the fiction, real and imaginary risk, horror and joy, death and life. This double requirement—an inheritance from Nietzsche's view of tragedy as requiring both the Apollinian illusion and the Dionysian "reality"—will devolve upon the following imperative, which is not only that of sacrifice and eroticism, but is that which drives Bataille's writing, and which he sees as the core of all sovereign literature: the experience that cannot be lived must be Communicated in a way that reveals to the living the invasion of its own impossible death, a revelation experienced not as knowledge, but as *pleasure* or enjoyment: it is not the horror of death, but "joy" that "tears one apart" in anguish.[127] Sacrifice, in the end, *is a fiction*. It need not be directly or physically lived, rather, it needs a representation to be approached: "I understand by sacrifice not only the ritual, but *every representation* or account in which the destruction (or its threat) of a hero or of a being plays an essential role"[128]—as, for instance, in tragedy. Correlatively, the imperative behind (tragic) literature is *sacrifice:* "[T]he fictional nature of the novel helps us bear what, if it were real, might exceed our strength and depress us. We do well to live vicariously what we don't dare live ourselves . . . we should *take pleasure* in the feeling of loss or endangerment it gives us."[129] Literature inherits the place left by the decline of sacrifice.[130] But with this notion, may Bataille be seen as climbing down from the heights of anguish to live sacrifice from his easy chair? Has his paroxysmal language of dislocation finally led us to a narcissistic catharsis permitting one to retire into self-sufficiency? Is he finally pulling his true Hegelianism out of the hat, moving from agonizing experience and absolute rending to pure self-certainty? Has he altered his notion of sacrifice, succumbed to the impossibility of expending without reserve, and finally divorced his symbolic system from the labyrinth of the unruly body from which it arose, and whose passions repeatedly defy the coherence of meaning? Is his game finally up, having laid his bluff on the table?

In a word, no. Yet in a sense, I do not believe these are even the right questions to ask, for on the one hand, they hold to the image of Bataille as some apostle of perpetual catastrophe, and on the other, they forget that a representation can be a passageway, and in the right conditions of intensity can be devastating, as Hegel and Nietzsche understood so well. Even if their paths diverge, Bataille understood what Hegel indicated, namely that the death and loss in question, if only for a moment, can be without limit, and Bataille has never, save for a few intemperate moments, intended to dissolve the tension that results from the conflict between human, individual consciousness, and inhuman, absolute loss. If the point of no reserve is not reached at the price of anguish for the individual who wants to remain identical in time, identical with its own anticipated future, then the movement of life does not reach the point of intensity where one feels as if one is dying. Without this intensity, self-consciousness may know its link with inevitable death, know what it is, but it knows itself abstractly. And while Bataille insists on the fact that the experiences about which he writes must be directly lived, there is nevertheless a way to live them without living them, to die without dying. In a very revealing handwritten note attached to the "Notes" for the article "Communication,"[131] he states:

> This text is not finished: what should have emerged . . . is that the necessity of sacrifice should not be understood in a literal sense [*crossed out:* it is a ques-

tion of *the mystical complicity with the death of one's fellow being* and not of really renewing the savage practice . . .] but as the expression of the nature of things which more ancient man found in their rites. It is a question of *complicity with death* and only of *that which* is revealing itself in anguish to the mind, not of acts to accomplish.

This little note is of capital significance for the understanding of the ties that bind mystical experience with eroticism and eroticism with sacrifice. Yet it leaves us with one final question to ask—what is revealed?

It cannot be refuted that Bataille, while following Nietzsche, has as well retained both the working structure of, and impulse for, Hegelian self-consciousness as a confrontation with death's manifestation:

> [B]y associating it with sacrifice and, thereby, with the primary theme of *representation* (in art, in festivals, in performances), I have sought to demonstrate that Hegel's reaction is fundamental human behavior. . . . It is not Hegel alone, it is all of humanity which everywhere always sought, obliquely, to seize what death both gave and took away from humanity.[132]

Bataille himself does not hesitate to repeat, through his account of sacrifice, Hegel's structure of self-consciousness, where the abysmal disclosure of death is revealed only to be sublimated, one's own pure negativity experienced only to be transcended, the impossible is found in an external image, yet eventually is made possible without entering the arena of impossibility:

> Ultimately it is not ruination, let alone death, it is joy that the pursuit of ruination attains in the sacrifice. We draw near to the void, but not in order to fall into it. We want to be intoxicated with vertigo, and the image of the fall suffices for this. . . . So not only is trickery necessary in order not to die, we must avoid dying if we wish to attain joy. . . . Not that we should turn away from death, on the contrary: stare at it, look it straight in the face, that is the most we can do.[133]

If he follows Hegel's imperative to the end, it is with the following disclaimer, the one that exposes the twist Bataille gives to the Hegelian theory of Desire.

We know that self-consciousness relies on the recognition that Desire desires itself in its object. It comes to know itself as the truth of Desire, and finally to recognize the absolute identity—complicity—of subject and object. At this point—the complete fulfillment of Desire, the end of the history of Desire—Desire desires nothing, and the Wise Man is satisfied in knowing that the highway of knowledge has reached its destination. What Bataille insists upon, however, is that this knowledge leaves us dissatisfied, always leaves something to be desired. For what Desire recognizes when it recognizes itself, is anything but its *self*—it is itself as it can never see itself. It is itself as absolutely other, effectively unknowable. What is finally recognized is that we are bound to something that, insofar as we remain tied to our individuality and our self-certain knowledge, we can never recognize. And furthermore, should self-consciousness somehow manage to completely assimilate into the consciousness of *self* what is manifest in the other who dies, self-consciousness will—for all intents and purposes—be dead. Defying this possibility, Bataille views self-consciousness—Desire—as insatiable, for it is the consciousness of nothing that could ever satisfy it.

At the limit drawn by the fulfillment of Hegelian Desire, when Desire desires nothing, Bataille will simply repeat Hegel with greater urgency— Desire (still) *desires nothing!* Desiring nothing that could satisfy it, Desire becomes insatiable and unrelenting. In the end, Desire persists—but is unemployed. With nothing to do, humanly, it searches for pleasure—the useless and expressive form Negativity takes when there is no task to accomplish. But pleasure is banal if it merely satisfies. The excessiveness of Desire's dissatisfaction with pleasure will push it farther in the erotic search for a pleasure that puts one at risk, that exposes pleasure's complicity with death and defilement—of the other.

4.3 THROUGH THE MIRROR

Stumbling upon the uncanny coincidence between enjoyment and death, satisfaction and dismemberment, we have come to "the essential point of the problem," the problem that not only will bring us to the unity of mysticism, eroticism, and sacrifice, but one which occupied Bataille through the entirety of his work: "[H]ow can it be that distress was turned to joy—something that should have been shattering turned into exuberance?"[134] How is anguish transformed into ecstasy, isolation and individuation into communication and self-loss? With this question we are moving beyond the concern to merely locate the place assigned to death in consciousness, to the extent that we are even able to relate ourselves to, and integrate into consciousness, that which may outstrip consciousness. What is implied is an attempt to challenge the common attitude toward death, which is accepted—as Americans like to say—as being as unavoidable as taxes, but against which every possible attempt is made to eliminate from life. It is an attempt to move toward the sacred, toward "an apotheosis of that which is perishable,"[135] a divinization of finitude revealed in the anguishing yet affirmative destruction of the finite being as-individual, an affirmation of the negative in-and-for-itself— that is, for nothing.

Now, the principles we hold to so as to live as individuals may very well be too strong for those subterranean elements that threaten our existence to be faced directly, or to be revealed, as he is fond of saying, "in spite of ourselves." In and of itself, this is not necessarily undesirable. Yet Bataille believes that this resistance, while necessary to fulfill the vital requirements of life, nevertheless diminishes the self-conscious awareness of the human condition, of our persistent links with a side of life that humanity in former times lived in a very real manner. And while there is no question of going back, he nevertheless advocates and practices the voluntary revival of those abominated, religious elements—those life-affirming signs of death which our moral principles, indeed our very principle of individual identity, err in striving to eliminate from life.

Consequently, he posits the need for a willful, *complicitous* or identificatory deception—a fiction, a spectacle. As he says, "[I]t is question of our identifying with some character who dies, *and of believing that we die, although we are alive.* Furthermore, pure and simple imagination suffices";[136] or again: "This difficulty [to live at the moment one dies] proclaims the necessity of *spectacle,* or of *representation* in general, without the practice of which it would be possible for us to remain alien and ignorant in respect to death, just as beasts apparently are. Indeed, nothing is less animal than fiction."[137] The world of fiction and imagination fills the void left by the intolerance for ritual sacrifice, it allows for the recognition of our negativity, the "manifestation" of the abysmal truth of desire in a time when negativity has no productive manner in which to manifest itself.

I believe that Borch-Jacobsen has pinpointed the dynamic at work for Bataille:

> [T]he manifestation of death (the "realization" of desire) requires a whole theatre. More precisely, it requires the whole distance of theatrical representation—that is, the protective spacing that permits one to fulfill desire *in effigy,* without suffering its consequences. Only a specular identification . . . allows one to *see* oneself dead.[138]

Now, in fact, this is very close to the classic notion of *tragic* spectacle in which the hero undergoes the worst that fate has to offer and lives it for the spectators who, because of the pathos aroused in them, can feel that they themselves were strong enough to withstand the sufferings portrayed, can fulfill their desire to be heroes, and nevertheless emerge unscathed. This, however, only pertains to what Nietzsche—in his *Birth of Tragedy*—specifies as the Apollanian form of art which serves to conceal the horrific character of life by transforming it into beautiful images of noble individuality. The cathartic aspect of this form is actually the delight in an illusion that is recognized as an illusion, the knowledge of which creates a protective distance on the abysmal aspect of existence that poses a threat to our individuality. The enjoyment involved is thus the survival of the *principium individuationis,* a redemption *from* the "reality" of life through a conscious falsification of its horror: "Apollo overcomes the suffering of the individual . . . pain is obliterated by lies."[139] By bringing the abysmal chaos of existence into a harmonious form, a rhythmical harmony, the dangerous was rendered not only livable, but cathartic and enjoyable. In a sense, death was brought on stage to render it harmless, or better, beneficial. This is not, as both Nietzsche and Bataille agree, the point of sacrificial tragedy, and when Bataille in turn resorts to spectacle, to sacrificial fiction, it is not "to put life in proportion to the impossible *in order to evade it,* as does nature in tragedy, following Aristotle's theory of purgation."[140] But rather, again following Nietzsche, to see what both supports and is veiled by the cathartic Apollinian illusion, the chthonic primordial unity, the realm of life-affirming destruction fatal for the individual. For in Nietzsche's theory, the Dionysian art of tragedy, while equally an illusion, does not simply protect the spectator from personal involvement. Rather, by destroying one illusion—that of individuality—it reveals "a further dimension of reality which otherwise remains inaccessible,"[141] the admittedly metaphysical "eternal joy of existence" behind the phenomenon.

Indeed, if the fictional transposition which proposed to fulfill desire in effigy did so without touching the life in which this desire was housed, truly letting it be satisfied with the illusion, it would in fact be—as Borch-Jacobsen concludes—a failure, a comedy.[142] This is not what Bataille is proposing. Rather, he wants to expose the classic, *tragic* sense of subterfuge—in which death is seen solely as frightening, *serious,* and to be kept at an enjoyable distance—as a comedy. For while it is legitimate that "the death of an *other*" is "the image of one's own death,"[143] even the identificatory ruse cannot get around the fact that there is no abolition of the fundamental repulsion among beings, the establishment of difference or transcendence above the ground of immanence. In contrast to Nietzsche's early theory of tragedy from which Bataille drew so much, and even in contrast to what Bataille often seems to be proposing, there is no "metaphysical comfort"[144] of sinking into a harmonious union with the One behind beings. There is no *satisfactory* substitution for death: "If you die, it is not my death."[145] My *own* death is, for me, unpresentable. It is a comedy, therefore, to assert that one can both accede to one's own death, and survive as an intact individual; it is a comedy to claim that one can live one's death without exceeding the circle of representation. More specifically, and even more comic, is to be *satisfied* with a representation; to believe an image can reveal, and thus allow one to know, death—in which nothing is revealed; to believe one can satisfy one's desire to die through an image.

What Bataille calls the comedy of the tragic, however, is actually its efficacy: it is that identification allows one to take the death of another so seriously that one forgets one's own suffering, one's own finitude, and at the same time feels the cathartic joy of having passed through death and emerged on the other side. This joy is the "minor" reaction "that the impossible produces when sympathy does not put one in play personally," where one feels neither oneself, nor in fact the fictional hero, to be actually endangered or at risk: "[I]n this case the impossible leaves the core of the possible intact."[146] Oddly enough, however, Bataille's way out of this "minor" comedy is through . . . comedy, in the sacrificial forms of eroticism and literature.

For it is indeed a comedy to believe that one truly *"dies in seeing himself die,"*[147] through a simulation of the play with death, but this is precisely what he is proposing: by heightening the sense of identification to the point of Communication, suggestive of a sort of nonspatial, "mystical" hyper-identification, the spectacle (the other put to death) can present the unpresentable "beyond" of discontinuous existence, can present one to oneself *as other*, as dead, as nothing. Thus, one would seem to be able to see the inaccessible "beyond" of the self, the unknowable death awaiting us all.[148] Yet despite the affirmation of this Hegelian mirror-play of self-consciousness, one may perceive it as harboring an attempt by Bataille to project this process beyond the plane of representation, to in fact pass *through* the looking-glass to an affirmation of that which cannot be made present. It is in fact specifically in the *joy* of passing *through* the mirror, or facing a shattered mirror which no longer reflects a unified, stable image of the self—which presents oneself to oneself as profoundly other; it is passing through representation beyond the plane of representation itself, *to the point* of actually putting one's own vital equilibrium in danger, that the spectacle "opens itself like a theatre curtain onto a beyond of this world . . . transfigur[ing] all things and destroy[ing] their limited meaning."[149] We are talking of an experience that, in short, does not belong to the realm of "possibility."

And if it exceeds "possibility," then—despite the irreducibility of an *other*—it must reject the social, the ethical, the economic. It takes place in solitude and silence. For even if the moment of unleashing violence follows the momentum of its own imperative, should it come to light it is powerless to resist the force of social integration, the imposition of a moral meaning—its unwitting reward. Such is the lesson that Kierkegaard taught us through Abraham, who was ready to sacrifice his son *despite himself*, and who thus had to do so without mediating his act, without words or justification, without making it tragic and without making himself a hero. This lesson Derrida accurately identified so as to view Abraham's acceptance of sacrifice as "a sacrifice of the economy" itself, a "general economy of sacrifice."[150] By sacrificing the economy of sacrifice, refusing to allow his actions to be seen, heard, understood, and thus integrated, Abraham's decision was, from the perspective of the ethical, the most immoral imaginable, was outright murder.[151] Yet at the same time, owing to his sovereign disinterest in the judgment of others, his renunciation of the foreknowledge belonging to the tragic hero, his decision was in fact the "most moral," without calculation or hope for recompense—hopes that are based on concern for oneself. In short, his perspective was thoroughly *an*-economical. This sacrificial destruction of the meaning of sacrifice—lacking the practice of either sacrifice or tragedy—is finally to be found in eroticism, and will receive its most adequate expression in laughter, where some final questions will be brought to the fore.

To make a final run at this *an*-economy of sacrifice, to attempt to specify its ontological core, its initial and terminal foundation, we will turn to an account of eroticism tinged with mysticism, which may ultimately be identified as an experience of divinity, of the sacred, the point where horror and joy coincide. This point, I believe, is situated beyond the dualism of the subject and object, just as "original" intimacy was situated anterior to that dualism which negated it. The beyond and the origin of the subject-object correlation are fundamentally linked, such that at the extreme limit of the mutual transcendence of the subject and object, when each side of the equation is pushed to the height of tension in confrontation with one another, the distance may collapse into a momentary fusion which may be seen as the inverse image of the original unity.

Now the dialectic I am proposing—Intimacy, Transcendence, Intimacy—is not altogether dissimilar from the one we have repeatedly encountered—Substance, Subject, Substance. Indeed, for both, the initial point is natural immediacy, the middle is arduous knowledge, and the final is divine immediacy. The profound difference, however, is that the final term of the former is not a point of stoppage, but is rather where the final point of the latter—absolutely satisfying knowledge—is expended and dissolves. The whole process is left to begin again. There is indeed so much preparation to get to the point of having learned nothing but how to unlearn, how to reach a moment of innocence and desperate play which leaves one profoundly altered. This is perhaps the greatest game of all—to know and yet not to know, to finally be powerless.

If I have described this dialectic in an arcane fashion, this is not to say that it cannot be rigorously delimited, for it is nothing but the *an*-economic dialectic of sacrifice and eroticism, or in a word, Communication. Now if intimacy, the absence of subject and object, is an immediate experience, it is only so through putting at risk the terms of mediation, the subject and object. It is therefore immediate only as the end of a dialectic, the negation of a negation. To restate matters: original, natural intimacy is negated with the formation of distinct subjects and objects, a mutual transcendence which must in turn be negated for sacred intimacy—the nothingness or pure ecstasis beyond every subject and object—to be revealed. Intimacy is therefore reached only by means of a detour, which may alternatively be called sacrifice or eroticism. Bataille:

> It's important to me to show that with "communication" or physical lovemaking, desire takes nothingness as its object. It's the same with any 'sacrifice'. . . . The beyond of my being is first of all nothingness. . . . It reveals the presence of another person. Such a presence, however, is fully disclosed only when the

other similarly leans over the edge of nothingness or falls into it (dies). "Communication" only takes place *between two people who risk themselves.* . . . This way of understanding things gives a similar explanation to both sacrifice and the works of the flesh. . . . Sacrifice itself and its participants are in some way identified with the victim. So, as the victim is being put to death, they lean over their own nothingness. . . . In sensuality as in death, moreover, nothingness in *itself* isn't what attracts us . . . [rather], *a transposition is required* in order for us to be attracted to nothingness.[152]

Indeed, a transposition, or more precisely, a *substitution* is required if life is to recognize its desirous complicity with nothingness and death. The erotic object is the substitute, the victim, the representative of the nothingness of the subject, which is projected onto the object of desire.

Not all physical lovemaking, however, falls into the category of Communication, does not reveal intimacy, for these elements do not come into play if there is too much respect for the individual *as individual.*[153] For, unwittingly, respect—just like the respect for the transcendent "God"—turns the individual into a separate, distinct *thing*, untouchable and never at risk. Eroticism, meanwhile, requires a sovereign disrespect for the individual as individual. Expanding this notion further—placing the lover-become-thing into the moral and economic "world of things"—we may say the path to erotic intimacy requires a temporary sacrifice of our ties to economic goods or particular pleasures altogether, even pleasure itself, as a prerequisite for the search for the nothing but Desire itself, for the "dark God" that lies hidden in the object.[154] For when the object ceases to be a distinct, economic object opposing a subject, an object to which a value-in-itself is attributed, and thus becomes a matter of indifference or (Sadean) apathy, it is then possible to destroy the object as object and return it to its sovereign, meaningless intimacy—the *beyond* of subject and object, the *before* the subject and object. "Hyper"-identification, however, dispels the notion that it is merely a matter of an object, for it entails that the subject itself is at risk.

The movement and experience we have just identified as belonging to eroticism, however, is in fact very close to the mystical experience of ecstasy, burning before the nothingness of GOD. And having taken the detour through sacrifice and spectacle as a path to divinity, it seems that the mystic night, in which GOD is directly encountered in the void of determination left by the absence of God, is not so utterly void of objects after all. "Truly, truly, you long for the night. *But you have to take the indirect way.* . . ."[155] This is the way of eroticism. Yet eroticism, every bit as much as its spiritual counterpart, mysticism—which apparently rushes headlong into the night, into the absence of every object—seems the most direct path of all. It is physical, its object is immediate, it is *there*, in your arms, above you, beneath you. Yet at the same time, the beloved is simply the sacrificial circle, the site of an immolation, the place of Communication with the beyond of individual being, with one's absence, one's nothingness, as revealed through the death or absence of another.

It is, I believe, because Bataille recognized the abominable potential of what he advocates, as well as the possibility that the anguish tied to the erotic principle—the object must be destroyed—would be too great to ever allow one to accede to sovereign eroticism, that he turned to fiction as an expression of what cannot be both lived and survived. Indeed, intimacy itself—the absence of subject and object, the opening of the ground beneath one's feet— is no idyllic state. In itself it cannot even be desired. It requires the detour, and literature, in a sense, is a detour around the detour. If we briefly look at two examples of his erotic fiction, however, we may quite directly perceive how he seeks to reveal the essential. The texts I will focus on are *Ma mère (My Mother)* and *Madame Edwarda*,[156] and I will be aiming to show only two things: the first is the play of transgression and the law of substitution; the second is how transgression of the law may be divine. The point is to see how the game of life and death, satisfaction and dissatisfaction, is played within, and at the limits of, the realm of representation.

The law of substitution is the law of the father. The father is the barrier erected to unlawful desire, and marks the entry of desire into the play of substitutions, into language. The only way to approach the signified of desire— the mother—directly, would be to escape the father's rule, and thus to escape language which, like sexuality, lives through substitution, always circling around its object, but never penetrating the thing itself. Language and knowledge substitute for, and separate one from, pleasure. This tension between escaping and accepting the rule, pleasure and knowledge, is most visible in the language of *Ma mère*, yet is as well revealed by the fact that nearly all of his erotic texts were written under a pseudonym, quite literally erasing the name of the father.[157] I believe the real significance of this erasure to be the following: if he eradicates the name of the father, it is in fact to become the father.

Denis Hollier,[158] specifically with respect to *Madame Edwarda*, perceptively suggests another reason for the different authorships, one that is in keeping with what I emphasized above: the separation of knowledge and pleasure. He points out first that erotic fiction confined to itself is not a transgression. It is, rather, in relation to a theoretical discourse, one of authority and knowledge, that it receives its transgressive nature. The fact that the theoretical discourse here precedes the erotic serves to show that eroticism is not a moment superceded to the benefit of knowledge, but rather that discursive knowledge runs aground in the erotic, which "marks the dissolution of knowledge in its own blind spot."[159] Secondly, it is only the theoretical text, the sphere of discursive knowledge, that bears the name of the father. If one is truly to know, to know desire through debauchery and transgression, the name of the father must be erased (*Ma mère* was also written by Angélique). That is, the "proper" name may only belong to a text in which the "proper" identity and integrity of the author is retained.

Now, in *Story of the Eye*, the most transgressive and poetic of his novels, the *consciousness* of the game with the father is lacking, although the father certainly is not. The poetry of *Eye* proceeds in a manner remarkably similar to dream-work. There is an unconscious reality or desire (we know that Bataille was not conscious of the source of his images) that is too disturbing to be directly presented, but which is thrown into the machinery of poetic production in an attempt to express itself. This is why the father is still alive—the law, castration, will not permit one to accede to the object of desire, one must substitute. The resulting images are disfigurations and distortions, not only of the eye, but of its function—knowledge. In this text Bataille cannot escape the father, for he does not realize that the father is there. He can only transgress the discourse of knowledge which prevents access to pleasure, to the forbidden referent that drives the promiscuous play of language. Here he effectively, and unknowingly, accomplishes merely in poetry what Hollier has suggested in theory—the transgression of knowledge with the erotic.

In *Ma mère*, the situation is quite different, for unlike in *Eye*, where language was forced to trace a circuitous trajectory by the law, which compelled the repression of the object sought, in *Ma mère* the law is absent from the start, the father is already dead. When, therefore, the child (Pierre)—who is trying to penetrate the riddle of his mother's body from which he arose, who desires to know the cause of the (mother's) desire—says to his mother, "I would like to know what you know" (197), and we later discover that he is really asking, "Mother . . . I want to know what you want" (213), it is not the name of the father that is forthcoming. This leaves open the possibility that the boy will indeed come to know what the mother wants, and while she in fact wants him "to know," she is—at least originally—cautious about directly disclosing the truth: ". . . you must not learn it from me" (197). For indeed, she knows that the truth can kill.

In her attempt to simultaneously shield her son from, and awaken him to, what she knows, she procures substitute objects for him; first her own lover, Réa, and later the girl Hansi who, we are told, is "insignificant." Whereas in *Eye* the linguistic substitutions unconsciously produce and replicate the displacement of objects, here the language reveals a conscious and deliberate attempt to represent the same substitutive play in the Oedipal drama. But with the father gone, the castrating law that drives one into linguistic displacements is no longer in force, and the real desire behind the law is brutally exposed. Thinking he had his object in the substitute, Pierre soon comes to realize the misrecognition of his Desire: "I was resigned to no longer see in her but the access—by a detour—to what was inaccessible for me in my mother" (224). In this game of displacement driven by impossible access Bataille unmistakably reveals the poetics of sexuality.

The vain search for the signified through the labyrinthine play of signifiers, the failure of which is the life-blood of signification, has now quite literally become the play of signifier-lovers substituting for the ultimate ungraspable object: the mother's desire—whose unattainability is the lifeline of sexuality. Correlatively, the "insignificance" of the substitute lover shows not only the unsatisfactory nature of words, but the fact that every erotic object, every sacrificial victim, is but a lure perched on a more ungraspable intimacy: any word and any lover will suffice because none can grant the impossible satisfaction: "[I]ndifferently I could have satisfied it in the arms of someone else. My mother and I easily put ourselves in the state of the woman or the man who desires . . . but I did not desire my mother, she did not desire me" (235). As we attempted to specify above, while an object is required for Desire, this object—while deceptively promising gratification—is simply an invitation to ruin, to the loss of oneself—and the object—in the ecstasis of Desire itself, in a love that, again reminiscent of our discussion above, is "impersonal," or mystical:

> That's when you were conceived . . . your scoundrel of a father had nothing, or next to nothing to do with the story . . . you are not his son but the fruit of the anguish I felt in the woods. You come from the terror I that experienced when I was naked in the forest, naked as a beast, from the terror I enjoyed . . . you were born of this pleasure. . . . I believe I have never loved except in the forest . . . I loved nothing. I didn't love myself, but I loved immeasurably. I have never loved anyone but you, *but what I love in you, make no mistake about it, is not you.* I believe I love nothing but love, and in love itself, only the anguish of loving. (221–22, emphasis added)

Divine love and its ecstasy emerge in the absence of the loved object. The individual is but a sign pointing to its nothingness:

> For, nearing death, one doesn't see death;
> but stares *beyond,* perhaps with an animal's vast gaze.
> Lovers, if the beloved were not there
> blocking the view, are close to it, and marvel . . .[160]

It should be noted, however, that the choice of a unique and irreplaceable lover is an essential component of the movement beyond the particular individual. Passionate love for an individual who holds out the promise of satisfaction necessarily lives in the anguish of losing that individual, it heightens the passion and can send one into the ruinous abnegation of self. The point is that the specific individuality of one person is the necessary fuel to the loss of one's own individuality:

> Its irreplaceable individuality is a finger that points to the abyss. . . . To those who avidly desire laceration, individuality is necessary. Laceration wouldn't

be *itself* if not a laceration of a particular person, a person chosen for his or her plenitude. . . . Hence this deep paradox: it's not simple laceration that intensely lacerates us, but rich individuality . . . abandoning us to anguish. . . . The greatest vertigo comes from the beloved's uniqueness.[161]

Yet if eroticism is to attain divinity, then we must see that erotic desire only seems to have a definite object, whereas actually this object is "an indefinite presence. God and a woman who is loved are parallel [i.e., distinct objects]. Contrasted to them would be nothingness [i.e., GOD] and a woman's nakedness (irrespective of any particular woman)."[162] The search for GOD in eroticism leads us to *Madame Edwarda*.

Madame Edwarda, written by "Pierre Angélique," reads like a mystical tract under the guise of an erotic novella.[163] The theoretical preface (written by Bataille) leaves no doubt as to the significance of the book: to "rediscover God" (12). The assumption that God has been lost seems to be presupposed from the start. But this does not change the fact that the projection of one's existence toward some "point" is required for a religious framework, and that the nature of this point, as well as attitude of the subjective pole, determines the result of this projection. For Bataille, the positing of a benevolent and transcendent God mirrors the structure of a subject facing a clear and distinct object, or the confrontation with an intact mirror—it solidifies the subject. Bataille's view of divinity reverses this structure. If God is to be "rediscovered," it is by "bringing God himself into play,"[164] that is, by putting the notion of God *at risk* through the projection of one's existence toward a point that provokes an ecstatic response, a point that mirrors the excessiveness of God. One "rediscovers" God in excess, in ecstasy, in the "identity of extreme pleasure and extreme pain, the identity of being and death"—the "little death" *(petite morte)*, that is—a moment in which one feels oneself to be dying.

Let us now turn briefly to Pierre Angélique's tale, his perverse catechism. The story itself is simple, divided into two scenes: the narrator stumbles into a brothel (the Mirrors), where he encounters Mme. Edwarda who, spreading her legs, exposes herself to him in the café, and then they go up to a room; the second part consists of Edwarda racing out into the street, delirious, with the narrator following after her, and they eventually encounter a taxi driver with whom she makes love while the narrator watches. End of story. Starting casually, the story quickly moves to the confrontation with and affirmation of God's *presence*. Sparing Bataille's description, what occurs is that Edwarda lifts a leg, pulling apart her thighs to afford a better view, and declares: "You see . . . I am GOD" (21). In his distress, the gazer begins to pull away, aware that she is not only opening her thighs but that her action was an "opening to the consciousness of a laceration *[d'une déchirure]*" (Preface, 10). "Don't you shield your eyes," she commands, "you've got to see: look!" (21, trans. modified). It is not surprising that one should turn away, run from one's own distress, but there is an opposing determination to look it in the eye, to see that from which our integrity was shielding us.[165]

After exposing the presence of GOD quite literally down-below, there is an ascension in the form of mounting the stairs to her room: "Mme. Edwarda went on ahead of me . . . up into the clouds" (21). They make love surrounded by mirrors, a broken, fragmented image of an animal coupling. The mirror no longer offers an image that assures the unity of self. But this is as well the turning point for Bataille to pull off his mystical slight of hand. The anguished tension felt when one toes the border of the limits of self in the face of a specific object of desire, when one is at the edge of the sacrificial circle, is dissipated in the act of love. That is, repeating the structure of Eckhartian mystical experience wherein one must clear the ground for God by letting go of self and "God," we see here that what was the desire for a specific object (Edwarda, "God") has become a passageway to a sovereign absence of desire, absence of self and absence of "God." "That pleasure, in the end, overturned us" (22). The liberation from individuality is the passageway to GOD.

To state the matter succinctly, whereas Edwarda first manifests God's transcendent presence, she then reveals God's transparent absence. The pages that follow, as we track the elusive Edwarda through the streets in the black night, are on a level with one of Eckhart's sermons, almost consciously and explicitly drawing upon the mystic's language itself:

> She was entirely black, simple, as anguishing as hole: I realized . . . that indeed, underneath the veiling garment she wore, she was now absent. I then knew . . . that She had not lied, that She was GOD. Her presence had the unintelligible simplicity of a stone: in the middle of the city I had the feeling of being in the mountains at night, surrounded by a lifeless solitude. . . . I felt that I was free of Her. . . . I trembled, perceiving before me what is most barren in this world. . . . I was amazed to grasp it all so well. . . . I accepted, I desired to suffer, to go farther, as far as the "void" itself, even if I should be destroyed. I knew, I wanted to know, avid for her secret without doubting for an instant that it was death that ruled her. . . . Her nakedness now had the absence of meaning and at the same time the excessive meaning of a death-shroud. Strangest of all—and most disturbing—was the silence in which Mme.Edwarda remained enclosed: in her suffering there was no more possible communication and I was absorbed in this barrenness [absence d'issue]— in this night of the heart which was no less than a desert nor less hostile than the empty heavens . . . (24–26)

It is in the silence of ecstasy, where no possibility for communication remains, that Communication takes place. Fleeing like the object anguish desires to attain, Edwarda provokes her pursuer into a vertiginous sliding away from the narrow horizon of self, an absorption to the outside, ecstasis without object: "Edwarda's contortions tore me from myself and threw me into a black beyond" (27). Thrown into a region of silence, of sovereign "indifference" to self and to desire, we encounter GOD.

It would make sense that he end the story here, with both characters lost in the black void beyond particular beings. But he does not conclude at this point, adding a final scene in which Edwarda has an erotic encounter with a taxi driver, *watched* by the narrator. If this is not purely gratuitous, and we must assume it is not, then there must be some point Bataille is making by including it. I believe that what guides his final maneuver is the realization that there are only two options open to humanity: death or dissatisfaction. In the scene just described, the individuals (Edwarda and the chauffeur) have ecstatically submerged themselves in the absolute, have completely relinquished their subjectivity in a fusion equivalent to death. And while they do not actually die, having only the feeling of dying, I think that to account for the final scene requires us to connect it with the notion that without mediation, without the maintenance of limits, the assenting of life to death is a pure acquiescence to death. This is not Bataille's point. The narrator—Bataille, we assume—has *watched a spectacle* of individuals lost in ecstasy, and through this spectacle, has participated in their absence. Bataille thus implicitly asserts that it is the through the death of an *other* that one's own death, the night of non-knowledge, is suddenly there. The immediate fusion of subject and object is not a pure, irrevocable, loss of the subject. Despite appearances, an economy of life is maintained. But in this economy, and through its relation to insensate moments of meaningless expenditure, life is awakened to its connection with what lies beyond the economy of life—the sacred.

I would suggest that Mme.Edwarda's final throes of erotic abandon, in which she reveals herself as sacred through the presentation of a sacrificial spectacle to the narrator-viewer, is in fact a fictional transposition of another image imprinted in Bataille's mind—that of a Chinese torture victim, photographs of which were curiously enough given to Bataille by his psychoanalyst (Adrien Borel) in 1928. This horrific series of photographs depict a Chinese man bound to a pole, his limbs being cut from his body and holes bored into his torso while his eyes are rolled heavenward, an incongruous expression of ecstasy on his face. It is with this photograph before him—an image of not only of disfigurement and violence to the human form, but as well of painful enjoyment *(jouissance)* at the literal rips to the integrity of this form—that Bataille began writing. And it is specifically this contradictory representation of suffering and rapture that was "decisive" for Bataille: "This photograph had a decisive role in my life. I have never stopped being obsessed by this image of pain, simultaneously ecstatic and intolerable."[166] As we have seen in his fiction, Edwarda was the point, the "object" of desire which provoked the anguished ecstasy in which GOD was rediscovered. And as Bataille says of himself, "I didn't choose God as an object, but humanly, the young Chinese."[167] It is in is facing this image, this broken mirror, and somehow experiencing it as love and friendship with the victim, that Bataille perceives, at the extreme limit, the *divine* coincidence of extreme joy and pain. It is facing this image that Bataille experiences erotic and sacrificial Communication of beings united by wounds.[168]

There is a final note to sound, however, with respect to *Mme. Edwarda*, which is that Bataille takes care to confirm the meaninglessness of the final scene, as well as that of the entire book, by denying the seriousness of these dramatic evocations. In a self-parodying gesture, he says, "Monsieur Nonsense is writing and understands that he is mad: it's awful. But his madness, this nonsense—how it has all of a sudden become so 'serious': would that of itself be of some 'meaning'?" His answer: "No, Hegel has nothing to do with the 'apotheosis' of a madwoman . . ." (30). The erotic comedy has taken us beyond the serious. In the end, one has not died, but has seen enough to be able to laugh at the tenacity with which one held to life and its calculations for the future, with what anguish it avoided the joy of letting go, letting life itself be consumed and burned. In the end, "sovereignty (the absolute degree of putting at risk) . . . laughs at itself . . . for *the sovereign operation also needs life* . . . in order to be in relation to itself in the *pleasurable* consumption of itself. *Thus, it must simulate, after a fashion, the absolute risk,* and it must laugh at this simulacrum."[169] The final word of sacrifice . . . is laughter.

Laughter—In Place of a Conclusion

To see tragic figures founder and to be able to laugh at the spectacle, despite the profound understanding, the emotion and the
sympathy that one feels, that is divine.
                                    —Nietzsche, *The Will to Power*

I laugh when I think that my eyes persist in demanding objects
that do not destroy them.
                        —Bataille, The Practice of Joy before Death

We have come to our final point, the point with which—if we were to have
followed Bataille's scheme—we should have started . . . laughter.[1] Indeed,
Bataille does not hesitate to propose laughter as the *arche* and *telos* of philosophy itself, "its very first and perhaps its ultimate given."[2] And if we cannot
accept that, then at least we may identify laughter as the central point of his
own "philosophy."[3] From the very beginning of his philosophical reflections he
believed that laughter would be the "grail" unlocking the very essence of
things. Reflecting back twenty-odd years (from the time of writing IE, 1943),
he recounts that:

> Laughter was revelation, it revealed the essence of things . . . [reading Berg-
> son's *Le Rire*, Bataille says, the theory fell short] . . . but the question, the
> meaning still hidden in laughter was from then on the key question in my
> eyes . . . the enigma that I would resolve at all costs (and which, once
> resolved, would itself resolve everything).[4]

If, in Bataille's view, laughter should "resolve" everything, perhaps it is due to
an awareness, not yet articulated, that laughter resolves nothing, which would
turn his adherence to the revelatory function of laughter into an implicit
Socratic admission that he knows nothing (laughter being an "effect" of not
knowing), that knowledge knows nothing if it fails to take account of the

209

unknowing from which it begins and to which it must return: ashes to ashes. Or still more accurately, laughter would accompany the revelation that occurs to the one who, "avid for knowledge . . . remains finally, in his *knowing non-knowledge*, something like the unexpected result of this operation [the 'work of knowing'].["](5) Already we may perceive not only the overriding critique involved in laughter, which is that of the hubris of knowledge and the subject's desire to know, but also one of its intrinsic forms, namely, a self-critical humbling of the one who claims to know in the face of something unexpected and perhaps overwhelming.

Is it thus the case that after all the "work of knowing" we have carried out thus far, all the discursive effort of making distinctions, arguments, conclusions, that we are no farther than the point from which we began, that we (philosophers) are so many dogs chasing their tails? Must we face the possibility that this has all been for nothing, a risible attempt to find some meaning for oneself by finding some meaning in the completion of a project that will mean . . . *ad infinitum?* In fact we do, but this may not be such a morbid proposal. In fact such an admission may carry its own unexpected levity and affirmation, if it is indeed possible to escape the gravity of another form of affirmation—that of individual sufficiency, which Bataille translates into the imperative of meaning. And it is the attempt to escape this imperative that will expose the relationship between the unlikely companions of sacrifice and laughter. This is not all that is at stake, however, for we must, according to Bataille's directive, find in laughter some final perspective. And to do so we shall be taken through a series of confrontations with the lead players on the stage—Bataille, Nietzsche, and Hegel.

But first of all, just how does it come to be that Bataille proposes "to solve the enigma of sacrifice [that is, *"the ultimate question"*] . . . in laughter"?(6) How is it that a phenomenon which is apparently so deadly serious, which occurs in and through the play with death, comes to be resolved in such apparent playfulness? Is Bataille simply following Goethe's praise of the ancients for treating the most profound pathos as mere aesthetic play, for their "profound superficiality," as Nietzsche translates? In part at least this playful attitude toward the abysmal will be seen as a constitutive element in laughter. Yet when we first look at Bataille's implausible association of laughter and sacrifice, we find that the disparity is not so pronounced once we remember that one of the primary reasons for bringing sacrifice to account was to question its moral, economic, or generally limited transcendent *meaning* in a system of goal-oriented, efficacious action (productive negativity). Or in a word, sacrifice was staged in order to question its seriousness. Which is precisely the perspective from which Bataille approaches laughter, namely as a phenomenon that "suspends" the Hegelian imposition of meaning, suspends indefinitely the imperative to perform the work of dialectics which sets its guiding limits on what can be lost in every game with death, the game laughter plays.

More fundamentally, however, to penetrate this enigma solely requires the recognition that laughter is presented as following, to the letter, the movement and structure of sacrifice, and consequently eroticism. Or, uniting these forms, the movement of Communication which ruptures the subject's isolation and individuation through a relation to an object that itself is ruptured. A movement—like that found in Nietzsche's vision of tragedy, and as well found in Hegel's critique of the isolated individual that takes itself as absolute—which reveals a "beyond" of the illusion of individuality itself. Yet Bataille sees sacrificial Communication in the Nietzschean light as retaining the advantage of being brought into play without the moral or economic compromises that come with intentionally relating its violence and violation to, or reconciling it with, some transcendent good, some future promise, by which sacrifice *maintains* its work. Laughter overcomes us in an instant, invades us, as Bataille often says, "in spite of ourselves," causing our being to lose its stability, its isolation, and undergo a "sliding" movement that begins and terminates with no particular aim in mind.[7] In this way, laughter will become the sign, the inarticulate speech, of sovereignty, of sovereign communication.

At first glance, however, the association of laughter with sovereignty can be misleading, as there is first of all the possibility to read Bataille's interpretation of laughter in the classic sense of originating from, and conditioned by, a position of "sovereign" superiority or aloof skepticism.[8] For indeed, laughter is the response provoked by the comic situation when someone else takes a fall—from grace, from the image of sufficiency or stability—when the banana peel inevitably plants the respectable person on his or her ass. In which case laughter is the result of distance, of not being personally involved with the other, or as Baudelaire aptly states it: "*I* do not fall; *I* walk upright."[9] Or—as Freud points out with the example of a condemned man who, while on his way to be dangled at the end of a rope one Monday morning, ironically states, "Well, the week's beginning nicely"—it arises from taking a distance on oneself, acting *as if* one's "precious" self is not at risk, *as if* we could rise above our situation and assert the "invulnerability" of our individuality which "refus[es] to be distressed by provocations of reality, to let itself be compelled to suffer."[10] The essential aspect of humour, and of tame laughter that accompanies it, is thus to reduce to nothing any threat to our *selves*, to *not get carried away* in an explosive pathological expression, as "there is no doubt that the essence of humour is that *one spares oneself* the affects to which the situation would naturally give rise and dismisses the possibility of such expressions with a jest."[11] Or as Bataille says—making our reading considerably more difficult—the laughter of the spectator who witnesses the fall of another, the laughter of the one who "remains upright," serves to "dispel the anguish" that would result if one actually saw oneself in the other, and thereby saw the fall as a possibility for oneself.[12]

Herein lies the point of ambiguity with respect to Bataille's notion of laughter. By stating that in laughter, the anguish that would arise from the risk to oneself is overcome, and in fact to present laughter from the position of an indifferent or even hostile spectator who is above the situation—and thus above any real sense of risk to oneself—he has done nothing more than reinsert the tragic theory of purgation into his theory of laughter, thereby affirming everything from which I have presented him as taking a distance. In an uncharacteristic moment, he even claims that there must be an acceptable "proportion of profit to loss"[13] if the loss involved is to be sustained. While the ramifications of this statement, which if upheld would send reverberations through the entirety of his work, must be considered, I do not believe that it is worthwhile to dwell on it at this moment, for immediately after presenting such a feeble account of the phenomenon in question he demotes it to a minor position and once again emphasizes the dynamic with which he started: the intimate association or identification of the spectator with the one who has revealed his vulnerability.[14]

That is, he reasserts the play that occurs between anguish and release we have identified in sacrifice, where "gaiety [or here, laughter, C.G.], connected with death, causes . . . is accentuated by, and in return exacerbates . . . anguish."[15] Anguish serves to increase the intensity of the explosive communication of laughter (self-loss)[16] which, insofar as it reaches a point of strained intensity, "does not entail a balance of accounts between profit and loss,"[17] and which may then accelerate the loss to the point of causing a trembling at the heart of existence itself. And while he continues, in the article "Sacrifice," to assert the function of "profit—the sense of superiority,"[18] which is to dispel anguish, at the height of laughter's convulsion the awareness of the protective spacing of viewing the spectacle from without is annulled, and Communication enters the picture: a "major sort of communication by which everything is violently called into question," which arises "only when death is at stake."[19] Thus, when he rhetorically asks, "[W]hat passes within those who burst into laughter upon seeing a fellow man take a fall? Can it be that their neighbor's misfortune brings them such joy?"[20] the answer can only be negative—exposing the falsehood of his own proposition of superiority—insofar as the neighbor's misfortune is not the issue, nor is the Schadenfreude thereby implied. Rather, the misfortune, the fallibility—and ultimately the finitude—of the other is but a term of mediation which reflects one's own misfortune, so that what is communicated between them, "that which is revealed in our laughter," in a paraphrase of Nietzsche, is a "fundamental accord between our joy and an impulse to self-destruction,"[21] or as he stated elsewhere, our "joy before death." As with a sacrifice, the communication that is laughter is not circumscribed solely within the destruction of an object, but "causes a slipping . . . [to the sacrifice of] the subject."[22] Yet can we be so certain that the sense of superiority is truly dispelled? For even with Nietzsche—whose view of tragedy had a decisive influence on Bataille's notion of laughter, sacrifice, and eroticism, and whose language of "sovereignty" was appropriated by Bataille as well—we find a shifting interpretation.

For while Nietzsche will always retain that in tragedy the spectator is presented with the terrifying spectacle of a noble individual being destroyed, and that this vision fills the spectator with "joy" at the feeling of a sense of oneness with the forces of destruction, the emphasis on the type of "joy" does not remain the same. In the early *Birth of Tragedy*, the emphasis rests on the redemption involved with destruction as a release from the source of all suffering, the principle of individuation. The destruction of the hero was thus for the spectator a catalyst for rapturous self-abandon and submersion of one's individuality in the satyrnalian chorus, a movement that we should have no difficulty perceiving in Bataille's vision. Years later when the text was reprinted, however, Nietzsche added a preface to the text, the "Attempt at a self-criticism," which relegated the notion of self-abnegation to the status of mere romanticism. The tragic confrontation with and joy in destruction is now a heroic confrontation, an assertion of individual strength in the face of the inevitable. No longer does the sovereign individual require redemption from itself, rather it *affirms* its *self* in suffering, by "staring death in the face," if you will—and here too we find echoes from Bataille. Furthermore, with this change in emphasis comes a transformation in the status of laughter. No longer is it the laughter that dispels the "absurdity" of limited individual existence and finds "metaphysical comfort" in the "annihilation of the ordinary bounds and limits of existence."[23] Rather, it is the defiant laughter of the hero in confrontation with its fate, the laughter of strength which is a laughter of disgust at the cowardice of those still in need of metaphysical comfort.[24] In the later theory there is neither a critique nor a limit posited to heroism and hubris—the forces of destruction are a springboard to the "sovereign" affirmation of the individual *as* a (higher) individual.[25]

Does Bataille take a definitive stance between tragic self-abnegation and sovereign, heroic affirmation? And correlatively, is his "sovereign" laughter a laughter that reveals a humbling of the individual in the face of something that exceeds and overwhelms it, and which reveals at the same time that the collapse of the individual opens to an affirmation—perhaps even "comfort"— of being beyond individuality? Or is his laughter that of mocking superiority with respect to those who hold to the "comfort" of metaphysics, with respect to those cowardly types who either turn away from death or strive to give it some human meaning so as to "dispel the anguish"? The question of mocking superiority may answered with a bit more clarity if we look to what I believe is the real issue Bataille is consistently trying to address, the reason he takes sacrifice onto the plane of Communication and laughter, and how in doing so he will be able to conclude that one can no longer take oneself as "more serious," as superior to, more stable, closed, perfect, "than the objects of his laughter."[26] For what ultimately justifies linking sacrifice to Communication, and then to the laughter that will express what is revealed in Communication, is the fundamental, even archaic, purpose behind sacrifice: the redressing of a wrong, an abuse or exploitation. And the wrong that humankind has done to itself, in Bataille's opinion, always comes down to the futile, though human, assertion of the "imperative presence," "the avidity for the dominion of . . . ,"[27] or the seriousness of, the *me*, the *ipse*, the self: mankind is *"guilty* of being a *self,"*[28] of hubris and humanistic *self*-assertion.

Does this not, however, reveal his affinity with another sense of the tragic, one that posits not only the need for a "sovereign" subject, but as well involves a dialectic of self-destruction *intrinsic* to the self-assertion of that sovereign subject? An affinity, that is, with the analysis of tragedy as found in Hegel? For whether it is a matter of Greek or modern tragedy—the differences between which, while significant, need not occupy us here—the core of tragedy for Hegel rests on a self-impelled downfall brought about by the self-oriented actions of self-assertive individuals, the onesidedness of which inevitably leads to conflict and catastrophe. It leads, that is, to the breakdown or "death" of the individual as individual and its entry into the community of spirits (rather than Nietzsche's primordial One). What we must examine further then is how the failure built into hubristic individuality is resolved, and in particular whether Bataille will finally side with the early Nietzsche and emphasize the sinking of individuality into the undifferentiated abyss; or whether he leans toward Hegel's claim that the Greek/Dionysian sacrificial spectacle only anticipates the appropriation of this destruction into self-consciousness; or then again, whether he somehow unites the two.

For we know that even if Bataille accepts the imminent dialectic of self-destruction implied in individuality, and posits this as an essential element of self-consciousness, he will not accept the Hegelian view that the destruction of particularity is a logical necessity internal to the universal spirit in which the living individual is but an external moment of alienation to be overcome in the self-mediation of the concept. The question, rather, is whether the breakdown of self-assured individuality—which is ultimately the source of laughter—points to a *dialectical* beyond-of-individuality which will be transformed, mediated, and neutralized by the cadence of the concept or the rational community; or whether the collapse of the individual points to something that, while eluding dialectics altogether, nevertheless contributes to self-consciousness, something of the order of heterogeneous, "non-logical difference," or "elements that are impossible to assimilate."[29] And furthermore, if it is the latter that provokes laughter, and this laughter is not simply a form of defiance in the face of that which is devastating, does laughter then indicate some final affirmation of the negative moment, even if it is a negative that does not dialectically convert itself into a positive? Does laughter finally *heal* an ontological wound that dialectics can only close by diminishing its impact?

This question, for the moment, remains open. What we may assert with certainty, however, is that sovereign existence is not the maintenance of inviolable mastery, a proud and defiant position that asserts the willful identification of the subject with itself and takes risks according to its self-determined principles. Nor are we dealing with an identity that merely circumnavigates difference in order to further develop its identity. Rather, sovereign existence is an ecstatic movement toward the unforeseeable and ungraspable, caught in the movement of "catastrophe—lived time"[30] by "objects" which violently dispel the illusion of sufficient existence, which expose human beings as mutually wounded, expose the precariousness of *me* perched above the void; "objects" that thereby subvert the presence, the projection, and the avidity for *self.* Or if we were to employ Heideggerian terminology, to which Bataille denied himself recourse primarily on grounds of methodology, we find that sacrifice, Communication, and laughter expose Being in order to put into question the limited, distinct, and individual *"being (one being),"* which Bataille calls "a movement closing over itself, uniting limited elements. Unity is the essential attribute of a being."[31] Or more specifically, we may identify Bataille's notion of Being itself as Communication,[32] acute intermingling and combination with other beings—intentionally provoked in sacrifice and tragedy, spontaneously overcoming us in sex and laughter—a definition that is based on his fundamental principle of human life: *"the principle of insufficiency."*[33] This principle, which guides Bataille's ontology of dissatisfaction, is but another way of asserting the wisdom of Lessing that it is better to desire—desire being the sign, indeed the equivalent, of insufficiency—than to be satisfied.[34]

Of course, this does not, indeed cannot, prevent the desiring individual from trying to find satisfaction, from projecting one's existence onto a point— whether it be a goal, a commodity, a lover, or God—onto a fixed object that reflects the illusion of completeness or perfection which one expects will satisfy one's own desire for completeness, invulnerability to time, and autonomy. And while, as he claims, "it is true that this isolated 'being'—foreign to what it is not—is the form in which existence and truth first appeared to you," and while "it is to this irreducible difference—which you are—that you must relate the sense of each object," nevertheless, as he invariably adds, "the unity which you are flees from you and escapes. . . . Thus, there where you would like to grasp your timeless substance, you encounter only a slipping, only the poorly coordinated play of your perishable elements."[35] The human being is, in this fundamental way, unhappy consciousness searching to deny itself as such, and effectively does so by perceiving each thing in light of the illusion of *self* (unity, *ipse*), by finding in its chosen objects the reflection of stability, an assurance, an *answer* to the quest for being, a means to take oneself "out of play." And the privileged object that answers this plea for permanence is, of course, God.

But then, taking on a rather "Left-Hegelian" slant by criticizing the content of the divine illusion as being mere human content, Bataille reasserts the core insight of *Guilty,* claiming that:

> Belief in God is belief in self. God is only a guarantee given to me. . . . We're reassured when something is stated clearly, and defining an immutable

SELF as the principle of our being and nature presents the temptation to make the object of meditation something clear. Such a definition projects what we are into infinity or eternity. (G, 45)

The big lie: existing in this world under these conditions and thinking up a God who's like us! A God who calls himself *me!* Imagine a God— a being distinct from others—calling himself *I*. . . . This kind of nonsense transposes a notion we have of ourselves onto a scale of totality. God is the kind of impasse that happens when the world . . . surrounds our *self* to give it the illusion of possible salvation . . . the God of theology is only a response to a nagging urge of the self to be finally *taken out of play*. (G, 85, author's emphasis)

Bataille's point, however, is not that of the Marxist-humanists, rather it is quite the opposite. For while such a critical conception of the divine has a legitimate basis given its context of condemning the desire for flight from the human condition—and on this count Bataille could not be more in agreement—it nevertheless transposes human autonomy into the absolute. Atheist humanism ultimately claims divine status for humanity ("man is the only god for man," as Marx claims), and ultimately the proponents of finitude end in denying the profound truth of finitude. Bataille meanwhile believes that "if we ceased to project the *self* on the absolute we'd be convulsed with laughter."[36] This may be read in two ways: as a counter to the Marxist/Kojève-style atheist humanism that projects the self-productive, self-assertive self into the status of the absolute, without bringing about a tragic downfall; and as a counter to the theological projection of the self above and beyond itself in a search for a stable, absolute object (God or the derivatives thereof) which— like a mother to her child—would answer the desire for satisfaction with its own sufficiency.

Now both of these perspectives, each in its own way, are not only tempting, but necessary. Why then the laughter which would result should they be abandoned? The answer lies in the tension between an ontic perspective of "representational thought" and its drive for complete self-determination in knowledge, and an ontological perspective that undermines the efforts of the knowing subject to render everything it encounters determinate. When boiled down, "representational thinking"—as it has come to be known and condemned—effectively takes the salvific methodologies of an anthropocentric strain of Christianity and hands them over to the human subject who then provides for its own salvation. That is, it posits the self-certain subject as the substance and efficient cause of all things, which transforms all entities into determinate objects as represented before cognition. Whether this involves the representation of a determinate God, or the representation of objects and other subjects as determinate, at stake is the positing of a separate and distinct object which may be brought under the control of the knowing subject—divide and conquer. And the critique of this form of thought, a critique that has become the mode of continental thought since Heidegger, is that the other is not represented *as other*, but rather as present within the thought of the subject, such that the representation is of no other, but rather is a reflection of the subject. In this way, nothing may be seen to strike at the walls of subjective certainty, to breach its self-sufficient closure, to put it at risk. And it is this steadfast insistence to hold to one's particular certainty and knowing integrity which, for Bataille, is not only profoundly laughable for its "fearful, timid attachment" to harmless determinacy that is "taken for what it appears to be," but is as well an ontological misrecognition of the truth of intimacy.

It is an error for its lack of insight to an *impersonal* and indeterminate intimacy (or Being as I claimed earlier) that both exceeds and precedes every determinate representation of self and other, and consequently it is an error for misrecognizing the impersonal ground of interpersonal relations. Which is not to say that the positing of a distinct subject and determinate object are not necessary, but rather to assert that they are necessary if only to exacerbate the anguish when the walls of isolation begin to crack, when one's existence begins to flow outside itself, to become other: ". . . the fragile walls of your isolation . . . the stabilized order of isolated appearances is *necessary* to anguished consciousness of the torrential floods which carry it away."[37] The representation of stable existences is thus necessary as a means to pass beyond the representation, and into unrepresentable intimacy. And the error is revealed when the represented object undergoes a sacrifice and falls from on high, exposing, through its wounds, the excessive nothingness that its appearance conceals. When, that is, it enters Communication: "The crucifixion, for example, is a wound by which believers communicate with God," but Bataille's "crucified" is not God, it is (the image of) a Chinese torture victim being ripped to pieces, a dignified woman in the throes of ecstasy,[38] both of which are greeted with a burst of laughter.

The laughter, however, as I again emphasize, does not arise from remaining at a distance from destruction, even if it is indeed seen through a representation or spectacle. Rather, it arises from the undermining of the separation between one isolated person and another, emerging from isolated existence by means of the image which betrays the error of self-determination: "[E]ssentially, the laugh comes from *Communication*."[39] That is—to repeat our opening quotation from Nietzsche—the laughter that greets the spectacle of a figure who founders, arises "*despite* the sympathy that one feels," which is ultimately to say that one laughs at *oneself* foundering, at *one's own* fallibility with which one is in complicity through the other who has betrayed the illusion of being integral, upright, sufficient. As in the dialectic of self-consciousness where each position of consciousness is taken as absolute until it breaks down and is exposed for what it really is, one laughs when one's own imaginary pretensions to absoluteness are exposed and brought to awareness in confrontation with something that exceeds one's comprehension. One laughs, in short, when one's finitude is affirmed. Laughter attests to "an apotheosis of that which is perish-able,"[40] it is the quintessential affirmation of an excess that cannot be reduced to ourselves, and a knowing awareness that our relation to this excess under-mines our sense of being at ease with ourselves and the world.

To illustrate the dynamic we have been analyzing, I shall now turn to an example of erotic revelation, which I believe will better situate laughter as a form of self-conscious knowledge. The example is found in *Eroticism* (106), and in keeping with the thrust of this text it is guided by the essentially reli-gious play of prohibition and the (sacrificial/sexual) violence of transgression. Here, the prohibition is expanded to entail the enclosure in individual separa-tion or "discontinuity," that has its "foundations" in the "anguish of death and pain" which "has bestowed on this wall of separation the solidity of prison walls."[41] Meanwhile, transgression, which brings death into life, has "depriv[ed] the creature of its limited particularity and bestow[ed] on it the limitless nature of sacred things."[42] As the scene goes, in the violence of sexual urges,

> [a] madness suddenly takes possession of one's being. Although that mad-ness is well known to us, we can easily imagine the surprise of anyone who . . . by some device, secretly witnessed the amorous transports of a woman who had struck him as particularly dignified. He would think she was sick, just as mad dogs are sick. As if some rabid bitch had usurped the place of the person who had received him with such distinction. Yet sickness is not putting it strongly enough; *for the moment the personality is dead.* For the moment its death gives the bitch free reign, and she takes advantage . . . *of the other's absence in death.* The bitch comes *(jouit)* . . . in response to this silence and this absence. The return of the personality [and it invariably returns, C.G.] would [put an end to her abandon].[43]

For a moment, having broken the chains of transcendence (the "completeness" of her personality, her dignified stability), her being has toppled over into nothing (absence), the "beyond of beings." She has undergone, in Hegel's terms, the "absolute liquefaction of everything stable." She has become a sac-rificial spectacle seen through a keyhole, communicating to the spectator the "unknown" and sacred regions of death which she has entered. The spectacle is different from a mirror. It undermines the ordinary state of knowledge with which we find ourselves in the world, the "order of things" in which we rec-ognize ourselves, by undermining the "optical perspective" of knowledge that "distinguishes a perceived object from a perceiving subject,"[44] thereby leading the spectator into the "unknown."

The "unknown" arises, that is, insofar as the object, here in ecstasy, is stripped of its objectivity and dissipates into absence, into "night":

> The desired spectacle, the object, in the expectation of which passion goes beyond itself . . . this object grows dim and night is there . . . but this night

which is substituted for the object and now alone responds to my anticipation? Suddenly I know: it is not an object, it is IT I was waiting for. . . . If I hadn't gone to IT as eyes go to the object of their love, if the anticipation of a passion hadn't searched for it, IT would only be an absence of light. Whereas my exorbitant gaze finds IT, *ruins itself in it* . . . and yet IT is nothing . . . in IT, I communicate with the 'unknown' opposed to the *ipse* which I am; I become *ipse*, unknown to myself, two terms merged in a single rending *(déchirement)*, barely differing from a void.[45]

Captivated by the object that is no object, seeking to possess it with the expectation of satisfaction, one comes face to face with IT, and is dispossessed, momentarily ruined. But the extremity of this dispossession is such that—barring grave misfortune—it cannot be maintained, so it is dissatisfying, and desire will continue to search for IT in another (substitute) object.

Yet what is glimpsed in this moment carries its own "transparency," and what is made transparent is the improbable notion which Bataille has apparently carried over from the early Nietzsche, namely, that "essentially all beings are only one," that there exists a "fundamental identity" or continuity between beings, yet it cannot resist the movement of "repulsion" (or transcendence) which separates beings and in fact renders them stable, knowable entities.[46] Or in a phrase that witnesses Bataille's translation of representational thought, "knowledge requires a certain stability of things known. The realm of the known is . . . a stable one, in which we recognize ourselves."[47] What is made transparent, more specifically, is that isolated, individual existence, the basis of all our projects, knowledge, our *meaning*, is not the whole story. And even though it cannot be annulled, it can be (dialectically) suspended: "Transparency isn't the abolition of individual isolation but transcends it. It is not a *state* of theoretical or fundamental unity, but chance that occurs in risk. . . . Not pure *unified being* but one that is separated is (chance's) object, a separated being that owes to chance alone (to itself occurring as a separate being) the power it has to deny separation. But this negation assumes the encounter with a beloved."[48] Whether it is a beloved or a noble individual tragically annihilated, the movement through representation to Communication is the same. But in this statement Bataille takes two steps away from Nietzsche, and perhaps one toward Hegel: no *abolition* of the subject in a "fundamental unity" with the *Ur-eine;* no *willful* affirmation of suffering. Rather, an immanent yet innocent breakdown of the subject in its justifiable desire for satisfaction, and a movement through the breakdown to a new level of self-consciousness, another possibility of being.

Nevertheless, Bataille is indeed making a rather curious association between lovemaking and the Being of beings. The point of issue, however, ultimately is this: our individual being, our lives, the ends we pursue for ourselves, the meanings we give ourselves, all of these are painfully fragile insofar as they rest on a truth that is not the whole truth, insofar as the being that defines and is defined by these ends, goals, meanings, can—at any chance moment—sink into the void which it denied in becoming a particular being. Consequently, the all-too-human attempt to deny the transience and potential meaninglessness of those truths which we hold to be self-evident, to hold to them as to a metaphysical ground, is based on a fundamental misrecognition—or perhaps better, forgetfulness—of our constituent finitude, and of our intimate yet impersonal bond with an otherness we cannot master. However, as Bataille claims, if we could cease to flee from ourselves and into goals that render our finitude opaque and unreal, if we could recognize that which is in fact implicitly revealed to us all the time (in lovemaking, in the arts, in tears, laughter, drunkenness), namely, the futility of holding to one's self as the principle of all existence, this recognition would free us "from the worries that erode life," would give to life "the infinite transparency of something freed at last from a burden of meaning," a freedom that has "as its condition that I laugh, principally, *at myself*."[49] Mocking one's own pretensions to sufficiency, laughter affirms the chances of life as exposed by our own fallibility, a fallibility itself affirmed when something genuinely other breaks through and shocks us into consciousness of our vulnerability: "Brief-tenured tragedy finally has always returned to the eternal comedy of existence."[50]

But why, finally, does Bataille posit laughter as the response to this transparency, to the moment one has one's eyes opened to one's own fallibility and finitude? One possible answer lies in the theory that laughter results from "the sudden invasion of the unknown," that in laughter "we pass from the domain of the known . . . the foreseeable, to that of the unknown and unforeseeable":

> We laugh, in short, passing very abruptly, all of a sudden, from a world in which everything is firmly qualified, in which everything is given as stable within a generally stable order, into a world in which our assurance is overwhelmed, in which we perceive that this assurance was deceptive . . . suddenly the unexpected arises, something unforeseeable and overwhelming, revelatory of an ultimate truth: the surface of appearances conceals a perfect absence of response to our expectations.
>   We perceive that finally, for all the exercise of knowledge, the world still lies wholly outside its reach, and that not only the world, but the being that one is lies out of reach. Within us and in the world, something is revealed that was not given in knowledge. . . . It is, I believe, at this that we laugh . . . this is what ultimately illuminates us; this is what fills us with joy.[51]

One problem with this theory, however, is its general nature, for the above explanation, while consistent, perhaps irrefutable, nevertheless can be applied to other phenomena—particularly tears—where one is equally overwhelmed by the felicitous or tragic invasion of the unanticipated. Another problem with the theory is quite simply the fact that it is a theory, whereas Bataille is trying to pinpoint an *experience*. Laughter is indeed unknowable from without, it is missed if not lived. But there is yet another problem, the most difficult to address and potentially fatal for the theory, which is in effect the voraciousness of dialectics itself. And while we may momentarily suspend our orientation among the things of the world—just as we may turn a trick of language, undermine the expected cadence of discourse to provoke laughter—the destruction (negation) involved is not absolute. We retain the conviction that, after all, nothing has been definitively overcome. So, does Hegel indeed have the last laugh?

He would, except for the fact that Bataille has never said anything otherwise. Or more accurately, Bataille has never claimed that the negative experiences he has described can erase the trace of the positive. What he does claim is that they contribute nothing to that positive—that in fact they *mean* nothing—but they are nevertheless as legitimate as those experiences that contribute to meaning. In a word, they are *sovereign*. And if we must persist in deriving some "meaning" from them, we nevertheless cannot refer beyond the experiences themselves, for their "meaning" is contained solely in themselves, their negativity affirmed for nothing . . . but affirmed nonetheless. Carrying this logic through, we may thus conclude that they are sovereign in their insignificance, yet as sovereign, they as well express the insignificance of meaning and knowledge. In *Theory of Religion*, where he is discussing the movement of productive work—or, as I have repeated so often, where he is asserting the discursive, dialectical movement of Hegelian knowledge—in which each thing receives its meaning in relation to something else, each end is a means to another end, he states that "the absurdity of an endless deferral [of meaning, C.G.] only justifies *the equivalent absurdity* of a true end, which would serve no purpose."[52] In the end, sovereign being, "just like servile being . . . has no other sense than its fundamental insignificance."[53] Sovereign being is laughable,[54] yet it is sanctified *despite* its absurdity.

Yet one does not, cannot laugh at oneself, unless one can take distance from oneself, or see oneself as other. Which will reintroduce our respectable woman who has slipped from herself and into absence, who has died to herself. She—the erotic, sacrificial object of desire, the image of death by dispossession—has become the object of laughter, "which is always NOTHING, substituted for the anticipation of a given object," a substitution that occurs in the *sovereign* moment "in which the anticipation is resolved in NOTHING."[55] The sovereign moment—and sovereignty, like laughter, only belongs to the moment—is when desire (anticipation) encounters dissatisfaction, when it is disappointed, when negativity is "unemployed," when there is no more object, goal, *sens* (meaning/direction), or end. Identifying with, seeing oneself in her as she founders into the beyond of her being (into nothing), I lose myself in that which lies beyond what I know, and laugh at the thought that I am sunk, laugh at the thought that this moment "means" as much as the book I am writing—finally, I laugh at myself, who can't go on yet must go on, who cannot face yet must face that it is for nothing. This is the risk, the chance one must take. Which is not really a risk at all. It is simply an acceptance of finitude, an acceptance that the promises of satisfaction are so many devices to stave off inevitable dissatisfaction; and yet it is as well an acceptance of the desire to escape one's finitude, equally recognizing that it is just as impossible to *refuse* giving our actions, our desires and our death a meaning, laughing at our *inability* to stop taking ourselves so seriously, and accepting that it is impossible not to search for satisfaction before death—the desire for which, perhaps, coming from its inaccessible character. One cannot do otherwise, despite oneself.

If it all ends in laughter, however, perhaps Bataille has failed, but failed in a way that he would find acceptable. That is, perhaps he has failed in the way sacrifice failed, its success lying precisely in its failure, its failure being that something is won *despite* it all being for nothing. No direct confrontation with the abyss, rather a confrontation with oneself as other, a way to live with what cannot be survived if confronted directly. Or, in a summation which once again undermines his manifest anti-Hegelianism, the process of individuation and collapse is a process of "*acquiring life by losing it* in communication with each other."[56] Which is why the arts, literature, those who manage to put into form an overwhelming content within us, became the focus of Bataille's admiration. For even if they confront us with it, like laughter they offer relief from what could otherwise drown us in misery. And is this not, despite the radicality with which I have sometimes been obliged to present it, the efficacy of his favored notions such as risk, play, chance? For the final term evokes levity, an escape from Kojèvian seriousness, the anguish of being a self in the world with all one's memories and responsibilities. An anguish and concern, which would crush the present with the future and past, would deprive us of life and withdraw us from chance or risk, would take us out of play, "but to take risks means to overcome anguish,"[57] it is "the refusal to take anything seriously,"[58] to escape the imperatives of self, to unlearn our burdens and get caught, if ever so briefly, in the intoxication of childish play.

Notes

INTRODUCTION

1. "Even if he has lost the world in leaving animality behind, man has nonetheless become that consciousness of having lost it which we are, and which is more, in a sense, than a possession of which the animal is not conscious," Bataille, AS I, 133.

2. Cf. Bataille, E, 7, and Heraclitus, Fragment XXVII, from *The Art and Thought of Heraclitus*, trans. Charles H. Kahn (Cambridge: Cambridge University Press, 1979).

3. Hegel's criticism of what he calls the "Reflective Philosophy of Subjectivity" (i.e., Kant, Fichte, Jacobi) or more generally, the philosophies of the understanding (including Descartes and Enlightenment philosophy in general) and their corresponding empirical sciences, is relentless. In brief, he sees them as proceeding from a fixed opposition of subject and object, which they fail to adequately (dialectically) overcome, rather subsuming the given "objective" data under the unity of subjective law. Thought is thus reduced to subjectivity, which dominates, but does not really know, objectivity. It is thus not true knowledge. On this basis he as well views the sciences as blind, for in asserting knowledge as subjective and human, they disclaim the ultimate source of knowledge—God. We shall give this further consideration below. On the "Reflective Philosophy of Subjectivity," see Hegel's *Faith and Knowledge*, trans. W. Cerf and H. S. Harris (Albany: State University of New York Press, 1977).

4. Cf. Bataille, G, 14–27, and 147–61 where, for instance, he claims that "Desire . . . is avid not to be satisfied," 51.

5. The reference to the Anaximander Fragment and its modern traces was brought to my attention by William Desmond in his *Speculation, Cult, and Comedy* (Albany: State University of New York Press,1992), 200 *ff.* The quotation above is found here.

6. *Hegel's Science of Logic*, trans. A. V. Miller (London: George Allen & Unwin, 1969), 611. Reference cited from John W. Burbridge, *Hegel on Logic and Religion* (Albany: State University of New York Press, 1992), 33.

7. Hegel, *Hegel's Logic*, trans. W. Wallace (Oxford: Oxford University Press, 1985), 172.

8. Bataille, G, 25.

9. Cf. Bataille, AS 3, 203–18.

10. Bataille, LE, 72.

11. Bataille, "Un-knowing and Rebellion," *October 36*, 86.

12. Phillipe Sollers, "Intervention," in *Bataille: Communications, Interventions* (Paris: 10/18, 1974), 10.

13. Bataille, N, 157.

14. Cf. J.-L. Nancy, *La communauté désoeuvrée* (Paris: Bourgois, 1986), which is an extensive reflection upon Bataille's thought.

15. "Bataille suffered from lack of recognition. The dynamic and influential thinking of the last twenty years [1965–85, C.G.] owes so much to him (and paradoxically owes so much of its influence to him) that we ourselves find it difficult to believe in that lack" (Denis Hollier, "Introduction" to Bataille's *Guilty*, x). Jacques Derrida claims that a number of his texts "(particularly '*La double séance,*' '*La dissémination,*' '*La mythologie blanche,*' but also '*La pharmacie de Platon*' and several others) are situated *explicitly* in relation to Bataille, also explicitly putting forth a reading of Bataille," in *Positions*, trans. Alan Bass (Chicago: University of Chicago Press, 1981), n.35, 105–106, author's emphasis. See as well the "Introduction" to *Bataille: A Critical Reader*, ed. Fred Botting and Scott Wilson (Oxford: Blackwell, 1998), 1–23.

16. Bataille's infamous *Histoire de l'oeil (Story of the Eye)* was written around 1928, but was written under a pseudonym, Lord Auch, and privately published in a collection of pornographic novels. The bizarre little text, "The Solar Anus," was written in1927 but not published until 1931, illustrated with etchings by André Masson who, coincidentally, would later lose an eye.

17. Anecdotal evidence from the thorough biography by Michel Surya, *Georges Bataille: la mort à l'oeuvre* (Paris: Séguier, 1987) has Bataille living a rather bohemian lifestyle, at one point lodging in the studio of Klossowski's younger brother—Balthus. For Bataille's response to Breton, cf. "The 'Old Mole' and the Prefix *Sur* in the Words *Surhomme* and *Surrealist,*" in VE, 32–44. For a history and analysis of the dispute between Bataille and Breton, cf. Michael Richardson, *Georges Bataille* (London: Routledge, 1994).

18. The various groups I am discussing here, as well as the manner in which he coalesced Marxism and primitive anthropology into fascism, shall be given further treatment below. Cf. Chapter 2.2, "Unholy Alliances," 90 ff.

19. Maurice Blanchot, *La Communauté inavouable* (Paris: Les Èditions de Minuit, 1983), 27.

20. Bataille, "The Practice of Joy Before Death" in VE, 239. The text reads "JE SUIS MOI-MÊME LA GUERRE," while his name *(Bataille)* means battle. The quotation is the opening line of section VI in the text, entitled "Méditation Héraclitéene," OC I, 557.

21. The date on which Bataille began to write *Guilty* (September 5, 1939, the date World War II began) was, as he claims, "no coincidence," 11. In his "Introduction" to

this text, Denis Hollier posits that the very personal and enigmatic title to this text is owed to the "lightness" Bataille felt in the midst of all the disaster, his lack of seriousness with respect to the war. While this is an essential aspect of Bataille's work, I believe it is—in a moment uncharacteristic for Hollier—an inaccurate interpretation of the title. I will offer what I believe is a better one later, but would like to suggest in the current context that—given its proximity to the death of Laure, with whom Bataille had an obsessive, stormy and, if Michel Surya is correct, rather abusive and treacherous relationship—Bataille may well have felt a guilty complicity with that death. In this sense I do not think his familiarity with Freud was insignificant to the title (cf. Freud's text, "Mourning and Melancholia"). In any case, he was certainly "guilty" of *using* that death as a source for his writing, a *profanation* of the dead if you will.

22. Although Bataille claims that his "true entrance into contact with the work of Hegel" took place "from 1933," it seems that he was interested in Hegel from as early as the end of 1925. Cf. *"Emprunts de Georges Bataille à la Bibliothèque Nationale, 1922–1950,"* OC XII, 562.

23. For an analysis of the extent to which Kojève's interpretation influenced French thought, including Lacan, Merleau-Ponty, and Sartre among others, see Vincent Descombes's *Modern French Philosophy*, trans. L.Scott-Fox and J.M.Harding (Cambridge: Cambridge University Press, 1980).

24. Jean Hyppolite, *Logic and Existence*, trans. Leonard Lawlor and Amit Sen (Albany: State University of New York Press, 1997), 6.

25. Bataille, "From the Stone Age to Jacques Prévert," in AM, n.p.153. The note continues as follows: "This interpretation, which reduced the difference between Hegel and Marx . . . also had the interest of an original position, and perhaps a decisive value."

26. Jean-Luc Nancy and Phillipe Lacoue-Labarthe, *The Title of the Letter: A Reading of Lacan*, trans. François Raffoul and David Pettigrew (Albany: State University of New York Press, 1992), 123.

27. Jacques Derrida, "From Restricted to General Economy," in *Writing and Difference*, trans. Alan Bass (Chicago: The University of Chicago Press, 1981), 253; reprinted in *Bataille: A Critical Reader*, 104.

28. Ibid., 253.

29. Bataille, OC VIII, 562.

30. As Joseph Flay claims with respect to Kojève's *Interpretation*, "Kojève's influence is unfortunate, for seldom has more violence been done by a commentator to the original. . . . The interpretation . . . simply does not work; it might be good Kojève, and might even be correct about reality, but it is not Hegel" (Joseph C. Flay, *Hegel's Quest for Certainty* [Albany: State University of New York Press, 1984], 299 n.1).

31. Mark C. Taylor, *Journeys to Selfhood: Hegel and Kierkegaard* (Berkeley: University of California Press, 1980), 21, n.64.

32. Allan Bloom, "Editor's Introduction" to K1, ix.

33. Philip T. Grier, "The End of History and the Return of History," *The Owl of Minerva* 21, 2 (1990): 132, 133. We should as well consider the views of those such as

Daniel P. Jamros, S.J., who finds that "the clearest and most thorough commentary for exegesis of selected points is that of Alexandre Kojève. But Kojève's interpretation has a number of serious flaws . . . ," in *The Human Shape of God: Religion in Hegel's* Phenomenology of Spirit (New York: Paragon House, 1994), 15; and Robert C. Solomon, who essentially aligns himself with Kojève's reading, *cf.* Robert C. Solomon, *In the Spirit of Hegel: A Study of G. W. F. Hegel's Phenomenology of Spirit* (New York: Oxford University Press, 1983). Bataille's assessment is as follows: "whatever opinion one may have of the correctness of [Kojève's] interpretation of Hegel. . . . No one today can claim to be educated without having assimilated its contents. (I would also like to underscore the fact that Alexandre Kojève's interpretation does not deviate in any way from Marxism . . .)" (Bataille, Appendix to TR, 124).

34. Errol E. Harris, *The Spirit of Hegel* (New Jersey: Humanities Press, 1993), 45.

35. Ibid., 59.

36. Jamros, *op. cit.*, 15.

37. Kojève, K1, 131.

38. Ibid., 134. The article to which he is referring is Koyré's "Hégel à Iéna (à propos de publications récentes)," initially published in the *Revue philosophique de France* 59, 118 (1934): 274–83; also published in *Revue d'histoire et de philosophie religieuse* 15 (1935): 420–58; also found in Koyré, *Études d'histoire de la pensée philosophique* (Paris: Colin, 1961), 135–73; (2nd ed., Paris: Gallimard, 1971), 147–89. All references will be to this final edition (1971).

39. Grier, "The End of History, and the Return of History," *op. cit.*, 136–37. One will note that the dialectic of the temporal dimensions with respect to the theory of two infinites as proposed in Hegel's Jena text on Nature (1804–05) disappears in the later *Natuurphilosophie* from the *Encyclopedia* (1817) and the Berlin Manuscript on Space and Time (1821–22). Time is no longer the infinite, but is negativity, and moreover, time in nature is not historical, but is rather the negativity provoking the shifts between being and nothing. We shall encounter this again in what follows.

40. Cf. Koyré, 150. Strangely enough, Koyré himself will in turn ignore his own cautionary advice.

41. As Koyré states, "[T]he theological dialectic is a dialectic of the eternal *[l'intemporel]*. The historical dialectic is that of time. The one implies the primacy of the past, for in the *nunc aeternitatis* everything is already realized; the other, the primacy of the future, since in the historical *nunc*, the present itself only has meaning in relation to the future that it projects before it, that it announces and which it will realize in suppressing it" (ibid., 160, n.1).

42. George L. Kline has as well suggested that Kojève's view of the primacy of the future in Hegel was influenced by his reading of Heidegger; cf. George L. Kline, "Presidential Address [to the Hegel Society of America], 1986]: The Use and Abuse of Hegel by Nietzsche and Marx," in *Hegel and his Critics: Philosophy in the Aftermath of Hegel*, ed. William Desmond (Albany: State University of New York Press, 1989), 1–34. See as well Catherine Malabou, "Negatifs de la dialectique entre Hegel et le Hegel de Heidegger: Hyppolite, Koyré, Kojève," *Philosophie* 52 (December 1996): 37–53.

43. Koyré, 177.

44. Ibid., 169–70.

45. Ibid., 168.

46. Ibid., 177.

47. Ibid., 189. Or again, "Hegelian philosophy, the 'system', would only be possible if history has terminated, only if it no longer has any future; only if time could stop itself," ibid.

48. Ibid., 188–89.

49. Ibid.

50. Hegel, *Phenomenology of Spirit* (PS) §801, 487. See also Hegel's Preface, where it reads, *"Was die Zeit betrifft . . . so ist sie der daseiende Begriff selbst"* ("In what concerns *time . . .* it is the existent Concept itself") PS, §46, 27. Cf. Kojève, K1, 101. Note that I have chosen to use the translation of Hegel's *Begriff* as "Concept" rather than following Miller's translation as "Notion."

51. Kojève, K1, 133. See in general the Eighth Lecture in the chapter, "A Note on Eternity, Time, and the Concept," particularly pages 130–40. Consequentially, human existence is time, while nature (Being) is just space. As Kojève reads it, there is no time without human existence in space (Cf. Kojève, K1, 133, 137, where he is commenting on Hegel, PS §807, 492). Yet this, in the words of John Burbridge, amounts to a "perverse reading of the text," insofar as it involves a critical omission. Hegel does state that Spirit intuits "its Being as Space," but the following line reads: "This last becoming of Spirit, *Nature,* is its living immediate Becoming." Thus, Nature is not static Space, but is Becoming (cf. Burbridge, *Hegel on Logic and Religion, op. cit.,* 166 n.1).

52. Hegel, PS §801, 487, translation modified, second emphasis added.

53. Burbridge, *Hegel on Logic and Religion, op. cit.,* 79.

54. For an excellent analysis of the relation between, and necessary unification of, the *conceptual* process of becoming, the *circular* movement of which is from being to non-being to being, and the *linear* structure of time which moves from non-being to being to non-being, see Burbridge, "Concept and Time in Hegel," in *Hegel on Logic and Religion, op. cit.,* 79–93.

55. Hegel, *Hegel's Lectures on the History of Philosophy* in three volumes, trans. E. S. Haldane and Frances H. Simson (New York: The Humanities Press, 1968), vol. 1, 92, emphases added. This is repeated in the Introduction to his *Lectures on the Philosophy of Religion,* where again he is critiquing the separation of the two forms of consciousness at issue: "[M]an has in his actual worldly life a number of working days during which he occupies himself with his own special interests, with worldly aims in general, and with the satisfaction of his needs; and then he has a Sunday, when he lays all this aside . . ." (Hegel, *Lectures on the Philosophy of Religion together with a work on the proofs of the existence of God,* trans. Rev. E. B. Speirs and J. Burdon Sanderson, ed. Rev. E. B. Speirs, in three volumes [New York: The Humanities Press, 1974], vol. 1, 7).

56. Hegel, *Philosophy of Religion, op. cit.,* 9.

57. Raymond Queneau, *Le Dimanche de la vie* (Paris: Gallimard, 1952); translated as *The Sunday of Life* by Barbara Wright (New York: New Directions, 1977). Not with-

out coincidence, Raymond Queneau—a member of the *Collège de Sociologie* along with Bataille, and collaborator with Bataille on his first article dealing with Hegel, "La Critique des fondements de la dialectique hégelienne," *La Critique sociale* 5 (March 1932): 209–14, reprinted in VE, 105–15—was also responsible for assembling Kojève's lecture notes into the form they would take in the *Introduction à la Lecture de Hegel*. Furthermore, Queneau opens his book with yet another reference to the "Sunday of life" in Hegel, this time from *Hegel's Aesthetics: Lectures on Fine Art* (Vol. III, III, ch. 1), from which he quotes, "[I]t is the Sunday of life, which levels everything, and rejects everything bad; men gifted with such good humor cannot be fundamentally bad or base."

58. Cf. Walter Benjamin, "Theses on the Philosophy of History," in *Illuminations: Essays and Reflections*, ed. Hannah Arendt, trans. Harry Zohn (New York: Schocken, 1968).

CHAPTER 1. BEYOND THE SERIOUS

1. "Whether through logic or epistemology, whether through Marx or Nietzsche, our entire epoch struggles to disengage itself from Hegel" (M.Foucault, *L'ordre du discours*, cited in V.Descombes, *Modern French Philosophy*, 12, *op. cit.*).

2. Alexandre Koyré, "Hégel à Iéna," *op. cit.*, 153; 153 n.1. The first text reads, "Or, le 'sytème' hégélien est mort, et bien mort."

3. Karl Rosenkranz, *Georg Wilhelm Friedrich Hegel's Leben: Supplement zu Hegel's Werken* (Berlin: Duncker und Humblot, 1844), xii. Cited in Emil Fackenheim, *The Religious Dimension of Hegel's Thought* (Bloomington: Indiana University Press, 1967), 4.

4. Bataille, G, 43–44.

5. Bataille, "Letter to X [Kojève]," in *The College of Sociology*, 90, and G, 108.

6. Hegel, *Phenomenology of Spirit* (PS), §26, 14.

7. "Without Hegel, I'd first have had to be Hegel—and I lack the means" (Bataille, G, 108).

8. Bataille, IE, 150.

9. In French the term *sens* connotes not only sense/meaning but also direction or aim. To lose sense or meaning amounts to the loss of one's way, being without direction.

10. Bataille, "The Obelisk," in VE, 219, emphasis added.

11. Bataille, "*Hegel, la mort et le sacrifice,*" OC XII, 339.

12. J. Derrida, "From Restricted to General Economy," *op. cit.*, 253.

13. I note here that Bataille's *jeu* may be translated as "play," "game," "risk," or "gambling," as when one has to put one's chips on the table: "*Messieurs, faites vos jeux.*" Bataille's *jeu* is literally a game of *chance*. The relation of these terms will eventually point to the essential in Bataille's thought.

14. Bataille, IE, n.p.109.

15. Hegel, PS, §80, 51.

16. Bataille, *"De l'existentialisme au primat de l'économie,"* OC XI, 286.

17. Bataille, IE, 43.

18. *"De l'existentialisme au primat de l'économie,"* 287.

19. For one text that emphasizes Hegel's attempt to unify the two moments of Kantian knowledge, transcendental and empirical subjectivity, see Howard P. Kainz, *Hegel's Phenomenology, Part One: Analysis and Commentary* (Athens: Ohio University Press, 1988), particularly 22, 26–27, 44.

20. Hegel, PS §17, 9–10.

21. Cf. Hegel, PS §796, 484 and §801, 487.

22. Immanuel Kant, *Immanuel Kant's Critique of Pure Reason,* trans. Norman Kemp Smith (London: Macmillan, 1933), 93.

23. Ibid., 29, author's emphasis.

24. Ibid., author's emphasis.

25. The failure to reconcile phenomena and noumena can be addressed in a variety of ways. In his *Critique of Judgment,* Kant points out that the failure of determinate judgment opens the way to reflective judgment—for example, when the sublime wreaks havoc on the cognitive forms of the imagination. In which case the particular event does not correspond with the given universal coordinates that situate it, so the rule for sensation must be found without doing violence to the indeterminacy of the given. And while Kant posits that this failure may lead to a nonconceptual (free) feeling, which points the way to an ordering Idea (Reason, Freedom) as if it was implied from the start, Lyotard, for example, emphasizes the potential inability to master the incommensurable and calls for the respect and recognition of something that at present remains beyond our grasp, heterogeneous and unknown. And if, on the other hand, the latter is the case—as it implies a more radical split between the given and our presentation of it—then the lack of coincidence between thought and its matter reveals the inevitable mutilation of the given carried out by our ordering concepts, the realization that things are not grasped but dominated. In citing Lyotard here I am referring particularly to his text, *The Differend: Phrases in Dispute,* trans.Georges Van den Abbeele (Manchester University Press, Manchester, 1988).

26. Cf. Charles Taylor, *Hegel and Modern Society* (Cambridge: Cambridge University Press, 1979), chapter 1, "Freedom, Reason and Nature." Reference cited from 2. The discussion that follows is based on this text.

27. Ibid., 6.

28. Ibid., 9.

29. Ibid., 10–11.

30. Ibid., 11.

31. Cf. Joseph C. Flay, *Hegel's Quest for Certainty, op. cit.,* chapter XI, "The Absolute Standpoint: A Critique," 249–67. For another critique of Hegel's assumption

of the "Absolute standpoint," see Judith Shklar, *Freedom and Independence: A Study of the Political Ideas of Hegel's Phenomenology of Mind* (Cambridge: Cambridge University Press, 1976).

32. This citation and the previous one from Flay, 253.

33. Flay approaches the issue a bit differently. His question concerns the warranty of absolute access to all domains of reality, all possible perspectives and frameworks of action, and as he tells us from the start, we "are led to see a basic error, grounded in the natural attitude itself, which denies validity to the project of articulating the structure of comprehensive intelligibility . . ."(252). The presupposition, formulaically announced, is as follows: "[T]he referents for the principle or ground of totality and for the principle or ground of intelligibility [i.e., Being and Thought, C.G.] are one and the same. The presupposition is that intelligibility and totality . . . are grounded in the same locus, and thus that there is such a thing as a comprehensive principle of intelligibility. . . ." Or as he states in more plain language, "[T]he presupposition is that the world out there is a whole and makes sense as a whole" (ibid.). Consequently, even if the commonsense natural attitude cannot actually access the ultimate intelligibility of the totality, nor would it have the means to articulate it should it find it, it nevertheless assumes what fully self-conscious philosophy articulates, namely, that everything "fits together meaningfully" (253). When it seems that the world fails to make sense, reference is made to that single locus of intelligibility—whether it be *Geist*, Nature, God, or some other 'cosmic spirit'—and the whole is reintegrated. But this, as Flay claims, only goes to show that "philosophical and theological projects are parasitic on common sense" (255). That is, they rely on the natural assumption that everything makes sense, and conclude that there is an absolute standpoint that transcends our particular lived experience, yet to which we nevertheless have access, and from which standpoint every experience is intelligible—an assumption that he believes "is not warranted" (257). I have considerably flattened Flay's articulate presentation of the issue here, but the basic theme holds.

34. Werner Marx, *Hegel's Phenomenology of Spirit: A Commentary Based on the Preface and Introduction*, trans. Peter Heath (Chicago: The University of Chicago Press, 1971), 107, emphasis added.

35. Jacques Taminiaux, in an essay that reveals the common *structure* of Hegel's and Heidegger's treatment of the issue of the relation of Being to beings, states, "I am inclined to think that right from the beginning, from the moment Hegel takes up the philosophical project, the proper subject matter of his thought lies in the theme of the difference, but that the way in which he relates to it entails the elimination of the difference. The key term that reveals how Hegel's involvement with the theme of the difference is, at one and the same time, the emergence and the elimination of the difference is: the Absolute. . . . The task of thought as envisaged and taken up in this word is indeed the difference, but when seen as the Absolute, the difference and the whole interplay of references connected with it are condemned to elimination. By definition, the Absolute is that which absolves itself from all reference . . . makes itself equal to itself, coincides with itself. . . . The difference, therefore, is absorbed into a conciliation in which it is eliminated and swallowed up in the indivisible unity of self-consciousness" (Jacques Taminiaux, *Dialectic and Difference: Finitude in Modern Thought*, ed. James Decker and Robert Crease [New Jersey: Humanities Press, 1985], 75).

36. Robert R. Williams, "Hegel and Heidegger," in *Hegel and His Critics, op. cit.,* 140. See as well his article, "Towards a Non-Foundational Absolute Knowing," *The Owl of Minerva* 30, 1 (Fall 1998): 83–101, where he repeats this characterization as follows (87): "Absolute knowing thus appears (formally at least) to be absolute autarchy. Hence all externality, including the subject-object relation, are supposed to be internal relations of absolute knowing. This means that all mediation by the other must in the final analysis be resolved into absolute self-mediation. This makes it look as if the other must be derived from a prior unity, and come to be through a diremption of that unity or identity . . . [as if] the other, the difference, serves merely an instrumental function whereby the unity mediates itself by itself. This account of otherness appears to reduce it to an 'internal relation'. The other and the difference apparently vanish." It is clear from this presentation ("supposed to be," "makes it look as if . . .") that Williams will reject such an account.

37. Cf. Joseph Flay's contribution to the discussion in his "Absolute Knowing and the Absolute Other," *The Owl of Minerva* 30, 1 (Fall 1998): 69–82. To put the debate into relief, compare Williams's articles cited above—where (in the latter) he claims no less than seven times in the last two pages that absolute knowing is not a production of the known, and in the former sees Hegelian comprehension of the object as closer to Eckhartian or Heideggerian *Gelassenheit,* or "letting the other be"—with Taminiaux's articles in *Dialectic and Difference.* See where Taminiaux comments on Hegel's famous phrase "pure self-recognition in absolute otherness," of which he claims that "only a hurried reader might be inclined to credit to a kind of Hegelian altruism . . ." (26).

38. Hegel, PS, §78, 49.

39. Hegel, PS, §18, 10.

40. Given our earlier remarks, the shadow of Koyré and Kojève on this reading should be evident.

41. Cf. Kojève, *Introduction* (K1), "A Note on Eternity, Time, and the Concept," notably 130–49. Here Kojève states, "Hegel's *whole* philosophy or 'Science', therefore, can be summed up in the sentence: '*Time* is the Concept itself which is *there (daseiende)* in empirical existence.'" (See my remarks in the "Introduction" on Kojève's alteration to Hegel's phrase). Kojève states explicitly his belief in Hegel's atheism in the second appendix to his *Introduction* (K2):

> *Il n'y a donc pas d'Esprit en dehors de l'Homme qui vit dans le Monde. Et 'Dieu' n'est objectivement réel qu'à l'interieur de ce Monde naturel, où il existe sous la seule forme du discours théologique de l'Homme.*
> *Ainsi, Hegel n'accepte la tradition anthropologique judéo-chrétienne que sous une forme radicalement . . . athée. L'Absolu-Esprit ou la Substance-Sujet, dont parle Hegel, ne sont pas Dieu. L'Esprit hégélien . . . est l'Homme-dans-le-Monde: l'Homme mortel qui vit dans un Monde sans Dieu . . .* (538–39).

He repeats this sentiment on page 550 of the same appendix, only adding that the Totality of Being is revealed by one of its (finite) parts, by the Spirit—the Being that reveals itself to itself—which is Man.

42. *"Je ne crois pas que Hegel fut pleinement l'athée qu'Alexandre Kojève voit en lui."* Bataille, *"L'au-delà du sérieux,"* OC XII, 315.

43. See for instance Fackenheim's *The Religious Dimension in Hegel's Thought, op. cit.*, where he emphasizes the essentially religious character of Hegel's entire philosophical endeavor to find the Absolute as present in the world. See as well Quentin Lauer's *Essays in Hegelian Dialectic* (New York: Fordham University Press, 1977), where he states (114), "there are those, of course, who, like Kojève, claim that Hegel did not believe in God at all or that his speculations did more to destroy than to establish God, but it is difficult to take such contentions seriously . . ."

44. Hegel, PS, §19, 10.

45. Ibid.

46. Hegel, *Lectures on the Philosophy of Religion, Vol.3, op. cit.*, 91. On the "speculative Good Friday," see n.48 below.

47. "For the true consciousness of Spirit the finitude of Man is slain in the death of Christ. This death of the natural gets in this way a universal signification, the finite, evil, in fact, is destroyed" (ibid., 96). For a similar account see PS §784–85, 475–76.

48. Ibid. We find the same notion at the end of *Faith and Knowledge*, where a speculative account of the death of God is addressed as being necessary to overcome the opposition of the finite and infinite : "But the pure concept of infinity as the abyss of nothingness in which all being is engulfed, must signify the infinite grief of the finite *purely as a moment of the supreme Idea, and no more than as a moment*. Formerly, the infinite grief only existed historically in the formative process of culture. It existed as the feeling that 'God Himself is dead.'. . . By marking this feeling as a moment of the supreme Idea, the pure concept must give philosophical existence to what used to be either the moral precept that we must sacrifice the empirical being, or the concept of formal abstraction. Thereby it must re-establish . . . the speculative Good Friday in place of the historic Good Friday. Good Friday must be speculatively re-established in the whole truth and harshness of its Godforsakenness" (Hegel, *Faith and Knowledge*, trans. W. Cerf and H. S. Harris [Albany: State University of New York Press, 1977], 190f., emphasis added).

49. Hegel, PS, §32, 19.

50. Ibid.

51. "This self-consciousness therefore does not actually *die*, as the particular self-consciousness is pictured as being actually dead, but its particularity dies away in its universality, i.e. *in its knowledge, which is essential Being reconciling itself with itself*" (PS §785, 475, emphasis added). With statements such as these, it becomes more and more difficult to accept the "nonfoundational" interpretation of the Hegelian Absolute.

52. Cf. Bataille, *"Hegel, la mort et le sacrifice," OC* XII, 330.

53. Bataille, *"Hegel, l'homme et l'histoire," OC* XII, 363.

54. Hegel, PS, §804, 490.

55. Bataille, G, 24.

56. Ibid., 42.

57. Bataille, IE, 108. For support regarding the contested notion of Hegel's predetermination of experience and his assertion of the necessity of its development, see

for example Judith Shklar, *Freedom and Independence, op. cit.*, where she recognizes Hegel's "organizing hand" (8), and claims that "Hegel has invented the links that tie his modes of thought together. . . . It is history as art, but since he does not defend his decisions they do seem arbitrary, though not random. The ordering is always made to seem plausible, even though there is no evidence to prove its necessity or advantages over other possibilities . . ." (9).

58. Cf. Bataille, *Méthode de Meditation* (MM), 204–205 and 213; IE, 52–55 and 108–11.

59. Bataille, "The Use Value of D.A.F. de Sade," VE, 96.

60. Hyppolite, *Logic and Existence*, 102, *op. cit.*

61. Ibid.

62. Cf. K1, n.p.199; 200; n.pp.212–15. The establishment of this argument comprises chapter 7 of K1, "The Dialectic of the Real and the Phenomenological Method in Hegel," 169–259.

63. Bataille, IE, 52, 101, emphasis added.

64. Denis Hollier, *Against Architecture: The Writings of Georges Bataille*, trans. Betsy Wing (Cambridge: MIT Press, 1992), 157.

65. Cf. Bataille, "Letter to X, Lecturer on Hegel . . . ," reproduced in *The College of Sociology*, 89–93, and the letter of 1944, reproduced in *Guilty*, 123–25.

66. Descombes, *Modern French Philosophy*, 30, *op. cit.*

67. Bataille, G, 124.

68. This statement is found in both letters. cf. *College of Sociology*, 91, and *Guilty*, 125. The change of emphasis between the first and second drafts begins after this point, the former being much more optimistic than the latter, though the solution is rather weak. Even if still facing resistance from the multitude of people who remain blind to its possibility, the unemployed man still: "understands that it is his good, not his bad, luck that brought him into a world where there was nothing left to do . . . [except] to be recognized by others. . . . Thus, once again, he discovers something 'to do' in a world where, from the point of view of actions, nothing is done any more. And what he has 'to do' is to satisfy the portion of existence that is freed from doing: It is all about using free time," 92. In the latter version, after the war and the night it exposed, the somewhat populist notion of "leisure time" as a possible solution is abandoned so that "the man of 'unemployed negativity' almost can't dispose of its effects anymore. . . . He confronts his own negativity as if it's a wall . . . since negativity has no more outlet."

69. The dialectic is also, and perhaps most accurately, the dialectic of the independence and dependence of consciousness. This fundamental aspect is curiously sidelined by Kojève, but is emphasized in most readings of the *Phenomenology*. See, for example (and there are many), Joseph Navickas, chapters 8 and 9 in his *Consciousness and Reality: Hegel's Philosophy of Subjectivity* (The Hague: Martinus Nijhoff, 1976); Joseph Flay, chapter 6 in *Hegel's Quest for Certainty, op. cit.*

70. Bataille, IE, n.p.109, author's emphasis.

71. There is little agreement about the status of this dialectic. Howard Kainz sees the master/slave as forms of self-consciousness (Kainz, *op. cit.*, 83ff.); Flay similarly claims that the terms *master* and *slave* only refer to the two aspects of self-consciousness, namely, independence and dependence (Flay, *Hegel's Quest*, 86ff.); Lauer views the dialectic as "metaphorical" (Lauer, *A Reading of Hegel's Phenomenology of Spirit*, 174ff.); while Charles Taylor provides an anthropological account (Taylor, *Hegel* [Cambridge: Cambridge University Press, 1975], 148ff., 216ff.) Still others (i.e., Baillie) read it as an analysis of medieval Catholicism (this was pointed out by Burbridge, *Hegel on Logic and Religion*, chapter 10).

72. See n. 75 below.

73. Bataille, IE, 39.

74. The most basic example of the duality of desire (alienation [non-being] and satisfaction [search for being]) is hunger. When hungry, one feels a lack of something and a dissatisfaction that induces action. Faced with an object that potentially may alleviate this state, one cancels the object's otherness through assimilation, thereby reestablishing the satisfied certainty of the subject, its independence from the external world. Desire in this sense represents the self-realizing movement of the subject toward independence from any object.

75. "With self-consciousness, then, we have entered the native realm of truth . . . self-consciousness is *Desire* in general" (PS, §167, 104–105). And further, "[S]elf-consciousness is thus certain of itself only by superseding this other that presents itself to self-consciousness as an independent life; self-consciousness is Desire" (PS, §174, 109).

76. Kojève, K1, 4.

77. Bataille, AS 1, 56, emphasis added.

78. Bataille, OC XII, 547. Please note—to avoid ungainly phrasing we will be presenting the situation as an actual conflict, and thus at times it will be difficult to avoid using personal pronouns. If I then rely on the masculine form, this is not to indicate that it is solely a masculine conflict, for it is a universal dialectic.

79. Navickas, *Consciousness and Reality, op. cit.*, 98.

80. "Originally, the master enjoys the recognition of the slave and feels completely independent. He has attained this position by holding his self-affirmation above his life. For if self-consciousness denotes independence, self-sufficiency, and self-determination, it is obvious that the subject must feel convinced of the unessential character of life and terminate his association with it. Only in the measure that consciousness experiences dependence, does life become problematic" (ibid., 103).

81. Hegel, PS, §187, 114.

82. Bataille, AS 1, 71.

83. Hegel, PS, §187, 113.

84. Bataille, "*Le paradoxe de la mort et la pyramide,*" OC VIII, 517. See as well AS 3, 216–20.

85. Bataille, OC VIII, 508.

86. Bataille, *"Hegel, l'homme et l'histoire,"* OC XII, 351.

87. Hegel, PS, §188, 114–15.

88. I note here that the primary significance of the fight for recognition is the realization of man's negativity, his transcendence of natural existence. *This negativity cannot be revealed in natural death.* As Bataille states: "In principle, death reveals to man his natural, animal being, but the revelation never takes place. For once the animal being that has supported him is dead, the human being himself has ceased to exist" (*"Hegel, la mort et le sacrifice,"* OC XII, 336). In short, the life and death struggle is not a matter of biological survival.

89. Hegel, PS, §189, 115.

90. Merold Westphal has presented the Hegelian risk of life in terms of Marx's use and exchange value, concluding that it falls under the C-M-C (Capital-Money-Capital) form wherein one use value is exchanged for a qualitatively superior use value. That is, something is given up (expended) but with the intention of receiving something of higher value. "Thus in the famous struggle for recognition . . . the risk of death is a rational risk in the C-M-C form. Life is the risk capital ventured in search of something better than life, namely recognition." He correctly concludes that when Bataille speaks of "meaning," he often has in mind the notion of profitable return. Cf. Merold Westphal, "Laughing at Hegel," *The Owl of Minerva* 28, 1 (Fall 1996): 49.

91. Derrida, "From Restricted to General Economy," 255–56.

92. Bataille, unpublished note to *"L'au-delà du sérieux,"* OC XII, 640. I shall have more to say on recognition in the following chapters, specifically in its relation to language and further with respect to the notion of "communication," an experience which I believe to be Bataille's transmutation of the Hegelian notion of recognition.

93. Kojève, K1, 19.

94. Cf. Hegel, PS, §191–194, 116–17, and Kojève, K1, 20.

95. As noted in the Introduction, we are now in the realm of Kojève rather than Hegel. If the slave truly attained Hegelian sovereignty, the slave ideologies of stoicism and skepticism, as well as the unhappy consciousness, would not follow. That is, it would not be necessary to ideologically hold fast to oneself as the center of the world, nor would this pass over to a feeling of having missed the essential moment of truth, and subsequently find oneself yearning for it.

96. Bataille, *"Hegel, la mort et le sacrifice,"* OC XII, 336.

97. Kojève, K2, 556.

98. Ibid., 551. Where we say "death," we could substitute "desire," for the fact of being revealed to oneself and recognized as desire (nothing), rather than as a fixed, given being (thing), allows for the possibility to die—and thus live—as a conscious human being, conscious, that is, of one's own nothingness.

99. These last two phrases are only ambiguously applicable to Heidegger, for whom being-toward-death is one's ownmost *(eigentlich)* possibility, is that which singularizes Dasein, but in so doing reveals its ecstatic character, with its ownmost possibility being impossibility.

100. M. Borch-Jacobsen, *Lacan: The Absolute Master,* trans. Douglas Brick (Stanford: Stanford University Press, 1991), 92.

101. Bataille, *"Hegel, la mort . . . ,"* 336. Kojève's implicit affirmation of the same difficulty is shown by his use of quotation marks when he refers to the "manifestation" of freedom through death, signifying an as-if structure to a manifestation that is in itself impossible.

102. As S. Kierkegaard claims, "[T]he Hegelian philosophy assumes no justified hiddenness, no justified incommensurability. It is, then, consistent that it demand disclosure [in the universal]," *Fear and Trembling /Repetition,* ed. and trans., Howard V. Hong and Edna H. Hong (Princeton: Princeton University Press, 1983), 82.

103. Bataille, *"Hegel, la mort . . . ,"* 336.

104. Kojève, K1, 21.

105. Heidegger, it should be noted, does not rely on this representational structure in order to affirm death as the horizon to which Dasein relates itself and its possibilities. Herein lies the source of some obfuscation when trying to bring the issues surrounding the relation to death into focus.

106. Kojève, K2, 549.

107. Ibid., 556.

108. Kojève, K1, 21. This is a translation from Hegel, PS, §194, 117.

109. Bataille, *"Hegel, la mort . . . ,"* 336–37, second emphasis added.

110. Kojève, K2, 548.

111. Ibid., 550.

112. Hegel, PS, §32, 19. "Utter dismemberment" is Miller's translation of Hegel's *"der absoluten Zerrissenheit." "Déchirement absolu"* is cited from Bataille's *"Hegel, la mort . . . ,"* OC XII, 351, which refers to Hyppolite's translation of Hegel's *Phenomenology* (t. I, 29), which Bataille claims is in turn cited from Kojève's translation in his *Introduction à la lecture de Hegel,* 538–39. Derrida calls into further doubt the origin of the French translation in "From Restricted to General Economy," 131–32, n.13.

113. Ibid.

114. Bataille, *"Hegel, la mort . . . ,"* 344.

115. "[The slave's] consciousness is not this dissolution of everything stable merely in principle; in his service he *actually* brings this about. Through his service he rids himself of his attachment to natural existence in every single detail; and gets rid of it by working on it" (PS, §194, 117).

116. Navickas, *op. cit.,* 105, emphasis added. Hegel's phrase cited here is from PS §195, 117–18.

117. I am following the arguments laid out in PS, §195–96, 118–19. All references cited are from these paragraphs.

118. Kojève, K1, 25.

119. See particularly the final pages in the *Phenomenology* on "The Revealed Religion," just before the transition to "Absolute Knowledge," PS §785–87, 475–78. For commentary, see Burbridge's "God, Man, and Death in Hegel's *Phenomenology*," in his *Hegel on Logic and Religion, op. cit.,* 119–30.

120. Cf. Burbridge, 129. Burbridge ends his article, however, with an interesting conclusion that points Hegel himself in the direction of Bataille. After the reconciliation of man and God has occurred, he claims: "Barely has the result appeared, however, than the negative process continues, defining, isolating, and rendering precise the result that has been achieved, taking it as an immediate to be rendered determinate. *Thus no conclusion is final. It only opens up a new set of transitions*" (130, emphasis added).

121. Cf. *"Hegel, la mort . . . ,"* 338–39; *"La pur bonheur"* (OC XII, 478) and MM, 232–34. Also see J.Derrida, "From Restricted to General Economy," 106: "To stay alive, to maintain oneself in life, to work, to defer pleasure, to limit the stakes, to have *respect* for death at the very moment one looks *directly* at it—such is the servile condition of mastery . . ." (author's emphasis).

122. Bataille, *"Sommes-nous là pour jouer? ou pour être sérieux?"* OC XII, 115–16.

123. Bataille, *Theory of Religion* (TR), 41.

124. Charles Bukowski, "A Cat is a Cat is a Cat," in *You get so Alone at times that it just Makes Sense* (Santa Rosa: Black Sparrow Press, 1986), 237.

125. It is Kojève who emphatically claims that History is the history of the working slave. Cf. K1, 20 ff.

126. Bataille, TR, 41, emphasis added.

127. ". . . immer, überall,/ dem allen zugewandt und nie hinaus!/ Uns überfüllts. Wir ordnen. Es zerfällt./ Wir ordnens wieder und zerfallen selbst" (Ranier Maria Rilke, selection from "The Eighth Elegy" of *Duino Elegies* in *The Selected Poetry of Rainer Maria Rilke,* ed. and trans. Stephen Mitchell [Vintage International, New York, 1989]).

128. Guy Debord, *The Society of the Spectacle,* trans. Donald Nicholson-Smith (New York: Zone Books, 1992), §33, 24.

129. Ibid.

130. Bataille, TR, 52, emphasis added.

131. Bataille offers varying accounts of his terms *possible* and *impossible*. A general notion of each is as follows: "possible"—servile activity, prohibition, discursive knowledge, or generally that which serves life; "impossible"—excess, transgression, non-knowledge, death brought into life. For a theoretical description of these terms, cf. MM, 205–209.

132. Let us therefore not confuse this with an accurate, or even explicit, reading of Hegel in any sense. Hegel repeatedly and relentlessly criticizes this sort of mechanistic, means-ends rationalism. It is totally at odds with his way of thinking. Bataille will, nevertheless, take some of his Kojèvian lessons on Hegel and in turn see Hegel as implicated in the type of rationalism he is attacking. We should thus keep in mind here that Hegel per se is not the target, but is, rather, guilty by association. We should also

mention that Heidegger, among others, was not exempt from this sort of reading of Hegel as a Cartesian; see Heidegger, *Hegel's Concept of Experience*, trans. K. R. Dove (New York: Harper & Row, 1970), 27ff. For a more contemporary reading of a similar sort, see Tom Rockmore, *Hegel's Circular Epistemology* (Bloomington: Indiana University Press, 1986).

133. Cf. Bataille, "On Nietzsche: The Will to Chance," *October 36*, 52.

134. See our previous discussion of Hegel's attempt to overcome just this sort of fragmented totality as influenced by the doctrine of "expressivism."

135. Ibid.

136. Bataille, IE, 46, author's emphasis.

137. Bataille, TR, 26.

138. Here we are confronted with the tension in Hegel's thought referred to above. On the one hand, the unfolding of the system through history is nothing less than time itself, accomplished by the finite individual. This is what Kojève emphasizes. But the meaning of time is in effect its cancellation in the infinite reconciliation of the finite and infinite (Absolute). This as well points to two different desires: the one that provokes the restlessness of the finite being transcending itself toward the world, and the other that appropriates the finite world, returning out of difference into an identity composed of differences overcome. Furthermore, this final reconciliation would not imply profane existence, but rather a cancellation of the profane as a moment of divine existence.

139. Bataille, IE, 81.

140. Derrida, "From Restricted to General Economy," 259, *op. cit.*

141. Adorno, *Negative Dialectics*, trans. E. B. Ashton (London: Routledge, 1990), 159–60. Bataille's critique of Hegel is analogous to that of Adorno who rails against the positivity of Hegelian dialectics. The quote is taken from the following, "To negate a negation does not bring about its reversal; it proves, rather, that the negation was not negative enough. . . . The thesis that the negation of a negation is something positive *can only be upheld by one who presupposes positivity . . . from the beginning*" (emphasis added).

142. Bataille, "Initial Postulate," *The Absence of Myth* (AM), n.p.95, emphasis added.

143. Catherine Malabou, "Négatifs de la dialectique," *op. cit.*, 53, n.52.

144. Bataille, MM, n.p.215.

145. *"L'au-delà du sérieux"* is the title of an article found in Bataille, OC XII, 313–20.

146. Bataille, G, 150.

147. Bataille, "Un-Knowing and Rebellion," *October 36*, 86–87.

148. Bataille's reading of Huizinga's *Homo Ludens: A Study of the Play Element in Culture* is to be found in the article *"Sommes-nous là pour jouer? ou pour être sérieux,"* OC XII, 100–25.

149. "Any game can at any time wholly run away with the players. The contrast between play and seriousness is always fluid. The inferiority of play is continually being offset by the corresponding superiority of its seriousness. Play turns to seriousness and seriousness to play" (Huizinga, *Homo Ludens*, 8).

150. Cf. Huizinga, 19, 18. Here he states, "This identity of ritual and play was unreservedly recognized by Plato as a given fact. He had no hesitation in comprising the *sacra* in the category of play." The reference he cites in a number of instances is Plato's *Laws*, vii, 803–804 and 796. For an analysis of the origins of philosophy itself as play, see Chapter IX in *Homo Ludens*, "Play-Forms in Philosophy," 146–57.

151. Cf. Bataille, *"Collège de sociologie,"* OC II, 366; reprinted in *The College of Sociology*, 335.

152. Huizinga, *Homo Ludens*, 10.

153. With this in mind Huizinga draws upon Mauss's study of the *potlatch* (58ff.). In *potlatch* he sees evidence of the clearly agonistic basis of cultural life. As we will see when we turn to Mauss, entering the game is taking up the dare, obliging one to reciprocate. On the etymological connection of risk, danger, and obligation, cf. 39–40.

154. Bataille, *Eroticism* (E), 108.

155. "Or il est difficile de dire exactement que les interdits n'ont de sens que le jeu. Nous pourrions même être tentés d'apercevoir ici les limites de la pensée de Huizinga: tout serait jeu dans la culture à l'exception des interdits. Je crois au contraire que les interdits témoignent dès l'abord de l'exubérance humaine, ce ne sont pas vraiment des jeux mais les réactions résultant d'un heurt de l'activité utile, sérieuse, et du mouvement intempérant qui nous anime au-delà de l'utile et du sérieux" (OC XII, 109, modified in translation).

156. Huizinga, *Homo Ludens*, 45, emphasis added.

157. Bataille states, "Cette opposition au travail me semble au reste de nature à montrer que le jeu se trouve moins évidemment qu'il ne semble—et que Huizinga ne l'admit—dans l'animalité. Je crois que le travail est nécessaire à la pleine affirmation du jeu" (OC XII, 114). Furthermore, "Tout un mouvement de culture, en effect, a pour base le jeu, la libre effervescence et les rivalités démesurées, qui nous portent déraisonnablement à défier la ruine et la mort. Mais le travail, la négation de ce premier mouvement, n'eut évidemment pas moins de part à l'ensemble de traditions, de conduites, de notions qui, sous le titre de culture, sont aujourd'hui objet d'enseignement" (OC XII, 113).

158. OC XII, 124.

159. Ibid., 122.

160. Ibid., 113.

161. Ibid., 117.

162. "[P]lay, if it is no longer inferior, tolerated, serious, leads to the inoperable spirit *(à l'esprit désoeuvré)*, to the sovereign spirit. . . . The serious has only one *meaning:* play, which no longer has any meaning, is only serious insofar as 'the absence of meaning is also a meaning . . .'" (Bataille, *Méthode de meditation* [MM], OC V, 234, author's emphasis).

163. Bataille, IE, 35.

164. Bataille, G, 159.

165. "La clé est la vérité de l'interdit, la certitude qu'il n'est pas en nous venant du dehors, ce qui nous apparaît dans l'angoisse au moment où nous transgressons l'interdit" (Bataille, *"L'érotisme ou la mise en question de l'être,"* OC XII, 403).

166. Ibid., 404, emphasis added.

167. Bataille, *Eroticism* (E), 36. See as well OC XII, 403.

168. Cf. Jacques Taminiaux, "Hegel and Hobbes," *Dialectic and Difference: Finitude in Modern Thought,* 26–33.

169. Kojève, K2, 547, 550.

170. Cf. Bataille, IE, 129. Here the emphasis is not strictly on the issue of time but on the isolation involved with work (becoming a thing among things) in contrast to the communication involved in the unleashing of excessive desire: "But instead of embracing this unleashing of oneself, a being stops in himself the torrent which gives him over to life, and devotes himself, in the hope of avoiding ruin . . . to the possession [knowledge] of things. *And things possess him when he believes to be possessing them.* . . . Servitude, inextricable downfall: the slave frees himself from the master through work (the essential movement of *The Phenomenology of Spirit*), *but the product of his work becomes his master"* (emphasis added).

171. Bataille, *On Nietzsche* (N), 91.

172. Bataille, G, 96.

173. See Descombes, *Modern French Philosophy,* 14, *op. cit.*

174. Bataille, OC XII, 106.

175. Bataille, AS 3, 219, author's emphasis.

176. Ibid., 219–20.

177. Bataille, OC XII, 111–12.

178. I give a reminder that both risk and questioning are implied in the phrase *"mettre en jeu."*

179. Bataille, G, 82.

180. Cf. Bataille, "Un-Knowing, Laughter, and Tears," *October 36,* 90–91.

181. Nietzsche, *Thus Spoke Zarathustra: First Part* in *The Portable Nietzsche,* trans. Walter Kaufmann), 139. Bataille cites this quotation in *On Nietzsche,* 151. I find it telling that Bataille's most sustained writing on risk and chance is to be found in his text *On Nietzsche.*

182. Bataille, G, 72. In reference to the section in *Zarathustra* "On the Three Metamorphoses," which advocates becoming a child, Bataille claims that "the *will to power* is the lion: but isn't the child the *will to chance?"* (N, 151–52).

183. Bataille, AS 3, 206. This is a translation of Goethe's comment on death that it is "an impossibility that suddenly changes into a reality," found in his *Conversations with Eckermann.* The phrase, "anticipation dissolves into nothing," is regularly found in AS 3.

184. Bataille, G, 51, emphasis added.

185. Bataille, IE, 80, emphasis added.

186. I am borrowing here from a phrase from Stéphane Mallarmé, "Un coup de dés jamais n'abolira le hasard" (A throw of the dice will never abolish chance).

187. Cf. Merold Westphal, "Laughing at Hegel," *op. cit.*, 48. Credit is due here to Westphal's brief, yet accurate, assessment of Bataille, although it is, as he acknowledges, based entirely on Derrida's essay, "From Restricted to General Economy."

188. Bataille, N, 150.

189. Bataille, OC X, 659.

190. Bataille, N, 110.

191. "If one now wants to represent . . . the 'grail' obstinately pursued through successive, deceptive, and cloudy depths, it is necessary to insist upon the fact that it could never have been a *substantial* reality; on the contrary, it was an element characterized by the impossibility of its enduring. The term *privileged instant* is the only one that, with a certain amount of accuracy, accounts for what can only be encountered *at random* in the search; the opposite of a *substance* that withstands the test of time, it is something that flees as soon as it is seen and cannot be grasped" (Bataille, "The Sacred," in VE, 241, author's emphasis).

192. Bataille, "On Nietzsche: The Will to Chance," *October 36*, 53, emphasis added.

193. Bataille, *"L'au-delà du sérieux,"* OC XII, 314.

194. Bataille, "On Nietzsche: The Will to Chance," *October 36*, 54.

195. Ibid., 55.

196. Bataille, "The Sorcerer's Apprentice," *VE*, 231.

CHAPTER 2. THE END OF UTILITY

1. The more sober-minded Heidegger as well did not hide his disdain at the hubris of humanity. In *The Question Concerning Technology,* Heidegger posits the unity of the "Christian, humanistic, Enlightenment, bourgeois, and socialist morality," all of which he sees as based on the view of the human *subiectum* as the self-certain "ground" for all things that can be represented, known, and controlled. This subject views itself as the source of light by which entities are illuminated, a 'disclosure' of entities that makes them conform to the expectations imposed upon them.

2. Bataille, AS 2, 15.

3. The "symbolic" referred to here is not—to my knowledge—from the pen of Bataille, but rather from Baudrillard, for whom Bataille's notion of nonproductive expenditure is essential, and perhaps essential to the point that his early works are a "reworking of Bataille's model of the general economy. . . ." Cf. Julian Pfanis, *Heterology and the Postmodern: Bataille, Baudrillard, and Lyotard* (Durham: Duke University

Press, 1994), 77. For a general assessment of Bataille's influence on poststructuralism and postmodernism, see as well Pfanis, "The Issue of Bataille," in *Postmodern Conditions,* ed. Andrew Milner, Philip Thomson, and Chris Worth (Munich: Berg, 1990), 133–55. The texts by Baudrillard in which Bataille's influence is most readily perceptible are: *For a Critique of the Political Economy of the Sign* (1972), trans. Charles Levin (St. Louis: Telos Press, 1981), and *Symbolic Exchange and Death* (1976), trans. Iain Hamilton Grant (London: Sage, 1993). See as well Jean-Joseph Goux, *Symbolic Economies: After Marx and Freud,* trans. Jennifer Curtiss Gage (Ithica: Cornell University Press, 1990).

4. Marcel Mauss, *The Gift: Forms and Functions of Exchange in Archaic Societies,* trans. W. D. Halls (New York: W.W. Norton, 1990). Mauss's *'Essai sur le don'* first appeared in *L'Année sociologique, 1923–24,* and—to my knowledge—was first read by Bataille in 1931, though he was already well acquainted with the work done by Mauss in association with Henri Hubert, most notably their *'Essai sur la Nature et la Fonction du Sacrifice,'* published in 1898.

5. Mauss, *The Gift,* 80.

6. For critical readings of Mauss's *Gift,* see in particular Lévi-Strauss's "Introduction to Mauss," and Marshall Sahlins's *Stone Age Economics* (Aldine, Chicago, 1974), chapter 4, "The Spirit of the Gift." The substance of these criticisms (as well as those of Firth and Johansen) lies in a reinterpretation, if not a total rejection, of the very core of Mauss's study, the notion of the *hau* as the magical force driving the exchange of gifts. We shall encounter this notion below.

7. *"La Notion de Dépense"* was first published in *La Critique sociale 7* (January 1933): 7–15, and reprinted in OC I, 302–20. I shall be referring to the translation by Allan Stoekl in *Visions of Excess.* I shall also refer to the posthumously published *Textes se rattachant à "La Notion de Dépense,"* from OC II, 145–58. This article, along with those addressing the same duality of existence represented through the problematic of consumption, lays the groundwork for his later, elongated treatment in *La Part maudite (The Accursed Share).*

8. Cf. OC I, 153–59. Translation taken from *October 36,* 3–9.

9. Cf. Bataille, AS I, 59.

10. Cf. Jürgen Habermas, "The French Path to Postmodernity: Bataille between Eroticism and General Economics," trans. Frederick Lawrence, *New German Critique* 33 (1984): 88–89, reprinted in *Bataille: A Critical Reader,* 167–90.

11. Bataille uses this term, created from the verb *consumer,* which means to consume or burn in the manner of a fire, to highlight its distanciation from the standard *consommer,* which means to consume in the manner of eating, drinking, or using fuel.

12. Quotations from this article will be indicated by their page number in *Visions of Excess.* Those from the *Textes se rattachant à "La Notion de dépense"* are indicated by (OC II) followed by page number.

13. VE, 118.

14. Sahlins, *Stone Age Economics,* 4, *op. cit.*

15. Max Horkheimer, "The End of Reason," in *The Essential Frankfurt School Reader*, ed. Andrew Arato and Eike Gebhardt (New York: Continuum, 1982), 28.

16. VE, 124.

17. OC II, 147.

18. At this early point Bataille apparently adheres to a strictly communist line of thought, either not having envisioned or simply refusing to see the logical consequences of market capitalism as did, for instance, Thorstein Veblen—when there is excess production, excessive and useless consumption is sure to follow. This form of consumption is simply divorced from a religious/community structure.

19. OC II, 153, emphasis added.

20. VE, 120.

21. VE, 117.

22. Ibid.

23. Mauss, *The Gift*, 72.

24. Denis Hollier, *Against Architecture: The Writings of Georges Bataille*, trans. Betsy Wing (Cambridge, Mass.: The MIT Press, 1989), 49.

25. M. Sahlins, "The Original Affluent Society," *Stone Age Economics, op. cit.*

26. Sahlins cites a number of reasons for this lack of concern with reserving supplies. First and foremost is their unwavering *confidence* in nature to provide for them; this results in two further reasons, their lack of agricultural development—which implies that resources in one area would quickly be depleted—and their consequent need for continual *movement* to more bountiful locales. Following *economic* logic, "storage would be superfluous," because it would contradict the wealth obtained through mobility, anchoring them in an area with diminishing returns; following *moral* logic, food accumulation and storage would be unachievable as it would be seen as hoarding in a society that relied upon sharing for survival. Besides which, the accumulation of objects had yet to become associated with status.

27. Sahlins cites some interesting examples such as the Tikopians or Fijians who know no linguistic distinction between "work" and "ritual," their equivalent importance manifested in one common term, and the Australian Aborigines (Yir Yiront) who do not discriminate between "work" and "play" (63–64).

28. As Sahlins claims, in their self-confidence they were "oriented forever in the present," with a "studied unconcern" beyond the present, unfamiliar with the subtleties of a calculated response to unforeseen circumstances, (29–31).

29. Here I am following the arguments of Ernst Cassirer in his book, *The Philosophy of Symbolic Forms, Vol. 2: Mythical Thought*, trans. Ralph Manheim (New Haven: Yale University Press, 1955), hereafter indicated by PSF. Bataille only made a few references to Cassirer, specifically to this text *(Mythical Thought)*. The most significant reference is found in "The Psychological Structure of Fascism," VE, 160, n.7, where Bataille affirms Cassirer's notion of primitive consciousness as being equivalent to his own guiding notion at that time—heterogeneity. We also find a passing reference to Cassirer's analysis of primitive thought in a much later article (1951) on J. Huizinga's *Homo Ludens*, OC XII, 104. On Bataille's analysis of Huizinga, see above, 61 ff.

30. Cf. Cassirer, PSF, 228–31. I shall discuss the latter gulf—divine and profane—in section 2.3.

31. Cf. Cassirer, PSF, 212–18.

32. Cassirer, PSF, 222–23, emphasis added.

33. Mauss, *The Gift*, 20.

34. Mauss notes the double sense of the word *gift* in a variety of languages, meaning at the same time gift and poison, as well as noting that in various folklore exist the theme of the fatal gift. (*The Gift*, 59–64). The doubling of meaning is a common feature of most expressions that signify sacred things, as sacred things are those that participate in and cross between two realms of existence. That is, they are profane things transported into the sacred world through a destruction of their profane value.

35. Sahlins, *Stone Age Economics*, 160. For a more extensive analysis these issues, cf. chapter 4, ibid.

36. Cf. Bataille, AS I, 69.

37. Cf. Bataille, AS I, 70–71.

38. This is not only Bataille's view, as Mauss claims, "the potlatch, the distribution of goods, is the basic act of 'recognition'. . ." (*The Gift*, 40).

39. Bataille, AS I, 70.

40. Mauss, *The Gift*, 73–74

41. J.Habermas, citing the same problem of the interested nature of potlatch, states that the "sovereign disdain for use-values is already overtaken at this level by the calculative acquisition of power. This practice bears within itself the contradiction between sovereignty and purposive rationality," "The French Path to Postmodernity," *op. cit.*, 95.

42. Bataille, AS I, 70.

43. Mauss, *The Gift*, 122, n.201. Bataille repeats this formula in "The Notion of Expenditure," 122, and again in AS I, 70.

44. Bataille, AS 2, 141. This principle is repeated on many occasions, this being merely its clearest formulation.

45. Bataille, AS I, 190, author's emphasis.

46. He did, of course, go on to write two more volumes, following his economic study with and anthropological one *(The History of Eroticism)* and a moral one *(Sovereignty)*.

47. For Hegel's definition of self-consciousness as desire, see PS (§166–76, 104–11).

48. Bataille, AS I, 73, author's emphasis.

49. Ibid.

50. Cf. *Visions of Excess*, 137–60.

51. This "other" he is referring to here is not the Jewish population, but rather the lower, base classes.

52. "The simple fact of dominating one's fellows implies the *heterogeneity* of the master, insofar as he is the master; to the extent that he refers to his nature, to his personal quality, as the justification of his authority, he designates his nature as *something other* [i.e., sacred, C.G.], without being able to account for it rationally" (VE, 145).

53. VE, 153.

54. VE, 157.

55. VE, 157. He repeats this notion in his article "The Notion of Expenditure" where he speaks of the worker's Revolution as being "capable of exerting a force of attraction as strong as the force that directs simple organisms toward the sun" (VE, 128). What are we to conclude then when he defines fascism as a "condensation of power" (VE, 154)? The notion of "affective" identification of the masses with a leader is taken from the principles laid out in Freud's *Group Psychology and the Analysis of the Ego*, a text essential to any understanding of fascism. We shall encounter the notion of "affective identification" again in later chapters.

56. As an example of this structure of inevitability, see "Celestial Bodies" in *October 36*, 75–78. Here he posits a strict opposition between the Earth's avidity to "use" all the energy given to it, and the Sun's unlimited expenditure—its "extraordinary loss," its "constant internal annihilation of [its] very substance." His conclusion is simply that "existence in avidity attains, when fully developed, a point of disequilibrium at which it suddenly and lavishly expends; it sustains an explosive loss of the surplus of force it has so painfully accumulated" (78).

57. In his 1935 speech to the Contre-Attaque group, "Popular Front in the Street," Bataille in fact advocates the unleashing of subversive violence, a *potlatch* of mass power.

58. Bataille, "The Sacred Conspiracy," VE, 180–81.

59. Cf. Bataille's article from 1930, "The Use Value of D.A.F. de Sade," VE, 91–102.

60. Bataille, "The College of Sociology" (1939) *The College of Sociology 1937–39*, trans. Betsy Wing, ed. Denis Hollier (Minneapolis: University of Minnesota Press, 1988), 338.

61. Bataille, "Sacrifice," *October 36*, 66.

62. Cf. VE, 61–72; OC I, 258–70.

63. "Sacrificial Mutilation," VE, 63.

64. "But it is no less striking that, in our day, with the custom of sacrifice in full decline, the meaning of the word [dislocation], to the extent that it implies a drive revealed by an *inner experience*, is still as closely linked as possible to the notion of a *spirit of sacrifice*" (VE, 67, author's emphasis).

65. VE, 70, author's emphasis.

66. Bataille, "Sacrifice," *October 36*, 62.

67. Bataille, "The Jesuve," VE, 73.

68. On ritual and moral sacrifice, cf. Bernard Baas, *Le désir pur: Parcours philosophiques dans les parages de J.Lacan* (Louvain: Éditions Peeters, 1992), in particular the chapter entitled *"Le sacrifice et la loi"* (120–61).

69. I use the term *hypothetical* here with reference to Kant's hypothetical imperative (the end justifies the means; or the desired effect determines the will, which thereby acts not according to freedom of will but from material principles guided by self-love) as opposed to the autonomy of the formal, categorical imperative (practical law) which is not subservient to any external justification, which is purified not only of empirical considerations but of self-love and concern for others. Cf. Immanuel Kant, *Critique of Practical Reason*, 33 ff., 93 ff.

70. Bataille, *Theory of Religion* (TR), 56.

71. Bataille, AS I, 129, author's emphasis.

72. TR, 56.

73. Ibid.

74. E. Levinas, *Time and the Other (and additional essays)*, trans. R. A.Cohen, (Pittsburgh: Duquesne University Press, 1987), 64, cited in R.Visker, "Levinas's Intrigue of the Infinite," in *Truth and Singularity: Taking Foucault into Phenomenology* (Dordrecht: Kluwer Academic Publishers, 1999), 250. This quotation in fact deals with things, but is contrasted with the relation to the ethical Other, which in turn refers to "God." The discussion of transcendence here was prompted by Rudi Visker's pertinent questioning regarding the manner in which Bataille uses this notion, and whether or not Bataille's usage may not be more properly delineated with reference to the notions of "transascendence" (closer to the mystical notion of God whose original position is withdrawal "to the point of absence," yet with which the subject can "participate") and "transdescendence" (closer to the *il y a* which would annihilate the subject who submerges (descends) into it), cf. Visker, ibid. I would suggest that Bataille's notion of "intimacy" hovers between these two notions, which—significantly—may devolve one upon the other.

75. Cf. PS §206–230, 126–38; on the "Cult," sacrifice and unhappy consciousness, cf. §714 *ff.*, 432*ff.*

76. The presentation of Hegel's "Unhappy Consciousness" offered here is informed by the analysis given in Desmond, *Beyond Hegel and Dialectic, op. cit.*, 100*ff.*

77. "In Hegelian *self*-recognition in absolute otherness, the otherness is in fact not absolute, since finally the other is a dialectical mirror which mediates *self*-recognition" (ibid., 113–14).

78. Henceforth, our use of "transcendent" or the "transcendent God" will refer to the type of transcendence whose difference has been domesticated, which gives itself to the desiring subject.

79. TR, 20.

80. TR, 22, author's emphasis. For a description of animal immanence, that sphere lacking distinct, transcendent objects and articulate language, see TR, chapter 1, "Animality," 17–25, and *"Schéma d'une histoire des religions,"* OC VII, 407–12.

81. Cf. Henri Hubert and Marcel Mauss, *Sacrifice: Its Nature and Functions*, trans. W. D. Halls, fwd. E. E. Evans-Pritchard (Chicago: University of Chicago Press, 1981) and Max Weber, *The Protestant Ethic and the Spirit of Capitalism*, trans. Talcott Parsons (London: George Allen & Unwin, 1976).

82. Bataille, AS I, 131, author's emphasis. While Bataille specifies this as the problem of Calvinism as it leads to capitalism, it is in fact a problem that adheres to sacrifice as a whole.

83. Hubert and Mauss, *Sacrifice*, 99.

84. Bataille, TR, 46, author's emphasis.

85. Cf. Ernst Cassirer, *The Philosophy of Symbolic Forms*, 221–22.

86. The identity of the sacrifier and victim, as well as the connection of the victim to the divine realm in which it participates, is a presupposition in Hubert and Mauss's study. This identity, as we will see, is both essential and problematic.

87. Bataille, TR, 51.

88. Cf. Cassirer, *The Philosophy of Symbolic Forms*, *op. cit.* I shall be paraphrasing from 200–203.

89. Bataille, TR, 54.

90. Hubert and Mauss, *Sacrifice*, 100.

91. Ibid.

92. Cf. M. Mauss, *"Essai sur les variations saisonières des sociétés Eskimos. Étude de morphologie social,"* cited in Roger Callois, *L'Homme et le sacré* (Paris: E. Leroux, 1939; Gallimard, 1950). Drawing on Mauss's studies, particularly in chapter 4 *("Le Sacré de transgression: théorie de la fête")* Callois attributes a "mystical efficacy" to the festival (here festival and sacrifice are more or less identical), a "rejuvenating" or "revitalizing" effect that adheres to the paroxysmal suspension of order.

93. On sacrificial destruction involving the rebirth of the victim and sacrifier, the assurance of the (future) life of those involved, see *Sacrifice*, chapter 4, "How the Scheme varies according to the Special Functions of the Sacrifice," 61–76. The point of this chapter is summarized in the following: "In a word, just as personal sacrifice ensured the life of the person, so the objective sacrifice in general and the agrarian sacrifice in particular ensure the real and healthful life of things" (75).

94. Bataille, TR, 54–55, emphasis added.

95. Friedrich Nietzsche, *The Genealogy of Morals*, in *Basic Writings of Nietzsche*, trans. and ed. Walter Kaufmann (New York: The Modern Library, 1968). This text is of particular importance when charting the moral development of the spirit of sacrifice.

96. Nietzsche, *Genealogy of Morals*, 502–503.

97. Ibid., 504, emphasis added.

98. To chart the parallel developments in the divine and human worlds, I will rely mainly on Bataille's *Theory of Religion*, though he charts a similar development in *La limite de l'utile* (OC VI, 181–280), *"Schéma d'une histoire des religions"* (OC VI, 406–42), *"Sade et la morale"* (OC VII, 445–52), and *The Accursed Share*.

99. Hubert and Mauss, *Sacrifice*, 77. Cassirer shares this view: "The meaning of sacrifice is not exhausted by the sacrifice *to* the god; rather, it seems to stand out fully and reveal itself in its true religious and speculative depth where *the god himself* is sacrificed or sacrifices himself . . ." (PSF, 230).

100. Hubert and Mauss, *Sacrifice*, 101.

101. Nietzsche, *Genealogy of Morals*, 528.

102. Cassirer, *The Philosophy of Symbolic Forms*, 230–31.

103. Ibid.

104. Hubert and Mauss, *Sacrifice*, 101.

105. Bataille, *On Nietzsche*, 33–34.

106. Cf. Immanuel Kant, *La religion dans les limites de la simple raison*, trans. J. Gibelin, éd. Vrin (1983); Fourth Dissertation, second section, paragraph one, 186–87. Cited in DP, 138–40.

107. Bataille, AS I, 120, author's emphasis, translation modified. Original text in OC VII, 166.

108. B.Baas, *Le Désir Pur,* 140, *op. cit.,* author's emphasis.

109. Bataille, AS I, 122.

110. Ibid.

111. Weber, *The Protestant Ethic*, 108, *op. cit.*

112. This notion actually is Calvinistic. Weber claims that "the religious believer can make himself sure of his state of grace either in that he feels himself to be the vessel of the Holy Spirit or the tool of the divine will. In the former case his religious life tends to mysticism and emotionalism, in the latter to ascetic action. . . . Calvinism belonged definitely to the latter. . . . Since Calvin viewed all pure feelings and emotions, no matter how exalted they may seem to be, with suspicion, faith had to be proved by its objective results. . . . It must be a *fides efficax*, the call to salvation an effectual calling" (Weber, ibid., 113–14).

113. Ibid., 109.

114. Bataille, AS I, 122. Cf. Weber, 81: "That this moral justification of worldly activity was one of the most important results of the Reformation . . . is beyond doubt, and may even be considered a platitude."

115. Bataille, AS I, 124. Bataille's thought on the development of moral consciousness is recognized and aptly stated by Habermas: "Bataille finally reaches a critique of morality which forms a bridge to Max Weber's sociology of religion. It covers the development of religion from archaic rites to world religions . . . and interprets it as a path of ethical *rationalization*. Luther and Calvin mark a watershed in a religious evolution in which basic religious concepts are moralized and, along with this, religious experiences are spiritualized. The holy . . . is domesticated and split apart" (J. Habermas, "The French Path to Postmodernity," *op. cit.,* 184, author's emphasis).

116. Cf. Weber, 106, 116–17.

117. Bataille, *Theory of Religion*, 76–77, emphasis added.

118. J.Habermas, "The French Path to Postmodernity," *op. cit.*, 185.

119. Jean-Joseph Goux, "General Economics and Postmodern Capitalism," in *Bataille: A Critical Reader, op. cit.*, 198–99, emphasis added.

120. Bataille, *On Nietzsche*, 42, author's emphasis.

121. Even the earliest sacrifices were connected with "the most conservative cares—like the maintenance of life and work. In fact, what [sacrifice] intends to establish has relatively little to do with the instinct behind it. . . . Good was always the ultimate end of sacrifice, so the whole process was really mutilated: it was almost a failure" (LE, 70–71).

122. Bataille, LE, 182.

123. Bataille, *"Hegel, la mort et le sacrifice,"* OC XII, 334.

CHAPTER 3. LOGOMACHY: THROUGH DISCOURSE TO POETIC SILENCE

1. Bataille, IE, 80. "In the 'system', poetry, laughter, ecstasy are nothing. Hegel gets rid of them in a hurry: he knows of no other end than knowledge" (IE, 111).

2. "[The Unhappy Self-consciousness] knows what the validity of the abstract person [i.e., Stoic independence or Skeptical consciousness, C.G.] amounts to in reality and equally in pure thought. It knows that such validity is rather a complete loss; it is itself this conscious loss of itself and the alienation of its knowledge about itself. . . . The Unhappy Consciousness . . . is . . . the tragic fate of the certainty of self that aims to be absolute. It is the consciousness of the loss of all *essential* being in this *certainty of itself* . . . it is the grief which expresses itself in the hard saying that 'God is dead'" (PS, §752, 454–55, author's emphasis).

3. Bataille, *"Hegel, la mort et le sacrifice,"* OC XII, 342, author's emphasis.

4. On servile discourse as the loss of sovereignty, cf. Derrida, "From Restricted to General Economy," 262 ff.

5. Bataille, MM, 199.

6. Bataille, *Conférences, 1951–1953, "L'enseignement de la mort,"* OC VIII, 207, author's emphasis.

7. Bataille, G, 41.

8. "Previously, I designated the sovereign operation under the names of *inner experience* or *extremity of the possible*. Now, I am also designating it under the name of *meditation*. The change in words signifies the bothersomeness of using any words at all (*sovereign operation* is the most loathsome of all the names: in a sense, *comic operation* would be less deceptive)" (Bataille, MM, 219, author's emphasis).

9. Bataille, G, 118.

10. Cf. Sartre's criticism of Bataille in *"Un nouveau mystique," Situations I* (Paris: Gallimard, 1947).

11. Bataille, "Surrealism and God," AM, 183, author's emphasis.

12. Rainer Maria Rilke, selection from "The First Elegy" of *Duino Elegies.*

13. Cf. Maurice Blanchot, *The Space of Literature,* trans. Ann Smock (Lincoln: University of Nebraska Press, 1982), 238–39.

14. "Things are what they are only because of the meanings words give them . . . we could not live without these things which are words, just as we could not live without these words which are things. But words and things enclose us, stifle us; and it is very difficult for us to escape from them, to find ourselves beyond words and things" (Bataille, "Surrealism and God," AM, 182).

15. E.Cassirer, *Language and Myth,* trans. Susanne K. Langer (New York: Dover Publications, 1953), 32.

16. Bataille, MM, 210.

17. Bataille, G, 47.

18. Bataille, "René Char and the Force of Poetry," AM, 130.

19. Bataille, "Un-knowing and its Consequences," *October 36,* 83.

20. Bataille, *"De l'existentialisme au primat de l'économie,"* OC XI, 299.

21. Bataille, G, 102.

22. Bataille, IE, 68.

23. Bataille, *Conférences, 1951–1953, "L'enseignement de la mort,"* OC VIII, 201.

24. This citation and the following from G, 118.

25. Walter Benjamin, *The Origin of German Tragic Drama,* 36.

26. Allen S. Weiss, *The Aesthetics of Excess* (Albany: State University of New York Press, 1989), ix.

27. "Man, who essentially only differs from Nature insofar as he is Reason *(Logos)* or coherent Discourse . . . is himself not given-Being, but creative Action (= the one who negates the given *[négatrice du donné]*). Man is only dialectical or historical (= free) movement revealing Being through Discourse because he lives according to the *future,* which presents itself to him in the form of a *project* or an "aim" *(Zweck)* to realize by action that negates the given, and because he is himself only real as Man insofar as he creates himself by this action as a *work (Werk)*" (Kojève, K2, 533, author's emphasis). As remarked above, this reading of the *Logos* according to an ontological dualism between Nature and Discourse is specific to Kojève, and is a view which Hyppolite, among many Hegel scholars, rejects.

28. Bataille, MM, 196.

29. "The practical difficulty of inner experience stems from the faithfulness of a dog which man shows to discourse" (Bataille, Notes to IE, 181).

30. Bataille, IE, 58, emphasis added.

31. Bataille, *"La souveraineté de la fête et le roman américain,"* OC XI, 524. The quotation comes from the following context:

The question I have asked is that of the *sovereignty* of discourse, which where it occurs implies the reduction of man to a thing. . . . I have posed the question badly in that my own language is discursive, but I would not know how to avoid this contradiction . . . in every way we get ourselves stuck: how [are we] no longer to give sovereignty to consciousness? Consciousness denies itself the totality of the world and it piteously negates that which exceeds it. . . . It emasculates everything, it mutilates the world, but what is there to do? That I enter into its game in order to fight it with its own weapons, I resemble it. . . . I am in this manner a small speaking man, making speech his law. (author's emphasis)

32. Bataille, IE, 55.

33. Bataille, *"Le roman et la folie,"* OC XI, 528.

34. Bataille, *"L'au-delà du sérieux,"* OC XII, 319, author's emphasis.

35. Bataille, IE, 108.

36. See, for instance, Hans-Georg Gadamer, *Truth and Method,* trans. Garret Barden and John Cumming (New York: Seabury Press, 1975), "Language as a Horizon of a Hermeneutic Ontology," 397–447. Though Gadamer's concern is somewhat different (hermeneutic experience), he holds to the position that language and thought always point beyond themselves, and thus even the Hegelian-style developmental knowledge Gadamer affirms never achieves its goal (absolute knowledge), but rather opens to new horizons.

37. Ibid., 107.

38. Bataille, *"De l'existentialisme au primat de l'économie,"* OC XI, 282.

39. Bataille, IE, 109.

40. "It is only if I knew all that I might claim to know nothing. Only possession of this discursive [absolute] knowledge would give me an ineradicable claim to have attained un-knowing. As long as I misunderstand things, my claim to un-knowing is an empty one. . . . The fact remains that while recognizing that I cannot attain absolute knowledge, I can imagine knowing everything—that is, I bracket my remaining curiosity" (Bataille, "Un-Knowing and its Consequences," *October 36,* 81, translation modified).

41. Bataille, IE, 109.

42. Ibid. This question, though distinct from it, is admittedly in the spirit of Heidegger's question from *What is Metaphysics:* Why is there Being rather than Nothingness?

43. Hollier, *Against Architecture, op. cit.,* 65ff.

44. Ibid.

45. Bataille, IE, 82, author's emphasis.

46. Daniel Paul Schreber, *Memoirs of My Nervous Illness,* Memoir #312.

47. "The (conscious) Desire of a being is what constitutes that being as I and reveals it as such by moving it to say "I. . . ." "Desire is what transforms Being, revealed

to itself by itself in (true) knowledge, into an 'object' revealed to a 'subject' by a subject different from the object and 'opposed' to it. It is in and by—or better still, as—'his' Desire that man is formed and is revealed—to himself and to others—as an I, as the I that is essentially different from, and radically opposed to, the non-I" (Kojève, K1, 3–4).

48. Freud, *Project for a Scientific Psychology*, Part I (SE I), 339. I am taking some liberty with this phrase which occurs in the context of sleeping and wakeful life: "One shuts one's eyes and hallucinates; one opens them and thinks in words." My use of "prehistorical" is as well a reference to Freudian terminology as it refers to the zone of primary identification, the "emotional" tie established with another person prior to a proper differentiation of an ego and alter ego. I acknowledge however that I am taking some liberty here as well in that strictly speaking it is difficult to ascribe primary identification to an absolutely undifferentiated and objectless state.

49. Bataille, MM, 231.

50. Bataille, TR, 96, author's emphasis.

51. Ibid., 96–99.

52. Lacan, "The Mirror Stage," in *Ecrits: A Selection*, trans. Alan Sheridan (London: Routledge, 1989), 2.

53. Remember: "This Substance is, as Subject, pure, *simple negativity*, and is for this reason the bifurcation of the simple. . . . Only this self-*restoring* sameness, or this reflection in otherness within itself—not an *original* or *immediate* unity as such—is the True" (PS §18, 10, author's emphasis). Furthermore, "The True is the whole. But the whole is nothing other than the essence consummating itself through its development. Of the Absolute it must be said that it is essentially a *result*, that only in the *end* is it what it truly is" (PS §20, 11).

54. "Now, if Truth *(Warheit)* is the correct and complete "revelation" (= description) of Being and the Real by coherent Discourse *(Logos)*, the True *(das Wahre)* is Being-revealed-by-discourse-in-its-reality. It therefore does not suffice for philosophy to describe Being; it must again describe Being-revealed and take account of the fact of the revelation of Being by Discourse" (Kojève, K2, 529–30).

55. Kojève, K2, 531.

56. Kojève, K1, n.p.157.

57. Bataille, *De l'existentialisme au primat de l'économie*, OC XI, 278, author's emphasis. This comment refers us back to Koyré who, as we heard above, claims, *"Or, le 'system' hégélien est mort, et bien mort,"* in his "Hégel à Iéna," 153.

58. Kojève, K1, 186, author's emphasis. Derrida repeats this sentiment in his article, "The Pit and the Pyramid: Introduction to Hegel's Semiology," when he says that Hegelian discourse is a second, conscious history added on to the history of work, that discourse is history (work) comprehended. Cf. Derrida, *Margins of Philosophy*, trans. Alan Bass (Chicago: The University of Chicago Press, 1982), 72.

59. Kojève, K1, 190.

60. Kojève, K2, 546.

61. This is not, however, our only task, for we must as well identify how the apparently distinct levels of discourse are in a sense made of a piece. I offer here Kojève's account of how these levels in principle dovetail into one another, although our analysis shall trace a slightly different path. Kojève states, "[Absolute] philosophy describes, on the one hand, the path which leads from the birth of Discourse (= Man) within Being (= Nature) up to the advent of the Man [i.e., Hegel] who will reveal the totality of Being by his Discourse, and it is, on the other hand, itself this Discourse which reveals the Totality. But this Totality implies the Discourse which reveals it, as well as the processes of the becoming of this Discourse. So, in arriving at the end of the philosophical description, one is thrown back toward its beginning, which is the description of its becoming" (Kojève, K2, 531–32).

62. The limitation of our discussion of sense-certainty to problems of language should be recognized as an interpretive gesture, for language only informs part of Hegel's discussion. If, for instance, we look to Hegel's "Subjective Spirit" in his *Philosophy of Mind*, trans. A. V. Miller (Oxford: Clarendon, 1971) *[Encyclopaedia of the Philosophical Sciences III]*, §446–64 where he treats the same issue, we only find language eventually emerging in the process of ascension from sensation to thought, which moves through the stages of intuition (attention and externalization) and representation (recollection, imagination, and memory) before it reaches thought proper. Symbols, signs, and language (verbal and written expression) are treated in the third stage of imagination or the process of forming images (1.the mind's reproduction of images, 2.the relation of these images to its subjective aims, 3.symbolization and signification).

63. Hegel, PS, §97, 60, author's emphasis.

64. Cf. PS §100, 61.

65. Hegel, PS §110, 66.

66. Ibid.

67. Hegel, *Philosophische Propädeutik, Sämtliche Werke, Vol. 3*, Stuttgart, 1961, §59, 209–10. Cited in Derrida, "The pit and the pyramid: introduction to Hegel's semiology" in *Margins of Philosophy*, n.p.87, *op. cit.*

68. Man as work is time (history), the ability to transcend the present toward the future by way of the past; and man has as well been called the "empirically existing concept"; the negation of the spatial present and its being lifted into the concept (the word, as man = discourse) therefore raises the spatial object into a temporal existence, and in this manner the word becomes the time of the object. Cf. Kojève, K1, 139–40.

69. "If *Substance* conceived as natural static-given-Being has Identity (with itself) as its ontological foundation, the *Subject* of Discourse revealing this Being and itself, in other words Man, has Negativity as its final basis. . . . It is this Negativity . . . which splits *(scinde)* this Being into Subject and Object in creating Man opposed to Nature. But it is as well this same Negativity, realized as human existence within Nature, which re-unites the Subject and Object again in and by true knowledge or Discourse" (Kojève, K2, 531).

70. It is important to note that here, as above, we are working on the level of *Verstand*, the faculty dealing with finite entities that fixes and isolates them into determinate concepts, rather than with *Vernunft*, which flows between the isolated concepts,

resolving their contradictions in the attempt to coagulate them into a whole. But I should add that, in contradiction with Hyppolite, Kojève assigns both levels to the discursive faculty of man. We must bear in mind then that the priority Kojève gives to man's finitude, his creative action, and thus to negativity, work and discourse, against the correspondence of discourse and Nature, is an anthropological *interpretation* of Hegel. Hegel in fact is clear that the negative is *not simply an activity directed against substance* but that negativity is internal to substance itself. Cf. PS §37.

71. Hegel, PS §32, 18–19.

72. Kojève, K2, 542, author's emphasis.

73. Kojève, K1, 140. He is quoting Hegel from an unspecified section in chapter VII of the *Phenomenology*.

74. Bataille, *"Hegel, la mort et le sacrifice,"* OC XII, 332. The following quotations are found here.

75. Kojève K2, 542.

76. Kojève, K2, n.p.547, author's emphasis.

77. Hegel, PS §241, 146.

78. Cf. Hegel, PS §507–11, 308–11, author's emphasis.

79. Hegel, *Philosophy of Mind, op. cit.*, 213/459. He also claims here, "Speech, and its system, language—gives to sensations, intuitions, concepts, a second and higher existence than they naturally possess—invests them with the right of existence in the realm of representation." For comments on these quotations, see Derrida's "The Pit and the Pyramid," *op. cit.*

80. Lacan, *The Seminar of Jacques Lacan: Book I, Freud's Papers on Technique 1953–54,* trans. John Forrester (New York: W.W.Norton & Co., 1988), 248.

81. Ibid., 243.

82. This passage is from *Hegel and the Human Spirit: A Translation of the Jena Lectures on the Philosophy of the Spirit (1805–6), with Commentary,* ed. and trans. Leo Rauch (Detroit: Wayne State University Press, 1983), 89–91, 88–95. Passage cited from Borsch-Jacobsen, *Lacan: The Absolute Master,* n.p.276, *op. cit.*, emphasis Hegel's, brackets translator's.

83. Derrida, "The Pit and the Pyramid," 96, *op. cit.*

84. "Reason is language opposing general forms and common measures to things, or at least to a confused nature (since this confusion is immediately given in things); it is language opposing logical order to chance" (Bataille, G, 131).

85. Cf. Bataille, G, 85.

86. Ibid., 130–31.

87. Ibid., 134.

88. Ibid., 131–32, emphasis added.

89. Ibid., 132.

90. In the chapter that follows we will see how and why it is necessary that Hegel draw an equivalence between reason, *logos,* and God.

91. The "paranoid" nature of Hegelian Desire and Knowledge was originally proposed by Lacan, first in his text, *De la psychose paranoïaque dan ses rapports avec la personnalité* (Paris: Seuil, 1973), cited by Borch-Jacobsen in *Lacan: The Absolute Master,* 26–29, and then its repeated evocation in Lacan's *Écrits: A Selection, op. cit.,* 3–4, 17, 138, 294 *ff.;* see as well the commentary by Borch-Jacobsen in "Paranoid Knowledge," ibid., 57–61; and Julia Kristeva, "Bataille, l'expérience et la pratique," in *Bataille: Communications, Interventions,* from the colloquium, *Vers une Révolution Culturelle: Artaud, Bataille* (Paris: 10/18, 1972), 275–77.

92. Freud, "On Narcissism: An Introduction," P.F.L. 11, 91.

93. "When we think in abstractions . . . it must be confessed that the expression and content of our philosophizing then begins to acquire an unwelcome resemblance to the mode of operation of schizophrenics. . . . [A mode of thought which] treats concrete things as though they were abstract" (Freud, "The Unconscious," P.F.L. 11, 210).

94. Bataille, G, 78.

95. "The movement of poetry sets off from the known and leads to the unknown. It touches upon madness if it is achieved. But the ebb-flow *[le reflux]* begins when madness is near. What one takes to be poetry, in general, is only the ebb-flow: humbly, the movement towards poetry comes to rest within the limits of the possible. Poetry is, however one cuts it, a negation of itself" ("La volonté de l'impossible," OC XI, 21).

96. *The Impossible,* trans. Robert Hurley (San Francisco: City Lights Books, 1991).

97. In the scattering of unpublished notes on this text (OC III, 509–44) is found the following: "Call the book . . . the impossible . . . explain the title of the book in the preface . . . impossible in the sense of an absence of outcome *[d'absence d'issue]* . . . human existence in part belongs to the impossible . . . for example in *death* . . . and in *flesh* . . . no hidden meaning . . . above all no system. . . . Say what the impossible is . . . nevertheless [it is] out of the question that this be a philosophical definition . . ." (510–11).

In an abandoned attempt at the preface, he also states, "I come to say what leads me to now prefer the second title *L'Impossible.* The first only emphasizes the hatred of a so-called poetry linked to the taste for the possible, but this is not clearly stated. Again, *L'Impossible* is above all complete violence and unlivable tragedy. It is what exceeds the conventions of literary poetry" (512).

98. Bataille, "From the Stone Age to Jacques Prévert," AM, 137–54. Citations from 140, and 152.

99. Bataille is obviously referring to mainstream, pre-twentieth-century poetry, from which would be excluded poets such as Baudelaire, Blake, and Rimbaud, and authors such as Melville and Poe. It goes without saying that Bataille is making sweeping generalizations of poetry in order to stress his point. One must bear in mind, however, that the literature and painting of his time, along with certain antecedents, were launching attacks on both the subject matter, narrative style, and expression of what

had come before. The challenge of existing norms however can in no way be considered a new trend of the arts, as any familiarity with, for example, Cervantes or Voltaire makes explicit.

100. Bataille, *Manet,* OC IX, 103–64.

101. Bataille, *Manet,* 149.

102. For those unfamiliar with the two paintings, both depict the execution by firing squad of a group of men. The executed are on the left, the firing squad on the right, and more or less between them in the background are a group of spectators. The most striking difference is found in the stance of the executors: in Goya's painting they are driving forward with intensity, full of passionate determination, while on Manet's canvas the executors are upright, poised, and are carrying out their task in an almost bureaucratic fashion. One member of this group—apparently of lower rank judging from the uniform—is behind the line of executors examining his rifle, unconcerned and almost as if unaware of what is transpiring. The second notable difference is found in the depiction of the spectators: Goya's are *involved* in the scene and are clearly outraged at the event; Manet's are *separated* by a wall, rather lifeless. In each painting, one spectator in particular seems to represent the artist: Goya with head and body bent forward, face in hands with disbelief; Manet in a white shirt, causally leaning on the wall, resting his head on his arms as if contemplating a still life. In general tone, Goya's painting is much more rough and dramatic, its figures integrated in a composite whole; while Manet's is more geometric and studied, with the executioners in particular almost pasted onto the flat background.

103. Ibid., 131.

104. Ibid., 135.

105. The depiction of these two reclining nudes (Olympia and Venus) are structurally identical: both are lying on a bed, supported by pillows; right arms are extended from the shoulder, bent at the elbow, left arms positioned so that their left hands are covering the more delicate region; a dark curtain behind the bed splits the background, and where the curtain ends on the right the space extends in depth, etc. Much effort has been spent analyzing the additional figures on Manet's canvas—the cat on the bed and the servant—but they are unnecessary for our discussion. What is significant are the expressions on their faces: Venus the classic image of the feminine, demure yet not uninviting to the viewer; Olympia knowing and defiant, her eyes inspiring nearly as many words as the smile of da Vinci's unparalleled muse.

106. For a more comprehensive analysis of Holbein's painting, see Julia Kristeva's essay "Holbein's Dead Christ," in *Black Sun: Depression and Melancholia* (New York: Columbia University Press, 1989), 105–38.

107. Bataille, *Manet,* 145.

108. Ibid.

109. Bataille, "René Char and the Force of Poetry," AM, 138, author's emphasis.

110. Bataille, MM, 220.

111. "Men in former times did not submit without unease to the reduction their calculated activity imposed in the palpable world. This activity deprived the world of

poetry (it changed perceptible values into use values); it seemed necessary to prevent it, if for only one reason: what seems to us poetic today was at the same time experienced as dangerous—that is, as sacred. This is where the necessity for sacrifice comes in; sacrifice returns an element of use value to the world of sensibility." Or in other words, it delineates a domain of "interest confined to the instant itself. Like our ancestors, we must take objects away from productive activity to the *interest of the instant itself*" (Bataille, "From the Stone Age to Jacques Prévert," AM, 148, author's emphasis).

112. Bataille, IE, 135.

113. Ibid., 147.

114. Cf. Heidegger, *Being and Time*, trans. John Macquarrie and Edward Robison (New York: Harper & Row, 1962), 95–122. Hereafter BT.

115. I note again that Heidegger's concern is always with the Being of the being who makes use of equipment or signs, who is "fallen" into the horizon of reference in which it finds itself, rather than with the equipment itself.

116. Heidegger, BT, 102.

117. Bataille, MM, 222.

118. Bataille, IE, 135.

119. One may recall the fundamental principle guiding the analysis of work and the tool from chapter 1. Here I noted the dialectic in which the transformation of the world involves a transformation of oneself. If one subordinates the world through the use of a tool that transforms it into a world of things, one subordinates oneself, turns oneself into a tool, or a thing.

120. Bataille, IE, 5.

121. Derrida, "From Restricted to General Economy . . . ," *op. cit.,* 261.

122. Bataille, MM, 217, emphasis added.

123. Bataille, IE, 136.

124. Ibid., 135.

125. Ibid., 136.

126. Bataille, TR, 102, author's emphasis.

127. Bataille, IE, 146.

128. Ibid., 149.

129. Ibid., 148.

130. Cf. Bataille, MM, 220.

131. Theodor Adorno famously remarked that "to write poetry after Auschwitz is barbaric." "Cultural Criticism and Society," in *Prisms*, trans. Samuel and Shierry Weber (Cambridge, Mass.: The MIT Press, 1990), 34.

132. "Er ruft stecht tiefer ins Erdreich ihr einen ihr andern singet und spielt / er greift nach dem Eisen im Gurt er schwingts seine Augen sind blau / . . . Er ruft spielt

süßer den Tod der Tod ist ein Meister aus Deutschland / er ruft streicht dunkler die Geigen dann steigt ihr als Rauch in die Luft . . . ," in *Poems of Paul Celan,* trans. Michael Hamburger (New York: Persea Books, 1988), 60–62. The poem in the text is cited from the translation by John Felstiner in *Paul Celan: Poet, Survivor, Jew* (New Haven: Yale University Press, 1995).

133. Cf. Felstiner, *Paul Celan,* 118, *op. cit.*

134. Cf. V.Descombes's discussion of Lévi-Strauss and structuralism in *Modern French Philosophy,* 104–10, *op. cit.*

135. Bataille, MM, 210.

136. OC XII, 349–69. One finds similar notions in, for example, *"L'au-dela du serieux,"* OC XII, 313–20, and *"Le pur bonheur,"* OC XII, 480–87.

137. Bataille, OC XII, 359.

138. Bataille, N, 186.

139. Ibid., 150. Or as we saw above (section 3.2), the present (particular) is unavailable to thought because language cannot grasp it, can only utter the universal.

140. Bataille, "Surrealism and How It Differs from Existentialism," AM, 65–66.

141. Bataille, AM, 65, author's emphasis.

142. Ibid.,57–58.

143. Bataille, G, 118. The problem announced here relies on the following: "There can be *nothing* sacred. The sacred cannot be a *thing.* The instant alone is sacred, which is *nothing* (is not a *thing*). . . . What is sacred is ungraspable" (Bataille, "The Problems of Surrealism," AM, 99, author's emphasis). Bataille believes that surrealism ultimately failed the challenge, just as Sartre subsequently claimed that Bataille failed. Bataille announces this failure, stating that "the negation of things that surrealism is has itself become a thing. The glue of words makes an entity, a durable being . . . of what *is* not. . . . It would be necessary, in order to speak, that the word *being* should designate what the moment *is,* something which is impossible (surrealism, then, does not exist, since it cannot be named). But what, then, should the surrealists do? Keep silent!" (Bataille, "Surrealism and God," AM, 183, author's emphasis).

144. Bataille, "From the Stone Age to Jacques Prévert," AM, 148 author's emphasis. Allen Weiss, in his highly original *Aesthetics of Excess,* has articulated the same dynamic in accurate and agile fashion: "Meaning is thus the reduction of intensity to intentionality" (28).

Two further comments to note on poetry, sensibility, and sacredness: "What is strongly suggested to sensibility, and displaced to the process of intelligence, is always to some extent sacred, to some extent poetic" (149). Furthermore, in a footnote to this text (153), Bataille states: *"Donner à voir* is, of course, the title of a collection by Paul Éluard. It is the most accurate—as well as the most simple—definition of poetry: *what bestows sight.* Common prosaic language, on the other hand, does not touch the sensibility, and *bestows knowledge* even as it describes what is perceptible," author's emphasis.

145. Bataille, IE, 16.

146. In a text on silence as a rhetorical device from 1771 (*L'Art de se taire* or *The Art of Keeping Silent*), the Abbé Dinouart "catalogued the different modes of silence: prudent, guileful, complaisant, mocking, spiritual, stupid, approbative, scornful, political, humorous, capricious," indicating how silence was in fact a speech event. Reference to Dinouart from Allen Weiss, *The Aesthetics of Excess, op. cit.,* x.

147. Bataille, AM, 149. I reiterate: the present moment when evoked by Bataille involves absence, destruction of the distinct character of the object, an absence of difference between the subject and object.

148. Bataille, *The Impossible,* 158.

149. Bataille, AM, 147, author's emphasis.

150. Bataille, LE, 48.

151. Ibid.

152. Ibid., 47, first emphasis author's, second added.

153. Bataille, AM, 151, author's emphasis.

154. Bataille, N, 180.

155. Bataille, G, 117.

156. These quotations are from Celan's first major speech on poetry from 1958, "Speech on the Occasion of Receiving The Literature Prize of the Free Hanseatic City of Bremen," in *Paul Celan: Selected Prose,* trans. Rosmarie Waldrop (New York: The Sheep Meadow Press, 1986), 33–35. For interpretations and alternative translations, cf. Felstiner, *Paul Celan,* 114–18. The Heideggerian allusions here are not unintentional.

157. Ibid. Celan continues with some hope: "It went through. It gave me no words for what was happening, but went through it. Went through and could resurface, 'enriched' by it all."

158. Or, as he states in the unpublished notes to *L'Impossible,* "from the second title *[L'Impossible],* anticipation of a beyond of poetry: poetry shipwrecks *[la poésie échoué]*" (OC III, 540).

159. Bataille, MM, n.p.215, author's emphasis.

160. Ibid., n.p.194.

161. "If poetry is not accompanied by an affirmation of its sovereignty (giving the commentary on its absence of meaning), it will be like laughter and sacrifice, or like eroticism and drunkenness, *inserted* in the sphere of activity . . . *like children in the house. Within their limit they are minor sovereigns, which cannot contest the* empire *of activity*" (Bataille, MM, 220, author's emphasis).

162. Bataille, N, 184, author's emphasis.

163. Bataille, *"L'au-delà du sérieux,"* OC XII, 315, author's emphasis.

164. Bataille, N, 183, author's emphasis.

165. Bataille, IE, 8–9, author's emphasis.

166. Bataille, OC XII, 319.

167. Bataille, IE, 147.

168. *Ibid.*, 17.

169. Bataille, OC XII, 319.

170. Bataille, *"La volonté de l'impossible,"* OC XI, 21. Here he also claims, "I approach poetry with an intention to betray it: *the spirit of ruse is in me the strongest"* (20). A slightly altered and shortened version of this article is reprinted in the final section of *The Impossible,* "To be Orestes," 157–64.

171. Bataille, *The Impossible,* 163.

172. Ibid., 164.

173. "Je bois dans ta déchirure / j'étale tes jambes nues / je les ouvre comme un livre / où je lis ce qui me tue" (Bataille, *Le Tombe de Louis XXX,* OC IV, 161). This poem is the final stanza of another unpublished erotic poem, *Je mets mon vit . . . ,* OC IV, 14. Found among the manuscripts for *Le Tombe* was a photograph of a vulva which was supposed to be inserted between the page containing *Le Livre* and the title page of the next section, *La Méditation.*

174. Ibid., 149.

175. Notes to IE, 208.

176. To make matters a little less ambiguous, when referring to communication in Bataille's sense I shall capitalize. Communication shall be discussed in greater detail in the next chapter.

177. Bataille, LE, 188, 189.

178. Ibid., 199.

179. Bataille, G, 68. Lacan develops a similar notion in his analysis of the paradoxical relations of language and speech in "The function and field of speech and language in psychoanalysis," where he points to the paradox of the subject, the ego of modern man, who "loses his meaning in the objectifications of discourse. . . . For here is the most profound alienation of the subject in our scientific civilization. . . ." Namely, in the "common use of speech" or in the "common task of science . . . communication will be effective within the enormous objectification constituted by that science and it will allow him to forget his subjectivity . . . [it] will give him the wherewithal to *forget his own existence and his death,* at the same time to misconstrue the particular meaning of his life in *false communication"* (J.Lacan, *Ecrits: A Selection,* 70, emphasis added).

180. "The term poetry, applied to the least degraded and least intellectualized forms of expression of a state of loss, can be considered synonymous with expenditure; it in fact signifies, in the most precise way, *creation by means of loss,"* (Bataille, "The Notion of Expenditure," VE, 120, emphasis added).

181. Bataille, LE, 198–99.

182. Bataille, AS 1, n.p.197, author's emphasis.

183. Bataille, *Madame Edwarda,* n.p.12, author's emphasis.

184. Bataille, G, 8.

CHAPTER 4. MYSTICISM, EROTICISM, AND THE SACRIFICIAL RUSE

1. Bataille, LE, 72.

2. Bataille, E, 11.

3. Bataille, *"Hegel, la mort et le sacrifice,"* OC XII, 336.

4. Bataille, "A Preface to *Madame Edwarda,"* reprinted in E, 268, translation modified, emphasis added.

5. Cf. M.Blanchot, "Affirmation and Negative Thought," in *Bataille: A Critical Reader, op. cit.,* 45.

6. Kojève, K1, 76.

7. *Ibid.,* 77, author's emphasis.

8. Blanchot, "Affirmation and Negative Thought," 46.

9. Bataille, AS 2, 105, 141.

10. Bataille, *"Hegel, la mort et le sacrifice,"* 337.

11. Bataille, *Eroticism,* 57.

12. For the following argument, cf. Kojève, *L'athéisme,* trans. Nina Ivanoff, ed. Laurent Bibard (Paris: Gallimard, 1998), 179*ff.*

13. "Before God and for God, death does not signify the destruction of man; this is why the theist dying in God is not given to himself in the feeling *(tonus)* of terror. His end as 'man in the world' is not perceived in this light *(tonus);* he perceives this end as a passage into another life at God's side. . . . In theism, the terror of death is suppressed, because for a theist there is a Something in relation to which death is not an elimination. . . . [In death], the theist is given as affirmed in God, he is given to himself in 'being other' . . . but because this 'being other' is all the same a being (and *his* being), he is . . . given to himself in the light of the 'tranquil certainty' of his being" (Kojève, ibid., 188). This is, one must admit, a rather dubious notion, and one that is not necessarily consistent either with Christian experience, or with the notion of faith itself, which—*à la* Pascal or Kierkegaard—posits that one must simply believe despite the odds, without foreknowledge or advance reassurance.

14. For an account of the imagined "shapes" of the divine throughout the history of religion, see PS chapter VII. Any attempt to provide a precise phrasing of these final moments of Hegel's account of Spirit—and these attempts are manifold—always seems to leave one in the very state Hegel announces before absolute knowledge, where the words one uses—whether they come from God or Hegel—never quite seem to capture the content they try to express. Any individual attempt will therefore be inadequate.

15. We may clearly perceive Bataille as, on the one hand, following Kierkegaard's critique that Hegel so rationalized religion that it was no longer religious at all, and on the other hand, as partaking in the more general critique that Hegel simply went too far in integrating faith and intellect, for his integration became unlimited. Indeed, even "mystery" for Hegel is something completely different than we might imagine, for the

true "mystery" is just how the divine *fully discloses itself* in and to humanity. We will further address the notions "mystery" and "mystical" in Hegel as we continue. For a lucid account of the key notions of Hegel's religious consciousness from which these comments are drawn, see Quentin Lauer, "Human Autonomy and Religious Affirmation in Hegel," in his *Essays in Hegelian Dialectic, op. cit.*, 89–106.

16. Bataille, N, 53–54, author's emphasis.

17. Cf. Hegel's account of the Catholic Eucharist in *Lectures on the Philosophy of Religion, op. cit.*, 133. Though he does not actually refer to it as "fetish" worship here, it may easily be derived from his view on the mistaken identities of God in various religions.

18. Bataille, E, 275, trans. modified.

19. Bataille, *"Hegel, la mort et le sacrifice,"* 244–45, author's emphasis.

20. Bataille, TR, 50.

21. Bataille, *"De l'existentialisme au primat de l'économie,"* 282.

22. Bataille, *L'Abbé C,* OC III, 352–53.

23. Bataille, IE, 101.

24. Ibid., 52, trans. modified. This is also found in Appendix IV to N, in the context of Sartre's criticism that Bataille reifies non-knowledge as "the night," cf. N, 180–81.

25. Sartre, from *Un nouveau mystique,* reprinted in N, 181.

26. Bataille, IE, 117.

27. Bataille, G, 152.

28. Ibid., 104.

29. The very first lines of *Inner Experience* (3) contain the following: "By *inner experience* I understand that which one usually calls *mystical experience:* the states of ecstasy, of rapture, at least of meditated emotion. But I am thinking less of *confessional* experience, to which one has had to adhere up to now, than of an experience laid bare, free of ties, even of an origin, of any confession whatever. This is why I don't like the word *mystical."*

30. Bataille, IE, n.p.175.

31. Ibid., 3.

32. The mystic "night" is therefore a sort of tunnel to the light, witnessed for example in the writings of St. John of the Cross who speaks of "this obscure night through which souls pass in order to arrive in the divine light, in the perfect union of God's love," who loses himself "in order to arrive at the divine union." *La montée du Carmel,* éd.du Seuil, 1947, 19, 25. Reference cited by Robert Sasso, *Georges Bataille: le système du non-savoir. Une ontologie du jeu* (Paris: Les Éditions de Minuit, 1978), 98–99.

33. Bataille, IE, 3.

34. Cf. IE, 7. The notion that experience should be its own authority is an idea proposed to Bataille by Blanchot. On 53 of IE we find the following: "Conversation

with Blanchot. I say to him: inner experience has neither goal, nor authority, which justify it. If I destroy, burst the concern for a goal, at the very least a void subsists. Blanchot reminds me that goal, authority are the requirements of discursive thought; I insist, describing experience in its extreme form, asking him how he believes this to be possible without authority or anything. On the subject of this authority he adds that it must be expiated."

35. Bataille, AS 2, 170–71, author's emphasis.

36. M. Eckhart, Sermon 99, *Meister Eckhart*, trans. Franz Pfeiffer (London: John M. Watkins, 1956), 246, emphasis added.

37. With respect to Bataille's "atheology," I note that Bataille envisioned writing a magnum opus (between 1941 and 1944, including *Inner Experience, Guilty, Method of Meditation*, and *On Nietzsche*) entitled *La Somme athéologique (The Summa Atheologica)*, which he never completed. One should note the evocation of Aquinas's *Summa Theologica*, indicating that Bataille has in mind a displacement of the Judeo-Christian tradition which situates the realization of Spirit in the transcendent "beyond," in God. The reference to "beyond classical mysticism" is found in the article *"Hegel, la mort et le sacrifice,"* OC XII, n.p.333.

38. Bataille, "Un-knowing, Laughter, and Tears," in *October 36*, 99.

39. Hegel, PS §32, 19

40. Bataille, IE 25.

41. Ibid., 24–25.

42. Bataille, *"De l'existentialisme au primat de l'économie,"* OC XI, 292.

43. Bataille, IE, 102, 101.

44. Ibid., 107, author's emphasis.

45. Ibid.

46. Ibid.

47. St.Thomas Aquinas, *Sentences*, d.8, q.1, a.1.

48. Bataille, IE, 108.

49. Ibid.

50. Cf. Bataille, *"De l'existentialisme au primat de l'economie,"* OC XI, 297. Here he states that "total knowledge (dialectical or scientific) is also total night. An accomplished knowledge is only the most advanced point of knowledge, but if, beyond the most advanced point, it no longer has the least unknown able in its turn to become known, that which was otherwise unknown being decidedly related to the known, the known itself will be, in this completion, entirely related to the unknown."

51. Ibid.

52. This trend goes hand in hand with the Pietistic reform movement of the German Lutheran Church contemporaneous with the Enlightenment. In this movement devotion was renewed in the place of knowledge, severing the ties between *Andacht* (devotion) and *Denken* (thought).

53. Hegel, *Logic* §73, 107, *op. cit.* In this context, see the entirety of chapter V of the *Logic*, "Third Attitude of Thought to Objectivity: Immediate or Intuitive Knowledge," §61–78, 95–112.

54. Cf.Cyril O'Regan, *The Heterodox Hegel* (Albany: State University of New York Press, 1994), 31. For the main arguments in the pages to follow I shall be drawing extensively upon this text which has been an invaluable source of information for Hegel's theological notions and influences.

55. M. Heidegger, *The Basic Problems of Phenomenology*, trans. Albert Hofstadter (Indianapolis: Indiana University Press, revised edition 1988), 327.

56. With respect to the Romantic Intuitionist's denial of the cognizability of God, Hegel says, "I declare such a point of view and such a result to be directly opposed to the whole nature of the Christian religion, according to which we should know God cognitively, God's nature and essence, and should esteem this cognition above all else" (*Lectures on the Philosophy of Religion*, vol.1, cited in O'Regan, 31). On Christianity as the "revealed religion," cf. Hegel, PS, chapter 7.

57. Hegel, *Lectures on the Philosophy of Religion, op. cit.*, 84–85, emphasis added.

58. See for example Hegel's criticisms of the prevalent mode of thought in his times in the Preface to PS, §6–10. I should note however that his criticisms of Kant were less unequivocal than those of the Intuitionists.

59. Hegel, PS §785, 476.

60. "Divine Providence may be said to stand to the world and its process in the capacity of absolute cunning. God lets men do as they please with their particular passions and interests; but the result is the accomplishment of—not their plans, but his, and these differ decidedly from the ends primarily sought by those whom he employs" (*Hegel's Logic*, §209, 273, *op. cit.*).

61. Ibid., §36, 58, emphasis added.

62. Hegel, PS, §722, 437. In the *Logic* (§121, 82) Hegel claims that Mysticism is not what it is commonly thought to be, namely, the designation of "what is mysterious and incomprehensible," nor is it equal to the false understanding of "speculative" seen as the attribution of objective existence to that which simply exists in the subjective mind. These faulty conceptions are again based on adherence to the understanding *(Verstand)*, as he states, "[T]here is mystery in the mystical, only however for the understanding which is ruled by the principle of abstract identity," and further, "[T]he reason *(Vernunft)*—world may be equally styled mystical—not however because thought cannot both reach and understand it, but merely because it lies beyond the compass of understanding." Mysticism in Hegel's sense is properly speculative, is Reason, in that it forms a concrete unity of that which is opposed, so that fixed categories flow into one another and are unified.

63. I am again indebted to O'Regan for his thorough analysis of Hegel's reliance on the Christian doctrine of the Trinity, found in *Heterodox Hegel*, 63–140. Here O'Regan points out that it is really Jacob Boehme rather than Eckhart who influenced Hegel's view of God as revealed through Trinitarian differentiation: "If Eckhart espouses the hidden God, Boehme espouses the mystery of the self-revealing God. If

Eckhart points to the supereminence of the non-knowledge or unknowing possible on the level of divine simplicity, Boehme posits the supereminence of divine knowledge possible on the level of Trinitarian differentiation. It is, perhaps, Boehme who, in the theological tradition prior to Hegel, most radically posits the necessity of differentiation on the level of the divine. And it is Boehme . . . who also posits the necessity of return and the resolution of differentiation on the level of the divine" (118). See as well Dale M.Schlitt, *Hegel's Trinitarian Claim: A Critical Reflection* (Leiden: E.J. Brill, 1984).

64. Hegel, *Lectures on the Philosophy of Religion*, vol.3, 1824 MS E192, G 125. Reference cited in O'Regan, HH 65.

65. O'Regan, HH 94.

66. Maître Eckhart, *Sermons, 31–59*, trans. Jeanne Ancelet-Hustache (Paris: Éditions du seuil, 1978), Sermon 46, 102. All further reference to Eckhart's sermons shall be taken from this edition.

67. See Eckhart, Sermons 6,13,44.

68. Eckhart's commentary on the Book of Exodus has been translated by J. M. Clark and V. Skinner in *Meister Eckhart. Selected Treatises and Sermons* (London, 1958), 225–30.

69. Quote from the legend cited in Cassirer, *Language and Myth, op. cit.,* n.p.48.

70. Eckhart does not capitalize GOD as I have done. I simply want to avoid confusion.

71. Cf. Eckhart, Sermon 48, 114: "Je dis donc: quand l'homme se détourne de lui même et toutes choses créés—autant tu agis ainsi, autant tu es uni et bienheureux en l'étincelle dans l'âme qui ne touche jamais le temps ni l'espace. Cette étincelle refuse toutes les créatures et ne veut que Dieu dans sa nudité, tel qu'il est en lui-même. Ne lui suffit ni le Père, ni le Fils, ni l'Esprit saint, ni les trois Personnes dans la mesure où chacune d'elles demeure dans sa particularité." He repeats this twice in the same paragraph.

72. Eckhart, Sermon #36a, 34.

73. Eckhart, Sermon #36b, 39, emphasis added.

74. Bataille, from the unpublished fourth revision of the Preface to *Madame Edwarda*, OC III, 493. In *On Nietzsche*, however, Bataille has the following enigmatic formulation: "Not to speak about God is to be afraid of him, is to still feel uncomfortable about him (about his image or place in the interconnections of reality and language . . .) is to put off till later the examination of the emptiness he represents, put off shattering it with laughter" (66).

75. "This is absolutely true: all time must have disappeared when this birth begins for nothing restrains this birth as much as time and the creature. It is a certain truth that time cannot have any contact with God and with the soul because of their nature. If the soul could be touched by time, it would no longer be the soul, and if God could be touched by time, he would no longer be God. . . . In order that God be born in the soul, all time must have disappeared . . ." (Eckhart, Sermon 38, 49).

76. Eckhart, Sermon 31, 9.

77. Eckhart, Sermon 31, 10.

78. Eckhart, Sermon 32, 14.

79. Eckhart, Sermon 36 b, 38, emphasis added.

80. Eckhart, Sermon, 37, 44.

81. Eckhart, Sermon 42, 77. There are two things to note with respect to the atemporal status of the knowledge and union with God. The first is its admitted affinity with the Platonic notion that all ideas exist in the soul from eternity prior to and irrespective of the soul's knowledge of them. The second is Eckhart's notion that the divine birth occurs anew at every moment, in the present moment which contains all that previously was and will be. The "now of eternity" which is not touched by time is nevertheless called the "plenitude of time."

82. Eckhart, Sermon 52, 148.

83. Cf. O'Regan, HH, 248.

84. Bataille, E, 269.

85. Bataille, "Un-knowing, Laughter and Tears," *October 36,* 99.

86. Freud, "Beyond the Pleasure Principle," *On Metapsychology: The Theory of Psychoanalysis,* P.F.L. 11, 284–86.

87. Bataille's comments on Levinas are in reference to the text *De l'existence à l'existant* (Cf., "De l'existentialisme au primat de l'economie," OC XI, 279–306). The particular aspect of the *"il y a"* that interested Bataille (see n.p.293) was the common ground it shared with his own notion of intimacy (Being), the loss of subject and object, the cancellation of self in communication with the beyond of beings. Rightly or wrongly, Bataille says, "the *il y a* is apparently the ineffable of the mystics" (296), and supports this view with a statement from Levinas: "[R]ather than to God, the notion of the *il y a* leads us back to the absence of God, to the absence of all being" (Levinas, *De l'existence à l'existant,* 98. Reference cited by Bataille, 296). The absence of being is where Being arises, rendering the being absent.

88. Bataille, IE, 5.

89. Bataille, OC XI, 291, emphasis added.

90. This is where Levinas comes under Bataille's criticism, for despite the affinity of the *"il y a"* with Bataille's own notion of inner experience, Bataille believes that Levinas alters the intimacy of the experience by placing it within discourse, by his attempt to philosophically determine the state of pure existence through its formal effects, thereby inserting into the sphere of objects that which only has its place outside of it (Cf. OC XI, 293–94). This tendency is also identified as belonging to existentialism, which is why Bataille distances himself from the existentialists.

91. Bataille, E, 252.

92. Bataille, IE, 52.

93. Bataille, *"Le non-savoir,"* OC XII, 286, author's emphasis.

94. Hegel, PS, §16, 9.

95. Cf. J. P. Sartre, *"Un nouveau mystique,"* *op. cit.* The main lines of argumentation in Sartre's critique are: that Bataille is a mystic who has claimed to see God but simply refuses to articulate God in the language of those who have not shared this experience; that Bataille hypostatizes non-knowledge, reifies ignorance. Bataille may say "I know nothing," and then knowledge stops, beyond which is nothing. But if this non-knowing becomes the night of non-knowledge, it once again becomes positive, one can see it, hence know it—for to think that one does not know is still to think, and inner experience is thus another knowledge.

96. Bataille, *"Le non-savoir,"* OC XII, 287, emphasis added.

97. F.Nietzsche, *The Birth of Tragedy Out of the Spirit of Music,* in *Basic Writings of Nietzsche,* trans. and ed. Walter Kaufmann (New York: The Modern Library, 1968), §2, 38.

98. Cf. Lacan, *Les complexes familiaux dans la formation de l'individu* (Paris: Navarin Editeur, 1984). Reference drawn from citation in Borch-Jacobsen, *Lacan: The Absolute Master, op. cit.*, 64–71.

99. "You are right [to be afraid]. But you will only pull through it by facing up to what frightens you" (Bataille, *Ma mère*, 192). *Ma mère (My Mother)* is the second part of the project *Divinus Deus,* of which only the first part *(Madame Edwarda)* was published during Bataille's lifetime. The incomplete project is published in OC IV, *Madame Edwarda* in OC III.

100. "What then is the essential meaning of our horror of nature? Not wanting to depend on anything, abandoning the place of our carnal birth, revolting intimately against the fact of *dying,* generally mistrusting our body, that is, having a deep mistrust of what is accidental, natural perishable—this . . . leads us *to represent* man independently of filth, of the sexual functions and of death" (Bataille, AS 2, 91, author's emphasis).

101. Ibid.

102. Hegel, PS, §32, 19.

103. Bataille, MM, 205.

104. "The desire for destruction when it is directed *inwards* mostly eludes our perception . . . unless it is tinged with eroticism."; "It must be confessed that we have much greater difficulty in grasping that instinct [Thanatos, the death instinct]; we can only suspect it, as it were, as something in background behind Eros, and it escapes detection unless its presence is betrayed by its being alloyed with Eros" (Freud, *Civilization and its Discontents,* P.F.L. 12, 311–13). See in this context, *Beyond the Pleasure Principle,* and *The Ego and the Id,* P.F.L. 11, 380–88.

105. For the following definitions, see Appendix V to *On Nietzsche,* 188–89.

106. Bataille, AS 1, 56. The term *second self* is found, not insignificantly, in the following context: "No one can make a *thing* of the second self that the slave is without at the same time estranging himself from his own intimate being, without giving himself the limits of a *thing.*"

107. Bataille, LE, 26, first emphasis added.

108. Bataille, Appendix V, in N, 188.

109. Bataille, AS 3, 213.

110. *"Hegel, la mort et le sacrifice,"* 335. This seemingly ubiquitous quotation is taken from the Preface to PS, section 32, 19. It should be noted that Bataille does not follow Hegel's interpretation of sacrifice as given in the *Phenomenology* (cf.Chapter VII, "Religion," section B, "Religion in the form of Art" (a) "The abstract work of art" [433–35]), where there is a dialectic of mutually beneficial renunciation on the part of the Cult—which relinquishes its possession and enjoyment of the sacrificed thing—and on the part of the divine Being—who sacrifices its own essence to self-consciousness. Hegel's sacrifice is a classic dialectic of exchange, a sacrificial economy in which renunciation serves the Positive for the Spirit, yields a gain on the march to the Identity of the I and the Absolute. Bataille, perhaps reacting to its classical structure, says of Hegel's interpretation that "it no doubt makes sense in the development of the chapter, but it strays from the essential and, from the point of view of the theory of sacrifice, it is, in my opinion, of less interest than the implicit representation which is given in the text of the Preface . . ." (ibid., 334–35).

111. B.Baas, *Le désir pur, op. cit.,* 133.

112. Bataille, *"Hegel, la mort,"* 342, author's emphasis.

113. "The domination of activity is that of the *possible,* it is that of a sad emptiness, an atrophying *(dépérissement)* in the sphere of objects. . . . The simple truth: *servile* activity is *possible* . . . ," leading Bataille to exclaim, "LEAVE THE POSSIBLE TO THOSE WHO LOVE IT," MM, 209, author's emphasis.

114. Bataille, *"Hegel, la mort,"* 344.

115. Bataille, MM, 208, author's emphasis.

116. Ibid.

117. Bataille, LE, 192, emphasis added.

118. Bataille, *Conférences: 1951–1953, "L'enseignement de la mort,"* OC VIII, 208.

119. Cf. Bataille, *"Le rire de Nietzsche,"* OC VI, 310–13.

120. Hegel, PS, §808, 492.

121. Bataille, *"Hegel, la mort,"* 337.

122. Ibid., 338–39.

123. Bataille, *"Hegel, l'homme et l'histoire,"* OC XII, 359.

124. Kojève, K1, 5.

125. Kojève, K2, 551, author's emphasis.

126. Bataille, G, 155, author's emphasis.

127. Bataille, *"Hegel, la mort,"* 342.

128. Bataille, MM, 218, emphasis added.

129. Bataille, AS 2, 106, author's emphasis.

130. "Literature follows religion and is its heir. The sacrifice is novel, a story, illustrated in a bloody fashion. Or rather, a rudimentary form of theatrical representation . . ." (Bataille, E, 87, translation modified).

131. This article is included in IE, 93–98. The following quotation from the "Notes" is found in IE, 196, the first emphases are added, the last is the author's.

132. Bataille, *"Hegel, la mort,"* 337, author's emphasis.

133. Bataille, AS 2, 109. Note, I have substituted "sacrifice" where the text reads "festival."

134. Bataille, "Attraction and Repulsion II," *The College of Sociology, op. cit.,* 123–24.

135. Bataille, "The Practice of Joy before Death," VE, 237.

136. Bataille, *"Hegel, la mort,"* 337, emphasis added. A similar idea is expressed by Freud: having noted the modern tendency to eliminate any real sense of death from life, he states that "it is an inevitable result of all this that we should seek in the world of fiction, in literature and in the theatre compensation for what has been lost in life. There we still find people who know how to die. . . . There alone too the condition can be fulfilled which makes it possible for us to reconcile ourselves with death: namely, that behind all the vicissitudes of life we should still be able to preserve a life intact. . . . In the realm of fiction . . . [w]e die with the hero with whom we have identified ourselves; yet we survive him, and are ready to die again just as safely with another hero" ("Thoughts for the Times on War and Death," P.F.L. Vol. 12, 79).

137. Bataille, *"Hegel, la mort,"* 337, author's emphasis.

138. M.Borch-Jacobsen, *Lacan: The Absolute Master, op. cit.,* 95, author's emphasis.

139. Nietzsche, *The Birth of Tragedy,* §16, 104, *op. cit.*

140. Bataille, *"Le rire de Nietzsche,"* OC VI, 311.

141. Stephen Houlgate, "Hegel and Nietzsche on Tragedy," in *Hegel, Nietzsche, and the criticism of metaphysics* (Cambridge: Cambridge University Press, 1986), 187.

142. "With respect to the deadly truth of desire, no specular image can . . . be anything but a decay: the more I identify with such and such an image of my desire, the more I avoid my 'self' as pure desire of death. . . . Under these conditions, how could such an image ever 'become one' with the 'assumption' of my desire? On the contrary, that image would actually be its *méconnaissance*, its denial and refusal" (Borch-Jacobsen, *Lacan: The Absolute Master,* 96).

143. Bataille, *"Hegel, la mort,"* 341, author's emphasis.

144. Nietzsche, *The Birth of Tragedy,* §17, 104.

145. Bataille, E, 14.

146. Bataille, OC, VI, 311.

147. "In the sacrifice, the sacrificer identifies himself with the animal that is struck down dead. And so he *dies in seeing himself die.* . . ." "But," Bataille hastens to add, "it is a comedy! At least it would be a comedy if some other method existed which could reveal to the living the invasion of death" (*"Hegel, la mort,"* 336, author's emphasis).

148. Cf. OC IV, 535: "This beyond [of individual existence] can be placed before the self as a spectacle." Bataille does indeed seem to draw his notion of identification from, and to accede to, Nietzsche's metaphysical claims from the *Birth of Tragedy*, where it is claimed that in Dionysian tragedy, "each [man] feels himself not only united, reconciled, and fused with his neighbor, but as one with him, *as if* the veil of māyā (illusion) had been torn aside . . ." (§1, 37, emphasis added); "Dionysian art, too, wishes to convince us of the eternal joy of existence: only we are to seek this joy not in phenomena, but behind them. . . . We are really for a brief moment primordial being itself . . ." (§17, 104, op. cit). The tension in both Nietzsche and Bataille is between the claim that the experience itself is an illusion, and the claim that illusion yields to reality.

149. Bataille, *"Hegel, la mort,"* 338.

150. Derrida, *The Gift of Death,* trans. David Wills (Chicago: University of Chicago Press, 1996), 95.

151. Cf. Kierkegaard, *Fear and Trembling, op. cit.,* 30, 55, 57, 66, 74.

152. Bataille, N, 20–23, final emphasis added.

153. In the following analysis, one should be aware of my reliance on the categorical, Kantian notion of respect as distinct from the respect for particular pathological objects, and the possibility for this categorical respect—due to its formality, its disinterestedness—to slide into ultimate disrespect, as revealed in de Sade. The *summum* of Kant's *summum bonum* (sovereign good) is "that condition which is unconditioned, i.e., is not subordinate to any other *(originarium)*." Cf. I. Kant, *Critique of Practical Reason,* 135. Sovereignty implies disregard for self and others.

154. "[T]he sacrifice signifies that, in the object of our desires, we try to find evidence of the desire of the Other that I call here *the dark God"* (J.Lacan, *The Four Fundamental Concepts of Psychoanalysis, op. cit.,* 275, author's emphasis).

155. Bataille, G, 151, emphasis added.

156. *Ma mère* (OC IV, 175–276); *Madame Edwarda* (OC III, 7–31). *Ma mère* is the second part of the project significantly entitled *Divinus Deus,* of which only the first part, *Madame Edwarda,* was published during Bataille's lifetime. The incomplete project is published in OC IV. Both of these texts are included in an English-language volume, trans. Austryn Wainhouse (London: Marion Boyers, 1995), but the translation is, to say it gently, unsatisfactory. All references shall be to the texts in *Oeuvres Complètes.*

157. For example, *Story of the Eye* was written by Lord Auch, *Le Petit* by Louis Trente, *Divinus Deus* (including *Madame Edwarda* and *My Mother*) by Pierre Angélique, and the opening pages of *Guilty* by Dianus. Censorial concerns aside, each pseudonym has its particular significance, the most compelling and humorous being Lord Auch, which he explains as follows:

> The name Lord Auch refers to a habit of a friend of mine; when vexed, instead of saying *"aux chiottes!"* [to the shithouse], he would shorten it to *"aux ch'."* Lord [English in orig.] is English for God (in the Scriptures): Lord Auch is God relieving himself. (*Story of the Eye,* 76)

I think we may justifiably remind ourselves of the Christian theme, "God the Father."

158. Cf. Hollier, *Against Architecture, op. cit.,* 153–59.

159. Ibid., 154.

160. R. M. Rilke, excerpt from "The Eighth Elegy" of *Duino Elegies, op. cit.* The original reads:

Denn nah am Tod sieht man den Tod nicht mehr und starrt *hinaus,*
vielleicht mit großem Tierblick.
Liebende, wäre nicht der andre, der die Sicht verstellt, sind nah daran und
staunen . . .

161. Bataille, G, 157–58.

162. Bataille, N, 58.

163. I would propose that the same can be said of *Ma mère.* For instance: "Then, in the depths of corruption and terror, I continued to love [my mother]: I entered that delirium in which it seemed to me I was lost in GOD" (193); "There was in her and for me a love resembling the one that, as the mystics say, God reserves for his creature, a love appealing to violence, never leaving room for repose" (236).

164. *"C'est le sens, c'est l'énormité, de ce livre* insensé *[Madame Edwarda]: ce récit met en jeu. . . . Dieu lui-même"* (Preface to *Madame Edwarda,* 12). I should note that my reading here somewhat distorts the text, for Bataille is saying here that all of God's *attributes* are brought into play, but this indeed risks the notion of God.

165. "But I will never forget that there is something violent and wonderful associated with the will to open one's eyes, to look square in the face of *what is happening, of what is [ce qui arrive, ce qui est].* And I would not know *what is happening* if I knew nothing of extreme pleasure, if I knew nothing of extreme pain! Let us be clear about this. Pierre Angélique takes care to say it: we know nothing and we are in the depths of the night. But at least we can see what deceives us, what diverts us from knowing our distress, or more exactly, from knowing that joy is the same thing as suffering, the same thing as death" (10, author's emphasis).

166. Bataille, *The Tears of Eros,* trans. Peter Connor (San Francisco: City Lights Books, 1989), 206.

167. Bataille, G, 46.

168. "A god torn by wounds and a woman at the edge of pleasure transcribe ecstasy's outcry. It is easy and even inevitable to transcribe it; we only have to fix our gaze on what's in front of us. But in attaining the object in my outcry, I know I've destroyed what deserves to be called 'object'. . ." (G, 46–47).

169. Derrida, "From Restricted to General Economy," *op. cit.,* 107–108, emphasis added.

LAUGHTER—IN PLACE OF A CONCLUSION

1. "Philosophical reflection must, I think, consider laughter first" (Bataille, "Unknowing: Laughter and Tears," *October 36,* 92), from *"Conférences sur le non-savoir,"* OC

VIII. "I take my starting-point in laughter and not, as did Heidegger in *Was ist Metaphysik?*, in anguish . . . (anguish is a sovereign moment, but in flight from itself, negative) . . ." (MM, n.pp.116–17).

2. Bataille, "Un-knowing: Laughter and Tears," 93.

3. "Insofar as I am a philosopher, mine is a philosophy of laughter. It is a philosophy founded on the experience of laughter, and which does not even make any further claim" (ibid.). As previously mentioned, he elsewhere designates his philosophy as "play" (cf. "Un-knowing and Rebellion," *October 36*, 86–87), and still elsewhere as one of "chance." Yet he always comes back to laughter.

4. Bataille, IE, 66.

5. Bataille, G, 25, emphasis added.

6. Bataille, "Sacrifice," in *October 36*, 62, 68.

7. "As soon as I try to grasp my substance I sense only a sliding. . . . This radiant spell of laughter in which we lose ourselves has no exact location; it has no precise point of departure, no definite direction, but when it occurs, the separation of the withdrawn individual from a world of sudden flashing movement instantly ceases. An individual's fall only has to reveal the illusory nature of stability, and the witness of the fall passes, *with him*, from a world in which all is stable to one of slips and slides" (Bataille, "Sacrifice," 66, 69, emphasis added).

8. In his article, "The Laughter of Being," Borch-Jacobsen identifies certain instances where Bataille is seen to fall into the standard interpretation of laughter as an expression of superiority, for which he gives Hobbes's formulation from *Human Nature*, par.13, as an example: "The passion of laughter is nothing else but sudden glory arising from a sudden conception of eminency in ourselves, by comparison with infirmity of others, or with our own formerly." Cf. *The Bataille Reader*, 146–66.

9. C.Baudelaire, *"L'Essence du rire,"* in *Variétés critiques* (Paris: Grès, 1924), vol. 2, 100. Cited by B.-Jacobsen, 156.

10. S. Freud, "Humour," in *Art and Literature*, P.F.L. 14, 428–29. In this text, as well as in *Jokes and their Relation to the Unconscious* (P.F.L. 6, 302), Freud also points out the pleasure-economy of humor, where there is an "economy of expenditure upon feeling," as too high a quantity of energetic cathexis results in pain and suffering, while the less intense the pleasure is, the more liberating the humor seems to be.

11. Freud, "Humour," 433, emphasis added.

12. Bataille, "Sacrifice," 70. He also states here that: "What is dispelled is the possibility of anguish, rather than a real, true experience of it. The loss, the downfall usually does not elicit laughter from the individual who falls, he gains nothing by it. The [one] who witnesses a fall, on the other hand, gains in seeing himself as superior, for he remains upright. This helps to dispel that anguish which might make him see a resemblance between the falling man and himself, and that he himself might fall."

13. Ibid.

14. "The man who unwittingly falls is substituting for the victim who is put to death, and the shared joy of laughter is that of sacred communication" (ibid., 68).

15. Bataille, *"Hegel, la mort et le sacrifice,"* 342.

16. ". . . anguish in some form is necessary: when anguish arises, then laughter begins" ("Sacrifice," 70). He repeats this notion to the letter in *"La limite de l'utile,"* OC VII, 275. Cf. as well, *Guilty,* Chapter 4 "The Divinity of Laughter," particularly section 3, "I'm Trembling, Laughing."

17. Bataille, "Sacrifice," 72.

18. Ibid.

19. Cf. "Sacrifice," 68. Bataille continues to connect this with laughter, stating, "Now, of all the sorts of intense communication, none is more common than the laughter which stirs us in (each other's) company. In our laughter, our lives are quite constantly released in a facile form of communication . . ."

20. Ibid.

21. Ibid., 70.

22. Bataille, IE, 208.

23. Nietzsche, *The Birth of Tragedy,* §7, 59–60, *op. cit.*

24. Nietzsche, "Attempt at a self-criticism," 26–27, *op. cit.*

25. For a more extended discussion of Nietzsche on tragedy, cf. S. Houlgate, "Hegel and Nietzsche on Tragedy," *op. cit.*

26. Bataille, "Sacrifice," 72.

27. Cf. the article "Sacrifices" in VE, 131. This crucial early text (1933) is not to be confused with the article "Sacrifice" which we have been following. A revised edition of this article is found in IE (69–74) under the title "Death is in a sense an Imposture": that is, death only has importance when regarded from the position of a *self* that regards itself—despite the "infinite improbability" that it *is* at all—as the foundation of existence, which evades the fact that its existence is only as a "self-that-dies."

28. "And what about the fact that I can tell I'm laughing, guilty of being a *self*? Of not being someone else? Of not being dead?" Found on page 55 of *Guilty,* this gives a clue to the book's enigmatic title: despite what he asserts as the structure of human life, that it is composed of waves rather than particles, that it negates itself by directing it toward some end, he is guilty of taking himself as an individual, of writing, trying to assert himself in the completion of a project. We must remember, of course, that guilt is ontological—it cannot be avoided.

29. Bataille, "The Psychological Structure of Fascism," in VE, 140–41.

30. Bataille, "Sacrifices," VE, 134.

31. Bataille, OC VI, 443, author's emphasis.

32. This notion is frequently found in Bataille's writings, particularly in *La Somme athéologique.* For a succinct account, cf. the article "Communication," in IE, 93–98.

33. Bataille, "The Labyrinth," in VE, 172, author's emphasis. A revised version of this article is found in IE (81–93), entitled "The Labyrinth (or the Constitution of Beings)."

34. In Lessing's case this refers to the search for truth, which was given preference over possession of truth itself.

35. Bataille, IE, 94.

36. Bataille, G, 45, author's emphasis.

37. Bataille, IE, 95, emphasis added.

38. See below, citation from E, 106.

39. Bataille, G, 140, author's emphasis.

40. Bataille, "The Practice of Joy before Death," VE, 237.

41. Bataille, E, 98.

42. Bataille, E., 90. Here he reveals the identity of sacrifice and sexuality (from a uncompromisingly male position, although the roles are reversible): "The lover strips the beloved of [her] identity no less than the blood-stained priest his human or animal victim. . . . Together with her modesty she loses the firm barrier that once separated her from others and made her impenetrable."

43. Bataille, E, 106, emphasis added, trans. modified. In a virtually identical paragraph from *Guilty* (27), we find the following: "The illusion of completeness which I'm (humanly) aware of in the body of a woman with her clothes on: as soon as she's even partly undressed, her animal nature becomes visible and (while I'm watching) *hands me over to my own incompleteness*. . . . The more perfect, the more isolated or confined to ourselves we are. But the wound of incompleteness [i.e., finitude, C.G.] opens me up," emphasis added.

44. Bataille, IE, 124.

45. Ibid., 124–25, emphasis added.

46. Cf. Bataille, N, 72–73,

47. Bataille, "Un-knowing: Laughter and Tears," 89.

48. Bataille, N, 73.

49. *Ibid.,* 60–61, emphasis added.

50. Nietzsche, *The Gay Science,* cited by Bataille in N, 53.

51. This and the two previous quotations, "Un-knowing: Laughter and Tears," 91–92.

52. Bataille, TR, 28–29, emphasis added.

53. M.Borch-Jacobsen, "The Laughter of Being," 159, *op. cit.*

54. As Borch-Jacobsen aptly states it: "Laughter bursts forth . . . at the sudden revelation of the relativity of everything. Sovereignty is finite (insignificant, insufficient, deprived of being). And finitude, inversely, is sovereign (it is being). This revelation is profoundly comic, in fact, since it debases even the sovereign being . . . " (ibid., 160).

55. Bataille, AS 3, 234, author's emphasis. These quotations are an (unquoted) reformulation of Bergson's definition: "Laughter proceeds from an expectation which

is suddenly resolved in nothing" (*Le Rire*, 65) (unlike Bataille, I will acknowledge M.Borch-Jacobsen for bringing this to my attention), which is in turn a reformulation of Kant's definition: "Laughter is arising from a strained expectation being suddenly transformed into nothing" (I. Kant, *Critique of Aesthetic Judgment*, trans. J. C. Meridith [Oxford: Clarendon Press, 1911], 199).

56. Bataille, G. 27, emphasis added.

57. Bataille, N, 71.

58. Ibid., 91.

Bibliography

Works by Georges Bataille

Oeuvres Complètes. Paris: Gallimard, 1970–1988:

I. *Premiers Écrits, 1922–1940:* Histoire de l'oeil, L'anus solaire, Sacrifices, Articles. Présentation de Michel Foucault.

II. *Écrits Posthumes, 1922–1940.*

III. *Oeuvres Littéraires:* Madame Edwarda, Le Petit, L'Archangélique, L'Impossible, La Scissiparité, L'Abbé C., L' Être indifferérencié n'est rien, Le Bleu de ciel.

IV. *Oeuvres Littéraires Posthumes:* Poèmes, Le Mort, Julie, La Maison brûlée, La Tombe de Louis XXX, Divius Deus, Ébauches.

V. *La Somme Athéologique, I:* L'Experience intérieure, Méthode de méditation, Post-scriptum 1953, Le Coupable, L'Alleluiah.

VI. *La Somme Athéologique, II:* Sur Nietzsche, Mémorandum, Annexes.

VII. L'Économie à la mesure de l'univers, La Part maudite, La Limite de l'utile (Fragments), Théorie de la religion, Conférences 1947–1948, Annexes.

VIII. L'Histoire de l'érotisme, Le Surréalisme au jour le jour, Conférences 1951–1953, La Souveraineté, Annexes.

IX. Lascaux ou La Naissance de l'art, Manet, La Littérature et le mal, Annexes.

X. L'Érotisme, Le Procès de Gilles de Rais, Les Larmes d'Éros.

XI. Articles I, 1944–1949.

XII. Articles II, 1950–1961.

Texts and Collections in English Translation

L'Abbé C, trans. Philip A. Facy. London: Marion Boyers, 1989.

The Absence of Myth: Writings on Surrealism, ed. and trans. Michael Richardson. London: Verso, 1994.

The Accursed Share, Volume 1, *Consumption,* trans. Robert Hurley. New York: Zone Books, 1988.

The Accursed Share, Volume 2, *The History of Eroticism;* Volume 3, *Sovereignty,* trans. Robert Hurley. New York: Zone Books, 1991.

The College of Sociology, 1937–39, trans.Betsy Wing, ed. Denis Hollier. Minneapolis: University of Minnesota Press, 1988.

Erotism: Death and Sensuality, trans. Mary Dalwood. San Francisco: City Lights, 1986.

Guilty, trans. Bruce Boone. San Francisco: The Lapis Press, 1988.

"Hegel, Death, and Sacrifice," trans. Jonathan Strauss. *Yale French Studies* 78 (1990): 9–28.

The Impossible, trans. Robert Hurley. San Francisco: City Lights Books, 1991.

Inner Experience, trans. Leslie Anne Boldt. Albany: State University of New York Press, 1988.

Literature and Evil, trans. Alaister Hamilton. London: Calder & Boyars, 1973.

My Mother, Madame Edwarda, The Dead Man, trans. Austyn Wainhouse, intro. Yukio Mishima. London: Marion Boyers, 1996.

"Extinct America" (1928), "Slaughterhouse" (1929), "Smokestack" (1929), "Human Face" (1929), "Metamorphosis" (1929), "Museum" (1930), "Counterattack: Call to Action" (1936), "The Threat of War," "Additional Notes on the War," "Toward Real Revolution" (1936), "Nietzsche's Madness" (1939), "On Nietzsche: The Will to Chance" (1949), "Van Gogh as Prometheus" (1937), "Sacrifice" (1939–40), "Celestial Bodies" (1938), "Un-knowing and its Consequences" (1951), "Un-knowing and Rebellion" (1952), "Un-knowing: Laughter and Tears (1953), "The Ascent of Mount Aetna" (1939), "Autobiographical Note" (1958). *October 36* (1986): 1–110.

On Nietzsche, trans. Bruce Boone. New York: Paragon House, 1992.

Story of the Eye, by Lord Auch, trans. Joachim Neugroschal. London: Penguin Books, 1982.

Theory of Religion, trans. Robert Hurley. New York: Zone Books, 1992.

The Tears of Eros, trans. Peter Conner. San Francisco: City Lights, 1989.

Visions of Excess: Selected Writings, 1927–1939, ed. Allan Stoekl, trans. Allan Stoekl with Carl R. Lovitt and Donald M. Leslie Jr. Mineapolis, Univesity of Minnesota Press, 1985.

SELECTED BIBLIOGRAPHY

Adorno, Theodor W., and Max Horkheimer. *Dialectic of Enlightenment,* trans. John Cumming. London: Verso, 1986.

———. *Hegel: Three Studies,* trans. Shierry Weber Nicholsen. Cambridge: The MIT Press, 1993.

———. *Negative Dialectics*, trans. E. B. Ashton. London: Routledge, 1990.

———. *Prisms*, trans. Samuel and Shierry Weber. Cambridge: The MIT Press, 1990.

Aquinas, St. Thomas, *Introduction To St. Thomas Aquinas, The Summa Theologica, The Summa Contra Gentiles*, ed. Anton C. Pegis. New York: The Modern Library, 1948.

Arendt, Hannah. *The Human Condition*. Chicago: University of Chicago Press, 1958.

Aristotle. *Nicomachean Ethics*, trans. Martin Ostwald. Indianapolis: The Liberal Arts Press, 1962.

Baas, Bernard. *Le Désir Pur: Parcours Philosophiques dans les parages de J.Lacan*. Louvain: Éditions Peeters, 1992.

Barthes, Roland. "The Metaphor of the Eye." In *Critical Essays*, trans. Richard Howard. Evanston: Northwestern University Press, 1972.

Baudrillard, Jean. *Le sociéte de consommation: ses mythes, ses structures*. Paris: Gallimard, 1976.

———. *Symbolic Exchange and Death*, trans. Iain Hamilton Grant. London: Sage, 1993.

———. "When Bataille Attacked the Metaphysical Principle of Economy," trans. David James Miller. *Canadian Journal of Political and Social Theory* 15 (1991): 63–66, reprinted in *Bataille: A Critical Reader*, ed. Fred Botting and Scott Wilson. Oxford: Blackwell, 1998, 191–95.

Benjamin, Walter. *Illuminations: Essays and Reflections*, trans. Harry Zohn, ed.Hannah Arendt. New York: Schocken Books, 1968.

———. *The Origin of German Tragic Drama*, trans. John Osborne. London: Verso, 1990.

Blake, William. "The marriage of heaven and hell." In *William Blake: A Selection*, ed. Michael Mason. Oxford: Oxford University Press, 1994.

Blanchot, Maurice. "Affirmation and the Passion of Negative Thought." In *The Infinite Conversation*, trans. Susan Hanson. Minneapolis: University of Minnesota Press, 1993, reprinted in *Bataille: A Critical Reader*, 41–58.

———. *"La Communauté négative."* In *La communauté inavouable*. Paris: Les Éditions de Minuit, 1983.

———. *The Space of Literature*, trans. Ann Smock. Lincoln: University of Nebraska Press, 1982.

Borch-Jacobsen, Mikkel. *Lacan: The Absolute Master*, trans. Douglas Brick. Stanford: Stanford University Press, 1991.

———. "The Laughter of Being." *Modern Language Notes* 102 (1987), reprinted in *Bataille: A Critical Reader*, 146–66.

Botting, Fred, and Scott Wilson, editors. *Bataille: A Critical Reader*. Oxford: Blackwell, 1998.

Burbridge, John W. *Hegel on Logic and Religion: The Reasonableness of Christianity*. Albany: State University of New York Press, 1992.

Callois, Roger. *L'homme et le sacré*. Paris: Gallimard, 1950.

Cassirer, Ernst. *Language and Myth*, trans. Susanne K. Langer. New York: Dover, 1953.

———. *The Philosophy of Symbolic Forms, Volume 2: Mythical Thought*, trans. Ralph Manheim. New Haven: Yale University Press, 1955.

Celan, Paul. *Poems of Paul Celan*, trans. Michael Hamburger. New York: Persea Books, 1988.

Comay, Rebecca. "Gifts without Presents: Economics of "Experience" in Bataille and Heidegger." *Yale French Studies* 78 (1990): 66–89.

Debord, Guy. *The Society of the Spectacle*, trans. Donald Nicholson-Smith. New York: Zone Books, 1992.

Derrida, Jacques. "From Restricted to General Economy: A Hegelianism without Reserve." In *Writing and Difference*, trans. Alan Bass. London: Routlege & Kegan Paul, 1985, reprinted in *Bataille: A Critical Reader*, 102–38.

———. *The Gift of Death*, trans. David Wills. Chicago: University of Chicago Press, 1996.

———. "The Pit and the Pyramid: Introduction to Hegel's Semiology." In *Margins of Philosophy*, trans. Alan Bass. Chicago: University of Chicago Press, 1982.

Descartes, René. *Discourse on Method and Meditations on First Philosophy*, trans. Donald A. Cress. Indianapolis: Hackett Publishing Co., 1985.

———. *Discourse on Method, Optics, Geometry, and Meteorology*, trans. and intro. Paul J. Olscamp. Indianapolis: Bobbs-Merrill, 1965.

Descombes, Vincent. *Modern French Philosophy*, trans. L.Scott-Fox and J. M. Harding. Cambridge: Cambridge University Press, 1980.

Desmond, William. *Beyond Hegel and Dialectic: Speculation, Cult, and Comedy*. Albany: State University of New York Press, 1992.

Eckhart, Meister. *Meister Eckhart*, trans. Franz Pfeiffer. London: John M. Watkins, 1956.

———. *Parisian Questions and Prologues*, trans. and intro. Armand A. Maurer. Toronto: Pontifical Institute of Mediaeval Studies, 1974.

———. *Sermons 31–59*, trans. Jeanne Ancelet-Hustache. Paris: Éditions du Seuil, 1978.

———. *The Essential Sermons, Commentaries, Treatises, and Defense*, trans. and intro. Edmund Colledge and Bernard MacGinn. London: SPCK, 1981.

Fackenheim, Emil. *The Religious Dimension of Hegel's Thought*. Bloomington: Indiana University Press, 1967.

Felstiner, John. *Paul Celan: Poet, Survivor, Jew*. New Haven: Yale University Press, 1995.

Flay, Joseph C. "Absolute Knowing and the Absolute Other." *The Owl of Minerva* 30:1 (Fall 1998): 69–82.

———. *Hegel's Quest for Certainty*. Albany: State University of New York Press, 1984.

Foucault, Michel. "A Preface to Transgression." In *Language, Counter-Memory, Practice: Selected Essays and Interviews*, ed. and trans. Donald F. Bouchard and Sherry Simon. Ithica: Cornell University Press, 1977, reprinted in *Bataille: A Critical Reader*, 24–40.

Freud, Sigmund. *Civilization and its Discontents*, trans. James Strachey. In *The Standard Edition of the Complete Psychological Works of Sigmund Freud* (SE), *The Penguin Freud Library* (P.F.L.) *Volume 12*. Middlesex: Penguin Books, 1985.

——— . *Beyond the Pleasure Principle*, trans. James Strachey. P.F.L. 11.

——— . *The Complete Letters of Sigmund Freud to Wilhelm Fliess, 1887–1904*, trans. Jeffery Moussaieff Masson. Cambridge: Belknap Press, 1985.

——— . *The Ego and the Id*. P.F.L. 11.

——— . "Humour." In *Art and Literature*. P.F.L. 14

——— . *The Interpretation of Dreams*, trans. James Strachey. P.F.L. 4.

——— . "Thought for the Times on War and Death," trans. James Strachey. P.F.L. 12.

Goux, Jean-Joseph. "General Economics and Postmodern Capitalism," trans. Kathryn Ascheim and Rhonda Garelinck. *Yale French Studies* 78 (1990), reprinted in *Bataille: A Critical Reader*, 196–213.

——— . *Symbolic Economies: After Marx and Freud*, trans. Jennifer Curtiss Gage. Ithaca: Cornell University Press, 1990.

Grier, Philip T. "The End of History and and the Return of History." *The Owl of Minerva* 21:2 (1990): 131–44.

Habermas, Jürgen. "The French Path to Postmodernity: Bataille between Eroticism and General Economics," trans. Frederic Lawrence. *New German Critique* 33 (1984), reprinted in *Bataille: A Critical Reader*, 167–90.

Harris, Errol E. *The Spirit of Hegel*. New Jersey: Humanities Press, 1993.

Hegel, G. W. F. *Faith and Knowledge*, trans. W. Cerf and H. S. Harris. Albany: State University of New York Press, 1977.

——— . *Hegel's Lectures on the History of Philosophy*, in 3 volumes, trans. E. S. Haldane and Frances H. Simson. New York: The Humanitities Press, 1968.

——— . *Hegel's Logic*, trans. William Wallace, fwd. J. N. Findlay. Oxford: Oxford University Press, 1985.

——— . *Lectures on the Philosophy of Religion together with a work on the proofs of the existence of God*, in 3 volumes, trans. Rev. E. B. Speirs and J. Burdon Sanderson, ed. Rev. E. B. Speirs. New York: The Humanities Press, 1974.

——— . *Phenomenology of Spirit*, trans. A. V. Miller, fwd. by J. N. Findlay. Oxford: Oxford University Press, 1977.

——— . *Philosophy of Mind*, trans. A. V. Miller. Oxford: Clarendon, 1971.

Heidegger, Martin. *Being and Time*, trans. John Macquarrie and Edward Robison. New York: Harper & Row, 1962.

———. *Hegel's Concept of Experience*, trans. K. R. Dove. New York: Harper & Row, 1970.

———. *Nietzsche, Vol. Four, Nihilism*, trans. Frank A. Capuzzi, ed. David Farrell Krell. San Francisco: Harper & Row, 1982.

———. *The Basic Problems of Phenomenology*, trans. Albert Hofstadter. Indianapolis: Indiana University Press, revised edition 1988.

Heraclitus. *Fragments*. In Kahn, Charles H., *The Art and Thought of Heraclitus: An Edition of the Fragments with Translation and Commentary*. Cambridge: Cambridge University Press, 1979.

Hollier, Denis. *Against Architecture: The Writings of Georges Bataille*, trans. Betsy Wing. Cambridge: The MIT Press, 1992.

———. "The Dualist Materialism of Georges Bataille," trans. H. Allred. *Yale French Studies* 78 (1990), reprinted in *Bataille: A Critical Reader*, 59–73.

Horkheimer, Max. "The End of Reason." In *The Essential Frankfurt School Reader*, ed. Andrew Arato and Eike Gebhardt. New York: Continuum, 1992.

Houlgate, Stephen. *Hegel, Nietzsche, and the Criticism of Metaphysics*. Cambridge: Cambridge University Press, 1986.

Huizinga, Johan. *Homo Ludens: A Study of the Play Element in Culture*. London: Routledge & Kegan Paul, 1980.

Husserl, Edmund. *The Crisis of European Sciences and Transcendental Phenomenology*, trans. David Carr. Evanston: Northwestern University Press, 1970.

Hyppolite, Jean. *Logic and Existence*, trans. Leonard Lawlor and Amit Sen. Albany: State University of New York Press, 1997.

Jamros, Daniel P., S.J., *The Human Shape of God: Religion in Hegel's* Phenomenology of Spirit. New York: Paragon House, 1994.

Kainz, Howard P. *Hegel's Phenomenology, Part One, Analysis and Commentary*. Athens: Ohio University Press, 1988.

———. *Hegel's Phenomenology, Part Two, The Evolution of the Ethical and Religious Consciousness to the Absolute Standpoint*. Athens: Ohio University Press, 1988.

Kant, Immanuel. *Critique of Practical Reason*, trans. T. K. Abbott. Amherst: Prometheus Books, 1996.

———. *Immanuel Kant's Critique of Pure Reason*, 2nd ed., trans. Norman Kemp Smith. London: Macmillan, 1933.

Kierkegaard, Søren. *Fear and Trembling* and *Repetition*, ed. and trans. Howard V. Hong and Edna H. Hong. Princeton: Princeton University Press, 1983.

Kline, George L. "Presidential Address [to the Hegel Society of America], 1986]: The Use and Abuse of Hegel by Nietzsche and Marx." In *Hegel and his Critics: Philosophy in the Aftermath of Hegel*, ed. William Desmond. Albany: State University of New York Press, 1989.

Kojève, Alexandre (Alexandre Kojevnikov). *Introduction to the Reading of Hegel: Lectures on the Phenomenology of Spirit,* assembled by Raymond Queneau, ed. Allan Bloom, trans. James H. Nichols Jr. Ithaca: Cornell University Press,1993.

———. *Introduction à la lecture de Hegel, Appendix II, "L'idée de la mort dans la philosophie de Hegel."* Paris: Gallimard, 1947.

———. *L'athéisme,* trans. Nina Ivanoff, ed. Laurent Bibard. Paris: Gallimard, 1998.

Koyré, Alexandre. "Hégel à Iéna (à propos de publications récentes)." In *Études d'histoire de la pensée philosophique,* 2nd ed.. Paris: Gallimard, 1971), 147–89.

Kristeva, Julia. *Black Sun: Depression and Melancholia,* trans. Leon S. Roudiez. New York: Columbia University Press, 1989.

———. *Powers of Horror: An Essay on Abjection,* trans. Leon S. Roudiez. New York: Columbia University Press, 1982.

———. "Bataille, l'expérience et la pratique." In *Bataille: Communications, Interventions,* from the colloquium, *Vers une Révolution Culturelle: Artaud, Bataille.* Paris: 10/18, 1972.

Lacan, Jacques. *Écrits, A Selection,* trans. Alan Sheridan. London: Tavistock/Routledge, 1989.

———. *The Ethics of Psychoanalysis, 1959–1960, The Seminar of Jacques Lacan,* ed. Jacques-Alain Miller, Book VII, trans. Dennis Porter. London: Routledge, 1992.

———. *The Four Fundamental Concepts of Psychoanalysis,* ed. Jacques-Alain Miller, tr. Alan Sheridan. Penguin Books, London, 1994.

———. *The Seminar of Jacques Lacan: Book I, Freud's Papers on Technique, 1953–54,* trans. John Forrester. New York: W.W. Norton & Co., 1988.

Lauer, Quentin. *Essays in Hegelian Dialectic.* New York: Fordham University Press, 1977.

Lyotard, Jean-François. *The Differend: Phrases in Dispute,* trans. Georges Van den Abbeele. Manchester: Manchester University Press, 1988.

———. *Discours, figure.* Paris: Klincksieck, 1985.

Malabou, Catherine. "Negatifs de la dialectique entre Hegel et le Hegel de Heidegger: Hyppolite, Koyré, Kojève." In *Philosophie* 52 (Dec. 1996): 37–53.

Marx, Werner. *Hegel's Phenomenology of Spirit: A Commentary Based on the Preface and Introduction,* trans. Peter Heath. Chicago: The University of Chicago Press, 1971.

Mauss, Marcel. *The Gift: The Form and Reason for Exchange in Archaic Societies,* trans. W. D. Halls, fwd. Mary Douglas. New York: W.W.Norton, 1990.

Mauss, Marcel, and Henri Hubert. *Sacrifice: Its Nature and Functions,* trans. W. D. Halls, fwd. E. E. Evans-Pritchard. Chicago: University of Chicago Press, 1981.

Moyaert, Paul. *Ethiek en Sublimatie: Over De ethiek van de psychoanalyse,van Jacques Lacan.* Nijmegen: SUN, 1994.

———, and Jan Hendrik Walgrave. *Mystiek en liefde.* Leuven: Universitaire Pers, 1988.

Nancy, Jean-Luc. *La communauté désoeuvrée.* Paris: Bourgois, 1986.

———, and Phillipe Lacoue-Labarthe. *The Title of the Letter: A Reading of Lacan,* trans. Francois Raffoul and David Pettigrew. Albany: State University of New York Press, 1992.

Navickas, Joseph. *Consciousness and Reality: Hegel's Philosophy of Subjectivity.* The Hague: Martinus Nijhoff, 1976.

Nietzsche, Friedrich. *Basic Writings,* ed. and trans. Walter Kaufmann. New York: The Modern Library, 1968.

———. *Thus Spoke Zarathustra,* trans. Walter Kaufmann. New York: The Viking Press, 1966.

———. *The Will to Power,* trans. Walter Kauffmann and R. J. Hollingdale, ed. Walter Kaufmann. New York: Vintage Books, 1968.

O'Regan, Cyril. *The Heterodox Hegel.* Albany: State University of New York Press, 1994.

Pfanis, Julian. "The Issue of Bataille." In *Postmodern Conditions,* ed. Andrew Miller, Philip Thomson, and Chris Worth. Munich: Berg, 1990, 133–55.

Queneau, Raymond. *Le Dimanche de la vie.* Paris: Gallimard, 1952.

Richardson, Michael. *Georges Bataille.* London: Routledge, 1994.

Richman, Michele H. *Reading Georges Bataille: Beyond the Gift.* Baltimore: The Johns Hopkins University Press, 1982.

Rilke, Rainer Maria. *The Selected Poetry of Rainer Maria Rilke,* ed. and trans. Stephen Mitchell. New York: Vintage International, 1989.

Sahlins, Marshall. *Stone Age Economics.* Chicago: Aldine, 1974.

Sartre, J. P. *Situations I.* Paris: Gallimard, 1947.

Sasso, Robert. *Georges Bataille: le système du non-savoir: Une ontologie du jeu.* Paris: Les Éditions de Minuit, 1978.

Shklar, Judith. *Freedom and Independence: A Study of the Political Ideas of Hegel's Phenomenology of Mind.* Cambridge: Cambridge University Press, 1976.

Sollers, Phillipe (with Roland Barthes, Denis Hollier, Jean-Louis Houdebine, Julia Kristeva). "Intervention." In *Bataille: Communications, Interventions,* from the colloquium, *Vers une Révolution Culturelle: Artaud, Bataille.* Paris: 10/18, 1972.

Sollers, Phillipe. "The Roof: Essay in Systematic Reading." In *Writing and the Experience of Limits.* New York: Columbia University Press, 1983.

Surya, Michel. *Georges Bataille: la mort à l'oeuvre.* Paris: Séguier, 1987.

Taminiaux, Jacques. *Dialectic and Difference: Finitude in Modern Thought,* ed. and trans. Robert Crease and James T. Decker. New Jersey: Humanities Press, 1985.

Taylor, Charles. *Hegel and Modern Society.* Cambridge: Cambridge University Press, 1979.

Taylor, Mark C. *Journeys to Selfhood: Hegel and Kierkegaard.* Berkeley: University of California Press, 1980.

Van Haute, Phillipe. *Psychoanalyse en filosofie: het imaginaire en het symbolische in het werk van Jacques Lacan.* Leuven: Peeters, 1989.

Visker, Rudi. *Truth and Singularity: Taking Foucault into Phenomenology.* Dordrecht: Kluwer Academic Publishers, 1999.

Weber, Max. *The Protestant Ethic and the Spirit of Capitalism,* trans. Talcott Parsons. Boston: George Allen & Unwin, 1978.

Weiss, Allen S. *The Aesthetics of Excess.* Albany: State University of New York Press, 1989.

Westphal, Merold. "Laughing at Hegel," *The Owl of Minerva* 28:1 (Fall 1996): 39–52.

Williams, Robert R. "Hegel and Heidegger." In *Hegel and his Critics,* 135–57.

Index

knowledge, 30, 34, 37–38, 50, 54, 129, 139, 223n. 3
recollection, 132
reiteration of extent that is dead, 25, 130, 252n. 57
Sunday of life, the, 18–19, 67, 227n. 55
unhappy consciousness, 99–101, 165, 249n. 2
See also absolute rending; economics; knowledge and non-knowledge; negativity; sacrifice; self-consciousness
Heidegger, Martin, 13–14, 32–33, 36, 76, 92, 144, 174, 176, 217, 235n. 99, 105, 238n. 132, 241n. 1, 251n. 42, 257n. 115, 271–72n. 1
Herder, Johann Gottfried von, 31
Holbein, Hans, the Younger, *The Body of the Dead Christ in the Tomb*, 142
Hollier, Denis, 9, 40, 83, 126, 202–3, 224n. 15, 225n. 21
Horkheimer, Max, 82
Houlgate, Stephen, 269n. 141, 273n. 25
Hubert, Henri, 85, 96, 102, 104
Huizinga, Johan, 61–64, 239n. 149, 150, 153, 155
Hyppolite, Jean, 12, 36, 39, 250n. 27

identification, 49, 197–99, 201, 212
impossible, the, 56, 237n. 131, 255n. 97
incompletion (insufficiency), principle of, 4, 126, 158, 168, 215, 274n. 43
individuation, principle of: 44, 53, 56, 68, 95, 103, 112, 134, 184, 197, 210, 214, 215, 218; downfall and alteration of, 74, 101, 103, 185, 196, 214 (*see also* intimacy); insignificance of, 5, 211, 213, 219; loss of, 6, 65, 71, 94, 134, 162, 201
inner experience: 8, 20, 41, 48, 60, 65, 96, 183, 267n. 90. *See also* intimacy
intimacy, 1, 8, 55, 84, 94, 142, 161, 165, 167, 191, 200, 202; and consciousness, 98–99, 186; and self-consciousness, 72, 128, 169, 186; as Being, 7,

158, 217, 266n. 87; search for lost, 11, 72, 98, 102, 163, 167; and violence, 107

Jacobi, 39, 175, 223n. 3
Jamros, Daniel P., S.J., 226n. 33

Kainz, Howard P., 229n. 19, 234n. 71
Kant, Immanuel, 18, 29, 30–31, 39, 109, 175, 223n. 3, 229n. 25, 246n. 69, 270n. 153
Kierkegaard, Søren, 25–26, 110, 199, 236n. 102, 261n. 15
Kline, George L., 226n. 42
Klossowski, Pierre, 10
knowledge and non-knowledge: 3–4, 6, 168–69, 174, 251n. 40, 264n. 50. *See also* non-knowledge
Kojève, Alexandre: 10, 28, 51, 60, 123, 171, 261n. 13; criticisms of, 13–15, 19, 40, 225n. 30, 226n. 33, 232n. 43, 235n. 95; humanist anthropology of, 12–19 passim, 36, 39, 52, 231–32n. 41, 254n. 70; ontological dualism of, 12, 15, 17, 39, 233n. 62, 254n. 70; primacy of future in, 15–16, 56, 227n. 51 (*see also* Koyré). *See also* discourse; master-slave dialectic
Koyré, Alexandre, 15–17, 25, 226n. 40, 41, 228n. 2, 252n. 57
Kristeva, Julia, 9, 255n. 91, 256n. 106

Lacan, Jacques, 9, 123, 128, 135–36, 191, 255n. 91, 260n. 179, 270n. 154
Lacoue-Labarthe, P., 225n. 26
Lauer, Quentin, 232n. 43, 234n. 71
laughter, 26–27, 45, 69, 200, 211–14, 217, 221, 271–72n. 1, 272n. 7, 8, 273n. 19, 275n. 55; and anxiety, 211–13, 273n. 16; and sacrifice, 210–11, 273n. 14; and self-consciousness, 218, 220; and sovereignty, 211; Bataille's philosophy as, 209–10, 272n. 3
Laure (Collete Peignot), 11, 225n. 21
Leiris, Michel, 10–11
Lessing, G.E., 215